THE KINGDOM OF GOD

THE KINGDOM OF GOD

The Message of Jesus Today

John Fuellenbach

ORBIS BOOKS

Maryknoll, New York 10545

Third Printing, May 1998

The Catholic Foreign Mission Society of America (Maryknoll) recruits and trains people for overseas missionary service. Through Orbis Books, Maryknoll aims to foster the international dialogue that is essential to mission. The books published, however, reflect the opinions of their authors and are not meant to represent the official position of the society.

Library of Congress Cataloging-in-Publication Data

Fuellenbach, John.
    The Kingdom of God : the message of Jesus today / John Fuellenbach.
        p. cm.
    Includes bibliographical references and indexes.
    ISBN 1-57075-028-9 (alk. paper)
    1. Kingdom of God.   I. Title.
BT94.F84 1995
231.7'2—dc20
                                  95-20982
                                   CIP

Contents

Part 2

THE KINGDOM MESSAGE OF JESUS

Part 3

THE KINGDOM AND JESUS CHRIST

Foreword

For over twenty years, my main fascination in theology has been the central message of the preaching of Jesus—the Kingdom of God. The more I meditate on it, read, and lecture about it, the more I come to see what Jesus sought to convey and the vision to which he desires to draw us.

Wherever I present Jesus's message of the Kingdom, whether to students, priests, religious, or lay people, it invariably has the same effect. It is as if the message of Jesus is discovered for the first time. This grand vision of Jesus about God, the world, humankind, and creation as a whole fills people with enthusiasm, joy, and hope. Whether they come from Manila, Delhi, Melbourne, Cape Coast, Chicago, or Rome, the central realization is the same—the Kingdom becomes a reference point to which they can relate all other topics in theology, a horizon against which all can be seen as a unified whole.

This book is a summary of what I have taught over the past two decades. During that time many students and friends have asked me to publish my lectures and conferences. The book you hold in your hands is a completely new version of one published in 1987 in the Philippines. Although the basic content is the same, large sections are completely new and virtually everything from the old one has been reworded and updated.

I hope these pages will spark a little of the enthusiasm and joy for God's Kingdom that the world badly needs today. Jesus, after all, did understand his message as good news for the whole world.

This book is dedicated to all those in whom I was privileged to ignite new fervor for the marvelous vision that Jesus has brought into the darkness of our world and to all who labor to make the Kingdom present.

To Father August Moelle, SVD, my teacher of thirty years ago, I owe a special word of thanks for kindling in me interest in the Kingdom of God.

Introduction

The Challenge of Jesus' Message Today

A RETURN TO THE ORIGINAL MESSAGE

There are times in the history of our faith when we are compelled to ask fundamental questions that touch its very roots. What in fact did Jesus really bring us? Is the message the Christian churches preach and proclaim today still the message Jesus preached? Or is their proclamation of the message so encrusted with traditions and secondary concerns that people of our time can hardly see the real issues addressed by his preaching?

The difficulty is that often our self-image with its corresponding worldview can be biased or even false. Furthermore, our common self-image as a cultural and societal group with its corresponding worldview can become so biased that, without realizing it, we are unable to read and understand the biblical message correctly. Every worldview is constantly in danger of becoming an ideology if it pretends to be the only valid way of perceiving reality and of directing human action and behavior. The essence of ideology is precisely the selective inattention that refers only to those facts that aid the maintenance of our own status in society and facilitate the suppression of everything that might threaten it. We can persist in this direction even at the expense of our fellow human beings.[1] We would do well to heed Walter Brueggemann's observation that a "dominant culture, now and in every time, is grossly uncritical, cannot tolerate serious and fundamental criticism, and will go to great lengths to stop it."[2]

Have we perhaps fallen into the trap of perceiving the word of God with this same rather selective inattention? Do we refer only to those aspects of our faith which make us feel comfortable about the way we live, while ignoring anything that could question how truly Christian our way of life is? In other words, does our own cultural frame of mind prevent us from reading the Bible correctly? Have we succumbed to that numbness that prevents us from seeing any alternatives to the present state of things?

1

In the seventies the following story concerning the famous painting *Nightwatch* by Rembrandt circulated in art journals. The painting is known for its contrast of lightness and darkness. In order to preserve the painting every generation had added a new coat of varnish over it. As a result the painting gradually became so overlaid that its bright colors became increasingly dull. When chemists were able to remove these layers of varnish without damaging the painting, the effect was astonishing. The colors returned to their original brightness. The reaction of the art world, however, was mixed. While many were amazed at the painting in its original colors and freshness, others simply said, "This is not my Rembrandt anymore." They had become so accustomed to looking at the painting through the layers of varnish that they found the original strange and offensive to the eyes.

Could it be that we are so used to looking at revelation through so many layers of varnish that the original message, stripped of all protective covering, sounds strange to us and even offends our feelings?

Have the prophets, whose task it would be "to nurture, nourish, and to evoke a consciousness and perception alternative to the consciousness and perception of the dominant culture around us," left us?[3] Looking at the church in America Brueggemann made an observation which could be applicable to many other churches as well:

> The contemporary American church is so largely enculturated to the American ethos of consumerism that it has little power to believe or to act. The internal cost of such enculturation is our loss of identity through the abandonment of the faith tradition. Our consumer culture is organized against history. There is a depreciation of memory and a ridicule of hope, which means everything must be held in the now, either an urgent now or an eternal now. Either way a community rooted in energizing memories and summoned by radical hopes is a curiosity and a threat in such a culture. The church has no business more pressing than the re-appropriation of its memory in its full power and authenticity.[4]

Our faith, particularly as organized religion, is challenged everywhere in the contemporary world. In the West we are faced with the challenge of a totally secularized world that radically questions the relevance and meaningfulness of the Christian faith in its present form. Can faith only be a private affair of the heart vis-à-vis technology and economics, or can it offer an alternative to the way consumer society perceives reality? In Latin America the "non-person" whose situation is marked by utter dependence and oppression looks at traditional faith and asks, Does the Christian message have anything to say that could help us overcome our situation through a liberating praxis inspired by the gospel? Or, is the message of Jesus as it has been preached to us for centuries absolutely irrelevant to our plight and our clamoring for freedom? In Asia the great religious traditions older than Christianity itself look at us and ask, What can Christian faith and its tradition offer us that we do not have already? Is Christianity only another subtle attempt at Western domination?

Some years ago the German Bishops' Conference appraised this crisis and expressed its solution with these words: "The way out of the crisis that we are facing today can only be the way into fellowship with the Lord."[5] The direction suggested is correct. We have to go back to the roots of our faith, to our relationship with the Lord himself, and admit that there are times in history when nothing else can be done, other than to go back to the original message and pursue a fresh path. The old ways only leave us wandering around in circles, confused and exasperated.

Many people of this age, inside and outside Christianity, ask, Who was this Jesus of Nazareth? The question is not based on any dogmatic interest but plain curiosity. People want to know what Jesus was like as a real person in history who after his death made such a stir. Jesus' public life was very brief: one year or two and a half. Moses led his people for forty years, Buddha taught for forty-five years after his enlightenment, and Muhammad for about twenty years. Jesus' ministry, in comparison, was like a meteor flashing momentarily, though brilliantly, in the night sky.[6] What was it that Jesus did or said that has inspired millions of people through the centuries to follow him and to give everything for him and his mission? What was it that he communicated so powerfully that people fell as under a spell, leaving everything to follow this man from Nazareth?

Jesus himself expressed his mission in these words: "I came to bring fire to the earth and how I wish it were already kindled!" (Lk 12:49). Jesus was driven by a vision that he compared with "fire." It was definitely not to be understood as a theoretical worldview. Jesus' vision aimed at a radical transformation of the world that would upset everything and in no way leave people in peace. As he himself put it: "Do you think that I have come to bring peace to the earth? No, I tell you, but rather division" (Lk 12:51). What is this fire he came to throw into this world and with which he himself was apparently burning?

To ask this question is to search for the key that unlocks for us the real message of Jesus, to seek the overriding arch that binds it together. The most basic historical fact of Jesus' life is the symbol which dominated all his preaching, the reality that gave meaning to all his activities, that is, the *Kingdom of God*. The synoptic gospels summarize Jesus' teaching and preaching with the "lapidary phrase":

The time is fulfilled, and the kingdom of God has come near;
repent, and believe in the good news (Mk 1:14-15; Mt 4:17; Lk
4:43).

The Kingdom is so central to Jesus that it led Karl Rahner to the
observation that "Jesus preached the Kingdom of God, not himself."[7]
In his teaching Jesus appears as the representative (Lk 17:20-21), the
revealer (Mk 4:11-12; Mt 11:25-26), the champion (Mk 3:27), the
initiator (Mt 11:12), the instrument (Mt 12:28), the mediator (Mk
2:18-19), and the bearer (Mt 11:5) of the Kingdom of God.[8] We could
even say with Jon Sobrino that "The topic of Jesus' preaching was not
himself nor was it just God; it was God in his relation to the world."[9]

Almost all exegetes and scholars are in agreement on this point: the
center of Jesus' preaching and teaching is the Kingdom of God. The
word *kingdom* occurs 160 times in the Christian scriptures, with 120
occurrences in the synoptic gospels. Indeed, the formula *kingdom of
God* or *kingdom of heaven* occurs over one hundred times in the gospels in the following distribution: Matthew, fifty-five times; Mark,
fourteen times; Luke, thirty-nine times. On the lips of Jesus we find
the phrase ninety times. The word *church* is used only twice: Matthew
16:18 and Matthew 18:17. This fact led to A. Loisy's often quoted
polemical comment: "Jesus preached the Kingdom of God and what
came out was the Church."[10]

The Kingdom is not only the central theme of Jesus' preaching, the
reference point of most of his parables, and the subject of a large
number of his sayings, it is also the content of his symbolic actions. A
large part of his ministry consists of such activities as his table fellowship with tax-collectors and sinners as well as his healings and exorcisms. In his communion with the outcast Jesus lives out the Kingdom, demonstrating in action God's unconditional love for undeserving
sinners.[11]

After the Resurrection we do find a shift in the preaching of the
Kingdom of God. As Rudolf Bultmann expresses it: "He who for-
merly had been the bearer of the message was drawn into it and became its essential content. The proclaimer became the proclaimed."[12]
Though the shift is real, it is not an early falsification of the message.
Consequently, it should not be over-stressed. In Paul and other writings of the Christian scriptures, the Kingdom notion does not disappear; nor is it replaced by other concepts. Although the word itself
does not remain in center position, as it did in Jesus' message, the idea
nevertheless reappears in a number of texts, taking on its own shade
of meaning. The symbol Kingdom of God remained an element of the
early church's proclamation.[13] To postulate that there are two central
topics in the Christian scriptures, the Kingdom of God before Easter
and Jesus the Christ after Easter, has some legitimacy, but both phrases

are so intrinsically interwoven that they should not be contrasted one against the other.

THE NEED FOR A RELIGIOUS SYMBOL

In our age, which has been called an age of broken religious symbols, there is an urgent need for a new religious symbol which can cut through all cultural barriers. The symbol Kingdom of God, standing as it does for a very rich religious experience, may perhaps meet this need. John Brown remarks:

> Among the central concepts of the great religions, that of the Kingdom of God may be the most hopeful, for while it recognizes the reality of death and injustices, it affirms that a just and living transcendent reality is entering history and transforming it.[14]

A. Schweitzer states it this way: "As for humankind today the realization of the Kingdom of God here on earth has become a matter of survival or extinction."[15] There are two reasons which justify the choice of the Kingdom of God as our religious symbol.

First, the crisis of Christian identity asks for a radical inquiry into the origin of its history. We need a fresh look at the main topic of Jesus' proclamation and ministry, the Kingdom of God. Any theological treatise (e.g., church, Christ, sacraments) has to be treated and developed from this center of Jesus' preaching lest we get lost in all kinds of needless explanations and useless speculations. Thus, Wolfhart Pannenberg writes:

> In the New Testament, however, Jesus' message of the imminent Kingdom of God precedes every Christology and every new qualification of human existence and thus becomes the foundation of both. Christological and anthropological interpretations cannot be imposed upon the preaching of the Kingdom, but must themselves be judged in the light of the Kingdom. This resounding motif of Jesus' message—the imminent Kingdom of God—must be recovered as a key to the whole of Christian theology.[16]

Second, we experience in our world today a general drive toward a highly complex social organism, the shrinking of the globe into one earthly society. To understand and discern such a drive we need a religious symbol that is both broad and deep enough to focus and illuminate this process, a symbol that will give meaning to humankind's most noble aspirations and hopes for this world, and yet, at the same time will also transcend all inner earthly expectations. The religious symbol Kingdom of God may well fulfill this function. It is the most powerful symbol of hope in the religious and social history of humankind.

THE WORLD IN WHICH WE LIVE

If we look at the drama of human history, we discover two opposite forces at work. There is a self-destructive force at work in every individual, to which the individual, as well as the whole of society, can easily succumb. We see this negative, destructive force at work today in many ways: in the rising nationalism of the newly liberated countries of the former communist world, in the tribalism and anarchy into which many African nations seem to collapse, and in the Western consumer mentality with its "me" culture, which seeks maximum fulfillment regardless of the fate of others. For millions of people on this earth there seems to be no hope for a better future; things for them can only become worse. Yet, there is also another force:

> But concurrently with wars, animosities and divisions among people and countries, another trend, with equally objective causes, is gaining momentum—the process of the emergence of a mutual interrelated and integral world.[17]

Which of these two forces will win? Can history give us a clue? Will the unquenchable thirst for justice which runs like a thread through the history of humankind finally overcome the self-destructive forces of war, hatred, oppression, and exploitation? Will the vision of the prophet Micah one day come true?

> They shall beat their swords into plowshares,
>   and their spears into pruning hooks;
> nation shall not lift up sword against nation,
>   neither shall they learn war any more;
> but they shall sit under their own vines and
>   under their own fig trees,
> and no one shall make them afraid;
>   for the mouth of the Lord of hosts has spoken.
>   (Mi 4:3-4)

Will hope in a world of justice and peace find fulfillment? Leonardo Boff believes that despite historical reality, hope remains indestructible:

> As attested to by all cultures and civilizations the world has known, there is a principle of hope at work wherever people

have lived that generates great excitement and utopian visions in spite of the fact that of the 3400 years of recorded human history 3166 were years of war and the remaining 234 were years of preparation for war.[18]

Perhaps hope's time has come. Future generations might regard us as fortunate because we were privileged to live in one of history's rare moments of great importance. Something is happening in our days that seems to be a culmination of what others have hoped for, dreamed of, and lived for, but did not live to see. Ideologies are collapsing at an amazing speed, and old enemies are appearing to become friends. What is behind all this? What is its driving force?

Over the last decades a process of social awareness has taken place which affected and is still affecting all human beings. An unquenchable desire for universal brotherhood/sisterhood, a world of justice and peace, of equality and participation is becoming increasingly felt and articulated. The greatest single mental change happening today is a sharpened sensibility toward unjust and oppressive structures on all levels of human society. In particular, the many liberation movements which have emerged over the last decades give expression to the increasing awareness of entire groups of people to their oppression by others and to their determination to rid themselves of these inhuman conditions. This process expresses itself in the almost desperate search for a new social, political, and economic order, one which can reverse the dreadful march toward impending total destruction, and thus, alter the direction of history. Never before have we had such an opportunity to construct for the whole human family a new world order where justice and peace for all is not a mere dream or utopia, but a plausible reality. These events have led to the following observation:

> We have entered a new stage in the history of humankind, in which a vision is being shaped of a community that is more extensive than any offended group, that includes all sides, that is passing beyond tribalism into a recognition of a new interdependence. During this century we have arrived at a revolutionary understanding of God.[19]

How should we interpret these movements, these experiences, these changes? How do they relate to our faith as Christians? The words of the South African theologian Albert Nolan are instructive:

> All these experiences of going beyond some limitation or restriction are experiences of God, because God is transcendence. God's voice is the call of transcendence that challenges us to go further, to do more, to try harder, to change our lives, to venture out into

new areas and into the unknown. . . . God is out there calling us to move beyond the system, beyond sin, beyond suffering, beyond our narrow and limited ideas of what is possible.[20]

The church has come to realize that it must take history much more seriously and open itself up to a more evolutionary worldview. The change that has occurred in theology over the last fifty years reflects the shift in worldview well expressed by Vatican II:

And so mankind substitutes a dynamic and more evolutionary concept of nature for a static one, and the result is an immense series of new problems calling for a new endeavor of analysis and synthesis (*Gaudium et Spes* 5).

With the opportunity come also more challenges. Yet the church, more recently, has recognized these liberation movements as originating from God's entrance into the process of history itself:

Thus the quest for freedom and the aspiration to liberation, which are among the principal signs of the times in the modern world, have their first source in the Christian heritage. This remains true even in places where they assume erroneous forms and even oppose the Christian view of man and his destiny. Without this reference to the Gospel, the history of the recent centuries in the West cannot be understood (*Instruction on Christian Freedom* 5).

This awareness is relatively new and requires an adequate interpretation in the light of the Gospel. The symbol Kingdom of God may provide us with an adequate key for understanding and interpreting these processes as signs of the time. Such movements, reflected upon in the light of the Word of God, can help us to see and interpret human history as a global development leading from bondage to freedom.[21]

THE NEED FOR A VISION

All purely humanistic movements, and Marxist utopian messianism in particular, base their thrust and vision on two characteristics: humankind's aspirations for brotherhood/sisterhood and the firm hope that this goal is attainable in the future. That these movements can inspire millions of people is due to their use of these most noble aspirations and hopes of humankind. Whatever objections one has to

Marxism, its effectiveness and appeal depend mostly on the fact that it has offered a global vision of the world. This vision has inspired millions of people to commit themselves to creating a better world where justice and peace would indeed be achievable. Karl Marx was animated by a deep and lasting concern for the plight of the oppressed class. He was inspired by an almost messianic conviction of his mission to lead humankind from bondage to freedom. Marx's basic question was, "How can man be free?" In this way he tried to express the deepest aspirations of the human person. He developed a strategy which he believed could make that dream come true, the ideology of Communism, which deceived millions of people and taught us once again that we cannot redeem ourselves. Indeed, Marxism must be understood as a secularized version of Jewish Messianism, and as such, would have been a replacement for religion.

Years ago I was working with some young people in the Philippines who were toying with the idea of joining the radicals in the hills, who were mostly Maoists. I asked one leader, "What is so attractive in Maoism that cannot be found in our Christian faith?" His answer: "Father, Maoism provides us young people in our present situation with four essential things: (1) a unified and coherent vision of the world, history and reality; (2) a definite goal to work for, live for, and die for; (3) a call to all people for a common fraternity; and, (4) a sense of commitment and a mission to spread the good news that there is hope for the hopeless. The fact is that the Christian faith in all its beauty seems to be unable to provide us with such a vision."

In frustration and sadness I had to watch these young and idealistic people be caught up in the vision of a destructive ideology, while I was unable to convey our own vision of God's Kingdom in a way which would have caught their imagination with the same enthusiasm and zeal. From that time on I knew that the only way to prevent people from committing themselves to all kinds of ideologies was to present our Christian vision in a form like the one the young man had just outlined for me.

What we have experienced over the last few years would have been unimaginable just a short time before. Communism collapsed under its failure to fulfill its promises of creating a just and a peaceful society. With an air of complacency the West could easily be led to say that it has won the Cold War and democracy has finally triumphed over communist dictatorships. This, however, would be an incorrect and incomplete interpretation of events:

> The world has become unipolar in terms of both ideology and power. This is to be regretted because, as the former Archbishop of Canterbury Runcie told the European Parliament in Novem-

ber 1989, while communism has failed, capitalism has not shown the capacity to liquidate mass poverty in the world, to eliminate the threat of war or to deal tenderly with our own earth.

Or as Boff put it: The collapse of authoritarian socialism does not pardon the sins and inherent perversity of capitalism which must be constantly condemned and especially now when it is feeling euphoric and triumphant.[22]

The fall of one ideology is no guarantee that it will not be replaced by another. The end of the Cold War and the fall of communism, for instance, does not mean that the West has won. Its own ideology of market-oriented democracy is not an automatic solution to the world's problems and to the fulfillment of the dream we have described. We need a vision of the world and of human society that transcends our present solutions and propels our imagination to new and broader horizons than we are accustomed to. Today we need a *global vision* that goes beyond ideology. It must prevent us from simply falling prey to new ideologies which lead to new oppression and destruction of human freedom instead of to the genuine humanization of the world. Our time continues to be characterized by an almost desperate search for new social and political approaches to reality that would guarantee a more just and equitable order for all human beings. In order to succeed in this project, we must understand better both our own inclination toward ideology and our own nature which rebels against it.

The tendency to succumb to ideology, no matter what its name, and to betray our freedom and human dignity lies in all of us. The playwright and first freely elected president of Czechoslovakia, Vaclav Havel, describes in a masterly way how both forces in human nature, the inborn thirst for freedom and justice as well as the profane trivialization of our dignity as humans, are at work wherever ideologies arise and crumble. In analyzing the rise and fall of the communist totalitarian system in Eastern Europe, Havel shows not only what forces were at work to create it, but also what led to its breakdown.

The essential aims of life are present naturally in every person. In everyone there is some longing for humanity's rightful dignity, for moral integrity, for free expression of being and a sense of transcendence over the world of existence. Yet, at the same time, each person is capable, to a greater or lesser degree, of coming to terms with living within the lie. Each person somehow succumbs to a profane trivialization of his or her inherent humanity, and to utilitarianism. . . . In everyone there is some willingness to merge with the anonymous crowd and to flow comfortably along with it down the river of pseudo-life. This is much more than a simple conflict between two identities. It is something far worse: it is a challenge to the very notion of identity itself.[23]

How is it possible for people to accept totalitarian systems which then violate their basic human dignity? For Havel, to opt for a totalitarian system is not just a decision between the system and the individual person. The dividing line runs straight through the heart of every person who has the capacity to be simultaneously the victim and the willing accomplice of his or her own oppression. "A totalitarian system happens because part of us wants it to be there: human beings can be accomplices in their own bondage, and the appeal of a totalitarian system is that it is nourished by the fear of human autonomy."[24] Havel continues:

> It can happen and it did happen only because there is obviously in modern humanity a certain tendency toward the creation, or at least the toleration, of such a system. There is obviously something in human beings which responds to this system, something within them which paralyses every effort of their better selves to revolt. Human beings are compelled to live within a lie, but they can be compelled to do so only because they are in fact capable of living in this way. Therefore not only does the system alienate humanity, but at the same time alienated humanity supports this system as its own involuntary master-plan, as a degenerate image of its own degeneration as a record of people's failure as individuals.[25]

But the unquenchable thirst for human dignity and freedom makes itself felt in the dissident voice of the powerless in the system. It withdraws from the control of the system and creates a network of integrity and free action which discloses to others the possibilities of responsible action still open to them. Havel explains:

> This power does not rely on soldiers of its own, but on the soldiers of the enemy as it were—that is to say, on everyone who is living within the lie and who may be struck at any moment (in theory at least) by the force of truth. . . . It is a bacteriological weapon, so to speak, utilized when conditions are ripe by a single civilian to disarm an entire division. This power does not participate in any direct struggle for power; rather it makes its influence felt in the obscure arena of being itself. The hidden movements it gives rise to there, however, can issue forth (when, where, under what circumstance, and to what extent are difficult to predict) in something visible: a real political act or event, a social movement, a sudden explosion of civil unrest, a sharp con-

flict inside an apparently monolithic power structure, or simply an irrepressible transformation in the social and intellectual climate. And since all genuine problems and matters of critical importance are hidden beneath a crust of lies, it is never quite clear when the proverbial last straw will fall, or what that straw will be. This, too, is why the regime prosecutes, almost as a reflex action preventively, even the most modest attempts to live within the truth.[26]

But can we Christians propose a vision to a disillusioned East, to an economically broken Developing World and to a Developed World trapped in consumerism? Do we have more to offer than economic progress within a consumer society? Can we develop upon the innate desire of all to live in the truth? There will be enormous disillusionment, particularly among the young, in the wake of the collapse of communism. But can we fill this emptiness with a global vision which is concerned with a world of justice, peace, and joy for all? Do we have a vision at all?

Every social movement or political experiment begins with a vision that animates it and pulls it forward. It is a vision that compels the response of those who share it. A common social vision is something people aspire to, are exhilarated by, and are willing to sacrifice for. It transforms present actions and interprets them in the light of future possibilities. The pope, as well as many political leaders, speaks about a new age, a new dawn for the human race, a new world order, a new vision for humanity. Such a cry for a vision becomes intensified by the impending deadline of a millennium. The ending of a century in the year 2000 will stimulate questions concerning the meaning of history as well as its future development. But how do visions originate? Where do they come from? The answers vary. Some will say a prophet is needed to present a vision. Thus, Brueggemann contends:

Prophets are essential not only for the church but for humankind as a whole as well. Only the prophet engages in imagining different possibilities. He never asks whether his vision can be implemented, for before all else must come a vision. Modern cultures are normally competent enough to implement everything but it seems impossible for them to imagine anything. The prophet's task is to keep alive the ministry of imagination, to keep on proposing alternative solutions and futures not yet conceived. The prophet must propose new visions in order to enthuse and energize people since it is the "Not Yet," the promised and that which is about to begin that can energize us, and not that which we already possess.[27]

This perhaps is why at times we seem to have no way out of our impasse: we have "no prophet and no king." But then, one could ask, where are our prophets and leaders? Perhaps we either do not recognize them or we have killed them.

Others believe people already have the vision; it only needs to be unearthed and brought into the open. But by whom and/or in what manner?

Since humankind can only survive if it has a vision of the future, several questions emerge: Who can present such a vision? Can Christian faith still offer a vision for our sin-permeated and disillusioned world? Or does our faith have nothing to say about this world except that it will end in total destruction? Can faith only console us by saying that the present suffering has a meaning and that the New Heaven and the New Earth will soon come? Does scripture itself not tell us that the darker the situation appears the closer we are to the end of the world? If we take the apocalyptic writers literally in their description of this age there is no future for this world. The closer we get to the year 2000 the more we will hear such views from many corners of the church but mostly from sectarian groups. But what about Jesus' own vision of reality? Does he have anything to say to our world today?

It is here that we as Christians could discover the explosive force of God's Kingdom in the historical unfolding of creation. The Kingdom could be seen as a hidden yet effective moral ferment within the body politic. It has a social momentum whose *kairos* will come when the circumstances are right for the movement of the Holy Spirit. To identify this "revolution" for justice, peace, and human rights as the Kingdom at work in the concrete situations of human history means to read the signs of the time from the commitment of faith. Robin Green sees our time as one of great opportunity and possibility:

> In a way without parallel in Christian history we have rediscovered a God who is totally immersed in our history, our suffering, our hope. . . . Above all else, we have entered a time when the fundamental character of humanity and the universe is being revealed as that of exchange and interdependence.[28]

The symbol of the Kingdom of God leaves room for interpreting its content as belonging to this world and as also proclaiming a historical future that is not deducible from the circumstances of present history. The future, as the Bible understands it, is something qualitatively new that lies beyond human planning and capability, something we can only allow to be given to us. Yet, this symbol takes this world and human effort in history seriously without surrendering the openness to a transcendent future in the fullness of God. For only God can ultimately guarantee the fulfillment of humankind's deepest aspirations. Benedict Viviano expresses the dynamic well when he writes:

> Our engagement in this struggle (to make the kingdom hope come true) can be without illusions because we know by faith that no human program by itself will bring in the eschaton. Our engagement can also be without ultimate despair, because we believe that, no matter how great our self-created horror becomes, God is faithful to his promise and he will bring the kingdom which has already drawn near to us in his Son.[29]

The correct interpretation of the Kingdom symbol will show that its content does not signify something that is purely spiritual or outside of this world. Leonardo Boff minces few words when he writes:

> It is a total, global and structural transfiguration and revolution of the reality of human beings; it is the cosmos purified of all evils and full of the reality of God. The Kingdom is not to be in another world but is the old world transformed into a new one.[30]

Here the Kingdom is viewed as the consummation of history, the final fulfillment of humankind's social destiny, the accomplishment of God's own intention for the whole of creation. We have, therefore, always to be on guard not to regard the Kingdom as a utopia that is situated only on the horizon of history. The Kingdom is a present reality at the heart of history. Thus, Charles Elliott proclaims:

> The Kingdom is not some kind of extra-terrestrial entity that will be superimposed on this world. Nor is it a process of spiritual or internal change that leaves the outer realities looking much the same. It is the liberation of the world we live in, know, touch, smell, suffer, from all that corrupts and destroys it.[31]

It is incarnated in history, in human society and in the world. Although the Kingdom of God is not purely and simply identical with the world, it is "identifiable" *in* the world. We could also say with Clodovis Boff that "the Kingdom shows itself in society, it is encountered in society: but this society is not the Kingdom."[32]

To understand the Kingdom as belonging to this world leads to a broader understanding of the concept of salvation. The universality of the salvific will of God (1 Tim 2:4) is a generally established datum of Christian theology. In the past this notion was considered more in terms of its quantitative and extensive aspect. Today we have come to understand it under a more qualitative and intensive aspect. It is viewed in terms of the intensity of the presence of God, and consequently, of the religious significance of human action in history. The distinction between profane history and salvation history is here viewed differently. There is only one human destiny irreversibly assumed by Christ, who is the Lord of history. Salvation is seen as an intra-historical reality; it embraces all human reality, transforms it and leads it to its fullness in Christ. The absolute value of salvation gives human history an authentic meaning. It aims at the transformation of history and at its fulfillment in the New Heaven and the New Earth. The Bible is seen as presenting creation not as a stage prior to the work of salvation but as part of the salvific process and indeed its first salvific act.[33]

This seems to have been the Kingdom message Jesus came to proclaim. This was the vision he wanted to communicate to us. It is a vision of God, the world, humankind, and creation as a whole, as well as of each individual human person. It is the most grandiose vision that the world has ever known. For this vision Jesus lived, labored, suffered, and died. And it is this vision he entrusted to his disciples: "As the Father has sent me, so I send you" (Jn 20:21).

THE CHURCH AS AGENT OF THE KINGDOM

The church as the community of those who have been chosen to carry on the vision that Jesus conveyed must define itself in relation to the Kingdom, which is meant for humankind and the whole of creation. Its mission is to reveal through the ages the hidden plan of God (Eph 3:3-11; Col 1:26)) and to lead humankind toward its final destiny. It must be seen entirely at the service of this divine plan for the salvation of all human beings and all of creation.[34]

The church is the place where the Kingdom makes itself present in a particular and concentrated way. "She becomes on earth the initial budding forth of that Kingdom" (*Lumen Gentium* 5). We can even say: (1) The church is an "initial realization" or a "proleptic anticipation" of the plan of God for humankind, that is, the fullness of the Kingdom; and, (2) it is a means (sacrament) through which this plan of God for the world realizes itself in history (*Lumen Gentium* 9 and 48).

Indeed,

The church is a Kingdom colony, a people of God on earth called and empowered by the Spirit to show forth the reality of the Kingdom *now* in assurance that the Kingdom will eventually come in fullness and that their faithful service contributes to that final fullness of God's reign.[35]

We must, however, constantly realize that the nature and mission of the church is always to be understood in relationship and subordination to the Kingdom of God. This relationship is admirably described by K. E. Skydsgaard:

> The Church owes its existence to the Kingdom of God and both conceptions belong closely together, so that it is hardly possible to reach a clear understanding of the nature of the Church without relating it to the basic New Testament conception of the Kingdom of God.[36]

The church is not the Kingdom now, because the Kingdom makes itself present outside the church as well. Her mission is to serve the Kingdom and not to take its place. Vatican II states clearly:

> While helping the world and receiving many benefits from it, the church has a single intention: That God's Kingdom may come, and that salvation of the whole human race may come to pass (*Gaudium et Spes* 45; see also *Lumen Gentium* 5).

This text replaces what was perhaps the most serious pre-Vatican II ecclesiological misunderstanding; namely, the identification of the church with the Kingdom of God on earth. This misconception accounts in many ways for the kind of ecclesial triumphalism that regards the church as beyond all need for institutional reform and conceives her mission as bringing everyone within her fold in order to assure salvation.[37]

The distinction between the Kingdom and the church bore immediate fruits in the development of post-conciliar theology, at least in two theological fields: in the theology of liberation and in the theology of religions. The symbol Kingdom of God provides the horizon for a solution for two theological problems. First, in the context of liberation theology, it supplies the bridge that connects the historical liberation of the oppressed in this world with the eschatological Kingdom still to come in fullness at the end. It shows how work for justice and liberation inside and outside the church is intrinsically linked with the Kingdom present now, since the ultimate goal of the Kingdom of God is the transformation of all reality.

Second, in the interreligious dialogue the Kingdom symbol furnishes the theologian with a broader perspective to enter into dialogue with other religious traditions. If the Kingdom is the ultimate goal of God's intentionality with all of humanity, then the question is no longer how these other religious traditions are linked to the church but rather how the Kingdom of God was and is concretely present in these religions.

The church, while accepting the distinction between the church and the Kingdom in principle, has been very eager lately to ensure that they are not pulled apart whether in liberation theology or in the interreligious dialogue. Some theologians, particularly in India, are afraid that we are heading toward a crypto-identification of church and Kingdom once again. In the words of Felix Wilfred:

> Since certain trends in liberation theology and in the theology of religions seemed to highlight the reality of the Kingdom at the expense of the Church and to distance themselves from the Church, the reaction (of the official Church) has taken the form of barring any access to the Kingdom except through the Church. Or to put it in another way, instead of understanding the Church in relation to the mystery of the Kingdom, this trend wants to understand the Kingdom of God in terms of the Church, and indeed turn the Church itself into the Kingdom.[38]

If such a trend gains the upper hand in Catholic theology today, one of the most powerful sources for the renewal of the church and its theology could be seriously stifled. Only if we maintain the distinction between church and Kingdom clearly and uncompromisingly can we understand how such a symbol can once again become *the* religious symbol of our time. It provides us, on the one hand, with a way to relate to this world and its destiny fruitfully and, on the other hand, with a way to enter into a more open and creative dialogue with other religious traditions and ideologies.

THE MAIN AREAS OF CONCERN

We find today five major areas of concern that have been mentioned and discussed in numerous religious conventions and general chapters over the past twenty years. They seem to capture the most urgent topics that Christian churches must address and come to grips with. They are the horizons against which we must proclaim the vision of Jesus, the Kingdom of God. The urgency of each area depends, of course, on the concrete situation both of the local church and of the individual Christian attempting to witness to a commitment to the Lord. These areas are the discovery of the Bible as the prayer book of ordinary people, solidarity with the poor, the immense problem of refugees and migration, inculturation and dialogue with other religions and worldviews, and the process of secularization.

The Discovery of the Bible as the Prayer Book of Ordinary People

One of the astonishing signs of our time is the enormous interest of ordinary people in the Bible as the word of God for them. They have come to discover the Bible as their book, the people's book. This book had been closed to them for many centuries. Religious authorities decided which parts lay people could hear and which were not for their ears or which might even be dangerous to their faith. Vatican II, in *Dei Verbum* (22 and 25), insists very strongly that the Bible must be made accessible to all the faithful and that they should be led into direct contact with the sacred text. The Bible is discovered as a book of life, a book that can give hope, strength, and joy even in the midst of abject oppression, violence, and destruction. It can give new hope for the future.

Because of this interest in the word of God, particularly among the poor in the developing countries, the Christian community will be called upon to show to what extent its commitment to the Lord lives from this Word and to what extent it can effectively communicate and share the word of God. This is especially important today because of the fundamentalists' interpretation of the Bible, which is being communicated so effectively by members of many sects. Can we stand up against the kind of fundamentalistic interpretation of the Bible that is effectively promoted by many sects? Are we able to unmask the ideological presuppositions on which such sectarian interpretations of scripture are based?

Solidarity with the Poor: The Issues of Justice, Peace, Liberation, and the Integrity of Creation

Almost all bishops' conferences, catechetical congresses, and religious congregations have made the preferential option for the poor one of the priorities of their resolutions. This option includes the issues of justice, liberation, peace, and ecology. The question remains, however, as to how deeply this option has really affected the life and the spirituality of the committed Christian and of ecclesial groups. The implementation of this option will be one of the acid tests of whether the Christian faith will be relevant and whether traditional churches and their institutions will survive. On this point seemingly all authors agree.

Whenever issues of justice are addressed, our relationship to nature can no longer be ignored. Questions concerning the integrity of creation or the issue of ecology are rightly seen as belonging to the concern for justice. Some theologians call it eco-justice, which Cobb defines as follows:

The word "eco-justice" expresses the determination to hold together the concern for justice as a norm for human relations and the awareness that the human species is part of a larger natural system whose needs must be respected.[39]

Philosophers, scientists, and even theologians for too long have come to interpret and see everything in purely anthropocentric terms. Notwithstanding the fact that the highest value in scripture is the human person, a purely anthropocentric view is unbiblical and can only lead to total destruction. At the present time, a profound shift is occurring in which we are moving from an anthropological view of theology toward a view which considers nature as the context of Christian theology. This shift is more apparent in less academic theology than in the writing of most scholarly theologians. The Bible, however, supports such a way of doing theology. Here the natural world is taken very seriously, not merely as the playground of humanity, but as a gift from God for the work of redemption. The issue of eco-justice has become a matter of survival for the human species. We will take up this topic in detail later.

The Immense Problem of Refugees and Migration

The number of refugees is daily growing so drastically that many consider it the most important of the five concerns listed. Never in history have there been so many refugees as in our age. Estimates speak of some 200-250 million such persons. There are about 13-15 million who are officially registered, and about the same number who are "illegal aliens" in different countries. It is understandable why some have called our century the century of refugees. One in every fifty human beings has crossed borders as a migrant or refugee according to official UN figures. All indications are that the number of refugees, migrants, and other uprooted people will continue to increase. This is precisely because the pressures bearing upon international migration continue to increase. Most migration today takes place as a result of compelling circumstances. These include not only the obvious situations of warfare, civil strife, persecution, and ethnic conflict affecting so many countries today. As is now widely recognized, international migration is also compelled by environmental degradation, the failure of developmental models and economic structures to provide basic employment and subsistence, and often the displacement of people in the name of development projects (e.g., in the areas of agriculture, hydroelectricity, mining, and forestry).

The rising hostility toward migrant workers and other foreigners in so many societies, obviously exacerbated by the traumas of recession and unemployment, appears to be an ominous and malignant cancer spreading across our societies. Therefore, authentic Christian faith must be lived in a world in which millions of people have no home and are making demands on the countries to which they immigrate or are deported. What is the church's attitude toward these people? How should people of the church respond to the urgent needs of these human beings?

Inculturation and Dialogue with Other Religions and Worldviews

God's world in the making is marked by great variety and vitality. This can be seen in the tremendous assortment of human activities and actions: economy, society, religion, worldviews, values, prejudices, language, art, poetry, technical achievement, modes of interaction, to name a few. The sum total is what we mean by culture. It is only by taking culture seriously that the presence of God can be fully perceived. Inculturation fuses the experience of the people into a new functioning synthesis in order that they may experience and express the presence of God anew in the context of their own traditions. These traditions are not static but are in a constant process of change.

If God is revealed through the religious experiences expressed in the different cultures, then dialogue among these cultures is a necessity. Dialogue recognizes the right to be different. It means accepting the validity of another's religious experience, even when that experience is quite different from one's own. It requires the willingness and ability to communicate honestly one's own religious experience to the other. It is the effort to be open to one another, to listen to the other, to share in one another's life.

The Process of Secularization

Secularization is a term that arose in the wake of modernization. In the past religion offered a holistic view of reality, providing the universal meaning for a society, and the means through which a people could understand the world and organize its communal life. Religious faith pointed to the ultimate goals of life, which determined the system of values that governed one's concrete choices in life. Religion can still function in this way. Modernization, however, introduced a process of differentiation within this holistic view of reality. Within this perspective, secularization may be understood as referring to the differentiation between the "sacred" and the "secular," and the growing independence of the "secular" from the "sacred." The role of religion is thus reduced to providing the "ultimate meaning" of life and reality.[40] Two other definitions of secularization may be instructive:

Secularization is a process through which religious authorities and institutions are forced to give up their traditional control of State and society and accept the plurality of the religions and ideologies within the framework of a secular State and a growing secular society dependent on rational discourse to understand and pursue what constitutes the common Good.[41]

Secularization is the process in which religious consciousness, activities, and institutions lose social significance. It indicates that religion becomes marginalized to the operation of the social system, and that the essential functions for the operation of society becomes rationalized, passing out of the control of agencies devoted to the supernatural.[42]

Even though this process is most evident in highly industrialized cultures, secularization is a process involving the world as a whole. Although both Muslim and Hindu society will be much more reluctant and resistant to such a process, they cannot avoid its impact. Secularization must be recognized as a new and vital stage in the world that God is making and not merely seen as a further sign of decadence.

Theologians on their part have pointed out that the problem which emerges within this process of secularization is the rise of secularism. Or we might say that the process of secularization has led many to the acceptance of secularism as an ideology. Secularism has no positive contribution to make in humanity's search for ultimate meaning. It denies transcendence, affirming the absolute autonomy of the "secular" world.

Although most people may not hold to the ideology of secularism, their practical behavior indicates otherwise. They are indifferent to the transcendent in life. For this reason some would like to define secularism as "loss of a sense for the transcendence." It is important to realize that secularism is in no way a scientific conclusion, but rather a philosophical position which one embraces.

Secularism, therefore, need not be the natural consequence of the processes of secularization and modernization. Sociologists now acknowledge that, while modernization has led to secularization, religion and the sacred are not disappearing, though they may be finding new forms of expression.[43]

The evaluation of secularization as an irreversibly negative process is, therefore, not shared by all. Some hold that this process must be more critically evaluated. Secularization to them is too closely related to the "mechanistic metaphor" in explaining the world process and is too easily identified with a process that will almost automatically lead humankind to optimal fulfillment.[44]

Amaladoss believes that secularization should be interpreted less as a crisis of faith and more as a moral crisis of desire:

> The discussion on secularization is focused too much on philo-sophical and theological questions and too little on concrete matters such as consumerism, social inequality, economic ex-ploitation. The essential question is whether the moral decline around us is the result of a secularized view of life. Or whether people in trying to justify their wrong moral options reject the higher, religious option, simply because it is inconvenient. The danger which threatens Christianity in Western Europe might perhaps be found less in the fact that people have had enough of faith than in the individual and collective selfishness character-izing our society: the urge for constantly more and better, mu-tual competition, the lack of social involvement, of love of one's neighbor.[45]

Amaladoss accepts the process of secularization as a necessary means of promoting communion in difference in a religiously pluralistic so-ciety. The differentiation of social institutions and the relative autonomy of other institutions from religion are inevitable consequences of mod-ernization and will and should continue. But this does not have to lead by necessity to secularism, which is an ideology. In order to assist society in seeing that religion is required for ultimate meaning, Amaladoss proposes the following:

> The only way of meeting the challenge seems to be to develop a new Great Tradition in which society is not seen as a totally autonomous secular sphere that is somehow cut off from vari-ous religions, but as a communion promoted through a method of dialogue and consensus, which leads not only to a conver-gence on values in mutual respect for varieties of beliefs and traditions but also to a secularization of every religion so that it learns to distinguish the absolute ground of its life and practice from the relative manifestations of it in symbols and action in the secular sphere.[46]

It is within these areas that we are called today to live out our Chris-tian commitment to the Lord. No one can claim to be a disciple of Jesus and consciously disregard these aspects. We cannot believe that we are true followers of the Lord in our time while leaving the con-crete world out of our commitment.

Part 1

THE KINGDOM BEFORE JESUS

Introduction

The expression *Kingdom of God* appears only once in the entire Old Testament in the deutero-canonical book of Wisdom 10:10: "She showed him the Kingdom of God and taught him the knowledge of holy things." Since the phrase occurs only in a deutero-canonical book, it is clear why non-Catholic scholars say it does not appear at all in the Old Testament. (There are, however, nine references in the Old Testament to the "kingdom" over which Yahweh rules, and forty-one references to Yahweh as "king.") The phrase *Kingdom of God* or *Reign of God* is therefore basically a New Testament formulation. Yet Jesus took this notion for granted. Consequently, it must have been something every Jew understood. As John Bright observed:

> But for all his repeated mention of the Kingdom of God, Jesus never once paused to define it. Nor did any hearer ever interrupt him to ask "Master what do these words 'Kingdom of God,' which you use so often, mean?" On the contrary Jesus used the term as if assured it would be understood, and indeed it was. The Kingdom of God lay within the vocabulary of every Jew. It was something they understood and longed for desperately.[1]

The notion underlying this concept of God's sovereignty has deep roots in the biblical tradition of Israel's history. The phrase was not invented by Jesus. Many scholars employ the notion as a comprehensive theologumenon, as a heuristic scheme devised to synthesize the manifold texts of the Old Testament. Such a scheme can be comprehensive and synthetic without being exclusive. Other systematic themes, for example, *Covenant* or *saving history*, could be used as a synthesizing tool for the diverse literature and thought that make up the Old Testament. Yet, many Old Testament scholars have been reluctant to impose any such theologumenon on the Old Testament because they believe that it would violate the essential pluralism of the book. Jesus, however, seemed to have raised the phrase *Kingdom of God* to the level of a heuristic scheme for understanding God's purpose in human affairs.[2]

But like most Old Testament thoughts, the notion of the Kingdom of God has no smooth evolutionary development. It is pluralistic and nonsystematic in its expression. In order to grasp the true meaning we must briefly present its background as it developed in the Old Testament and in late Judaism, which was the immediate context of Jesus' own preaching. At the time of Jesus there were three interpretations of this symbol, the first of which is considered to have been the most common one:

- the national-political expectation—"within history" (prophetic-eschatological)
- the apocalyptic expectation—"beyond history" (apocalyptic-eschatological)
- the ethical expectation—"present realization" (realized eschatology)

Each of these will be examined in turn.

1

The National-Political Expectation

THE NOTION OF KINGDOM IN THE OLD TESTAMENT

There are a number of strands of Old Testament theology which could be utilized as basic elements for synthesizing the whole salvific activity of Yahweh under the heuristic scheme Kingdom of God.[1] Rudolf Schnackenburg, in his now classic work on the Kingdom, lists three such theological strands present throughout the Old Testament that seem to provide the foundation for the emerging notion of the Kingdom of God at the time of Jesus. Others present five strands or more. First, there is the belief that God is King over all creation and, as a result of the Covenant, over Israel in particular. Second, one finds the liturgical celebration in which Israel experienced in a particular way the kingship of Yahweh over the chosen people. Third, there is the hope of a final decisive intervention of Yahweh on behalf of the chosen people in the near future in order to fulfill the promise made to the fathers and the prophets.[2] N. Lohfink adds two more strands by referring to Israel's experience with its monarchy and the shattering experience of the Exile. Both modified the idea of God's rule and Kingdom considerably.[3]

God Is King Over All Creation

The Old Testament describes Yahweh as King first and foremost when seen as the Creator, the King of the universe, the Victor over the monster of chaos, the Sustainer of the universe. God's kingship is implicitly affirmed in the creation story. In the first chapter of Genesis, Yahweh gives *dominion* to human beings over the created order. This dominion is actually a stewardship, not an absolute authority, since dominion derives from Yahweh alone. In short, it is creation theology that is fundamental to the idea of the Kingdom in Israel's religion.[4]

This notion of God as King of all creation seems to have been borrowed from the ancient Near East mythologies. Here creation is depicted as a great struggle in which God rescues the world from the primeval chaos and keeps it in existence by protective and life-giving "kingly rule and power."[5]

The idea then entered Israel's liturgical celebration. Here Yahweh is acclaimed and experienced not only as King of Israel, but in particular as the cosmic King who created the world by defeating the chaos of nothingness that stood in opposition to creation (Ps 74:12-17). The enthronement psalms are the most forceful example of this idea (Ps 93-99). In addition to the cosmic power of God displayed in the act of creation these psalms carry another universal notion—they acclaim Yahweh as King of all the nations:

> For the LORD is a great God,
>   and a great King above all gods (Ps 95:3).

Here it can be seen most clearly how far reaching and expansive the Old Testament roots are for the later metaphor of the Kingdom of God. The liturgical acclamation and celebration let the people experience Yahweh as King in their midst. The liturgy became a powerful impulse for hope in the final achievement and fulfillment of God's Kingdom in the future.[6]

God Is King Over Israel

Historically this might have been the most rudimentary experience of Israel. The sovereignty of Yahweh over the chosen people is experienced in Israel's own history of salvation through events such as the deliverance from slavery in Egypt, the guidance during the wilderness wandering, the conclusion of the Covenant, the gift of the land, the protection from the surrounding nations, and even the establishment of the monarchy and ultimately the return from exile. All of these events were viewed as acts of God's saving power on behalf of the chosen people.

This experienced care, protection, and love of God for the chosen people found expression in images and metaphors which described God as shepherd and redeemer, but most distinctly as father or mother. God's work is compared to that of a parent—father, mother, or both. Although called Father fourteen times and never called Mother, God is not to be thought of in categories of sexual identity. When God's work is compared to that of a parent, the language is warm, gentle, affectionate, nurturing, and caring, which is the sense of the image.[7] Two examples illustrate the biblical view:

> And I was thinking: How am I to rank you as my children? I shall give you a country of delights, the fairest heritage of all the

nations! I thought: you will call me Father and will never cease to follow me (Jer 3:19).

> Can a woman forget her nursing child,
>   or show no compassion for the child of her
>   womb?
> Even these may forget,
>   yet I will not forget you
> See, I have inscribed you on the palms of my
>   hands (Is 49:15-16).

Furthermore, it is in hymns like the "Canticle of the Sea" (Ex 15:1-18) or in the famous creed of Deuteronomy 26:5-9 that we get a hint of what the Bible means by saying God "reigns or rules" over God's people. It is within this array of images and songs that the notion of king takes its concrete shape.[8]

The Experience of the Monarchy

To understand the people of Israel one has to consider the way it came into existence. According to the Bible, the Hebrews were a group of slaves on the bottom rung of Pharaoh's society in Egypt. Who they were and who they became is best explained in the official creed. The oldest historical summary of the faith that we have from Israel is Numbers 20:15-16:

> Our ancestors went down to Egypt, and we lived in Egypt a long time; and the Egyptians oppressed us and our ancestors; and when we cried to the LORD, he heard our voice.

But the official creed became Deuteronomy 26:5-9:

> You shall make this response before the LORD your God: "A wandering Aramean was my ancestor; he went down into Egypt and lived there as an alien, few in number, and there he became a great nation, mighty and populous. When the Egyptians treated us harshly and afflicted us, by imposing hard labor on us, we cried to the LORD, the God of our ancestors; the LORD heard our voice and saw our affliction, our toil, and our oppression. The LORD brought us out of Egypt with a mighty hand and an outstretched arm, with a terrifying display of power, and with signs and wonders; and he brought us into this place and gave us this land, a land flowing with milk and honey."

This text is "the quintessence of Israel's faith, and it is neither accident nor exaggeration that it is entirely subsumed under the theme of liberation."[9]

Yahweh, their God, had decided to liberate them from their misery and oppression. The way Yahweh does this is unusual. God does not liberate them by changing Pharaoh's mind, by lifting their burden, or by giving them a just share in Pharaoh's society. No, Yahweh takes them out of this society of oppression and misery in order to create them into a new society of brothers and sisters. This society will be a "contrast society" or an "alternative community" to the social reality of Egypt, because it will not be ruled by domination, oppression, and dependence, but by justice and compassion. Israel is made into this new society on its way through the desert at Mt. Sinai. Made here into a new community, the people will enter the promised land, the land that flows with milk and honey, God's own land, in order to celebrate a "feast for Yahweh." The aim of the Exodus is to create a new people that will celebrate forever its God in a new society.[10] This new Yahweh-society will become a paradigm of how God envisions a human society and of what God will ultimately achieve in the future concerning all of humanity. Brueggemann explains:

> The call of Israel can only be understood as a new call of God to create an alternative social reality. . . . The radical break of Moses and Israel from imperial reality is a two-dimensional break from both the religion of static triumphalism and the politics of oppression and exploitation. . . . Moses dismantles the politics of oppression and exploitation by countering it with the politics of justice and compassion. The reality emerging out of the Exodus is not just a new religion or a new religious idea or a vision of freedom but the emergence of a new social community in history, a community that has a historical body, that had to devise laws, patterns of governance and order, norms of right and wrong, and sanctions of accountability.[11]

Because of this origin as a "contrast society" (Lohfink) or as an "alternative community" (Brueggemann), Israel revealed a marked tendency to avoid any similarity with its neighboring kingdom-states. These kingdoms and their social reality were too clear a reminder of their situation as slaves in Egypt. Israel's pre-political form of government was based on an egalitarian society and on charismatic leaders according to the Exodus tradition. To proclaim Yahweh as King would have meant to accept the corresponding form of government practiced in the states surrounding Israel. It would have meant to go back to the Egypt whence they had come.

Yahweh was the only Lord and Ruler in Israel; there could be no one to take Yahweh's place here on earth. Although there are pronouncements about Yahweh which easily suggest the vocabulary of royal language, these statements do avoid the explicit words. It was almost like a tabu that could not be broken.[12]

Israel's sociopolitical structure changed around 1000 B.C. when it accepted the governmental form of a kingdom under David and Solomon. This development became one of the major impulses for considering Yahweh as King. The language tabu was lifted and the royal vocabulary of the surrounding nations was easily transferred to Yahweh. Those who objected to this form of government still used the old vocabulary with its avoidance of any kingly titles applied to Yahweh.[13] The Bible itself remains careful about the introduction of a centralized rule. Although the monarchy is accepted by Yahweh and the king is given God's blessing together with a promise of divine protection, his authority was clearly understood to be limited by God's own sovereignty. Yahweh's ultimate reign over Israel is not relinquished in the presence of an earthly king.[14]

Eschatological Hope for God's Rule

Solomon was able to counter completely the contrast society that Moses envisioned and created. He made Israel once again into a Pharaoh-society. He banished the neighbor for the sake of reducing everyone to servants. He replaced Covenanting with consuming. "In tenth-century Jerusalem it is as though the whole revolution and social experiment of the Mosaic novum had never happened."[15] The verdict of God on this achievement was the eradication of the two kingdoms of Israel followed by the Babylonian Exile.

The disillusionment with the monarchy gave shape to a renewed theology of God's definitive reign over Israel. The prophets had already outlined a new form for a society of Yahweh in which Israel could exist without being an independent state, a society in which the will of God alone was decisive. The return from exile is seen as an act of God's powerful reign, and Israel's hope for restoration fuels its vision of a final salvation. At this point the notion of Yahweh's reign takes on eschatological tones, an aspect of capital importance for the New Testament use of the metaphor. The eschatological note is well expressed by Schnackenburg:

> The fundamental idea in the future hope of Israel is always the kingly rule of Yahweh, his victorious advent as king and his reckoning with his enemies. Yahweh's victory is followed by the manifestation of the kingship. He appears as king and takes possession of his realm.[16]

Jeremiah foresees a new Davidic ruler, the Messiah (Jer 23:5-6). Deutero-Isaiah speaks in exultant and expansive terms of Yahweh's liberation of Israel from exile and of a future hope for salvation (Is 43:14-21). The famous text of Isaiah 52:7-10 breathes a similar eschatological tone. While the return to Jerusalem is the immediate referent of these songs of praise, their scope extends to God's final eschatological salvation. Deutero-Isaiah in his vision of Israel's future goes back to the early beginnings with its anti-royal legitimation of Israel's existence. A future is envisioned when Yahweh will not be King over all the gods (there are no gods to be King over), nor King of all the nations. Yahweh will be King of Israel only. Israel will never have an earthly king again. The promises made to David and his descendants are transferred to the people as a whole. Yahweh as sole King of Israel will become the only principle of life for all the other nations, who will continue to exist with their respective forms of government. The people of Israel as God's chosen instrument will take over the role of king for all the nations. As such, Israel will become the absolutely necessary source of legitimation for all states and governments in the world.[17]

The frustrated hope for freedom and peace after the exile gave further impetus to the eschatological dimension of God's rule. What had not and could not be achieved by human effort finally would be accomplished by God's own intervention. This aspect of God's reign is elaborated in the apocalyptic writings of the Old Testament (e.g., the book of Daniel), but most vividly in the non-canonical writings such as the Assumption of Moses, the Testament of the Twelve Patriarchs, and 1 Enoch.

The "Societal Reality" of the Coming Kingdom

After the exile Yahweh exercises kingship over the chosen people through the Torah. Yahweh's kingship becomes visible in cultic celebrations. Over against this cultic vision of the future Kingdom the book of Daniel presents a world vision in which the great empires of the world are seen as the reference point of God's Kingdom here on earth despite their enormous corruption. These corrupt and deformed kingdoms are here envisioned as the foil against which the true Kingdom of God will soon emerge after judgment by fire. The great empires of the present are compared to beasts coming out of the sea, a symbol of the societal chaos of the time. The future Kingdom is then compared to a human creature, known as the Son of Man, who will come on the clouds of heaven. With his appearance society will become human again. The new Kingdom is so different from all historical experiences that its coming is described as life out of death. The rising of the dead will give all those who lived before the coming a chance to participate in this new Kingdom. This eschatological Kingdom of God, embodied in the reign of Israel expanding over all humankind, will be a Kingdom that embraces all of humanity. The issue here is not that God is once again proclaimed King but that God's kingship will be over a "societal reality." It will be a counter-reality against all societal constructions in the history of humankind, particularly against the terrible world empires of the Greeks.

It is not possible, therefore, to speak of a purely religious form of the coming Kingdom. The Old Testament idea of the Kingdom of God makes it impossible to claim that the phrase *Kingdom of God* always refers to God as King but never to a realm where God will be King.[18] The coming Kingdom was always seen as having a material side, particularly as envisioned in the restoration of Israel to her land. The "day" of God's coming,

> would be the event that would usher in the victorious kingdom and the universal reign of Yahweh (Is 2:2; Mi 4:1;). Israel would be returned to their homes (Hos 11:10-11), and the peace of Eden would descend on the world of nature (Is 11:6-9). Joy would be the constant delight of the believing participants in the kingdom (Is 60), and death would be swallowed up forever (Is 25:7).[19]

The spiritual side of the coming Kingdom is especially seen in the fact that the Spirit from on high would be poured out over all (Is 32:15; Jl 2:28-29) and that God's Torah would be written on the hearts of all believers (Jer 31:33; Ez 36:24-28). In short, the coming Kingdom of God cannot be seen as purely spiritual, universal, and eschatological. The historical and political element is an essential part of the notion itself. No Jew could ever envision a purely spiritual Kingdom without expecting as well a complementary historical and political realization on behalf of Israel. Jesus went beyond these physical and material aspects of God's Kingdom, but he definitely did not abandon them.[20]

THE KINGDOM IN LATER JUDAISM

Flavius Josephus in *Antiquities* tells us that the principal preoccupation of the Jews between the years 100 B.C. and A.D. 100 was "to be liberated from all kinds of domination by others, so that God alone might be served" (*Ant.* 17, 11, 2). The coming of God's final visitation on behalf of the people was something that people expected soon. Jesus never defined concretely what the Kingdom meant. Rather, he presumed that his audience had at least a vague and general knowledge of this symbol. At the time of Jesus, revelation as we understand it today had already ceased for almost two hundred years. Other trends and ideas had been developed in the period between the two testa-

ments. The question is, therefore, what did people concretely expect
about the coming of the Kingdom at the moment when Jesus started
to proclaim its arrival? In order to understand this situation we must
examine later Judaism.

There are three basic beliefs that are common to all Judaic writers
during 200 B.C.–A.D. 100 concerning the coming of God's eschatological
Kingdom in the near future.

First, the place of all eschatological hope for the coming of the
Kingdom is this world. Although the spiritual and moral dimension is
not denied, the political and historical one remains dominant.

Second, the awaited coming of the Lord is expected to remove all
that is a hindrance to God's kingship in the present. It will free Israel
from all oppressors and all the nations will be brought under the reign
of God. The idea of the coming Kingdom is always seen as the bringing about of an inner-earthly and glorious Kingdom of Israel in which
all nations would find their peace and wealth. This nationalistic aspect of the coming of God's Kingdom was commonly held.
Schnackenburg explains:

> The idea that dominated, the usual and ordinary idea, was that
> God would send the Messiah-king, the "son of David," and
> through him restore the kingdom of Israel, with the ancient glory
> of the re-united tribes, liberated from foreign occupation and
> poverty but at the same time restored to a true service of God
> and a holy fulfillment of the Law.[21]

This aspect will appear in the Kingdom message of Jesus as well.
Jesus aimed first of all at the restoration of Israel as the true benefi-
ciary of the breaking in of the Kingdom of God. This point should not
be overlooked; the coming Kingdom was meant first and foremost for
Israel, as is also evident in the teaching of Jesus. The restoration of
humankind was always seen in the context of the historically rooted
restoration of Israel.[22]

Third, the coming of God's reign is seen as God's own activity which
human beings can only graciously accept. However, the final restoration of Israel would not be realized without Israel accepting it willingly and actively. Therefore, the coming Kingdom does not exclude
humankind's cooperation. The belief was widespread that one could
hasten the coming of the Messiah through prayer and good works.
The coming Kingdom must be looked upon not merely as a gracious
gift but also as a task. At the very least, the Kingdom would not be
realized without a willed act of acceptance on the part of the people of
Israel.[23] This view was so common that it is safe to say that all the
disciples of Jesus expected up to the very end that Jesus would bring

about this kind of Kingdom. This attitude is illustrated by the following two texts:

But we had hoped that he was the one to redeem Israel (Lk 24:21).

Lord, is this the time when you will restore the kingdom to Israel? (Acts 1:6).

THE KINGDOM IN THE APOCRYPHA
AND IN THE QUMRAN COMMUNITY

The Apocrypha and Pseudepigrapha[24] are as diverse in their understanding of the coming Kingdom as are the Old Testament writings themselves. The idea underlying all conceptions of the Kingdom seems to have been that God is King of the universe, past, present, and future. It was expected that the Kingship of God would be manifested in an eschatological Kingdom. The common denominator of all eschatological formulations of the Kingdom was the rejection of foreign rule. The bringing about of the Kingdom of God, whether by a messiah or a direct heavenly intervention, implied the destruction of the kings and the mighty of this world.[25]

From the Dead Sea Scrolls we know that the Qumran community lived in the near expectation of the coming Kingdom. Through the new revelation imparted to the "Teacher" the meaning of the prophecies had become clear. What had been prophesied by Isaiah and other great figures like Moses or Habakkuk could be applied to their own community. They experienced the beginning of the Kingdom already in their midst and were sure that the ultimate fulfillment was close at hand. They kept themselves in constant readiness for the final battle when God would come and defeat the demonic forces that were now ruling the cosmos and history. After the defeat, all the glories of the new and perfect creation would be bestowed on them.[26]

It has been observed that the vision of the Qumran community concerning the coming Kingdom portrays, at least in a couple of points, some striking similarities to that of Jesus' vision of God's coming reign. Several remarks may be made in regard to this topic.

First, great significance was given in Qumran to the ritual of the "messianic banquet," which the community celebrated regularly in anticipation of the great end-time banquet in which the Anointed One of Israel would soon be present to lead the community to final deliverance. One of Jesus' distinctive activities was his regular celebration of festive meals, which he regarded as celebrations of the presence of the Kingdom now.[27]

Second, the Qumran community structured its leadership in terms of twelve representatives of the twelve tribes. This was done in anticipation of the imminent fulfillment of the coming Kingdom. Jesus' election of the twelve apostles provides explicit evidence that he aimed at the restoration of the twelve tribes preparing Israel for the final coming of God's reign.[28]

Third, the community at Qumran lived in constant watchfulness and readiness for the imminent apocalyptic battle against the power of evil which would precede the coming of the new age. The coming of the Kingdom is imaged in connection with the holy war, the conflict of the Children of Light and the Children of Darkness. The similarity to Jesus with this eschatological conflict has been seen in Jesus' practice of exorcism. His exorcisms are to be understood as the beginning of the eschatological battle. Jesus is doing battle with the Evil One. His driving out of the evil spirits is evidence of the fact that Satan is being rendered powerless and his kingdom "plundered" (Mt 12:29). The eschatological conflict so much addressed in the Qumran War Scroll is taking place here and now. The Kingdom has come with Jesus.[29]

However, in spite of all similarities, one cannot overlook the difference that exists between Jesus' view of the coming Kingdom and that of the Qumran community. The Kingdom vision of Jesus could be described as "social, political, personalistic (respectful of individual freedom), universal in intent, transcendent in origin, earthly in realization, present in sign, and future in its fullness." The vision of the Qumran community was "social and political, but differs as being national rather than universal in its aims; militaristic, vindictive, violent, and somewhat more deterministic in its means, with no hints of love of enemies or forgiveness of sins." Although the Kingdom is seen as transcendent in origin and earthly in realization, the chief agent for its realization is Michael and not the mysterious Son of Man. In spite of these differences many scholars maintain that the Qumran ideas of the coming Kingdom do find a striking resonance in the teaching of Jesus.[30]

In conclusion, we can say that the roots of the intertestamental view concerning the coming Kingdom are deeply embedded in the Old Testament, in the Covenant tradition of Israel, and in the "plan" of God in regard to Israel and the whole of creation. Also, the Kingdom language, as in the Old Testament, remains historical and contains an irreducible national-political element.

THEOLOGICAL INTERPRETATION

The Purpose of Israel's Election

The history of humankind is the history of salvation. God is revealed in history as the One who intends to lead the whole human race and, through it, all creation to its final destiny, into God's own glory. "Again and again he offered a Covenant to man and taught him to hope for salvation" (Eucharistic Prayer IV). Although God is disclosed in all religions as the One who wants to save, the concrete form of this saving purpose unfolds explicitly and tangibly in the history of the people Israel. The simplest and most programmatic statement of the promised plan of God is found in Genesis 12:3: "In you all families of the earth shall be blessed." W. C. Kaiser unfolds some of the import of this idea when he writes:

> Included in that promise to Abraham was God's word that he would be and do something for Abraham, and therefore God would be and do something for all the nations on the earth. Among the earliest things he promised to do were these: he would send in Abraham's seed the man of promise; he would grant Israel an everlasting inheritance in the land of Canaan; and he would graciously give the gospel—i.e., "all people on earth will be blessed through you" (cf. Gn 12:3).[31]

This plan is expressed in the Covenant formula: "he may establish you today as his people, and that he may be your God" (Dt 29:13). This phrase should be regarded as an identification card for Israel as God's chosen people. On this formula rests the *Berit* (Covenant) which guarantees the very existence of Israel as a nation.[32] This phrase clearly reveals God's ultimate intention for the whole of humankind. The fulfillment of this intention is expressed in the Book of Revelation in the following way:

> And I heard a loud voice from the throne saying,
> > "See, the home of God is among mortals.
> > He will dwell with them as their God;
> > they will be his peoples,
> > and God himself will be with them;
> > he will wipe every tear from their eyes.
> > Death will be no more;
> > mourning and crying and pain will be no
> > > more,
> > for the first things have passed away."
> And the one who was seated on the throne said, "See, I am making all things new"(Rv 21:3-5).

The people of the Old Testament Covenant are considered both witness to and revelation of this plan. Their call and election by Yahweh are described accordingly (Ex 19:4-7; Dt 7:6-12). They are "designated for the worship of Yahweh."

Worship is seen as a celebration of what the people had received in the Covenant. It is a manifestation of life. This new life seeks its expression in adoration, thanksgiving, and praise (Is 43:21). This life received in the Covenant is "already" an anticipation of that future reality which God has destined for the whole human race. Through what Yahweh is doing for the people in the present is revealed what Yahweh has in store for humankind, history, and the whole of creation.

As it was for the Old Testament people, the idea of worship as celebrating in an anticipatory manner the final goal of creation (union and communion with God) is an essential aspect for the New People of God, the New Covenant, as well. The definition of the New Testament assembly as the "New People of God" is expressed in 1 Peter 2:9 as follows:

> But you are a chosen race, a royal priesthood, a holy nation, God's own people, in order that you may proclaim the mighty acts of him who called you out of darkness into his marvelous light.

Or,

> You have made them to be a kingdom and
> priests serving our God (Rv 5:10; 1:6).

People are called into the service of Yahweh to be mediators of God's saving activity for the nations. The election of Israel out of many nations is a calling for the nations. This contains three aspects. First, Israel is a passive witness of God's power, glory, and might (Is 44:23). Through Israel the nations will recognize who Yahweh is. Israel is a shining sign for the whole world (Is 62:1ff.). Since Yahweh is in the midst of the chosen people, Israel becomes the center of Yahweh's salvific activity. From here it flows over into the whole world (Ez 47:1-12). Israel is not only the recipient but also the source of blessing for all the nations on earth. That is the very reason it was called: "[that] in you all the families of the earth shall be blessed" (Gn 12:2ff.).

Second, the active role of Israel as mediator for all the nations is most explicitly expressed in being a servant. The idea of being a servant of God is essential in order to understand the election of Israel and any election by God. God's intention with creation will never be accomplished without the cooperation of those God chooses. Being elected by God means to be ready to be a servant, that is, a person God has asked to be a visible representative through whom God will accomplish the divine plan. It is not the one chosen one who will do the work, but God through this person. All God asks is that the one chosen trust in the divine presence in his or her life and let God accomplish the divine plan, working through the person's own gifts, talents, and activities. In God's hands the servant becomes, so to speak, transparent; he or she assumes the "concrete shape" through which God can reach creation and be present there, the saving will manifest.

The perfect example in the Old Testament of what it means to become a servant of God is Moses (Acts 7:20-45). His vocation story is a paradigm of how God accomplishes the divine purpose through people. Yahweh reflects aloud:

> "I have observed the misery of my people who are in Egypt; I have heard their cry on account of their taskmasters. Indeed, I know their sufferings, and I have come down to deliver them from the Egyptians" (Ex 3:7-8).

In order to accomplish the promise, God chooses Moses, one of the oppressed, to be God's agent of liberation:

> "I will send you to Pharaoh to bring my people, the Israelites, out of Egypt" (Ex 3:10).

When Moses objects to this selection, the only reassurance he receives is "I will be with you." This phrase will be the leitmotif throughout God's redeeming actions in history: to national leaders such as Joshua (Jos 1:9) and the Judges (Gideon in Jgs 6:16), to kings (Solomon and David in 1 Kgs 1:37), to prophets (Jeremiah in Jer 1:8) to Jesus (Acts 10:38), and finally to the church (Mt 28:20). All those whom God chooses will have to trust in this "I will be with you"; no other assurance is given.[33] The importance of a servant in God's plan with humanity can be seen most clearly in that it is ultimately through the "Ebbed of Yahweh" (*the* servant) that God will accomplish salvation for the whole world (Is 49:6; 52:13-53:12).

Third, any election follows the pattern: "to be with him and to be sent out to proclaim the message" (Mk 3:14). Whomever God chooses is called first to "be with him." God establishes with that person the intimacy and relationship which God intends to establish with the whole group. This person or this community is drawn into a relationship with God, within the condition of this present world, which God has in store for the whole human race: union and communion with humankind and creation as a whole. After this the person or the community is "sent out" to communicate to others what has already been received. They become the mediators of God's saving intention. There is no election without a call to active participation in the saving activity of God for the whole of humankind and creation.

The *why* of Israel's election remains the same for the New Israel, the New People of God, the church. The church has its roots in the "election of Israel." It carries on the mission of Israel as it finds its fulfillment in Jesus Christ.[34]

The Emergence of Eschatological Hope

The history of Israel, however, became a history of a broken Covenant. When the unfaithfulness of the Covenant people reached its peak, Yahweh did the seemingly unexpected thing—cancelled the Covenant: "You are not my people and I am not your God" (Hos 1:9). With this the existence of Israel as God's people was put into question. Israel's assets were reduced to nothing. The prophets seemingly created this vacuum in order to sweep away all false security. They then filled it up with their message of the new things Yahweh would do. Total annihilation could not be Yahweh's last word. There had to be some other possibility in the light of Israel's faith in and history with Yahweh. As the prophets saw it, this cancellation of the Covenant was done not to abandon the people but to open the way for something *new*: "I am about to do a new thing" (Is 43:19).

From then on, everything had to be expected from the future. What had previously been possession now became expectation. There will be a decisive intervention of God in the history of Israel that will, once and for all, make the promise of the Covenant a true reality. This is the basic message of the prophets Isaiah, Jeremiah, Ezekiel, and Hosea. All Israel can do is to hold onto this promise of God's final intervention with hope.

How New Is the New?

The new is understood as a break so deep that what follows cannot be understood merely as the continuation of what preceded. However, the new takes its form from the old saving acts: a New Covenant, a New People, a New Exodus—all basic themes of the old saving acts and institutions. The old must come to an end in order to give way to the new. Yet there is continuity in the discontinuity. This promise of Yahweh, of a final act on behalf of Israel, became the topic of theological thinking, of intense prayer, of political groups and apocalyptic visionaries. Mostly, though, it was thought of in terms of a national-political reality. However, it did begin with the idea of a transformed world which included a renewal from within: a new heart (Ez 36:24-28); a New Covenant (Jer 31:31-34); a New People of God which would include the whole of humankind as expressed in the famous pilgrimage of the nations to Jerusalem (Is 2:1-5f; 19:16-25); the dead who will come to life to participate in the New Creation (Is 26:19; Ez 37). The belief in the resurrection of the dead and life after death, however, was only developed as an explicit doctrine of Israel's faith in the apocalyptic writings.

A peculiar feature of the new vision is the function of the "nations." The foreign nations play a decisive role in the destruction of Israel and are therefore drawn into the field of Yahweh's work of judgment and blessing. Here the horizon of Yahweh's future action is broadened; it will extend to the nations as well. The annihilation of Israel paves the way for something ultimately new, having happened for the sake of greater perfection. This we could call *the prophetic expectation*, a new intervention of Yahweh on behalf of the chosen people. It will be the last one, at the end of history, but still "within history."[35]

2

The Apocalyptic Expectation

CHARACTERISTICS OF APOCALYPTIC LITERATURE AND WORLDVIEWS

Prophecy and apocalypticism are deeply interrelated. It is not as if the prophets died and apocalyptic writers took over. The most common feature is that both addressed very concrete historical-political situations. They both proclaimed a God who was very actively present in such situations. The situation out of which apocalypticism arose, however, was a situation of persecution and violent repression of the Jewish faithful who would not compromise their faith by acquiescing to reform. They were looking desperately for "divine revelations" that would explain to them why they had to suffer such intolerable situations and what plan God had for their deliverance. Most scholars agree that the apocalyptic books of the "Assumption of Moses, 1 Enoch, and the Book of Daniel were written in the time and in connection with the Hellenistic reform under Antiochus Epiphanes."[1] The context in which apocalypticism could arise is well described in the following passage:

> Apocalypticism as a general orientation in society, or at least influential groups within it, could arise out of and address situations in which Jewish faith was pushed to the brink of despair. In what were, to some, seemingly hopeless situations, such an orientation enabled people not only to endure in their traditional faith, but even to take action against overwhelming odds, such as the persecution by the Hellenistic armies of Antiochus Epiphanes.[2]

The seed for such literature can be found already in such passages as Ezekiel 38-39, Zechariah 9-14, certain parts of Joel, and Isaiah 24-27, which are embedded in prophecy. But it was in connection with the Maccabean Revolt that this seed was brought to full flower. The first, and the greatest, of apocalyptic writings is the book of Daniel, written against a background of persecution, terror, and death. It must have made a deep impression in the mind of the Jewish people because it alone won for itself a place within the canon of the Hebrew scriptures.[3]

The prophetic hope of the coming of the Kingdom always involved a catastrophic breaking in of God as well as continuity and discontinuity with the old order. For the apocalyptic writers the stress is definitely on discontinuity. The final intervention of God will bring a world totally transformed, a transfigured universe. Their eyes are fixed on what is "beyond history." The distinction is made between the "present age" and the "age to come." It signifies the contrast between the present world and the future redeemed order. The age to come transcends history; it entails a New Heaven and a New Earth. Its content is a final cosmic struggle between God and the powers of evil. It envisions a cosmic catastrophe that includes the collapse of the visible world as well as of all human institutions, the defeat of the powers opposed to God, the beginning of the new world, the new age in which God reigns supreme. It means the resurrection of the dead and the final revelation of God himself.[4]

The present world is viewed as totally under the reign of evil. This view reflects the profound pessimism into which the Jewish people had fallen during the post-exilic period. Israel had never before been so faithful to the Law, and yet the messianic Kingdom promised by the prophets had not appeared. Instead of God, the wicked pagan nations were ruling Israel. The present was regarded as abandoned to the domination of evil and suffering.

A new interpretation was necessary: Why had the promise of the prophets not come true? The apocalyptic seers tried to discover in visions and dreams the secrets of the hidden world. Why was God so silent? What was the reason for such terrible suffering of the righteous on earth? When and under what signs would Yahweh come to usher in the Kingdom and put an end to the present situation of the people? The following characteristics mark the eschatological expectations of the apocalyptic writers, revealing their answer to the problem set before them: dualism, present and future as unrelated, pessimism, and determinism.

Dualism

The Bible does not accept a metaphysical dualism in the sense of two independent principles, one good and one evil. However, Jewish dualism does combine a *cosmological dualism* (good-evil; light-darkness)—which sees the world in the grip of two conflicting spirits, God and Satan (Belial)— and an *eschatological dualism*—which limits the struggle between these two powers to this age and sees the complete triumph of God in the age to come. Evil is experienced as a reality which involves the human race but remains metaphysically independent. In the *Book of Watchers* sin derives from a "contamination" or vitiation of nature with respect to human beings and material things. Some angels damaged the order of nature as it had been ordained by God. In the *Book of Dreams* it is the leading rebel angel who is the true and proper principle of evil. He is seen as a creature who rebelled against God and encouraged other angels and humans to do the same. Others see the original fall in the disclosure of heavenly secrets about science and art and especially about the construction of arms. Science has given humans a sense of power and with it the ability to crush other beings.[5]

The prophets saw a contrast between the world God wanted and the world as it actually existed. The world is seen in the light of Genesis 2-11. It is a world that is penetrated by the *no* our ancestors had given to God (Gn 2-3); a world in which brotherhood had been killed (Gn 4:1-16); a world in which the technical skills given to humankind had been used to reach the heavens so as to become once again like God. This was done through exploitation and oppression of fellow human beings (Gn 4:17-11:9). But the prophets always saw nature and history as God's creation and under his sovereignty. Only now they lay under the curse of sin and the burden of evil.

The overwhelming experience of undeserved and inexplicable evil and suffering on the part of Israel led the apocalyptic writers to sharpen the contrast between the world in its present state and God's world, between the present sinful order and the future redeemed order of God's Kingdom. They developed the Old Testament idea of evil spirits into a dualism without, however, making it absolute. With the exception of Enoch, there is no truly transcendental dualism in all of Jewish literature.

Present and Future as Unrelated

With the overemphasis on the evil of this age, the apocalyptic writers, in contrast to the prophets, could no longer see how history is connected with eschatology. The continuity between the present world and the world to come is practically lost. Present and future are considered as two unrelated entities. The old and the new no longer have anything in common. The world to come could appear only when this world disappears. There had to be a break with the space/time continuum.[6]

Pessimism

Consequently, the apocalyptic writers display a strong pessimism about their age. The blessings of the Kingdom cannot be experienced in the present. This age is abandoned to evil and the righteous can only submit patiently to suffering in the hope of the new age to come. God remains the Lord of the world but seems to let it run its course without any intervention. The image of God becomes rather deistic. The solution to the problem of evil is relegated completely to the future coming of the Kingdom. The Fourth Book of Ezra, in particular, is shot through with a profound pessimism about the fate of humankind and creation. There is no hope for the present world nor any solution to its troubles. There is a basic mistrust of human beings and their capabilities. Everything is expected from God. The all pervasive dimension of evil led the apocalyptic writers to have little belief in God working with human beings. To that extent they seemed to believe only in God and not at all in humanity.[7]

Determinism

Amos and Deutero-Isaiah explicitly unite all history into a single plan, conceived and controlled by God. The apocalyptic writers expanded it into a whole doctrine. They related all the data of history and traced the connection among them in the divine purpose underlying history. They looked at the world from the view of eternity and saw in its apparent confusion an order and a goal. God had made the cosmos and God had a purpose for it and the power to achieve this purpose. God is not only in control of history but is the one who takes initiative in history and will lead it to its final goal. They worked out history in vast periods, not only systematically but deterministically. God had determined these periods and there could not be any deviation in the way they would occur. The different divisions of history showed clearly the unfailing purpose of God. Since these events were fixed, the calculation of time became a very important part of the apocalyptic writers. They wrote as if they were in the last days.[8]

The secrets revealed to the seers refer to the last things concerning God's purpose for the universe from creation to the end. The revelation of these secrets is meant to help the pious discern the signs of the approaching end and to strengthen them in their faith. The account of history given under symbolic devices is normally very clear up to the age in which the author himself is actually living. But from then on the accounts become obscure, the actual predictions begin, and the tempo of events is quickened, for the end is at hand. The content entails the overthrow of the wicked and the triumph of the righteous, either in this world or the life to come, in an earthly kingdom or in a heavenly, in their physical bodies or in renewed spiritual bodies. The Messianic Kingdom, temporal or eternal, is ushered in and heralds or inaugurates the age to come, when God's purpose will triumph and God will live with the people evermore. The practical purpose was to inspire the nation with new courage and with fresh hope in the ultimate victory of good over evil and the triumph of God and the Kingdom over all the powers of darkness.

The imagery used is most often taken from a mythological background concerning the combat between the Creator and the great monster, which symbolizes the chaotic deep or the cosmic ocean, the place of mystery and evil. Furthermore, frequent use is made of wild beasts and birds of prey to symbolize the nations of the Gentiles: lions, tigers, wolves, dogs, hyenas, wild boars, foxes, squirrels, swine, falcons, vultures, eagles, and ravens. Another symbolism is that of numbers, especially the numbers 3, 4, 7, 10, and 12, or multiples of these. Each has a peculiar religious significance in the Old Testament. A special importance is attached to the number 7, denoting completion and perfection.[9]

Despite all their effort to strengthen and encourage the people in their predicament of suffering and persecution, the apocalyptic writers offered little hope for this world. The way of this age is predetermined and must run its course to completion in total destruction and annihilation. The Kingdom of God must await the appointed time. God waits for the time decreed. As a consequence of such a view, apocalyptic eschatology despaired of history, since it was completely dominated by evil. Hope was related only to the future. The harsh experience of evil and suffering in the present made it impossible to believe that God would come into this world for a final "visitation." God became the God of the future and the future world.[10]

THE POSITIVE CONTRIBUTION OF APOCALYPTIC

The positive contribution of apocalyptic writings consists particularly in two things. First, the New Heaven and the New Earth comprise a totally transformed universe that includes all of creation. Second, there is a universalism of salvation that no longer restricts salvation to Israel alone but offers it to all human beings.

The apocalyptic writers took over the broad lines of prophetic eschatology, although they added modifications and new stresses. Particular emphasis was placed on the belief in life after death, which went far beyond anything to be found in the prophets. Furthermore, particular interest was placed on the final judgment, which was no longer confined to the living but was extended to include all of the dead, taking on the character of individual judgment. In short, the apocalyptics "did not lose sight of the prophetic teaching concerning the future hope, but enlarged it and enriched it out of their own religious insight and experience."[11]

Concerning the coming of God's Kingdom there was a tension between the worldly, national, and political elements on the one hand,

and otherworldly, universal, and transcendent elements on the other; this could not be easily resolved. While the prophets maintained a balance between the two, the apocalyptic circles put the emphasis strongly on the dualistic, cosmic, universalist, transcendental, and individualistic aspects. It is within this context that the name Messiah appears as an eschatological figure chosen by God to play a leading role in the coming of the Kingdom. Depending on the group's basic stance, the Messiah was perceived either as a predominantly this-worldly, national, and political figure, or a predominantly transcendental, eternal, and universal one.[12]

3

The Ethical Expectation

THE YOKE OF THE KINGDOM

The pious in particular believed that the Kingdom of God was a reality which did reach into this world. This found expression in the phrase: "To take upon oneself the yoke of the Kingdom." It expressed a certain attitude of mind. By reciting the Shema "Hear, O Israel . . . " [Dt 6:4-5]) the pious rabbi opened his mind and heart unconditionally to God's holy will. This act was seen as the "receiving of the Kingdom of God." Its intention was perfect unity with God. Whenever a Jew obeyed a precept of the Law and thus showed himself subject to the author of the Law, there the Kingdom of God was present.[1] What that could mean in the concrete situations of life is related in the death-story of Rabbi Akiba:

What a typical Rabbi longed for was that sublime moment when the daily profession of a long life might be confirmed by act. When R. Akiba, who died the death of a martyr, was in the hand of his torturers, he joyfully "received upon himself the yoke of the kingdom of heaven" (by reciting the Shema). When asked why he did so, he answered, "All my life I have recited this verse ('And thou shalt love,' etc.), and have longed for the hour when I could fulfil it. I loved him with all my heart, I loved him with all my fortunes. Now I have the opportunity to love him with all my soul. Therefore I repeat this verse in joyfulness." And thus he died. There is no indication of despair in Akiba's death, but also no thought of a crown of martyrdom awaiting him for this glorious act. He simply fulfills a commandment of love, and he rejoices in fulfilling it. It is "a love unto death," suffering no separation.[2]

KINGDOM AS PRESENT AND FUTURE

Judaism developed the following view: The kingship of Yahweh in this world depends, by God's own free choice, on a person's free acknowledgment of it. God wants to reign over free agents, and it is their free obedience he desires. The individual person thus becomes the center of the whole of creation. He or she is the one on whom the kingship of Yahweh in this world depends, both by God's free choice and by the individual's free acknowledgment. This liberty, however, was abused by the free agent and so the world was forsaken by God. God was no longer the King of the earth. The light returned with Abraham, for he was the first to again call God "Master," King, a name which declares God to be ruler of the world. Before Abraham, God was only the King of the heavens, where his reign was unquestionably accepted. But since Abraham, God became the King of the earth once again since Abraham made that which rules the heavens the rule of his life, namely, God's will. But God will only be fully King of the earth if all human beings once again freely acknowledge him as such. How God's presence left the earth after Adam's fall and how it came back to earth is seen in Jewish literature as follows:

The principal location of the Presence of God was (meant to be) among the creatures down here. When the first man sinned, the Presence of God moved up to the first firmament. When Cain sinned, it went up to the second firmament. When the generation of Enoch sinned, it went up to the third firmament. When the generation of the flood sinned, it went up to the fourth firmament. When the generation of the dispersion (at the tower of Babel) sinned, it went up to the fifth. On account of the Sodomite it went up to the sixth, and on the account of the Egyptians in the time of Abraham it went up to the seventh.

But, as a counterpart, there were seven righteous men who rose up: Abraham, Isaac, Jacob, Levi, Kahath, Amram, and Moses. They brought the Presence of God (by stages) down to earth.

Abraham brought it from the seventh to the sixth, Isaac brought it from the sixth to the fifth, Jacob brought it from the fifth to the fourth, Levi brought it down from the fourth to the third, Kahath brought it down from the third to the second, Amram brought it down from the second to the first. Moses brought it down to earth (Genesis Rabbah to Gen. 3:8. XIX:IX).[3]

Experience, however, had shown that not even Israel was able to respond fully to the Presence of God among them and that the "pious would always be sparse." Yet, whenever one submits to the "yoke of the Kingdom," the great Shema, there God's Kingdom would break into this world. But only at the time of the Messiah would all the nations turn to one creed and subject themselves freely to the "yoke of the Kingdom." In fact some rabbis believed that if Israel would keep the great commandment for only one day the Kingdom of God would "explode" into this world. Or, if only *one* would keep it perfectly, the Kingdom would definitely come.[4]

The Pharisees believed that they could hasten the day of the Messiah by faithfully keeping the Law in terms of holiness and purity. The Essenes of the Qumran Community shared this view as well with the firm belief that, like the Zealots, they would have to take up arms to fight for the Messiah on the day of his coming. By entering the community and living the rules of the community in holiness and purity, one already participated in the coming Kingdom of God.

4

The Emerging Content of the Kingdom

A RELIGIOUS EXPERIENCE

What is contained in this symbol of the Kingdom? As we saw earlier, the phrase *Kingdom of God* stands for a very rich and multifaceted "religious experience" expressing Israel's personal relationship with Yahweh. The following elements are part of that experience and, therefore, form the basic content of the Kingdom symbol. God is conceived as creator of all that exists. That was an experience Israel shared with its neighbors. What was unique was Israel's experience of Yahweh as Lord of history, who acts on behalf of the chosen people, who cares, protects, forgives, heals, and makes a Covenant with them. All of this becomes part of what it means to say that God is King of Israel and all the nations.

The actual care and presence of God among the people are then expressed in symbols like father, mother, pastor, bridegroom. Of particular importance is the God image as revealed in Deutero-Isaiah: the God of compassion. The concrete functions of Yahweh as King who reigns among the people also enter into this experience: Yahweh creates a people, organizes their structure, feeds, protects, directs, corrects, redeems, and imparts justice to them. The exercise of justice is of special significance. It consists of the following: to integrate once again into the community of Yahweh the people who have cut the bond of union; to reestablish friendship and harmony; to lead all to participate again in the blessings of the community; to give to each what is due; to compensate; to give back; to declare who is innocent and who is guilty. The aspect of justice presents Yahweh as defender and avenger of the rights of the poor and the marginalized in society, "partial" to their rights. Ultimately, justice almost becomes a synonym for "compassion, mercy, and forgiveness." All this stands behind the meaning of the "religious experience" expressed in the symbol Kingdom of God.[1]

THE SABBATICAL JUBILEE TRADITION

The day of Yahweh's final visitation is often depicted in Jubilee language. Isaiah 27:13 and 61:1-2 envision the final coming of Yahweh on behalf of his people in this light. The arrival of the Messiah is foreseen as *the* great Jubilee, the year of release and liberation.[2]

The Jubilee institution, although seen by many as an idealistic and nonhistorical creation of exilic theologians, is concerned with the social structures of Israel, which are based on the Covenant idea. Israel was an egalitarian society in which all were regarded as equal on the basis of land and inheritance. The danger always existed that the more thrifty and shrewd would get ahead and gradually establish an aristocracy. Consequently, the egalitarian society would give way to an order where peasants would become dependent upon and ultimately exploited by these aristocrats. In order to avoid such a development, the legal system of Leviticus 25 was designed. Its noble purpose was a periodic restoration of the ideal. The Jubilee Year demanded that each person be brought back to his or her original property and family.[3]

The Jubilee concept focused on returning disinherited people to the land of their traditional family heritage. To this end those who had lost their property were to regain possession, those who were indebted were to be freed from their debts, and those who were enslaved were to be released from slavery and allowed to return home. Its intention was clearly an attempt to guarantee that the Covenantal egalitarian society should remain the basis of Israel's social structure. At stake was the honor of Yahweh and of the individual citizen, who was restored to inherited rights given to him or her as a member of the Covenant.[4]

The final visitation of Yahweh is expected to be the great Jubilee of Yahweh, the year of salvation (Is 27:13). The Messiah will proclaim the good news of the great Jubilee of Yahweh to his people and announce the everlasting peace to Zion.[5] Isaiah describes the event as follows:

> How beautiful upon the mountains
>   are the feet of the messenger who
>   announces peace,
> who brings good news,
>   who announces salvation,
>   who says to Zion, "Your God reigns."
> Listen! Your sentinels lift up their voices,
>   together they sing for joy;
> for in plain sight they see
>   the return of the LORD to Zion.

Break forth together into singing,
  you ruins of Jerusalem;
for the LORD has comforted his people,
  he has redeemed Jerusalem.
The LORD has bared his holy arm
  before the eyes of all the nations;
and all the ends of the earth shall see
  the salvation of our God (Is 52:7-10).

SUMMARY OF THE TRIPLE EXPECTATION

The three views: national-political, apocalyptic, and ethical seem to have been the most dominant at the time of Jesus. They were not kept neatly separated but were intermixed and presented with every shade of meaning. The symbol "Kingdom of God," therefore, was known to the audience that Jesus addressed. Although the symbol evoked all kinds of expectations in the minds of the people, the national-political view was definitely the most widespread. Even the other two views shared in it.[6] In the latest period of Old Testament thought the idea of the Kingdom of God had developed to the point where it could carry the full weight of being a great arch extending from the first chapters of the Bible to the last. Under it, all other elements and stories must find their place:

It is this conception of the kingdom, and the story of God's work in history to establish it, that gives unity to the Bible and significance to its various parts.[7]

The notion can, therefore, be suitably employed as a "heuristic scheme" that is able to synthesize the enormous range of Old Testament ideas and themes. The hope of the future Kingdom of God had become the concentrated focus of Israel's expectations. It was to this hope, modified and enriched by the development of the intertestamental period, that Jesus addressed the good news of the breaking in of God's Kingdom. This he did in such a manner that a careful reading of the gospels gives the impression that people found his proclamation most attractive, fascinating, and arresting (Mk 3:7-21).

5

The Kingdom of God
in Contemporary Exegesis

In contemporary discussion there are three different approaches to the Kingdom of God. Each one focuses on a particular aspect of the Kingdom depending on the initial point of reference. However different they may be, they are complementary rather than mutually exclusive. These approaches are Kingdom as concept, symbol, and liberation.[1]

KINGDOM AS CONCEPT

In the past many scholars would insist on regarding the phrase *Kingdom of God* as a concept. To treat it as a concept means to assume that it leads to one clear and consistent idea. For example, the Kingdom of God is the final, eschatological, and decisive intervention of God in the history of Israel in order to fulfill the promises made to the prophets. The concern was to find out what the phrase meant in the teaching of Jesus, although Jesus himself never defined the Kingdom with specific concepts.

Three conceptual interpretations have been offered. First, the Kingdom may be seen as a speculative theological concept that attempts to get behind Jesus' own understanding of the expression, determining its definitive meaning for all time. The *City of God* by St. Augustine could be viewed as a perfect example of this.[2] A second interpretation sees the Kingdom as an apocalyptic concept, which in turn is said to have completely determined Jesus' understanding of the Kingdom. Albert Schweitzer could be regarded as the exponent of this view. A third interpretation treats the Kingdom as a biblical concept with the "present-future" tension that can be found in Jesus' message of the Kingdom.

In the history of theology the Kingdom concept has been used by countless theologians and philosophers. Some names to be mentioned are Kant, Lessing, Hegel, Hobbes, and Locke, who offered an almost incredible variety of interpretations to this concept. The concept is here used like an empty vessel, which can be filled at liberty with the contents and beliefs of one's own choosing.[3]

KINGDOM AS SYMBOL

In recent times scholars have been insisting on treating the phrase *Kingdom of God* as a symbol rather than a concept. Kingdom as a concept is regarded as too narrow and misleading. The idea of seeing the Kingdom as a symbol evokes an entire series of ideas, because a symbol, by its definition, presents or elicits a whole range of concepts.[4] The symbol of the Kingdom evoked in Israel the remembrance of God's activity, whether as creator of the cosmos, the creator of Israel in history, or ultimately as agent of God's final intervention at the end of history. It is God's action in history on behalf of God's people and ultimately on behalf of creation as a whole that is the underlying referent to which all of Jesus' teaching leads. The symbol stands for a very rich and multifaceted religious experience expressing a personal relationship with God.

It is quite obvious that such a broad range of religious experiences can hardly be expressed in one clearly defined concept. Jesus himself never defined the Kingdom of God in discursive language. Some scholars have concluded that the Kingdom was not a commonly understood phrase because Jesus was pressed constantly to clarify his message of the Kingdom. He did so by presenting parables. This is instructive. For whether one agrees or disagrees that the phrase *Kingdom of God* was commonly understood, the parables emerge as "Jesus' choice of the most appropriate vehicle for understanding the Kingdom of God."[5]

KINGDOM AS LIBERATION

A new attempt has been made by liberation theology to treat the phrase *Kingdom of God* neither as concept nor as symbol, but as a referent for historical liberation. In such a context the term would definitely yield a different understanding. At issue is the world-transforming dimension of the Kingdom.[6]

The Historical Background

Liberation theology claims that the most adequate understanding of the Kingdom of God can be reached by focusing on liberation. In order to understand this claim it is necessary to grasp the frame of reference in which liberation theologians theologize. This context, according to liberation theologians, has grown due to the developments of the last two hundred years regarding humankind's self-understanding and its role in history. A new historical situation and a new human self-understanding call for a rethinking, they say, of how the Bible should be read. This new historical situation has been brought about by two simultaneous and mutually dependent historical events that coincided with a new intellectual consciousness known as the Enlightenment. The first is the Industrial Revolution, which revealed humanity's capability of transforming nature. The second is the French revolution, which in its turn demonstrated humankind's potential for transforming the social order. This new self-understanding characterizes the human person's awareness of his or her capacity to transform both nature and the social order, and thus his or her active role in the transformation of history.

This self-understanding entails above all a new way of being a human person in history whereby men and women are more in command of themselves and their destiny in history. But it also implies a new way of being a Christian in the world and of living the faith in society. It demands that the Christian live the faith in the context of the contemporary consciousness of the person being an active subject in the transformation of history. Persons will be fulfilled only in the measure that they actively participate in forging their own destinies.

From here a very different view of human history emerges. The Christian understanding of history is seen as an alliance between God and humanity. It is history between two partners, God and human beings. God is the master of history, but humankind is another actor in the historical drama.[7] God created humans to be free and responsible persons. It is only in such a view that the words Covenant, grace, sin, faith, and freedom make sense. As Berdyaev says:

> History must not be understood as a purely human or purely divine achievement, but rather as a reality to which God and man contribute at the same time. Humanity partakes in the human nature of Christ. . . . It is the starting point of its [the Christian mind's] understanding of history. The latter must be understood, not as an event apart, a symbolic, sacred event, but in its real divine-human process, in the tragic cooperation of God and man, a cooperation whose force and intensity leads to the actual transformation of existence.[8]

History from such a perspective is conceived of as the "kingdom-process," wherein God's intervention is to be received as a gift and human cooperation is to be understood as a task. God's intervention is an appeal to open ourselves to the Lord and to our fellow human beings, to face historical reality in order to transform it in the spirit of the gospel. The secret of history is that it will not end in nothingness but in ultimate fulfillment.

As Christians we hold firmly to the fact that free will determines the flow of history. God enters into a partnership with us, God's creatures, with the sole intention of leading us into the fullness of a personal relationship. History is, so to speak, a love story in which God runs after creatures in the hope that they will finally come to realize that they find their ultimate fulfillment only in divine love. But the influence of the organic process of history as a factor that conditions all human actions must also be accepted and addressed. If we admit a "kingdom-process" and concede that it is in some sense incarnated in human history, then we would be justified in using sociological analysis of the human situation as an interpretative tool for understanding this incarnation. Theology cannot be done independently from society and history.[9]

It is not enough to deal with history and the role of human beings in history solely in an abstract and metaphysical way. One has to analyze society and understand history as the place of God's self-revelation if we want to discover and to speak about God in a meaningful mode for people today.

Theology on the whole has responded to this challenge raised by the new historical situation and the new human self-understanding. Much of contemporary theology in the First World derives its modernity from the fact that it takes seriously this question: How does one believe in a world where God has become an apparently superfluous hypothesis? In responding to this challenge first-world theologians have addressed themselves consciously or unconsciously to the nonbeliever.[10]

Liberation theology, on the other hand, takes seriously the question posed by the poor and oppressed as they struggle to free themselves from oppression and create a more just society.[11] It seeks to respond to the challenge coming from the nonperson, that is, the human being who is not considered human by the present social order. It asks how to proclaim to the nonperson "that God is love and that this love makes us all brothers and sisters." It is therefore not the nonbeliever but the nonperson whom liberation theology addresses.[12]

The problem, which is often not understood by those living in the First World, is that the new human self-understanding became the context out of which emerged the "bourgeois society," the dominant class. Its interests and values are stamped on modern society and, in turn, contribute to the situation of the nonperson in the Third World. For this reason liberation theology is theology from the underside of history, that is, theology from the perspective not of the dominant but of the dominated classes of society.[13]

The key phrase of the Bible, *the Kingdom of God*, is here examined from a different perspective than that of concept or symbol. Certainly the focus is distinctive. It is not reason and faith, but rather faith and transforming praxis that build the context of the question. In the words of E. Schillebeeckx: "The hermeneutics of the Kingdom of God exist especially in making the world a better place. Only in this way will I be able to discover what the Kingdom of God means."[14] What really is at stake here is the world-transforming dimension of the Kingdom of God. All who treat the Kingdom as concept or symbol normally stress the existential, individual, spiritual dimension of faith. While not denying these aspects, liberation theology views the Kingdom more in its historical, social, and political dimension, as well as in its world-transforming power. We must remember, however, that these three approaches are not mutually exclusive. Each focus highlights a dimension of the Kingdom of God.

The Hermeneutical Approach[15]

Liberation theology joins the general disenchantment of contemporary theology with a purely historical-critical approach to interpreting the Bible, a disenchantment expressed in the search for alternative models of interpretation. Historical criticism is concerned only with the *author* meaning of the text, that is, with what the original author intended to say. This is understood as an objective entity existing independently of the concerns of the interpreter. The content is culturally neutral, universally valid, and permanently relevant.

However, the real question is: How do we discover the meaning of the text today? How does the text disclose itself to us in our time? The question is not so much what the text meant in the past, but what it means now. In terms of liberation theology the question may be posed as follows: How can we discover the historical dimension of God's message and move that message away from all abstract universalisms so that the biblical message may be "more responsive to the geography of hunger, the culture of violence, the language of the voiceless masses, the world of oppression, and the structure of an unjust social order."[16]

The Proposed Solution

Scholars have proposed different solutions for resolving these two very different approaches to the text. S. Prabhu uses the "I-Thou" relationship as his starting-point. Hermeneutics is the conversation between the "I" of the interpreter and the "Thous" of the text. This kind of dialogical hermeneutics calls for a reciprocal openness between interpreter and text. The text is open to the questions the interpreter brings and the interpreter is open to the truth-claims of the text. S. Prabhu develops a distinctive approach relying on Gadamer, yet presupposing the work done by Ricoeur regarding the reading of any historical text. Ricoeur distinguishes among *author* meaning—what the author may have intended the text to mean; the *text* meaning—what the text actually means; and *listener* meaning—what the listener understands it to mean. Once the text is fixed in writing it is free from its origin and is open to new relationships. The written text is now autonomous:

• It is detached from its author. The mental intention and the verbal intention do not overlap.

• It is detached from the original addressees of the discourse. It is now open to an infinite number of readers and so to different interpretations.

• It is detached from the precise dialogical situation in which it was originally set. It becomes open to new references which offer new ways of experiencing reality.

The text itself confronts the interpreter with a history and a direction no interpreter can ignore. Every meaning brought out of the text can only be a further disclosure of the world behind the original meaning. This world in the biblical texts is ultimately an original religious experience which the text intended to communicate to all future audiences. The expression of this experience, which is the original meaning of the author, cannot be given up without violating the message of the text.[17]

Severio Croatto, a Latin American scholar, situates hermeneutics in the context of semeiotics, the science of signs, of which language in the narrow sense is the most comprehensive expression. Language, and therefore any text, contains a richness of meanings that cannot be reduced to only one. There is what could be called a surplus of meaning. A closure of meanings occurs through a particular linguistic performance when one meaning is selected from the many potential meanings by the original author and his or her addressees. Once that author dies and the addressees disappear, the closure of meaning comes to an end and is converted into an openness of meanings available to any reader in another context. Therefore, to read a text leads not only to a rediscovery of the original meaning but also to the production of meaning out of the reservoir of meaning implied in the text. As Croatto sees it, the text has not only a context-backward sense in the original historical context of the first closure meaning, but also a context-forward sense from which the text can be read so as to produce new meanings. This does not mean the imposition of an alien meaning on the text, because the meaning that is produced is potentially contained in the text's reservoir of meaning. The text itself remains normative.[18]

S. Schneiders suggests an analogy. The reading of a text from a given context-forward is like a contemporary artist's creative rendition of a classical musical score which, while producing a new interpretation that goes beyond the intentions of the composer, nevertheless must remain faithful to the score itself.[19]

By remaining faithful to the score, liberation theology regards its context-forward perspective as privileged because the Bible's own origin is marked by a profound liberation experience. Liberation hermeneutics appears to be more faithful to the biblical text and exhibits a closer harmony with the kerygmatic nucleus of the Bible. Liberation theologians are aware that this is a biased reading of the Bible, but all seem to agree that no one can read the Bible in a purely neutral and impartial way. Every reader approaches the Bible from a definite context-forward perspective which expresses the particular way in which he or she conceives of reality and correspondingly acts. It can, therefore, be said that understanding the Bible is no longer a matter of seeking a bias-free reading but of opting for the bias appropriate for the right reading of the Bible.[20]

The hermeneutics of liberation theology is quite simply the reading of the Bible from the perspective of the poor and oppressed, from the perspective of those who are persecuted in the cause of right, from the perspective of the condemned of the earth—for theirs is the Kingdom of Heaven.[21] Liberation theology, however, does not regard its hermeneutics as one alongside other possible ways of reading the Bible. It claims that it is the only way the Bible ought to be read, if it is to be read correctly at all. It is the hermeneutical key that unlocks the real meaning of the Bible.

It is from this perspective that the appeal of liberation theologians to the biblical theme of the Kingdom of God must be understood. Leonardo Boff, for example, suggests that "the Kingdom of God implies a revolution of the human world." Segundo insists that events of liberation in history stand in causal relationship to the Kingdom of God. Such an intimate connection between the Kingdom of God and the need for concrete action for liberation has even been recently affirmed by the church's magisterium.[22] In conclusion, we can say that the focus on the Kingdom of God as liberation raises different questions than the other two ways of considering the Kingdom. For liberation theology the nucleus of attention is the world-transforming dimension of the Kingdom of God.[23]

"MODEL" AS HERMENEUTICAL KEY TO THE KINGDOM

Over the last twenty-five years the concept of a theological model has been introduced into theology. Although this way of scientific investigation is mostly a tool employed by the empirical sciences, its use in theology has become acceptable. Why an empirical approach like "model" can be applied to theological topics at all might well indicate what has happened to theology over the last fifty years. In the words of B. Lonergan:

> Theology has become largely an empirical science, in the sense that Scripture and Tradition are not premises but data. The steps from data to interpretation are long, arduous, and at best, probable. An empirical science accumulates information, develops understanding, masters more of its material and, out of this, new insights and more comprehensive views will emerge.[24]

Model thinking in theology can prevent us from making concepts and symbols into idols. It helps us to realize that the infinite can never be captured in the finite structures of language. It opens an almost infinite possibility to theological development and therefore goes beyond any purely conceptual definition or symbolic representation.

Since Avery Dulles published his book on the models of the church in 1974 many other scholars have followed in approaching theological topics with the hermeneutical tool of models. Today we find books discussing models of Christology, moral theology, original sin, inculturation, and so forth. Howard Snyder has followed this line by investigating the biblical phrase *Kingdom of God* under the theological concept of model.

What Is a Model?

A model is a conceptual and symbolic representation or system by which we try to grasp and express reality or part of reality.[25] A model is to some degree an intentional abstraction from reality in order to clarify issues. It is a relatively simple, artificially constructed case that is found useful and illuminating for dealing with realities that are more complex and differentiated.[26]

Dulles distinguishes between explanatory and exploratory models. An *explanatory* model serves to synthesize what we already know, or at least are inclined to believe. An *exploratory* model, on the other hand, can lead to new theological insights. This kind of model is new, at least for theology, since it works more with a hypothesis rather than with firmly established data.[27] Models do not have to be exclusive. Various models can balance or supplement one another. A chosen model normally has one or two secondary ones, rejecting only the polar opposite of the primary model.

According to Lambino, when choosing a model the following points should be regarded as important:

• *Inadequacy* of models. Each model comprehends a different area of reality; it does not exhaust reality. Reality is always greater and richer than any model which tries to grasp it.

• *Relativity* of models. Each model focuses on one aspect of reality. No single model can claim to be exhaustive or exclusive in the sense that it grasps and expresses the whole of reality completely. There is no model to end all models.

• *Responsiveness* of models. Each age of history and each historical community tends to develop a model which best responds to its perceived needs. In that sense we can say that a model is accepted if it accounts for a large number of biblical and traditional data and accords with what history and experience tell us about the Christian life.

• *Historicity* of models. When the historical situation changes, that is, if there is a shift in the human person's understanding of self, the need for new models arises.

• *Time limits* of models. In time every model reaches the limits of insight and new models will emerge.[28]

Models of the Kingdom

The Kingdom is a multifaceted reality; in order to grasp its meaning the hermeneutical tool of a model might be one of the best instruments to deal with the mystery behind its depth. The concern here in using models should be to get at the truth of the Kingdom. According to Snyder, a valid conception of the Kingdom must meet three tests: It must (1) be solidly grounded in scripture, (2) be true to the character of Jesus Christ as witnessed by scripture, and (3) be fruitfully relevant in our present age.[29]

Snyder then proposes the eight models of the Kingdom that can be discerned as being present in the tradition of the Christian churches: (1) The Kingdom as future hope: the *future* Kingdom; (2) the Kingdom as inner spiritual experience: the *interior* Kingdom; (3) the Kingdom as mystical communion: the *heavenly* Kingdom; (4) the Kingdom as institutional church: the *ecclesiastical* Kingdom; (5) the Kingdom as counter-system: the *subversive* Kingdom; (6) the Kingdom as political state: the *theocratic* Kingdom; (7) the Kingdom as Christianized culture: the *transforming* Kingdom; and (8) the Kingdom as earthly utopia: the *utopian* Kingdom.[30]

Each of these models suggests something different about the nature of salvation, the mission of the church, and the meaning of Christian discipleship. No model can claim to be fully biblical and fully adequate.

According to Snyder, there are six fundamental tension points or polarities that are central to the mystery of the Kingdom of God. The best model would be the one that holds in proper tension these six polarities. They are the following: (1) present *vs.* future (already—not yet); (2) individual *vs.* social; (3) spirit *vs.* matter (religious—political); (4) gradual *vs.* climactic (eschatological—apocalyptic); (5) divine action *vs.* human action (gift and task); and, (6) the church's relationship to the Kingdom (the tension in seeing the church and the Kingdom as essentially the same or as clearly different).[31]

Any theology of the Kingdom that dissolves these tensions, opting wholly for one side or the other, is to that degree unbiblical. A true Kingdom theology will in some way maintain and live with these tensions. Snyder lists three criteria in the form of questions for assessing the accuracy of the Kingdom models in respect to the Kingdom message of Jesus:

(1) Does Jesus Christ remain the ultimate reference point in a given model? Since he emerges more clearly from scripture than the profile of the Kingdom, the Kingdom must be interpreted in the light of Jesus Christ. Jesus embodies in his person all the six polarities.

(2) Does the model help generate and maintain a vital Christian community of worship, witness, and mutual interdependence, or does it undermine it? The Kingdom is a social reality and not merely a private hope or a mental theory.

(3) Does the model inspire and nurture redemptive Christian living in the world? The most faithful and useful models are those that undergird the church's mission in the world, promoting both an immediacy of witness and action and a certain patience based on the confidence that the Kingdom is fundamentally God's work, not ours.[32]

In our treatise on the Kingdom the concern of each model will be dealt with at length without following necessarily the models themselves. Since the six polarities are the biblical basis that leads to different models, they are of particular importance. While each model helps to focus more sharply on one particular aspect of the Kingdom as Jesus preached it, on a biblical basis one cannot opt for one model alone, believing that in so doing one has grasped fully the mystery behind it. As we will see, the Kingdom remains a mystery which will always need to be approached anew without ever claiming to have fathomed it fully. While the approach through models serves as an excellent way to grasp the different aspects of the Kingdom, its danger is that because of the many details presented through the model approach a comprehensive understanding of the Kingdom might not be reached.

SUMMARY

Biblical and theological discussion of the Kingdom in modern times distinguishes three points of reference: the Kingdom as *concept*, the Kingdom as *symbol*, and the Kingdom in relation to *liberation*. Each approach raises specific questions, which should not be seen as mutually exclusive. The first approach can be described as author-centered. Its question is: What did the authors of the Bible mean by this concept? The second can be described as text-centered. Its question is: What does the text itself mean and say today? The third can be described as reader-centered. Its question is: What does the phrase *Kingdom of God* have to say to the concrete situation of utter oppression and exploitation in which we now find ourselves? To put it another way, the first approach tries to get behind the text, the second stays with the text, and the third stands before the text.

In the context of faith and justice Avery Dulles uses a similar outline and calls the different approaches the intellectual approach (Kingdom as concept), fiducial approach (Kingdom as symbol), and performative approach (Kingdom as liberation).[33]

It might be worth noting how these three approaches are even linked to geographical areas. The discussion in terms of the first focus, the Kingdom as concept, was carried out largely in Europe (especially Germany and Britain); the second, the Kingdom as symbol, in North America; and the third, Kingdom as liberation, emerged from Latin America. The intention of liberation theology has been to recover the historical dimension of God's message and to move that message away from all abstract universalisms so that the biblical message may be more responsive to the world of oppression and its social structures.

Part 2

THE KINGDOM MESSAGE OF JESUS

Introduction

Against this colorful background of opinions and expectations concerning the final divine intervention in the history of God's people, Jesus presented his message of the Kingdom of God as having arrived with him. Why he used such a complex symbol, which could easily be associated with a great range of expectations and aspirations, remains an enigma for some scholars. They find it unusual that Jesus made this symbolic expression the center of his proclamation. They believe that Jesus chose it purposely and reshaped it according to his own genius. Therefore, it is important—so the argument goes—to look very closely at Jesus' proclamation of the Kingdom and to become aware of the uniqueness which his message of the Kingdom contains compared to the use of the term in the vocabulary of his time.

In addition, this perspective argues that we need to take into consideration that Jesus, as a man of his culture and his age, accepted the worldview of his contemporaries. That view was colored by the apocalyptic writings and expectations of the time. But having borrowed the phrase from his contemporaries with all its nuances, divergent connotations, and ideological underpinnings, Jesus had to purify it substantially. It had to be cleansed, first, from the Pharisees' belief that the Kingdom could be obtained by strict observance of the Law; second, from the Essenes' fervent faith that the Kingdom could be brought into the world only through a ritually pure life of withdrawal and asceticism; third, from the belief of the revolutionary movements that it could be brought about through armed struggle; and fourth, from the apocalyptic writers' search for telltale signs and the total destruction of the present world. Other scholars maintain that there was nothing completely novel in the preaching of Jesus, but that he assumed his listeners knew about the Kingdom of God and were waiting for its coming. The distinctive characteristic of Jesus' proclamation was that he made these presuppositions radical and made that point of view decisive.[1]

Jesus' own mentality, however, seems to have been formed most profoundly by the great prophets of the Old Testament, particularly by Deutero-Isaiah.[2] The content of that eschatological hope is well expressed in these texts:

> He shall judge between the nations,
>   and shall arbitrate for many peoples;

67

> they shall beat their swords into plowshares,
>   and their spears into pruning hooks;
> nation shall not lift up sword against nation,
>   neither shall they learn war any more.
>   (Is 2:4)

> He will swallow up death forever.
> Then the Lord GOD will wipe away the tears
>   from all faces,
>   and the disgrace of his people he will take
>   away from all the earth,
> for the LORD has spoken (Is 25:7-8).

It is Deutero-Isaiah that actually proclaims the coming of the Kingdom as something radically new:

> For I am about to create new heavens
>   and a new earth (Is 65:17).

Jesus shared this prophetic vision and understood his task of proclaiming the Kingdom in this context.[3] This is also affirmed in his frequent references to the religious tradition of Israel as "the Law and the prophets." New is that Jesus proclaimed this vision no longer as merely future or as an object of anxious expectation (Lk 3:15) but as having arrived with him. In 4:16-21 Luke has Jesus presenting his mission to his audience in line with the messianic expectation of Deutero-Isaiah (61:1-4). In Matthew 11:4-6 Jesus tells the disciples of John the Baptist how John should understand Jesus' mission by quoting the same prophetic text:

> When he came to Nazareth, where he had been brought up, he went to the synagogue on the sabbath day, as was his custom. He stood up to read, and the scroll of the prophet Isaiah was given to him. He unrolled the scroll and found the place where it was written:
>   "The Spirit of the Lord is upon me,
>   because he has anointed me
>   to bring good news to the poor.
>   He has sent me to proclaim release to the
>   captives
>   and recovery of sight to the blind,
>   to let the oppressed go free,
>   to proclaim the year of the Lord's favor."
> And he rolled up the scroll, gave it back to the attendant, and sat down. The eyes of all in the synagogue were fixed on him. Then

he began to say to them, "Today this scripture has been fulfilled in your hearing" (Lk 4:16-21).

Jesus answered them, "Go and tell John what you hear and see: the blind receive their sight, the lame walk, the lepers are cleansed, the deaf hear, the dead are raised, and the poor have good news brought to them" (Mt 11:4-5).

One must be careful not to "spiritualize and etherealize" this expectation unnecessarily, since eschatological salvation was understood as an all-embracing reality with a particular stress on the historical-political dimension. It meant first and foremost the restoration of the Covenant people in their relationship to Yahweh and their relationship toward each other on the social-economic-political levels.[4] Whatever ideas circulated concerning the Messiah, he was definitely seen as God's envoy, one who would restore justice and side with the poor and the weak against their oppressors. The fundamental hope was for the restoration of the people. Horsley summarizes this belief succinctly:

Informed by the tradition of the promise to Abraham, Isaac, and Jacob, that besides Israel's becoming a great people with land, all peoples would be blessed, the prophets imagined that a restored Israel would become the basis for justice eventually reaching to all the people (see especially Is 42:1-7; 49:1-6). It is important to note, however, that the fundamental concern is with the restoration of Israel, and that restoration means the establishment of justice.[5]

Therefore, the central message of Jesus, the Kingdom of God, must be seen as aiming first at the restoration of Israel to the Covenant ideal, which in turn would lead to the transformation of all human structures in favor of justice and the rights of the poor. By placing himself in the perspective of the great prophets and announcing the "great year of God's favor" as the ultimate visitation of God on behalf of his people, there is hardly any doubt that the restoration of justice belonged preeminently to his mission.[6]

6

The Language of the Kingdom

Parables in the Teaching of Jesus

Jesus never defined the expression *Kingdom of God* in concrete terms. He presented its meaning in symbolic actions such as table fellowship with sinners, healings, and exorcisms. But most of all he disclosed its significance in parables, similes, images, and metaphors. Jesus did not invent the parable form. Parables had long been used in Greece and Rome as well as in the stories and writings of Israel.[1] The rabbis also told parables and used them to illustrate, explain, and defend their interpretations of the Law.[2] The Hagada valued and esteemed the parables as follows: "Do not despise the parable. With a penny candle one may often find a lost gold coin or a costly pearl. By means of a trifling parable one may sometimes penetrate into the most profound ideas."[3]

PARABLES AS JESUS' CHARACTERISTIC TEACHING VOICE

Parables are the most characteristic form of Jesus' way of speaking. They are Jesus' own method and most appropriate vehicle for understanding the Kingdom of God. They are rightly regarded as authentic sayings of Jesus, and they put us dramatically in touch with his mind and, above all, with his imagination. The import of the parables as used by Jesus is well described by Eamonn Bredin when he writes:

We are dealing with an incredibly persuasive but provocative teacher who teaches about what he calls "the Kingdom of God" active in the lives of people. He is a teacher who, with amazing clarity and incisiveness, succeeded in enshrining his message in the haunting and unforgettable poetry we call parables. This poetry combines contrast and paradox, irony and humor, the

70

similar and dissimilar, profound insight and concrete usage in a very powerful way. In the teaching of Jesus, parables are found more frequently than other rhetorical forms and with the parables we are at the bedrock of the tradition about Jesus of Nazareth.[4]

The difference between the gospels and the "classic" literature of Greece and Rome is striking. Jesus portrays himself as a man who preached his message among the peasantry in Galilean villages. It is their world, their individual and social problems, which appear in his narratives and his parables.[5]

Yet the parables provide us with Jesus' own perception of the Kingdom and describe in symbols the effects which the Reign of God will bring about in the world both as present experience and as future promise. They question the present structures of reality and open up the possibility of envisioning reality in a totally different way. The most striking feature of the parables of Jesus is the fact that they do not present us merely with a theory about the Kingdom. Rather, they provide a vision of the Kingdom that calls for immediate action aiming at the transformation of the world in its present state.[6]

It is only by entering into the parables that the listener will be able to gain access to the same horizon of meaning within which Jesus experienced the ultimate "referent" symbolized by the Kingdom of God.[7]

SCHOLARLY VIEWS ON PARABLES

Scholars offer us various descriptions of the parable form:

A parable is one of those stories in the Bible which sounds at first like a pleasant yarn, but keeps something up its sleeves which suddenly pops up and knocks you flat. A parable is a comparison drawn from nature or from daily life, and designed to teach some spiritual truth, on the assumption that what is valid in one sphere—nature or daily life—is valid also in the spiritual world.[8]

"An earthly story with a heavenly meaning." The parable uses an earthly story to reveal a reality that is breaking in upon human experience. The story is told not to divert us from life but rather to disclose to us, as we participate in the parable, the nature of God's reign that, even as we hear it, impinges upon our time. It deals with the Reign of God, showing us how human life is affected when God brings in the divine Reign.

In the parable a comparison is made. Something that is not well known—or at least readily recognized—is compared with something that is better known. The word "parable" means to "throw beside" or "to compare." In a simile one thing is said to be *like* another: for example, "my love is like a red, red rose." A metaphor, on the other hand, says that one thing *is* another: "You are my sunshine, my only sunshine." In a simile or metaphor, two terms that are not quite comparable, are "thrown beside" one another causing the mind and imagination to struggle with the reality that is being disclosed. This produces insight and understanding that cannot be reduced to our conventional analytic manner of speaking. When the dissimilar is "thrown" side by side, the conventional language itself is temporarily put aside in order to jar the imagination into a fuller grasp of a reality.[9]

> Every parable is a story; this story conveys a lesson, so that the parable has a double meaning, the story and the lesson; the parable's purpose is to effect a change in the hearer, to lead to decision or action; and the lesson always is religious or moral.[10]

From these descriptions four principal points of the parable emerge: it tells a story (*narrative*); it has two levels of meaning (*topical or figurative*); its purpose is to persuade, convince, convert (*rhetorical*); and its lesson always has to do with the interrelationship between the divine and human (*religious, ethical*).[11]

It is evident that in order to understand the parables it is vitally important to rediscover the situation in which a parable was first told, the intention of Jesus, and the experience out of which it was spoken. In so doing it will become clearer that the parables are occasional narratives, spoken to specific groups of people on specific occasions. They show a familiarity with a whole range of social, cultural, and historical experiences. Many of them, however, are addressed to people who certainly did not share Jesus' vision of reality. The parables of Jesus constantly surprised and frequently shocked his audience.[12]

THE PARABLES IN EVERYDAY LIFE SITUATIONS

The parables begin within the everyday life of people. The characters and settings are familiar; they could be anyone and anywhere. They simply convey what most people do in similar situations. The ordinariness of these narratives means that the hearers identify with these people. The parables feel comfortable. They make contact with all, regardless of background, profession, religious or political beliefs. Their effectiveness lies in their constant appeal to the experience of either Jesus or his audience. Twenty-two parables begin with a question: "What do you think?," "Who among you?," "How?" The whole parable becomes a question that calls for an answer from the listener. It asks for the listener's opinion.[13] The dynamic between the question and the answer, the parable and the hearer may be described as follows:

> They [the parables] ask the hearer to become part of the narrative: "This is the kind of situation you could find yourself in. These are the sorts of people you know. This is your life. This man/woman is you." In these parables a metaphoric shift takes place, for something new and unexpected, an irritant that "does not, yet does" fit is always introduced into the story, and the familiar, the certain, the comforting, the expected are at risk. The ground begins to open beneath our feet; a rift occurs in the old conventions; the fabric of our world is rent. What had been taken for granted as certain—the security of old ways, snug familiarities, inherited prejudices, unquestioned presuppositions— are now being stripped away and we are freed to stand before the new vision of truth that is disclosed. But this new vision of truth is profoundly unexpected and surprising. It disorients and diseases and it may indeed be shocking and subversive.[14]

Parables often uncover people's hidden prejudices and wrong assumptions. Their first, most instinctive reaction to the story is irritation or even indignation and anger. Several examples will illustrate this dynamic. Jesus tells the parable about the last hired servants getting the same pay as those who had worked the entire day in the hot sun (Mt 20:1-16). Such behavior is unfair and outrageous, no matter how we twist the story. This overturns our assumption and makes us furious. Jesus adds insult to injury by saying: "Are you jealous because I am generous?" Of course we are! Why should others have things handed out while we break our backs? God should work on a straight commission system. Here lies the challenge. The parable stories are not meant only to indict, they are meant to invite. They are an invitation to search out the basis of our outrage. We must look for something deeper.

We have created a sense of personal worth or importance by comparing ourselves with others. We have a vested interest in the subtle inferiority of others. This generosity of Jesus is the last thing we want because it equalizes everything. It takes away our privilege, our earned reward, our basis for being better. It touches on our fundamental competitiveness and enviousness.

The same can be said about the Prodigal Son story (Lk 15:11-32). Why is the older brother so unhappy that he cannot call his brother "brother" anymore but refers to him as "this son of yours" (verse 30)? It is his need to be better; and, unless he gives up this need, he cannot say "my brother" anymore.[15]

Only if the older brother would love his younger brother with all his heart, that is, if he would accept the Father's attitude toward his younger brother, could he join in the celebration. Instead of counting the wrong the younger brother has done, he is asked to rejoice in the mere fact that he who was lost has come back, the beloved one has returned. Behind these parables appears the demand of the Kingdom that a disciple of Jesus "be merciful just as your Father is merciful" (Lk 6:36).

The story of the Good Samaritan (Lk 10:29-37) presents us with another beautiful challenge that Jesus posed to his audience. Eamonn Bredin's interpretation of this classic parable is worthy of direct citation:

> The historical setting is a Jewish audience. There are the two temple functionaries embodying a whole social and religious order. There are the Samaritans hated, loathed and despised by all. Jews despised their next-door neighbors as wretched, half-breed outcasts who had sold out on both their religion and their culture. To them the Samaritans were the scum of the earth. Orthodox Jews would have no dealing with Samaritans (Jn 4:9), they would cross and recross the Jordan rather than enter that province; some Rabbis believed that to accept any help from them would delay the redemption of Israel. With this in mind we must try to hear this story once again.
>
> I am asked to identify with the man going down to Jericho. That man is me! I am attacked, robbed and stripped. I am left lying half dead in the ditch and I hope for help from the priest who approaches. But he passes by. Why? Is he busy or afraid that if I am dead already he would become ritually unclean. The same with the Levite. The same reasons as the priests. The hearers of Jesus, who would have expected the appearance of a third and final character (there are always three) begin to anticipate. They know who is coming next and eyes begin to brighten. Jesus is a layman. Ah, now, I see; he is being slightly anti-clerical! So a Jewish lay person will come around the corner and all of us will rejoice and applaud. But Jesus introduces a characteristic twist or shift into the story. The surface innocence of the language breaks and reveals the inescapable barb beneath. It is not a Jew who comes down the road, it is a Samaritan! No sooner had that unspeakable word (spit in contempt!) been mentioned than the antagonism of his hearers became palpable. But ignoring the reaction the story goes on to tell, in loving detail, about the Samaritan and his actions. Then at the end the provocative throw-away question of Jesus is found: "Which of these three do you think proved neighbor to the man who fell among robbers?"

Since I have identified myself with the injured man, I as a Jew must say what could not be said, I must say what has been ruled out as unspeakable—the Samaritan is my neighbor! So I am being forced/freed to say what cannot be said. I am to put into words what sticks in my throat, to voice what chokes me, to join two words never before united in the entire history of separation between Judea and Samaria—the words "Samaritan" and "neighbor." This conclusion is revolting and sickening. It demands that my worldview, my familiar horizons, my understanding, my whole value system be called into question. All my familiarities, the lessons I learned from parents, grand-parents, and religious leaders, my very faith itself is radically questioned and completely turned upside-down in and through this story. But that is not the end of it. This story leads me further into what was previously unimaginable. If Jesus really had to tell a revolutionary story it would have been enough to have told it with the Samaritan in the ditch receiving help from me, the Jew. Now that kind of love of non-Jews would be sufficiently unthinkable! But this story says that my revered religious leaders, who should help me, refuse to do so and the Samaritan, who should have refused, comes to my assistance!

Jesus does not mention God in the whole story at all. Could it be that it is only when my circumscribed world of closed options, set judgments, predetermined positions, and guaranteed conclusions is torn asunder and turned upside-down, that there is room for God in my life?[16]

The parables are concerned with the behavior of the listeners. Their ultimate intent is a change of behavior as a result of a new outlook on reality. In the case of the parable of the Good Samaritan, all discrimination, all racism, all prejudice are condemned. Before God we are all brothers and sisters and the one who is in need becomes my neighbor no matter who he or she is. It is in analyzing such parables that we see clearly Jesus' attitude against any kind of discrimination.

Jesus did not use parables to convey general religious truth or to enter into debate with his listeners. Rather, he sought to win them over to his view. He wanted people to see how wrong their outlook was, inviting them to change their attitudes in the manner which the coming Kingdom demands.

For this reason the parables themselves may never be eliminated or ignored. Interpretations of the parables in discursive language must always remain secondary. They are not really necessary for an understanding of the parables. The parables are the preaching itself and should not be considered as merely serving the purpose of some lesson which stands independent of them. Herein participation precedes information. Jesus tries to communicate an experience to other people by assisting them to find their own encounter with the Kingdom and to draw from that experience their own way of life.[17]

By exploring the concept of time in more existential terms Crossan presents a further viewpoint of the parables. Strictly speaking we cannot say God acts *in* history and intervenes *in* time. It is, rather, the presence of God that, in calling to us for a response, creates our history and gives us time. Time is the present of God. Human time and human history arise from response to the eternal Being who is always manifest as the unexpected and the unforeseen, One who cancels our future projects by the advent of the ever new and unpredictable mystery of God. The coming of God discloses a different past from that which we presumed was objectively given before this coming. God's *advent* may ask for a radical reappraisal and even a reversal of our past. But it is this coming and this reversal that create the force of a present which is now really breaking into action. Instead of the objective and superficial succession of three moments of past—present—future, we are now open to a deeper and more eschatological present of three modes of advent—reversal—action.[18]

From such a perspective on time the parables of the Treasure and the Costly Pearl (Mt 13:44-46) provide the key which can unlock the other parables. They contain a threefold pattern that sums up the basic experience of the Kingdom: (1) the *advent* of the Kingdom as gift of God; (2) the *reversal* of the recipient's world; and, (3) the empowering of the recipient to *action*. For example, the parable of the Hidden Treasure shatters the individual's experience of reality by the sudden and unexpected *advent* of the treasure. The discovery brings a *reversal* in the lifestyle of the person. The decision to "sell all that he has" leads to a new form of *action*. All parables can be seen under this threefold scheme: (1) Jesus proclaims the *advent* of the Kingdom in history as something totally new and never experienced in this form before; (2) the realization of the Kingdom as a present reality now effects a *reversal* of the values of the person's life and a change in outlook; and, (3) it leads to *action*.

The thrust of all parables is, therefore, directly toward transforming action aimed at changing the present situation, and as a result, the world at large. What really drives the individual to action is the "joy" over the unexpected treasure, the great blessing of salvation, the experience of God's gracious giving that transforms life. Jesus is telling his listeners to realize God's gracious coming into the present enabling them to reverse their lives and become doers of a new kind of action. The parables of Jesus seek to draw us into the present of the Kingdom. They then challenge us to act and to live in accordance with this gratuitous experience.[19]

Although most parables refer to Jesus' Kingdom message, the collection of parables entitled *growth parables* in Matthew 13 and Mark 4 are of greatest importance for an adequate understanding of the Kingdom message. These are the Sower, the Growing Corn, the Mustard Seed and the Leaven, the Weeds Among the Wheat and the Net Full of Fish.

In order to perceive the real message of these parables all allegorizing should be put aside. While in an allegory the elements and characters of the story are defined and the ultimate purpose of the story is clearly explained, in the parable the meaning of the story is neither explained nor defined. It is true that the evangelists often transformed the parables of Jesus into allegories. The best illustration of this tendency is Mark's allegorization of the parable of the Sower (Mk 4:14-20). All the evangelists do this to some degree, especially by tacking on a summary or explanatory sentences to the end of the parable. In reading the parables, one must accept them strictly as parables, leaving aside the added allegorizing elements. The "point of comparison" between the picture and the content is the only point at issue.[20]

For example, the point of comparison in the parable of the Mustard Seed is the contrast between the minuteness of the Kingdom's beginning now and the magnitude of its completion later. Notwithstanding the tiny and inconspicuous beginning, the glorious end is certain. The narrator is not reflecting on the natural process of growth. He is judging by what he sees with his eyes. Jesus is saying that despite the insignificant beginnings, the image of the smallest seed, God's power will bring about a great harvest. The parable, interpreted in this way, stripped of all allegorization, is placed once again in its true setting. That context is the ministry of Jesus as the great eschatological act of God who comes to save God's people. It is the final and decisive intervention of the living God in human history for the salvation of humankind.[21]

CONCLUSIONS

Although Jesus' use of the phrase *Kingdom of God* as the center of his proclamation and mission was unique, it was based on the religious experience of his people. The God of the Old Testament is a God who cares, loves, forgives—a compassionate God. Every parable that Jesus offered is a vivid witness to this God. His audience could at least sense and in some way participate in the "new experience" Jesus offered, because the parables he employed constantly referred to Israel's experience with Yahweh in the past. For us it is important not to forget that the Old Testament God-experience expressed in the symbol

Kingdom of God remains present in the New Testament. To evoke and participate in this "old experience" has value for our own participation in the Kingdom as Jesus experienced it.[22]

Jesus proclaimed the nearness of the God of Abraham, Moses, and the prophets. He is the God who decided that the time had come to bring the long-awaited salvation to his people, to give life and to bring justice and peace with a marked inclination toward the poor and the outcast of society. The Kingdom's goal is to create one great family, one people where all will find their home in the family of God. Here all discrimination against any individual or group will have ceased. This is the vision Jesus came to bring. This is the Kingdom message.

7

The Basic Characteristics
of Jesus' Kingdom Message

The content of Jesus' vision of the Kingdom has been systematized in various ways despite its original presentation in parables and images.[1] Keeping in mind what Snyder calls the six fundamental tension points or polarities that are central to Jesus' Kingdom message,[2] we will present in the chapters that follow these basic characteristics: (1) the Kingdom as eschatological and apocalyptic; (2) the Kingdom as a gift and a task; (3) the Kingdom as religious and political; (4) the Kingdom as salvational and universal; (5) a definition of the Kingdom; and (6) the demand of the Kingdom: conversion. Each characteristic will be followed by a chapter that will explain the theological implications as well as the practical consequences that flow from such a view.

ESCHATOLOGICAL: THE KINGDOM IS AT HAND

The symbol *Kingdom of God* as an eschatological expression refers to the teaching concerning the end of the world. Prophetic eschatology had no concept of another world above and beyond this one. The eschatological visitation of God was expected within history. Apocalyptic eschatology, on the other hand, looked at the end of *this* world as a necessary condition for the new to come.[3] Jesus, being more prophetic than apocalyptic in his outlook, does not reject the later but synthesizes both dimensions.

Mark 1:14-15 indicates that with Jesus the time of waiting has come to an end and the Kingdom has broken into history. Jesus' word and action initiate the dynamic activity of God that aims at bringing total salvation to humanity and a complete transformation of the universe.[4] The programmatic proclamation of Jesus is presented in two pairs of parallel expressions that seem to be formulated along the synonymous parallelism of semitic verse. It reads:

a. The *time is fulfilled,*
b. And the *Kingdom of God has come near;*
c. *Repent,*
d. And *believe in the good news.*

There is a pair of *indicatives* (a and b) followed by a pair of *imperatives* (c and d). In each pair the second member, in typical semitic fashion, takes up and explains the first. So b explains a: the time is fulfilled *because* the Kingdom of God has come near; and d explains c: to repent means to believe in the good news. Some scholars insist that the core of passages b and c is an accurate transcription of what Jesus himself would have preached. But they regard the framework, a and d, as an explanatory addition by Mark or his tradition. Their argument is that the expression "the time is fulfilled" is typical of early Christian fulfillment apologetic, while "believe in the good news" distinctively echoes the language of the early Christian mission (Acts 11:17, 20, 21).[5]

Others are less critical about the first indicative. They agree that the composition of the text, as far as the formulation goes, definitely comes from Mark. But the content, which comes from the source Mark used, seems to have already included the first indicative. "The time is fulfilled" means the measure of time assigned by God for the fulfillment of the promise of the Kingdom has been filled up. Behind this conviction lies the Jewish apocalyptic view that history is not simply an endless repetition of the same cycles but is moving forward under God's guidance toward a goal. The time has become *really* full, not almost or nearly full. The unsurpassable future of God has begun. The time before the Kingdom is finished and the time of the Kingdom has come. The two phrases "is fulfilled" and "has come" emphasize the completed action. The decisive manifestation of the saving God about which the prophets spoke is taking place now. The difference is only that the first phrase, "is fulfilled," looks backward, and the second phrase, "has come," proclaims the beginning of the new. Mark wants to indicate that with Jesus the time of waiting has come to an end and the Kingdom has broken into history. In Jesus' word and action there is an initiation of the dynamic activity of God that aims at bringing salvation to completion in a transformed universe.[6]

The first sermon of Jesus in Luke 4:14-21 provides us with the Lukan parallel to the Markan summary of the central message of Jesus. The fundamental meaning of the two passages is the same. Luke, instead of using the phrase *Kingdom of God,* presents its reality under the symbol of the Jubilee release which brings final salvation.[7] Jesus quotes a passage from Isaiah which is an affirmation of Israel's hope, the promise of God's liberating and reconciling future. Viviano remarks in regard to this passage:

One can hardly ask for a better description of what the Kingdom of God come to earth would mean. This *is* the Kingdom.

Viviano then asks why Luke does not mention the Kingdom here but uses a substitution of an Old Testament quotation for a mention of the Kingdom. His answer:

> Others had spoken of the kingdom before Jesus, but no one had centered everything upon it in the way he did. Luke here failed to present Jesus in his uniqueness and in the fullness of his eschatological expectation. In a word, his text is politically richer but theologically poorer.[8]

The most critical statement in this section of Luke is: "Today this scripture has been fulfilled in your hearing" (Lk 4:21). Now, what would have come to the mind of a listener who heard Jesus speak these words or the words of Mark 1:14-15 ("The time is fulfilled, and the Kingdom of God has come near; repent, and believe in the Good News")? A listener somewhat familiar with the scriptures might think of the following texts, to mention a few:

> You will rise up and have compassion on
> Zion;
> for it is time to favor it;
> the appointed time has come (Ps 102:13).

> Have you not heard
> that I determined it long ago?
> I planned from days of old
> what now I bring to pass (Is 37:26).

The days are surely coming, says the Lord, when I will fulfill the promise I made to the house of Israel and the house of Judah. In those days and at that time I will cause a righteous Branch to spring up for David; and he shall execute justice and righteousness in the land (Jer 33:14-15).

The time has come; the day draws near (Ez 7:12).

> For I am about to create new heavens
> and a new earth;
> the former things shall not be remembered
> or come to mind.
> But be glad and rejoice forever
> in what I am creating (Is 65:17).

Jesus declares that what Isaiah had promised as God's final messianic future is now at work. Reconciliation and deliverance are not distant songs of a utopian future far removed from present reality. The promise is invading the world now in every relationship and circumstance of our lives. Horsley drives this point home when he writes:

> The thrust of Jesus' ministry, his practice and preaching, was to realize and to make others realize the presence of the Kingdom of God. Not only is Jesus confident that God is acting imminently to liberate and renew the people and to vindicate those who join in that renewal, but Jesus manifests and mediates God's saving activity in his own action and teachings. He declares in no uncertain terms that the Kingdom of God has come upon and is among the people, available to be recognized, received, and entered.[9]

Jesus manifests the dynamic presence of the Kingdom in history not only in words but particularly in his wonder-working activity. His demon-exorcisms, for example, demonstrate that God is penetrating the present and establishing the Reign right here and now. One often-quoted passage that clearly indicates that God is inaugurating a new era of history is Matthew 12:28: "But if it is by the Spirit of God that I cast out demons, then the kingdom of God has come to you." Other sayings of a similar tone include Luke 10:18, wherein Jesus sees Satan falling from heaven like lightning. These passages indicate that something is happening now. God is entering the present age in a totally new way in order to bring to fulfillment the promises made to the prophets.

Other scripture passages place the accent on Jesus' common practice of table fellowship and interpret his festive "eating and drinking" as a present celebration of the banquet of the Kingdom understood as an "active anticipation of banqueting in the fully consummated Kingdom of God." Jesus saw the consummation of this historically present Kingdom in the coming of the Gentiles who will sit at table with Abraham, Isaac, and Jacob (Mt 8:11).[10] According to Ladd, Jesus' view is that

> the Kingdom of God is the redemptive reign of God dynamically active to establish his rule among human beings, and that this Kingdom, which will appear as an apocalyptic act at the end of the age, has already come into human history in the person and mission of Jesus to overcome evil, to deliver all from its power, and to bring them into the blessings of God's reign. The Kingdom of God involves two great moments: fulfillment within history, and consummation at the end of history.[11]

"Has come near" in Mark 1:15, therefore, does not have the meaning Rudolf Bultmann gave it. For him, the Kingdom that Jesus preached is as near as a train pulling into a station or as an approaching rain cloud already pouring down rain in the distance.[12] As the incoming train and the coming rain determine people's action when they see them, so does the coming Kingdom challenge people to act. The Kingdom is not present in this way. Rather, correcting the metaphor, the train has already arrived and the rain is actually falling. Jesus does not announce the nearness of the Kingdom or merely heighten expectation. His mission is to bring people into the actual relationship with God that the coming Kingdom promises. It is the final act of salvation, the final decisive intervention of God on behalf of God's people. This cannot be stressed enough. Eschatology is a key word for theology, and the eschatological character of the Kingdom message must be the real point of departure.

The fact that the Kingdom of God is a present reality has never been denied in theological writings. But most of the time this "being present" has been so qualified that the future and not the present of the Kingdom seems to be the only concern. As Gerhard Lohfink puts it:

> In order to be fair to Jesus' message and praxis, one must, more than anything else, hammer out the *presence* of the *Basileia* that Jesus himself maintained. That God would establish his kingly rule in the future was believed by everyone in Israel during Jesus' time. Generally speaking, people lived in the end-time hope. Jesus' unmistakable uniqueness lay in the fact that with frightening awareness he could speak of fulfillment: The Kingdom of God is here and now. And he not only said it, but fulfilled it in messianic praxis.[13]

According to Lohfink, it is not enough to say that the Kingdom is present in the person of Jesus, or in his signs, or proleptically, in an anticipatory way. He is afraid that such expressions push the Kingdom off into the future once again.

As an "exegetical probe" for the presence of the Kingdom now, Lohfink discusses the parables of the Costly Pearl and Treasure in the Field (Mt 13:44-46), or as he calls them, "The time of the Kingdom present." He writes:

> This adventure does not happen in the sometime of a future yet to come, or a vague everywhere-and-nowhere somewhere, but where Jesus is and where Jesus gathers Israel together. The Kingdom of God is found and acquired here and now. The treasure and the pearl are not proleptically, anticipatorily, and dynamically acquired, but really acquired. The parable does not say that the Kingdom of God is like a merchant who acquires a costly pearl which he only temporarily has in his possession.[14]

APOCALYPTIC: THE KINGDOM WILL COME

The Present Age and the Age to Come

Although Jesus' basic thinking followed that of the prophets, he also used apocalyptic imagery to explain his Kingdom message. As we saw, the prophets viewed the present order of society, including nature and history, as being marred by evil. They looked for a new order to be brought about by the redemptive breaking in of God, a final visitation. But the place where God's Kingdom would be realized was still this world.

Apocalyptic writers concentrate on the all-pervasive evil in the present world to the extent that they can hardly see anything good. The present world is under the influence of evil, the prince of this world. As previously mentioned, the world is seen in the light of Genesis 2-11. It is a world that is penetrated by the "no" which the first human beings, Adam and Eve, uttered to God (Gn 2-3); a world in which brotherhood is crushed through violence and the domination of one brother over the other (Gn 4:1-16); a world in which human beings use technical skills to subdue nature, to exalt human potential, to exploit fellow human beings, and to make themselves above God (Gn 4:17-11:9).

The world, human history, and society are so afflicted and permeated by evil that no future other than total annihilation is possible. This worldview becomes so dominant in the intertestamental period that *this age* and *the age to come* become technical terms in the rabbinic tradition. Did Jesus share this view of things? At least he used their terminology:

Mk 4:19   "the cares of the world"
Mk 10:30   "now in this age . . . and in the age to come"
Lk 16:8   "the children of this age"

Jesus was in no way naive concerning the present state of human beings. He portrays a remarkable sensitivity to the all-pervasive presence of evil in human affairs, whether private or public. He certainly saw the beauty of creation (Mt 6:25-36) and the goodness of human beings, because they are God's children, but he could not be deceived when faced with evil in its life-denying and destructive force. Confronted by evil—individual, social, or cosmic—Jesus assumes an uncompromising attitude that aims at the total destruction of it.

Therefore, the Kingdom of God which Jesus preached reveals immediately that the world is deeply troubled and is not a place where the Kingdom of God is present. This could be called the *pessimistic* note of the Kingdom of Jesus. The Kingdom that Jesus brings into such a world breathes a spirit of conflict. Mark 1:16-3:12 stands under the theme of a power struggle between Jesus and the Evil One, between the Son of God and the demons. Jesus' entire mission is bent on overthrowing the demonic power structures who ask Jesus, "Have you come to destroy us?" (Mk 1:24). This undoubtedly reveals Jesus' universal purpose: He came to destroy not individual proponents of the powers of darkness, but the kingdom of evil proper (Lk 10:18). Jesus' whole public life is seen as a struggle against Satan. It begins with the temptation story (Lk 4:1-13) and intensifies through the entirety of Jesus' ministry. The hour of his passion is the climax (Jn 12:31; 13:2).[15]

Throughout the entire New Testament, including the teaching sections of Jesus, *this age* is viewed as an age in which Satan has been permitted by the sovereign purpose of God to exercise a tragic sway over humankind (e.g., Lk 13:16; 22:31). Only in the *age to come* will this power be broken completely. Jesus' ministry can only be fully understood against the backdrop of two opposing kingdoms: The Kingdom of God and the kingdom of evil. Or in the words of G. E. Ladd:

> It is indeed impossible to interpret the New Testament teaching about the Kingdom of God except against the background of a great spiritual struggle. . . . The Kingdom is God's dynamic power, and it must come because there are real spiritual enemies which oppose it, both human and superhuman. The coming of God's Kingdom means the invasion of the power of Satan and the overthrow of his kingdom. Otto is right to this extent: the coming of the Kingdom in Jesus must be interpreted in terms of a great struggle between mighty spiritual powers.[16]

The Power of Evil: Individual and Social Sin

Apocalyptic View

Apocalyptic writers portray a vivid awareness of the presence of the power of evil in all aspects of human life. That power is connected with the personification of Evil, called Satan or Belial. All evils people suffer and all evils they commit may be regarded as the manifestation in history of the power of the evil kingdom. Sin (singular) cannot be regarded only as the sum total of all the individual sins (plural) that people commit. Viewed from a broader perspective, sin is an objective situation which conditions human beings and leads them to commit further sin. Sin is a social, even a cosmic event, rather than merely an individual problem. Personal sin is considered as the echo of a voice that comes from creation, the creation that "was subjected to futility" and that will be "set free from its bondage to decay" (Rom 8:20-21). The problem of a person in the world is not simply that he or she commits isolated sins or gives in to the temptation of particular vices. It is, rather, that he or she is imprisoned within a closed system of rebellion against God, a system that conditions him or her to absolutize the relative and to relativize the absolute.[17] Theologically, the question to be asked is: Do we have to presume an evil exists independently of individual conscience and imposes itself on that conscience?

Yet it is important to realize that the apocalyptic dualism is first of all not so much to be seen as a cosmic struggle, but rather as a struggle between divine creative forces and demonic destructive forces concerning the control of the historical process in the world. The struggle explains what is happening here in the midst of human beings in their concrete historical situation. To transfer this struggle right away to the "cosmic" level ignores that Jesus and his contemporaries saw "Satan as having a certain dominion socially-politically, and the demons as controlling possessed persons." In this connection Horsley has a point when he comments

> that the violent struggle[s] between God and demonic forces are simply a symbolization or reflection of the violent social-political-religious conflict in which people were caught individually and collectively.[18]

This would mean that people understood their struggle on the social-political-religious level in the context of the broader spiritual struggle between God and the evil forces.

Anthropological View

The anthropological view argues that sin is to be found in the individual person and in the social situation. The personal (subjective) and the social (objective) are two dimensions of every sin. It is personal in the sense that only persons can commit sin; only persons can be guilty, only persons can be sinners. But all sin has a social dimension because it has social consequences. Sin affects other people and becomes institutionalized in the structures, laws, and customs of society. In turn, society then shapes and influences the sinner.[19]

Christian thought views humanity as being simultaneously graced and sin-permeated. This fact becomes manifest in the concrete life of the individual who is both selfless (graced) and self-seeking (sinful). When such persons gather in community their structures will reflect the same ambivalence. Thus one can understand the "collective egoism" that conditions human beings. Individual sinfulness creates sinful structures, and sinful structures in turn lead the individual to sin. Sin is a human, social, and historical reality which originates in a socially and historically situated freedom. We all know, if only dimly, how all our thoughts, feelings, and actions are extensively controlled by cultural, social, political, and economic powers, the very powers that are created and sustained by us. In a real sense we are the enemies of our own freedom. We regret ever having settled for these comfortable structures of inhumanity, although they are the creations of our own will. And even after recognizing the situation we do not work for new institutions that foster more freedom and justice. St. Augustine once said that "we willingly enter the bondage wherein we unwillingly find ourselves." It is also true that we willingly remain in the bondage wherein we unwillingly find ourselves. We wish we were not here, but we choose to stay.[20]

Social View

Theologically we refer in this context to "structural sin," which means the social objectification of sin. This view goes beyond the insight of the social dimension of sin already articulated in the anthropological view. The Medellín and Puebla Conferences have put particular stress on this aspect by describing the dreadful situation in their countries as a "situation of sin." It is the product of the economic, social, and political structures that give rise to this state of misery. There is a sin that is born out of the human heart and overflows into social relations. These relational structures, based on sex, age, class, and race (which Paul calls "principalities and powers") have a firm control over our lives. They favor the freedom of some persons to an inordinate degree while depriving others. Mechanisms of racism, sexism, and class, deeply ingrained in the dominant culture, insinuate themselves into individuals—their language, their actions, and their understanding of what is possible.

But there is also an evil which exists independently of individual conscience and which imposes itself on that conscience. This evil must also be overcome. Social sciences have made us aware of structural mechanisms in society that exceed all personal responsibility and decisions. We know today, better than ever, that there is sin that individuals and groups absorb from their environment, that precedes and conditions every conscious choice.[21]

The objection is often raised that we do not find any allusion to social and structural sin in the Christian scriptures. The most obvious reason is that the first-century worldview lacked the consciousness and theory to make them explicit. Masters and slaves existed, of course, but the psychological, sociological, and economic structures which arose from and thus perpetuated the master/slave relationship were independent of any conscious decisions of particular masters and slaves.

Furthermore, we must take into consideration that the early Christians lived in expectation of an imminent end to their age; this made such matters very unimportant. Later, however, when the end was postponed indefinitely, the demand that everybody should remain in the state to which he or she was called (1 Cor 7:20) readily became the banner of social conservatism. Such an interpretation, though theologically unfounded, became very effective in promoting an indifference to reforming social structures.

The constantly recurring question is, What lies at the root of the situation of sin? Is it individual egoism that produces the structures of sin, or do the autonomous structures foster egoism? If our focus is egoism, we will emphasize the education of conscience; if sinful structures are stressed, social change will have priority. Of course, the answer will not be either/or but rather dialectical: there is a "sin" that individuals and groups absorb from their environment and that precedes and conditions every conscious choice. And when individuals and groups become aware of such sin, yet opt to maintain the status quo, in effect they ratify this sinful situation.[22] The dialectical nature of the problem is succinctly described by Edward Schillebeeckx when he writes:

> Christian redemption is indeed liberation from sin. But liberation from sin also has a cultural context. In our time the Christian understanding of sin also includes the recognition of systematic disruptions of communication like sexism, racism and fascism, antisemitism, hostility to and sense of superiority. The Christian love which is the basis of community therefore also includes the necessity to recognize the need for deep involvement in present-day work of political, cultural and social emancipation.[23]

Conclusion

The Old Testament as a whole reveals that since the creation of the universe God is revealed as someone who sets free, who liberates creation from the onslaught of the evil forces which try to destroy and enslave all creatures. Throughout the New Testament, particularly in the teaching of Jesus, we find the same theme. It is essential to see that Jesus' ministry can only be fully understood in view of two kingdoms: the Kingdom of God and the kingdom of evil. All evils that people suffer and all evils they commit are regarded as the manifestation in history of the power of the evil kingdom. The breaking in of the Kingdom of God must be seen in terms of a dynamic force that invades the present age ruled by the powers of evil. Its sole purpose is to overthrow this evil kingdom. Its aim is to liberate the whole of creation that "was subjected to futility" and that will "be set free from its bondage to decay" when the Kingdom comes in its fullness (Rom 8:20). The presence of the Kingdom will show itself as a liberating force that aims at restructuring human society in terms of justice, peace, and joy (Rom 14:17). The difficulty for many is that they see this liberating power of the Kingdom only in individual and spiritual terms without realizing that it aims at the liberation of all social structures as well. One of the basic elements in the theology of the Kingdom of God is the radical nature of evil. God is and will always remain the Lord of history, but there are opposing forces which seek to frustrate God's Kingdom. Evil is so radical that it is greater than the human person. It can be overcome only by the mighty intervention of God.[24]

Jesus revealed in his exorcisms how deeply human beings can be caught and held prisoner by the powers of evil. One of the most vivid illustrations of this fact is found in the story of the Gerasene Demoniac (Mk 5:1-20). Several points may be highlighted. First, the situation of the man is described as one of absolute hopelessness. The effects of possession are portrayed in violent antisocial and self-destructive behavior of the person. He lives in the abode of the dead. He has been cast out from the community which had attempted to bind him. He has become an outsider, excluded from the community and from communication. No one dares to live with him, no one talks to him, no one loves him. He is a living dead, exiled, cut off, despised. Second, the mission of Jesus is clearly demonstrated to be the setting free and the leading back of the human person to full authenticity and dignity. This liberation is not a peaceful surrender of Satan, but consists of a struggle by the evil forces to maintain their control of the person. The actual "driving out" involves violent convulsions of the possessed person (Mk 1:24-26; 9:20-26). Third, the story reveals the Kingdom as a power that deprives evil of any place in the world. Not even in pigs will it find a place to stay. The coming Kingdom means the end of all evil. The presence of the Kingdom of God is seen as a dynamic force overthrowing the kingdom of evil and liberating the present age by restoring human beings to their true authenticity and dignity.

Jesus is the one who "crosses over" to this man, who communicates with him, who has compassion for him, who cares for him. He restores him to his human dignity; he reintegrates him into life and community. In this the true mission of Jesus is revealed. The man "whom no one had the strength to subdue" (Mk 5:4) is found by his countrymen "sitting there, clothed and in his right mind" (Mk 5:15). Since he can communicate again Jesus sends him back to those who had excluded him from the community. The nonperson has been made a person again. He is to proclaim to his countrymen, "How much the Lord has done for you, and what mercy he has shown you" (Mk 5:19).

With the coming of Christ the "cosmic conflict" is unleashed, and there will be no peace until it is over. The place in which we live is hotly contested territory. The Kingdom of God has really entered the world. And so it becomes an object that can and will be attacked, since the evil powers will not let themselves be overthrown easily. There will be defeat as well as victory. Individual battles are sometimes won and sometimes lost, but the war has been won.[25]

The Visibility of the Kingdom

The perplexing question remains: How can we claim that the Kingdom of God is here? If it really has broken into this world, can it be seen and experienced? Do we really see justice, peace, and joy realized in the world? Commenting on Mark 8:29, where St. Peter confesses that Jesus is the Messiah, Martin Buber writes:

> According to my faith it is not the case that the Messiah has appeared in a definite moment of history but his appearance can only mark the end of history. In the perspective of my faith, the redemption of the world did not happen nineteen centuries ago. On the contrary, we still live in an unredeemed world.[26]

Judaism as a whole will always confront our Christian faith with the perennially troubling question about where the signs of the Kingdom, as proclaimed by the prophets, are manifested. Looking at Christianity, Judaism may well say that if Jesus is the Messiah, then why haven't the actions of the Messiah been fulfilled? Judaism can say very simply: "It never happened; and if it did, it could not have been true. Nothing has changed since Jesus."[27]

Can it, therefore, be meaningfully stated in any sense that the messianic era has been inaugurated and that the Kingdom of God is present in our world? If we look the real world straight in the eye, can we see what Paul means when he says:

> "At an acceptable time I have listened to you.
> and on a day of salvation I have helped
> you" (2 Cor 6:2)?

Many would say that if anything is obvious, it is that now is *not* the day of salvation. The Kingdom does not seem to be here. The train may be near and the rain may be falling over there, to use Rudolf Bultmann's imagery, but the platform of the station is still empty and the soil on which we stand is still dry. How can we say with great certainty that the Kingdom of God has already arrived in our midst? How should we understand this?

Various answers have been given. Martyn paints the following picture by referring to the apocalyptic background of the Kingdom in the preaching of Jesus. The battles between the two ages are never "public events" in the normal meaning of that expression. They do not make the evening news. These battles are not fully visible to the naked eye. Why not? Because the invasion is not demonstrable in categories native to the *old age* or with the means of perception native to the *new age*. The breaking in is itself *revelation*. The breaking in of the Kingdom brings about an epistemological crisis, a crisis in the way we see and understand. We need to speak of *bifocal* vision. Eyeglasses are bifocal when a lens has two portions, one for near and one for far vision. To see the Kingdom with bifocals is to see both the old age, and God's invading new age. This is the crucial difference, the difference between single vision, by which one sees on one level, and bifocal vision, by which one is given the grace and the power to see simultaneously on two levels. Faith gives us this added vision. It is not that we do not see the unredeemedness of the world, that is, the forces of dehumanization and oppression which cause our world to appear so unredeemed and at times so God-forsaken. Faith enables us to see deeper, to go beyond the appearances of reality, and to discover there the real powers that guide history, the power of evil and the power of the present Kingdom.[28] Only with the use of our image of single and bifocal vision can we perceive the Kingdom at work, as well as the counter-forces that try to overcome it.

In the light of such realities it is understandable why many scholars would like to place such strong emphasis on the cross as the only fundamental reality for understanding history and our world. They are extremely skeptical of any claim that the Kingdom is embodied in this world, which is so full of injustice, oppression, and hatred. In the words of Karl Loewith: "Nothing else than the life and death of Jesus Christ, the 'Suffering Servant' who was deserted and crucified, can be the standard of a Christian understanding of the world's history."[29]

There is a danger that we might despair of thinking the human race will ever change and even can change. Yet the Christian faith has proven in history that people lived with great hope in the midst of conditions that seemed objectively hopeless. Cobb, commenting on the enormous change we have to undertake if we want to survive today, expresses it this way:

Christianity does not underestimate the strength of tendencies which in the course of history have become anti-human and now threaten our survival. Viewing our ordinary ways of feeling, thinking and acting in the light of Jesus, Christians have used language like "natural depravity." But we also recognize in ourselves a transcendence over genetic endowment and cultural conditioning that makes us both responsible and, in principle, free to change. We recognize in ourselves also a profound resistance to change, so that our freedom is not a matter of simple choice between good and evil. Our self-centeredness distorts our use of our freedom. But we discover that there is a power at work in us that can transform even our distorted wills. This transformation is not subject to our control but comes as a gift. We call it grace, and we can place no limits on the extent to which grace can make us into new men and women. Apart from the transforming power of grace, there would be no grounds for hope.[30]

Now the question is, Where are we in this apocalyptic war? On which front do we fight? The powers of God's Kingdom have invaded human history; Satan has received a preliminary but decisive defeat (Lk 11:14-22). Yet this invasion into the present age does not transform it into the age to come. However, the final outcome of the war is clear. The power of evil is now like that of a nightmare which is able to spread real fear but lacks a positive or creative ontological basis. As Karl Barth once put it: "They may rattle the bolt but they will not break down the door."[31]

The Experience of the Kingdom

In spite of all warnings and skeptical observations, the question which we as Christians must ask remains: If the Kingdom is already present in this world, can it be experienced? In response we can say that wherever a person opens up and allows the power of the Kingdom in, he or she should experience the Kingdom as a power that can give freedom, wholeness, meaning, and authenticity. We might choose different words in our time, but what really happens where the imminent Kingdom becomes effective is, in principle, the same as the prophets had foretold and Jesus affirmed when he gave an answer to the two disciples of John:

> Jesus answered them, "Go and tell John what you hear and see: the blind receive their sight, the lame walk, the lepers are cleansed, the deaf hear, the dead are raised, and the poor have good news brought to them" (Mt 11:4-5).

The New Testament writings in referring to the reality of the "in-between time" speak continually about "the first fruits," "guarantees," and "signs." Reference is made to the Holy Spirit who has been given and who enables us to experience these "first fruits." We should, therefore, not underestimate the presence of God's redemptive power in the world today. The key function of the Holy Spirit seems to be precisely to make us see and feel the redeeming presence of God's Kingdom now. It is in the power of the Spirit that "not only the creation, but we ourselves, who have the first fruits of the Spirit, groan inwardly while we wait for adoption, the redemption of our bodies" (Rom 8:23ff.). It is the Spirit who helps us see what is going on and to realize where the Kingdom has won or lost a battle in this world.

Many scholars have restricted the experience of the Kingdom here and now to the individual person as the only way of being sure of its presence at all. The inner peace, the joy, the experience of forgiveness and reconciliation are signs interpreted by the individual as sure indications of the presence of the Kingdom in his or her life. They are great gifts of God granted already now in the midst of an unredeemed world.[32]

But we must insist that the Kingdom of God is never presented simply as a private affair between God and the individual. It includes social reality, because its outreach embraces the whole of reality. While it is true that the salvation of the Kingdom exceeds all present experience, we must not lose sight of the connection between present experience and future fulfillment. Without the present experience of the Kingdom, its future fulfillment easily runs the risk of "appearing as a distracting pie in the sky when we die."[33]

The experiential aspect of the Kingdom as belonging only to the individual is constantly reinforced by reference to Luke 17:20-21:

> Once Jesus was asked by the Pharisees when the kingdom of God was coming, and he answered, "The kingdom of God is not coming with things that can be observed; nor will they say, 'Look, here it is! or 'There it is!' For, in fact, the kingdom of God is among you."

Here the difficulty is in the translation of *entos hymoon*. There are two possibilities: "among you" or "within, inwardly, in the midst of you."[34] Older interpretations are inclined to translate it as "inwardly," referring to an inner realm of grace within the heart, or "as a principle at work invisibly in the heart of individuals."[35] However, this translation, as Viviano has pointed out, has caused problems:

> Unfortunately the verse has been abused throughout history and led to an overly spiritual, depoliticized and trivialized interpretation of the Kingdom. First, it is a mistake to make this verse the starting point of our understanding of the Kingdom in the proclamation of Jesus. More programmatic verses (such as Mark 1:15) must be the basis. Secondly, on the strength of this verse it would be illegitimate to understand the Kingdom as a purely

religious blessing, the inner link with the living God. Of course
it is a religious blessing, it is a link with God. But it is also God's
way of addressing our social, political, earthly needs, of assert-
ing his rights and his will for justice over his creation. A purely
private, withdrawn spirituality is not a Kingdom spirituality.[36]

The translation which corresponds most closely with the view of
Jesus himself seems to be "it is already in your midst." Cyril of Alexandria translated the phrase as "it is in the scope of your choice and it
lies in your power to receive it."[37] Jesus tells his audience not to occupy themselves with trying to determine when and where the Kingdom of God is to appear, but rather to realize that the Kingdom is
"within their reach." It lies in their power to enter in and secure its
blessing. What is important for the listeners is to become aware that
the Kingdom of God has entered the present world in and through the
person of Jesus and that the possibility of experiencing its saving power
lies within the range of all who hear the good news. The stress here is
on the "already" over against the "not yet." Anyone who emphasizes
the future coming of the Kingdom must realize the working of the
Kingdom in the present in order to see its future become reality at
all.[38] The "not coming with things that can be observed" negates the
rational-empirical observation and fixing of signs as used by apocalyptic seers to discover the time of God's coming. Jesus returns here to
the prophetic understanding of the eschatological event. He is not
guided by apocalyptic speculations, which try to find God at work in
the clash of earthly armies and heavenly bodies in such a way so as to
determine the day of the final arrival of the Kingdom.[39]

Most important is how the Kingdom was present in the concrete
life of Jesus. As an interpreter of God who acted in accordance with
the lifestyle of the Kingdom of God, Jesus did not act from a blueprint
or a well-defined concept of eschatological salvation. Rather, he saw
in and through his own historical ministry of "going around and doing good," of healing and exorcising, the dawn of a distant vision of
definitive and universal salvation of all creation.[40]

From the viewpoint of the incarnation we can say that the manifestation of the Kingdom in this world takes place in and through the
ministry of Jesus. The newness of the Kingdom manifests itself visibly.
Here the Kingdom becomes an experience in the present and does not
remain a mere hope for the future. The activity of Jesus during his
earthly ministry, for example, his working of miracles, demonstrates
that God wants to repair the brokenness of human existence. The
signs of the Kingdom, exorcisms and healings, show us that salvation
must be seen as "integral and all-embracing." The behavior of Jesus
incarnates how the presence of the Kingdom affects all human relationships. Jesus' action, therefore, can be defined as a *sacrament* of

the Kingdom in its fullness as it makes itself visible on the horizon of human history. The sacrament of the Kingdom means a "sign pregnant with the reality of the future fullness of the Kingdom, like the dawn is a sign of a new day."[41]

How did Jesus enact the Kingdom? What kind of behavior was characteristic of him in which and through which one could see that the Kingdom had arrived? Different answers have been given to these questions. E. A. Johnson considers four characteristic behaviors and actions to be the most outstanding ones[42]:

First, Jesus called disciples to follow him. They left family and home, job and village, and formed a community around him. Composed of men and women they went with him wherever he went. Their basic mood was that of joy and true companionship. After his death they became the nucleus of the church.

Second, Jesus revealed a preference for the poor, the ostracized, the marginalized. He associated with sinners and outcasts, he healed sick people, he reached out to them and touched them, disproving that sickness was caused by sin. He restored them in body and mind and brought them back into life-giving relationship with other human beings. Exorcisms and healing miracles were nothing new to Jesus' audience (Mt 12:27; Mk 9:38). But Jesus saw in his exorcisms an indication that Satan's rule was already broken. Something was happening through his actions that his contemporaries expected only in the last days (as in Isaiah 24:21-22). Healing, restoration, and liberation were taking place in and through his ministry, which had been a hope cherished only for the age to come (Mt 11:5, referring to Is 29:18; 35:5-6; and 61:1).

Third, Jesus shared companionship both with his disciples and with a wider circle of those interested in him. Meals were his favorite means to demonstrate the future of the Kingdom having already arrived with him. Meals were joyful occasions to make everyone feel at home—no fasting but just feasting and enjoying one another's company. People found themselves at table with Jesus in a new kind of community, sharing with people they never thought they would even sit down with.

Jesus saw his practice of *table fellowship* in the light of the endtime. For him the meals already mirrored the character of the festive banquet of the new age (Mk 2:18-19; Lk 14:12-24), again using imagery which contemporaries would relate primarily to the hoped-for future (as in Is 25:6-9).

Finally, Jesus is both faithful and free regarding the great Jewish tradition of the Torah. His interpretation is new, yet in continuity with the past. What counts is people. His interpretative key is compassion and justice, not holiness and purity. Love is the heart of the Reign of God. By loving this way, Jesus himself creates a liberating lifestyle and exhibits a wonderful freedom to do good.

Through these actions Jesus demonstrates what the Kingdom is and how it "materializes" itself already in his behavior within the history of humankind. In acting and behaving as he does, the future of God's Kingdom becomes visible and effective in the present. It is, therefore, too narrow a view to explain the breaking in of the Kingdom purely in terms of individual experience. In the words of Ladd:

> The Kingdom of God cannot be reduced to the reign of God within the individual soul or modernized in terms of personal existential confrontation or dissipated to an extra-worldly dream of blessed immortality. The Kingdom of God means that God is King and acts in history to bring history to a divinely directed goal.[43]

In short, the Kingdom encompasses everything. It aims at the transformation of all human reality including the whole of nature. Animals, plants, and inorganic nature are all destined to participate in the *new earth* and the *new heaven*. The final consummation of the Kingdom will have cosmic dimensions (Is 11:6-9; Rom 8:19-23). The Kingdom of God, therefore, does not signify something that is purely spiritual or outside this world. Rather,

> it is a total, global and structural transfiguration and revolution of the reality of human beings; it means the cosmos purified of all evils and full of the reality of God. The Kingdom of God is not to be in another world but it is the old world transformed into a new one.[44]

This transforming power of God's final intervention is now breaking into the world. It moves into action, so to speak. The transfiguration of the cosmos is on the way.

Edward Schillebeeckx describes the experience of the Kingdom from another position. Through Jesus' redemption Christians experience:

> The freedom to accept that despite sin and guilt we are accepted by God;
> The freedom to be able to live in this earthly world without ultimate despair about our existence;
> The freedom to commit ourselves disinterestedly for others in the confidence that such dedication is ultimately of decisive significance (Mt 25);
> The freedom to accept experiences of peace, joy, and communication and to understand them as manifestations, however fragmentary, of the saving presence of the living God;

The freedom to join in the struggle for economic, social, and political justice;

The freedom to be free from oneself in order to be free for others, free to do good to others.

For Christians, all these experiences are a Christian experience of faith in the God who is revealed in Jesus Christ as the sacred mystery of all-embracing love. They are the experience of salvation from God. Christian redemption is indeed liberation from sin. But liberation from sin also has a cultural context. In our time the Christian understanding of sin also includes the recognition of systematic disruptions of communication like sexism, racism, fascism, anti-semitism, hostility, and arrogance. The Christian love which is the basis of community, therefore, also includes the necessity of recognizing the need for deep involvement in the present-day work of political, cultural, and social emancipation.[45]

THE KINGDOM OF GOD AS GIFT AND TASK

Questions often asked are: What kind of Kingdom did Jesus expect? Was it something that would fit into the general expectation of his day? Was it in line with other groups and movements which wanted to overcome Israel's profound identity crisis as the people of God? Did he, as they, want a profound "restoration of Israel" that would include a new Temple and a new social order with a place for the "outcast and Gentile" as well?[46] Was it to be a Kingdom in this world or totally otherworldly, transcending all inner earthly reality?[47]

These questions do not find unanimous answers among scholars. As we have discussed above, most will agree that Jesus did not exclude this world from the coming of the Kingdom. He seems to have shared more the prophetic rather than the apocalyptic expectation. There is good reason to assume that he saw his ministry in the setting of the Jubilee tradition, as bringing the final "year of favor" for his people. Notwithstanding these remarks, Jesus' emphasis is on the coming Kingdom as unmerited gift. The Kingdom is a gracious gift from God, who comes with unconditional love to seek out humankind and to offer ultimate salvation to all. The Kingdom cannot be brought about by faithful adherence to the Law, as certain rabbis believed; nor can it be forced into the present by armed violence, as the Zealots thought. It is a gift from God which people can only receive in gratitude and awe. God is coming toward us as unconditional love, seeking communion and intimacy. Since it is a gift of love, the only concrete description can be in terms of symbols and images. Its final coming is totally up to God; it will come as God sees fit. It cannot be foretold nor calculated. No human initiative can bring about the coming of the Kingdom. It is God's own powerful and sovereign act.[48]

The sayings and parables of Jesus present the gift-character of the Kingdom in clear and unambiguous language. It is God who makes the seed grow, by divine power and grace (Mk 4:26-29). This is the principal teaching of the "growth parables" (Mk 4). It is God who invites to the eschatological banquet. One may pray "your Kingdom come" (Mt 6:10), may cry out to God day and night (Lk 18:7), may prepare oneself and hold oneself in readiness like the wise virgins (Mt 25:1-13), may seek the Kingdom (Mt 6:33), but it is God who "gives" it (Lk 12:31). God decides whose it shall be (Mt 5). It does not come from our effort but from God's overflowing love for us. We can only accept it in gratitude and joy.

On the other hand, we must avoid the danger of viewing the Kingdom as coming completely without human assistance. This is a perennial temptation in many treatises on the Kingdom of God. Lohfink astutely identifies the pitfall in this way:

> There is one sentence in modern exegesis that is constantly repeated: The basileia is solely and exclusively God's act. This sentence is then frequently followed by something like this: Human beings must pray for the coming of the basileia, they must prepare and be ready for it, orient themselves toward it and asymptotically draw near to it, but they can do absolutely nothing to cause or hasten its coming, nor can they do anything to stop or hinder it. . . . Now obviously we do not deny that the basileia is God's act. However, does that say all that needs saying?[49]

What about human cooperation? Must we not also say that the coming of the Kingdom is "totally, completely, and entirely" the work of human beings? The gratuitousness of the Kingdom should not lead us to regard ourselves as merely passive objects. The Kingdom of God is ultimately a personal relationship between God and human beings. As in any personal relationship two-way traffic is always involved. We are challenged to respond, and it is through this response that the Kingdom becomes a reality in our midst. In the view of Viviano,

> The Kingdom of God is a future apocalyptic divine gift not built by human beings directly but given as a response to hopeful prayer, longing and hastening struggle.[50]

Jürgen Moltmann regards a totally passive attitude toward the Kingdom as an invalidation of everything that the New Testament says about Jesus. If Jesus is God and man, then we must say the Kingdom of God is the affair of Jesus. From here he concludes:

> As the affair of Jesus, the kingdom of God can be readily experienced and can also be readily practiced in his community. "Seek ye first the kingdom and righteousness, and all these things shall be yours as well" (Mt 6:33). The power of God is indeed experienced in the community of Jesus. And through this experience, human beings become "coworkers in the kingdom of God" called to perform the same messianic works as Jesus himself. As you go, preach this message: "The Kingdom of heaven is at hand. Heal the sick, raise the dead, cleanse lepers, cast out demons" (Mt 10:7-8). It is the intent of Jesus here to make the kingdom of God our affair as well as his. God is freedom, and to possess authentic freedom means to walk and work in the kingdom.[51]

But Moltmann places beside the work for the Kingdom what he calls the "enjoyment of the Kingdom," that is, the liturgical celebration. As he points out, Jewish tradition tells us that to celebrate the Sabbath is to possess "one sixtieth of the Kingdom of God," and every successful celebration of the Lord's day counts for more. It is good to "work and to pray" for the Kingdom but to "rest and to celebrate" should be seen as adding a note of completion to the Kingdom.[52]

Lohfink sees the task-character of the Kingdom most vividly explained in the parable of the Talents (Mt 25:14-30). It depicts human beings as active agents of the Kingdom of God. The parable of the Treasure in the Field offers a similar portrayal. In these parables Jesus not only tells us that the Kingdom is a pure gift, but he also affirms that it unfolds through the taking of incredible risks. In the gospel of John the interaction of God's works and those of believers is explained most explicitly. For John, God does God's work, yet Jesus also does the same work, and believers will do even greater works than Jesus has done (Jn 14:12). The evangelist is so sure of the theological accuracy of such a bold assertion that he emphasizes: "The Son can do nothing of his own accord, but only what he sees the Father doing" (Jn 5:19). Analogously, the same is true for believers. Thus, in accord with John's gospel, the coming of the *Basileia* is totally and completely God's work, and totally and completely the work of human beings.[53]

Jon Sobrino in his book on Christology offers a unique way of looking at the Kingdom as gift and task. He sees the Kingdom as establishing first and foremost a filial relationship with God. We are oriented vertically to God, and thus, we are his children. From this vertical orientation follows the horizontal relationship which makes us brothers and sisters. Both are essential and are of equal and primary importance. They belong to God as such. Brotherhood without sonship can indeed terminate in atheism, but sonship without brotherhood can lead to mere theism.[54]

This idea of divine sonship and human fellowship as explaining the Kingdom as gift and task is employed by G. Gutiérrez in a specific way. For him divine sonship is a gift while the creation of a profound human fellowship is a task. A dynamic unity exists between gift and task. The gift is accepted precisely by carrying out the task entailed by it. Creating a profound human fellowship means accepting the gift of divine sonship. The God of the Kingdom does not allow us to choose between the two aspects. Those who let the Kingdom into their life by becoming children of God will have to show the presence of the Kingdom by working to make all human beings their brothers and sisters. Here the gift of the Kingdom is sonship and the task of the Kingdom is the bringing about of this sonship in the horizontal dimension through the creation of a community of brothers and sisters.[55]

8

The Future of Evil and the Question of Eternal Punishment

Jesus' Kingdom message is set against the background of the two reigns: the reign of evil and the Reign of God. God is the Lord of history but there are hostile forces which seek to frustrate God's rule. Ladd describes the situation in the following terms:

> There are demonic forces manifest in history and human experience which move against the Kingdom of God. Evil is not merely absence of the good, nor is it a stage in man's upward development; it is a terrible enemy of human well-being and will never be outgrown or abandoned until God has mightily intervened to purge evil from the earth.[1]

Within the context of our previous discussion on the Kingdom, several questions arise: What will happen to that reign of evil? What is its future? Will it continue to exist once the Kingdom of God has come in its fullness?

A careful reading of scripture seems to indicate that the reign of evil belongs to this world. We must never underestimate its power, because it is able to push this world and human beings to total destruction. It is best described as a destructive power which shows its destructive effects in the alienation and sinfulness of humankind. It can influence human beings individually and collectively to perform abominable deeds.[2]

The power of evil, however, is only of a preliminary nature and will never be able to destroy either humankind or the whole of creation. But what will happen to those who have fallen prey to its power? What will be their state after death? In what does their punishment consist? Is there a place for the evil spirits and for the condemned? In short, is there hell and in what does it consist?

THE PRESENT DISCUSSION

Due to the way the question of hell and eternal damnation were treated in traditional theology over the centuries, this subject has virtually no appeal for most theologians today, or for the majority of believers. Many theologians either do not want to talk about it or completely dismiss its existence. Even forty years ago Rahner remarked that the doctrine of hell was beginning to be a truth which no longer had any existential meaning for Christians.

Through the centuries, however, the church has maintained this doctrine and has repeatedly restated it. Cardinal Ratzinger declares:

No quibbling helps here: the idea of eternal damnation which had taken ever clearer shape in Judaism of the century or two before Christ, has a firm place in the teaching of Jesus, as well as in the apostolic writings. Dogma takes its stand on solid ground when it speaks of the existence of Hell and of the eternity of its punishments.[3]

We cannot simply dismiss hell because it is no longer popular. "Hell Belongs to the Good News," was the title of a book written some years ago. Theology must come to grips with it in a way that will allow this gospel truth to be heard again.[4] Although there are many reasons for the current neglect of the subject, they seem to center on the following arguments, which we shall review.

THE TRADITIONAL PERCEPTION

Hell's negative standing has a long history. The early Church Fathers had differing opinions about hell.[5] For better or worse Augustine gave the church its traditional way of thinking about this subject. He saw hell as a condition of endless torment of conscious persons in body and soul. He defends his view vigorously in *The City of God* (chapter 21) and concludes against any objection that God plans to torture the wicked forever both mentally and physically. Augustine's main argument against any compassion on the part of God toward those who are lost is that, to do so, God would have to pardon the devil as well.[6] Augustine's notion of hell inspired millions of preachers and created the enormous flood of threatening proclamations of coming doom that was used so effectively by the church over the centuries. Particularly vivid were the physical and anthropomorphic descriptions of the eternal punishment awaiting those who through their actions or false belief would have to remain forever in that place of darkness and fire.[7] Such descriptions very often bordered on mere sadism, even if beautifully disguised in the poetry of Dante's inferno. As someone put it: "The sadism that helped to fill the churches of the past has helped to empty the churches of today." It is interesting to note, however, that the vivid and graphic imagination of hell is virtually a universal phenomenon. Buddhism, Hinduism and Islam, as well as the Judeo-Christian tradition, all enshrine in their scriptures and/or traditions breathtaking descriptions of the torment that awaits those who are doomed to hell.[8]

INCOMPATIBILITY WITH THE IMAGE OF GOD IN REVELATION

In the New Testament two series of statements run along side by side in such a way that a synthesis of both seems impossible to achieve. The first series speaks of being lost for all eternity; the second, of God's will and ability to save all human beings. It is important to observe that most of the statements that refer to the first series are found in the pre-Easter texts of the gospels, while statements that talk about a universal salvation can be found mostly in Paul and John. The difference seems to be explainable by the fact that the death of Jesus on the cross and "his descent into hell" opened a whole new view on the universality of Christ's redemptive suffering and death.[9] Thus we read in scripture passages such as the following:

And I, when I am lifted up from the earth, will draw all people to myself (Jn 12:32).

God our savior . . . desires everyone to be saved and to come to the knowledge of the truth. For
>   there is one God;
>   there is also one mediator between God
>   and humankind,
>   Christ Jesus, himself human,
>   who gave himself a ransom for all.
>   (1 Tim 2:4-5)

For the grace of God has appeared, bringing salvation to all (Ti 2:11) according to God's will "to reconcile to himself all things, whether on earth or in heaven" (Col 1:20), since God has decided "to gather up all things in him (Eph 1:10).

One could quote dozens of biblical texts which all seem to indicate that there is hope for the salvation of all. Karl Barth commenting on

Jesus' death, sees him as the one rejected by God in place of all sinners, "so that, besides him, no one may be lost."[10]

Notwithstanding such texts, the principal objections to hell as preached over the centuries arise from theology itself. Hell—so the argument goes—is not reconcilable with a God who loves all human beings with an unconditional love and who sent his Son into the world not to condemn it but to save it.[11] The problem here is the issue of God's justice in relation to his love. Since Augustine there has been a tendency to teach that the justice of God consisted in the fact that although God could have consigned the whole human race to hell, he graciously saved some from the conflagration. The objection to such an argument is:

> What purpose of God would be served by the unending torture of the wicked except sheer vengeance and vindictiveness? Such a fate would spell endless and totally unredemptive suffering, punishment just for its own sake.[12]

The indignation that many faithful feel concerning the traditional doctrine of hell may be quite forcefully expressed by the same author in these words:

> The concept of hell as endless torment in body and mind is an outrageous doctrine, a theological and moral enormity, a bad doctrine of the tradition which needs to be changed. How can Christians possibly project a deity of such cruelty and vindictiveness whose ways include inflicting everlasting torture upon his creature, however sinful they may have been? Surely a God who could do such a thing is more nearly like Satan than like God, at least by any ordinary moral standard, and by the gospel itself. How can we possibly preach that God has arranged things that a number of his creatures (perhaps a large number predestined to that fate) will undergo (in a state of complete consciousness) physical and mental agony through unending time? Is this not a most disturbing concept which needs some second thoughts? Surely the God and Father of our Lord Jesus Christ is no fiend: torturing people without end is not what our God does. Does the one who told us to love our enemies intend to wreak vengeance on his own enemies for all eternity?[13]

Great saints like Catherine of Siena and Thérèse of Lisieux agonized over the mere thought of people being condemned to hell forever. Thérèse of Lisieux found consolation in the thought, "I believe in hell but I think that it is empty."[14] Catherine of Siena wrote:

How could I ever reconcile myself, Lord, to the prospect that a single one of those whom, like me, you have created in your image and likeness should become lost and slip from your hands? No, in absolutely no case do I want to see a single one of my brethren meet with ruin, not a single one of those who, through their like birth, are one with me by nature and by grace. I want them all to be wrested from the grasp of the ancient enemy, so that they all become yours to the honor and greater glorification of your name.[15]

In general, the idea of such a punishing God seems too repulsive. On a closer examination of the growing understanding of scripture itself we see more clearly that God is not portrayed as a wrathful God or as a punisher of human beings. Most sins punish themselves in the sense that their consequences for the sinner are sufficient punishment. For example, ecological disaster is God's judgment on technocracy and greed, as war could be regarded as God's judgment on a corrupt civilization. The world is constituted by a moral order, and breaches of its pattern bring about their own fruits. The idea of judgment is bound up with a moral order that is very real, immanent, urgent, and even eternal.

What appears in the life of an individual or in the life of a whole nation as God's punishment and justice is, in light of God's Kingdom, God's ultimate offer of salvation. It is to be seen, within the limits of our historical existence, as God's constant attempt to lead us to a life more in harmony with the vision of the Kingdom.

The traditional arguments are challenged as resting not on sound biblical interpretation but rather on early Greek pagan influence and on Augustine's version of hell.

A basic presumption for the traditional view of eternal punishment is the idea of the immortality of the soul. As Jacques Maritain wrote: "The human soul cannot die. Once it exists, it cannot disappear; it will necessarily exist forever and endure without end."[16] Today such a view would be contested as not being grounded in the scriptures. Immortality is not inherent in human beings. Eternal life is a gift from God and not a natural right of any human being. Pinnock argues:

If souls are immortal, then either all souls will be saved (which is unscriptural universalism) or else hell must be everlasting torment. There is no other possibility since annihilation is ruled out from the start. This is how the traditional view of hell was constructed: add a belief in divine judgment after death (scriptural) to a belief in the immortality of the soul (unscriptural), and you have Augustine's terrible doctrine.[17]

However the main argument against the traditional view is that it rests basically on three deficient presuppositions.[18] The traditional view assumes: (1) that the Old Testament is, generally speaking, silent on the subject; (2) that the doctrine of conscious, unending torment, which developed during the intertestamental years, came to be the commonly accepted Jewish view at the time of Jesus; and, (3) that the New Testament language requires us to conclude that God will make the wicked immortal for the purpose of torturing them without end. Such assumptions are challenged today. First, the Old Testament, while not silent on the subject, is definitely silent about unending conscious torture. Second, the time between the Testaments maintains basically the same view, as Fudge has noted:

> The apocryphal books of 1 Esdras, 3 Maccabees, 1 Baruch, Epistle of Jeremias, Prayer of Manasseh and the addition of Daniel and Ester are silent on the subject. The book of Tobit, Sirach, Baruch, 1 and 2 Maccabees and the Wisdom of Solomon agree thoroughly with the Old Testament as they anticipate the total destruction of the wicked.[19]

Third, since the New Testament language on the subject of hell comes primarily from the Old Testament, the issue should be interpreted from the starting point of the Old Testament.[20] In their Old Testament setting the common phrases like "unquenchable fire," "undying worms," "the gnashing of teeth," "the smoke that ascends," "no rest day and night," "the cup of God's wrath," and "the lake of fire" strongly suggest being extinguished, going out of existence, being annihilated. Fudge explains:

> Whatever the case the symbols are clear in the light of previous Biblical usage. None of them refers to unending conscious torment in regular usage, and there is no reason to think any refers to it here. They all, on the other hand, have regular prophetic significance in many passages of Scripture and the meaning of them all converges on this description of a complete, irreversible destruction and extinction forever accomplished.[21]

Fudge examines all of these Old Testament expressions in detail. For example, the phrase "unquenchable fire" means normally "destruction that cannot be resisted"; to "quench" means to "extinguish" or "put out a fire." The traditional translation as "unending conscious torment" can in no way be maintained. The same could be said about Isaiah 66:24, where the phrase "worm [that] shall not die" appears. To understand "worm" as tormenting conscience or everlasting parasites means to ignore the whole context in which this chapter must be understood.[22]

Even the Pauline language, as well as other New Testament language, at face value best describes some kind of total destruction. Fudge concludes his study by insisting:

> If we ignore the Bible's own usage of its language, we can make these terms mean whatever we please. But if we let the Bible interpret itself, we have far less choice. For all of Scripture's language on this subject leads us time and time again to the same conclusion: The wicked will finally perish completely and forever in hell. None of the Bible's language suggests unending conscious torment for human beings.[23]

THE PSYCHOLOGICAL ARGUMENT

The idea that hell is not a respectable topic comes as well from clinical psychology and from ethics. By analyzing human freedom as concrete action rather than as abstract concept, psychologists have made us aware of the enormous limits and relativity of any free human act. They question the ability of any human being to make a choice in this life with such definitiveness that it would be final for all eternity.[24] Other reasons, although more theological, are also mentioned: How can a just God condemn people to eternal torment? How can the blessed experience joy in heaven if friends and loved ones are in hell? How can God's purpose with creation be frustrated?[25]

POSSIBLE EXPLANATIONS OF HELL

The problem here is not the existence of hell but the nature of that existence. It is the "eternal punishment" and the "eternal damnation" that are most difficult to accept. The idea of hell as eternal punishment is regarded as too repulsive and inconsistent with a loving God. As we saw, some scholars challenge the traditional view on the basis of scripture itself. There are three current explanations for hell, of which two allow for alternative views.

Hell as Annihilation

This position argues that hell consists not in eternal punishment and condemnation but in annihilation or loss of life. The most objectionable feature in the traditional idea of hell is that God seemingly keeps those whom he hates in existence and even raises them from the dead, not for their own good, since they are past redemption, but only so that they may be tormented. To supersede such reasoning, heaven and hell cannot merely be juxtaposed as opposites. The opposite of heaven is death, not hell. The words to be compared are *life* and *death*. On such a basis, hell must be conceived of as death, which means ultimately annihilation or extinction, rather than a "semblance of life" envisioned as eternal torment and punishment.[26]

The Bible tells us that life is going to triumph over death; it is a book of life. God is identical with life and love. God is eternal life and eternal love. There is nothing more dreadful for a living being to think of than its opposite: nonbeing, absolute void, nonexistence. From this position one could argue as follows. God offers us a share in eternal life, but we have to make this choice for life freely and determinately. This we do by choosing God and a life of love for God and our fellow human beings. Our life, as we know it from scripture, makes sense only if it is lived in trying to be loving. Once we see hell as loss of life, it could be viewed as being removed from the love of God forever by annihilation. Here hell means not sharing in eternal life, no longer existing, rather than being tortured eternally. This seems to be what scripture means by "second death" (Rv 20:6).

The objection to this position is often that this would be an insufficient retribution for sin, more like a half-way house between heaven and hell. People like Hitler and Eichmann deserve more than just going out of existence. However, one can argue that the basic notion of hell is the notion of the worst possible outcome for a human being. This is why we have reason not only to fear it, but to fear it more than anything else. Hell is not so much something inflicted on us, but rather something we lose. The greatest loss a human being can sustain is the loss of life itself, that is, death.[27] On the Catholic side, Schillebeeckx favors just such an interpretation. He holds that living with God now is the basis for eternal life, and absence from the life-giving community is the basis of eternal death. Extinction is the logical result of an unloving life. So the idea of a punishing God can be rejected, without rejecting the basic idea behind hell. He writes:

> If living community with God is the foundation of eternal life, then absence of this living community (not so much through theoretical denial of God as through a lifestyle which radically contradicts solidarity with fellow human beings and precisely in that way rejects God and loving communion with God) is at the same time the foundation of non-eternal life for these people. That seems to me to be the "second death" of the fundamental, definite sinner (if there is such a person). That is hell: not shar-

ing in eternal life nor being someone who is tortured eternally, but no longer existing at death. That is the biblical "second death" (Rv 20:6). This sanction is the result of one's own behavior and not a positive act of the punitive justice of God who sends sinners to an eternal hellish fire (however that may be imagined as an instrument of torture) there is just no ground for eternal life. These people have resisted God's holiness and are incapable of loving. No one in heaven will ever remember them.[28]

Our Christian hope is that God will secure life after death for those who in life "choose life," that is, who give to their life a direction of love which God in turn will lead to eternal life. Those who did not choose life will await the opposite fate; namely, eternal death, which is annihilation beyond all hope. At death our characters are fixed, partly by our actions and partly by the state of our understanding. The only possible change is that which the traditional notion of purgatory implies—God, who is wholly good, purges us of those characteristics which obscure the Beatific Vision. But the effect of that purging will be more or less radical depending on the place those characteristics have in our personality as a whole. Those whose hearts are fixed "where true joy is to be found" will emerge from the process purified, and moreover, truly themselves. Those whose hearts are fixed on evil will fade into nothingness. They will, in short, be annihilated. In this way eternal death comes not as an act of vengeance or retribution, but as an act of a God who wills only the good. From this perspective the idea of a punishing God no longer makes sense.[29] Schillebeeckx explains:

> The evil do not have eternal life; their death is in fact the end of everything; they have excluded themselves from God and the community of the good, nor does any new heaven await them on earth. They no longer exist, and cannot sense the happiness that good men and women then enjoy. But there is no shadow kingdom of hell next to the eternally happy Kingdom of God. . . . The blessed will be spared the fact that a stone's throw away from their eternal happiness, fellow human beings are being tortured for ever with whatever physical or spiritual pains. . . . The eschaton of the ultimate is exclusively positive. There is no negative eschaton. Good, not evil, has the last word. That is the message and the distinctive human praxis of Jesus of Nazareth, whom Christians therefore confess as the Christ.[30]

Karl Rahner stated the same idea, only more cautiously, by saying that all a person needs to know about hell is that "he cannot say that absolute loss as the conclusion and outcome of his free guilt is not a possibility with which he has to reckon."[31]

From his scriptural analysis Fudge concludes:

> We were reared on the traditional view—we accepted it because it was said to rest on the Bible. A more careful study has shown that we are mistaken in that assumption. Both the Old Testament and the New Testament instead clearly teach a resurrection of the wicked for divine judgment, the fearful anticipation of a consuming fire, irrevocable expulsion from God's presence into a place where there will be weeping and grinding of teeth, such conscious suffering as the divine justice individually required—and finally, the total, everlasting extinction of the wicked with no hope of resurrection, restoration or recovery. Now we stand on that, on the authority of the Word of God.[32]

Pinnock sums up his findings by saying:

> At the very least it should be obvious to any impartial reader that the Bible may legitimately be read to teach the final destruction of the wicked without difficulty.[33]

Hell as Mere Possibility

How many will be lost or will all be saved? The answer is difficult. Jesus never answered this question; he only told the one who asked to take salvation seriously. Origen was condemned in 543 because he denied the existence of an eternal hell in the sense that God would ultimately redeem those condemned to hell as well.[34] In the East, Gregory of Nyssa and others maintained a silent certitude that God's grace would reach all. Based on the solidarity with us which Christ assumed by becoming man, the Russian Orthodox Church held to this belief. They argued that there is hope of salvation for all creatures and that the compassion and immensity of God's love for his creatures will indeed effect that salvation. Von Balthasar explains:

> In the East Origen, Gregory of Nanzianzus and Gregory of Nyssa maintain with a secret and silent certitude of faith that God's grace will ultimately show mercy to every creature. This hope of redemption for all lives on today in the Russian faithful in a new, even deeper rooted form. It is based on the solidarity of all human beings. . . . For the Russian believer this is not a piece of Christian doctrine among others but forms the center and heart of his faith.[35]

The basis for this belief is often connected with the "descent of Jesus into hell," a theme the early Church Fathers refer to most often in connection with the liturgy of Holy Saturday.[36]

The only passage in the New Testament that mentions Christ's descent into the realm of the dead is 1 Peter.[37] Here Christ preached to the spirits in prison "who in former times did not obey, when God waited patiently in the days of Noah" (3:20). What is here meant are actually all the dead to whom Christ preaches repentance (4:6). In short, it means that the message of Christ can still reach those already dead.

Pannenberg, commenting about this universalist understanding of salvation in 1 Peter, concludes by saying:

> Christian interpreters were already toning down the full boldness of this idea even in the earliest period of the church. We can read again and again that Jesus preached in Hades only to the righteous men of ancient Israel, or only to men in general who were righteous during their life time. But 1 Peter goes further when it talks about the preaching of repentance. The tendency toward a universalist understanding of salvation, which is aimed at there, has found its full expression in the idea that Christ redeemed Adam—i.e. man per se—from the underworld, an idea which we find in Origen and which generally stands in the fore-front in paintings of Christ's descent into hell.[38]

Pannenberg regrets that this theological truth has been forgotten or in many ways just ignored. He continues:

> The meaning of the Christian acknowledgment of the conquest of the kingdom of death and Jesus Christ's descent into hell lies in the universal scope of salvation. Anyone who has grasped this can only regret that this particular article of the Apostles' Creed has recently come up against such special lack of understanding and has consequently frequently been rejected altogether.[39]

The scriptural text most often used for such a hope is Jesus own saying: "For nothing will be impossible with God" (Lk 1:37; 18:25-27).[40]

Other texts are often quoted. First, it is pointed out that God wants the salvation of everyone (Rom 11:32; 1 Tim 2:4-6). Second, it can be shown that the work of God's grace in Christ was designated for the salvation of everyone (2 Cor 5:14; Ti 2:11; Heb 2:9; 1 Jn 2:2). Third, texts can be cited in which God's total victory is proclaimed and in which it is said that everything will ultimately be reconciled to God:

For as all die in Adam, so all will be made alive in Christ (1 Cor 15:22; cf. 23-28).

In Christ God was reconciling the world to himself (2 Cor 5:19).

For in him all the fullness of God was pleased to dwell, and through him to reconcile to himself all things, whether on earth or in heaven, by making peace through the blood of his cross (Col 1:19-20; see also Rom 8:19-21; Eph 1:10,20-23).

Therefore, just as one man's trespass led to condemnation for all, so one man's act of righteousness leads to justification and life for all (Rom 5:18).

> Therefore God also highly exalted him
>   and gave him the name
>   that is above every name,
> so that at the name of Jesus
>   every knee should bend,
>   in heaven and on earth and under the
>   earth,
> and every tongue should confess
>   that Jesus Christ is Lord,
>   to the glory of God the Father (Phil 2:9-11;
>   see also Jn 1:29; 3:17; 12:32,47).[41]

From here the following argument can be made. At death or shortly thereafter a choice is offered to anyone who, because of limited insights, might have refused the Kingdom in this life. Human freedom is taken very seriously in scripture, yet our freedom in this world is so highly conditioned that it can hardly be proportionate to eternal condemnation. It seems highly improbable that a human being on earth already possesses the gift of freedom to such a degree that he or she would definitely reject God's offer of salvation.

Certain scriptural texts suggest that after death a process of growth and a painful alienation from the Kingdom will lead such persons finally to accept the Kingdom fully and unconditionally. These processes are limited and meant to bring a person to his or her final destiny. They are not regarded primarily as punishment for the past. Nonetheless, one needs to maintain the possibility that a human being could still reject such an offer and so face condemnation and annihilation. The possibility cannot be denied.[42]

Hans Urs von Balthasar expresses his position on the issue by a lengthy passage from a work of Edith Stein. Since I share the same view, I will include this passage, which in a marvelous way describes how God's infinite love will ultimately "outwit" all human resistance to this love without violating the human person's most precious gift, individual freedom:

We attempt to understand what part freedom plays in the work of redemption. For this is not adequate if one focuses on freedom alone. One must investigate as well what grace can do and whether even for it there is an absolute limit. This we have already seen: grace must come to man. By its own power, it can, at best, come up to his door but never force its way inside. And further, it can come to him without his seeking it, without his desiring it. The question is whether it can complete its work without his cooperation. It seemed to us that this question had to be answered negatively. That is a weighty thing to say. For it obviously implies that God's freedom, which we call omnipotence, meets with limits in human freedom. Grace is the Spirit of God who descends to the soul of man. It can find no abode there if it is not freely taken in. That is a hard truth. It implies—besides the aforementioned limit to divine omnipotence—the possibility, in principle, of excluding oneself from redemption and the kingdom of grace. It does *not* imply a limit to divine mercy. For even if we cannot close our minds to the fact that temporal death comes for countless men without their ever having looked eternity in the eye and without salvation's having ever become a problem for them; that furthermore, many men occupy themselves with salvation for a lifetime without responding to grace, we still do not know whether the decisive hour might not come for all of these somewhere in the next world, and faith can tell us that this is the case.

All-merciful love can thus descend to everyone. We believe that it does so. And now, can we assume that there are souls that remain perpetually closed to such love? As a possibility in principle, this cannot be rejected. In *reality*, it can become infinitely improbable—precisely through what preparatory grace is capable of effecting in the soul. It can do no more than knock at the door, and there are souls that already open themselves to it upon hearing this unobtrusive call. Others allow it to go unheeded. Then it can steal its way into the souls and begin to spread itself out there more and more. The greater the area becomes that grace thus occupies in a illegitimate way, the more improbable it becomes that the soul will remain closed to it. For now the soul already sees the world in the light of grace. It perceives the holy whenever it encounters this and feels itself attracted by it. Likewise, it notices the unholy and is repulsed by it; and everything pales before these qualities. To this corresponds a tendency within itself to behave accordingly to its own reason and no longer to that of nature of the evil one. If it follows this inner prompting, then it subjects itself implicitly to the rule of grace. It is possible that it will not do this. Then it has need of an activity of its own that is directed against the influence of grace. And this engaging of freedom implies a tension that increases proportionately the more that preparatory grace has spread itself through the soul. This defensive activity is based—like all free acts—on a foundation that differs in nature from itself, such as natural impulses that are still effective in the souls alongside of grace.

The more that grace wins ground from the things that had filled the soul before it, the more it repels the effects of the acts directed against it. And to this process of displacement there are, in principle, no limits. If all the impulses opposed to the spirit of light have been expelled from the soul, then any free decision against this has become infinitely improbable. Then faith in the unboundedness of divine love and grace also justifies hope for the universality of redemption, although, through the possibility of resistance to grace that remains open in principle, the possibility of eternal damnation also persists. Seen in this way, what were described earlier as limits to divine omnipotence are also canceled out again. They exist only as long as we oppose divine and human freedom to each other and fail to consider the sphere that form the basis of human freedom. Human freedom can be neither broken nor neutralized by divine freedom, but it may well be, so to speak, "outwitted." The descent of grace to the human soul is a free act of divine love. And there are no limits to how far it may extend. Which particular means it chooses for effecting itself, why it strives to win one soul and lets another strive to win it, whether and how and when it is also active in places where our eyes perceive no effects—those are all questions that escape rational penetration. For us, there is only knowledge of the possibilities in principle, and understanding of the facts that are accessible to us.[43]

Hell as State of "Anomaly"

It is safe to say that the majority of scholars today still retain the idea of an eternal existence for those who decided against life and for death.[44] Besides the longstanding tradition, their main biblical basis is often Matthew 25:46: "These will go away into eternal punishment." For them the text means "everlasting, conscious torment." The passage can be interpreted in this way. However, in the light of the other passages, it can also mean irreversible destruction. Pinnock understands the text in this way:

Jesus does not define the nature of eternal life or eternal death in this text. He just says there will be two destinies and leaves it there. One is free to interpret it to mean either everlasting conscious torment or irreversible destruction. The text allows for both possibilities and only teaches explicitly the finality of the judgment itself, not its nature. Therefore, one's interpretation of this verse in respect to our subject here will depend upon other considerations. In the light of what has been said so far, I think it is better and wiser to read the text as teaching annihilation.[45]

Contrary to this interpretation are those who believe that beings who, in their lives, opted only for themselves will get what they wanted. In that case they remain eternally an anomaly, for they are alone for themselves, and therefore, against themselves—sealed in an interminable pursuit of self. Many who hold this view do admit that some passages in scripture can be taken to imply the annihilation of the wicked at judgment. But they believe that the solemn seriousness of the warnings of eternal punishment found in the Bible does ultimately allow for such an interpretation. Brown states:

> We know that at the time of Christ it was the common understanding, first of the Jews, then of the Christians, that punishment, like reward, is eternal. From the passages of the Church Fathers onward, we see that even though several of the Fathers and their successors, medieval and modern, wanted to soften the fate of those who are lost, whether by "apokatastasis," a second chance or chances, or, most recently, by annihilation after the Judgment, these hopes simply cannot be maintained in the face of Scripture's repeated warnings.[46]

CONCLUSION

None of these theories denies the possibility of hell. The issue is not the existence of hell but how to interpret the apocalyptic and anthropomorphic language of scripture and tradition.[47] Jesus himself speaks fifty-two times of punishment and condemnation, and continually voices severe warnings to his listeners not to underestimate the judgment that will be passed on each one's life. For this author, the first and second theories seem most plausible. The first explains hell as annihilation or loss of life. As we saw, this view has a reasonable basis in scripture. The second assumption leaves open almost unlimited possibilities for any person to convert, whether at the time of death or even after death. This view is supported by the doctrine of Jesus' descent into hell and the orthodox silent belief in the salvation of all creatures. Such conversion in or after death is ultimately based on God's incomprehensible love; "For mortals it is impossible, but not for God; for God all things are possible" (Mk 10:27). This view knows that all human beings have to go through "judgment," that is, they will have to face their wrongdoing and make amends. All authors who opt for this view do not pretend to know for certain that all will actually be saved. But they ardently hope that God's infinite love will know how to save all human beings.

In conclusion we can say that evil will have no power anymore because the Kingdom will overtake it and finally put an end to it. It will have no future beyond this world once the Kingdom arrives in its fullness.

9

The Sermon on the Mount
and the Kingdom of God

The central message of Jesus' preaching and ministry was the Kingdom of God. Everything he said and did was related to this message and must be understood from this perspective. There are two important topics that are most relevant to anyone who wants to follow the Lord: prayer and rule of conduct; that is, how we should pray and what is the norm for our actions. To both, Jesus gave clear and definite answers. As to prayer, he gave his disciples the Our Father as the pattern of all prayers, according to his admonition: "Pray then in this way" (Mt 6:9). With regard to a disciple's conduct Jesus proclaimed what scholars call the Sermon on the Mount, with the clear instruction: "Unless your righteousness exceeds that of the scribes and Pharisees, you will never enter the kingdom of heaven" (Mt 5:20). The Our Father will be the focus of a later chapter. At this point, we will discuss the Sermon on the Mount as a particularly vivid expression of the Kingdom of God in action.

The Sermon on the Mount cannot be seen apart from the context of the Kingdom.[1] For this reason we will follow the presentation of Joachim Jeremias.[2] Today we know that the Sermon on the Mount, which Matthew presents as the first of his five discourses, is a composition of many sayings of Jesus. Matthew weaved these together into a coherent whole. We must envision each of these sayings as a summary of something like an all-day discussion or a sermon or of some important teaching that might have been an answer to a question. These isolated sayings were first gathered together in the form of an Aramaic Sermon on the Plain. From this, in turn, the Greek Sermon on the Plain in Luke and the Greek Sermon on the Mount in Matthew have developed.[3] It is called the Sermon on the Mount since Jesus proclaimed the message and norms of the New Covenant from an elevated location. Many exegetes believe that Matthew presents Jesus here as the new Moses. Like Moses who from a mountain, proclaimed the ten commandments which formed the basis of the Old Testament, so now Jesus proclaims the commandments which will build the foundation of the New Covenant. Davies and Allison explain:

> We have no doubt, especially in the light of the evangelist's undoubted interest elsewhere in Mosaic motifs, that the parallels between Mt 1-5 and the story of Moses are intentional. They require that the Jesus of the Sermon on the Mount is in some sense a new Moses.[4]

Luke has the Sermon on the Plain, which seems to be an earlier form of the Sermon on the Mount. It is shorter and differs significantly from that of Matthew.

INTERPRETATIONS OF THE SERMON ON THE MOUNT

Different answers have been given to the question of the true meaning of the Sermon on the Mount. Davies and Allison list seven approaches. (1) *The monastic interpretation*. The Sermon on the Mount is seen not as commandment but as evangelical counsel meant for those with a special religious calling. (2) *The absolutist approach*. The Sermon on the Mount is to be interpreted literally. (3) *The doctrine of the two kingdoms*. There are two realms in this world: the religious and the public realm. The Sermon on the Mount is addressed to the Christian (religious realms), not to the government (public realm). It articulates an individual morality; it does not prescribe public policy. (4) *The impossible ideal*. The Sermon on the Mount cannot be lived; its point is to teach the necessity of grace. (5) *The ethics of intention*. The Sermon on the Mount is not about what we should do but about what we should be. (6) *Christological interpretation*. The Sermon on the Mount is a way of preaching Christ. He alone lived his own words. The singular content of the Sermon on the Mount is Jesus and our confrontation with him. (7) *The historical-critical approach*. The Sermon on the Mount is analyzed with the tools of modern historical criticism. We are left with a summary of unrelated individual sayings.

Jeremias presents his own approach to the sermon after expounding what he considers to be the three basic positions: the perfectionist conception, the theory of the impossible ideal, and the theory of an "interim ethic." We will survey each of these in turn.

The Perfectionist Conception

In the Sermon on the Mount Jesus tells his disciples what he requires of them. He explains to them the will of God as it should determine their way of life. This is demonstrated in the six antitheses in which the old and the new conceptions of the will of God are contrasted with each other: "You have heard . . . but I say to you . . . " (Mt 5:21, 22). That phrase continues in chapters 5 through 7. Jewish scholars in particular who have analyzed the Sermon of the Mount insist that there is nothing in this sermon that one cannot find already in the Old Testament. Jesus only refined and radicalized the demands of the Old Covenant. He was a rabbi, a teacher of the Law, which he developed to its perfection.[5]

The Theory of the Impossible Ideal

If the first solution seems to be favored by Jewish scholars, this second solution seems favored by Protestant scholars. The intention of the Sermon on the Mount is to move us to despair. Who can live these demands? Who can fulfill them? It is argued that it is a great mistake to regard the Sermon on the Mount as capable of being fulfilled. The intention of Jesus in the Sermon is to lead his disciples to the realization that they can never achieve salvation through the Law. The Law reveals our incapacity to ourselves by driving us to despair, and it opens our eyes to the wonders of God's mercy. The Sermon on the Mount reveals the propaedeutic meaning of the Law: the Law prepares us for salvation.

The difficulty with this theory is that nowhere in the gospels can the idea be found that we are incapable of fulfilling the will of God. Jesus obviously expected his disciples, as well as anyone who would follow him, to keep these commandments. As Jeremias has correctly observed, such an interpretation can only be justified if one interprets Jesus in the light of Paul instead of interpreting Paul in the light of Jesus.[6]

The "Interim Ethic"

In the third position Jesus does not preach a long-term ethic, but rather his demands are rooted in the nearness of the end. God has given the human race a final opportunity for repentance and a chance for salvation, before the terrible end breaks upon history as the waves of the flood in the days of Noah. The Sermon on the Mount contains a "thoroughgoing eschatology." We are faced with the immediate end and are challenged to make a last-minute effort to radicalize our behavior, because the final judgment is drawing near. All the heroic demands of Jesus are valid only for the short period before the end, a period in which unheard of sacrifices must be made.

Certainly eschatology was at the very heart of all that Jesus did and said. Everything must be seen in the light of the breaking in of the

Kingdom. And yet, the Sermon of the Mount is neither an ethic for a death-hour nor the utterance of a voice from a world on the brink of catastrophe. Jesus was no fanatical enthusiast who envisioned everything in imminent apocalyptic and catastrophic imagery. For him the presence of the Kingdom is good news, and the offer of salvation is *now*. He did not proclaim an exceptional Law for a short, interim period. His words have validity for all times (Mk 13:31).

The difficulty with these three theories is that they all regard the Sermon on the Mount as Law. All situate Jesus in the sphere of late Judaism. The first makes him a teacher of the Law; the second makes him a preacher of repentance; the third makes him an apocalyptic figure. But the question is whether Jesus fits any of these categories at all.

THE IMMINENT KINGDOM
AND THE SERMON ON THE MOUNT

Exegetes distinguish today between kerygma and didache or between proclamation and teaching. Proclamation is the missionary preaching to Jews and Gentiles. Its content is the crucified and risen Lord and his return, like the statement in 1 Corinthians 15:3-5. Teaching is preaching to the congregation. While the kerygma is directed outward, the didache is directed inward. Every worship service started with a didache. Its content was instruction for Christian conduct of life; the content of the kerygma, sacraments, and the last things. The Sermon on the Mount should be regarded as a classical example of early Christian didache. It should be seen as catechetical instruction or teaching for the newly baptized. Accordingly, we have to conclude with Jeremias:

> If the Sermon on the Mount is a catechism for baptismal candidates or newly baptized Christians, then it was preceded by something else. It was preceded by the proclamation of the gospel; and it was preceded by conversion, by being overpowered by the Good News.[7]

All the demands of the Sermon on the Mount make sense once we accept the fact that they were preceded by the preaching of the here and now of the Kingdom of God. It was addressed to those who had let the power of the Kingdom into their hearts. Turning to Davies and Allison, we read:

> To those who avail themselves of this kingdom, it [the Sermon on the Mount] becomes a grace which motivates and empowers.

The Sermon on the Mount does not speak to ordinary people in ordinary circumstances. It instead addresses itself to those in the eschatological crisis, those overtaken by an overwhelming reality. This reality, if embraced, remakes the individual, begetting a new heart, a new life, a new creation.[8]

It was meant for people who had "turned around" and opened themselves to the Kingdom and whose lives were lived in the present under the influence of the Kingdom. The Sermon on the Mount is good news. It demonstrates that the Kingdom is here and that those who turn toward it will receive the power to live its demands. In short, we can say that, like the Lord's Prayer, the Sermon on the Mount must be seen in the eschatological context of the "already" and the "not yet."

10

The Religious and Political Character
of the Kingdom

Most scholars are quick to point out that the Kingdom in the preaching of Jesus has first and foremost a religious character. Schnackenburg expresses the position in this way:

> The salvation proclaimed and promised by Jesus in this reign and Kingdom of God is purely religious in character. Jesus entirely excluded the national and political-religious elements from his "basileia" concept and repudiated the widespread Jewish hope of a splendid Messianic Kingdom of Israel.[1]

Others admit that there is a political aspect to the Kingdom as preached by Jesus, but they either play it down or insist that there is a shift in his teaching itself. In the first part of his ministry Jesus seems to have stressed the national and political aspect of God's Kingdom by offering it to the Jews of his time. But gradually the Kingdom in Jesus' preaching becomes more universal and eschatological while losing all political and national foundations.[2] Or, a number of scholars argue that the Kingdom was present in some way in the person and ministry of Christ; yet, at the close of his earthly life, this principal teaching looked forward to the Kingdom as a future reality. Admitting that the beginning of Jesus' ministry stressed the "presence of the fulfillment," they still hold that "at the end of the synoptic kerygma everything is again focused upon the future. The coming of the Kingdom is then referred to in such an absolutely future sense as if it had not yet come."[3] The conclusions drawn from this are evident:

> First, the primary thrust of Kingdom power relates to the inner person. While any genuine transformation of the inner person must certainly affect outward behavior, the blessings of the Kingdom for today focus on the spiritual aspect of life and not the

material. The Scriptures that relate the Kingdom to the present refer to redemption and forgiveness of sin (Col 1:13-14), righteousness, peace and joy (Rm 14:17). . . . Secondly, the present Kingdom power is fundamentally a power displayed through outer weakness (2 Cor 12:9-10).[4]

Witness to the Kingdom power now takes two forms:

There is the power of persuasive love involved in personal salvation, and there is the power of coercive force involved in the domination of hostile powers. The power of persuasive love is operative through the presence of the Kingdom today. There may be occasional manifestations of the power of coercive force in miraculous actions, but that dimension of Kingdom power awaits the arrival of the King for its general and universal application.[5]

A number of theologians, while maintaining the religious character of the Kingdom, have recently challenged this exclusively one-sided approach. The term *salvation* in the ancient world meant "the peace and prosperity provided by the ruler or king." It was his task to "save" his people, first and foremost from external enemies, but also from internal want: evil structures, poverty, sickness, and oppression. The quality of a king was judged by the extent to which he could be called "savior." The same meaning of *salvation* may be found in the Bible. Since in Jewish society the social-political dimensions were inseparable from the religious, it is hardly possible to separate Jesus' announcement of salvation from every social-political dimension connected with this term.[6]

From such a perspective new attempts must be made today to "rescue Jesus from the prison of individualism and to bring him back into social life."[7] Some scholars seek to overcome the one-sided presentation of a purely religious Christ, and they question the ideological presuppositions of those who would insist that the quest for a historical Jesus was once and for all laid to rest.[8] According to Norbert Lohfink, the problem in traditional theology is that most treatises on the Kingdom waste no words on the Kingdom's social shape. The Kingdom has no place in the world. It was briefly evident in Jesus but now is a distant cloud in the air.[9]

THE TRADITIONAL APPROACH

In the more traditional view, both Catholic and Protestant, Jesus is understood to have excluded from his understanding the national and political expectations that were connected with the Kingdom. He re-

pudiated the widespread Jewish hope of a splendid Messianic Kingdom of Israel. For many this is an enigma. Pannenberg comments: "If
one turns to Jesus and considers the political character of the hope for
God's Kingdom it remains a riddle how in Jesus' message, this idea
could occupy the central place without leaving the faintest impression
of its political bearing."[10] From this, one can conclude that Jesus had
nothing to say about political matters, but that his message was a
collection of inspiring thoughts about God's love and forgiveness, a
message about God's nearness to all who seek him. Is this true? Is
Yoder correct when he claims that mainstream Christianity viewed
Jesus as having no position of his own on social and political issues?

Yoder summarizes this position in six points: (1) Jesus had an "interim ethic," expecting the end soon; (2) he was a simple rural figure
caring little about problems of complex organization; (3) he had no
social ethic because he had no power or control over the political and
social fortunes of his society; (4) he did not deal with social change
but offered new possibilities for self-understanding; (5) he was a radical monotheist who relativized all temporal values; and, (6) Jesus came
to provide forgiveness, not an ethic.[11]

The inadequacy of such a position as Yoder's has led to many solutions being offered to deal with the question of the political nature of
Jesus. Various exegetes have addressed themselves to it without coming to any consensus. What follows is a sample of these responses.

Pannenberg solves the riddle by insisting that the political reality of
the Kingdom of God entered this world precisely through the private
calling of individuals and by the proclamation of individual salvation
in early Christianity. For him, democracy presupposes freedom and
concern for each other and only then can it penetrate to the level of
social and political action.[12]

Oscar Cullmann takes a similar view. Jesus severely criticized the
social injustices in the existing order. He demanded a radical, individual change of heart, which would change one's relationship to God
and to one's neighbor. It is through this radical, individual change demanded by Jesus that one is led to a new order of human relations.[13]

Martin Hengel in *Was Jesus a Revolutionist?* answered this question with a no and a yes. On the one hand, "Jesus did not take part
with those who sought to improve the world by violence, a violence
which brings with it hate-filled defamations and escalates to bloody
terror." That is what most resistance fighters wanted and actually did
in the time of Jesus. On the other hand, Jesus did not justify the status
quo. He advocated a freedom that is revolutionary, a freedom that
leads a person away from himself or herself to one's fellow human
beings. It is concern for one's fellow human beings that makes one
political.[14]

Gerhard Theissen gives an analysis of all the radical theocratic movements in the time of Jesus that wanted to establish the Kingdom on their own terms. His conclusion is that,

> although the Jesus movement was theocratic (since it talked about the imminent Kingdom of God) it differed most clearly from all comparable radical theocratic movements by virtue of its ethos. The resistance fighters and Essenes demanded hatred of foreigners. This aggressive feature was lacking in the Jesus Movement. There were tax-collectors and zealots (collaborators with the Romans and resistance fighters) included in the most intimate group of disciples. All this points to a readiness for reconciliation which transcends frontiers and culminates in the requirement to love one's enemy (Mt 5:43f).

Thus, it is impossible to bring the Jesus movement into close connection with the resistance fighters.[15]

These views stress predominantly the spiritual and personal conversion which will initiate in turn a structural change. Surely, personal conversion is the first response to the Kingdom. But the question still remains: Can personal conversion penetrate the mechanisms of social and political structures in such a way that society will change automatically with the conversion of the individual person? Or must these structures not be addressed directly in order to be unmasked as sinful and then be changed?

A NEW APPROACH

Seeking Light from the Social Sciences

The principal characteristics of God's image in the Old Testament as it unfolds over the centuries of Israel's history with Yahweh could be summarized in three aspects. First, Yahweh is a God who *liberates*, not only in the spiritual sense of liberation from sin, but also in the sense of liberation from concrete slavery and oppression (as seen in the Exodus tradition). Second, God's main concern is with *justice* in order to restore the dignity of the impoverished person as demanded by the Covenant. This was the priority of the great prophets. Third, and most outstanding, Yahweh in the Old Testament is a God of infinite *compassion and mercy*, especially for those who suffer and are oppressed.[16] The image of a compassionate and merciful God became the focus of attention in the post-exilic period, particularly in the writings of Deutero-Isaiah and in the final edition of Hosea.[17]

In the final coming of Yahweh these attributes of God's image would reveal themselves to the full. These three characteristics have definite social and political implications since Israel was a theocracy. Religion and politics were not clearly separated but were rather closely intertwined. The question is: How far did Jesus affirm this God image of Israel's religion? The answer depends on the answers to the questions: What did Jesus expect? What was the coming Kingdom for him? Did it include a restoration of the present social and political order?

Most scholars would agree that the life and mission of Jesus must be understood first and foremost in the setting of the Old Testament Covenant. Apart from the Old Testament, Jesus does not make sense. He understood his mission in the context of Israel, and his intention was to lead Israel back to the ideal of the Covenant. In revealing the true image of the God of the Covenant, Jesus challenged the people to return to this God and to reach their destiny as true children of the Covenant. Luke seems to agree with this view by presenting Jesus' message as the fulfillment of the great Jubilee of Yahweh.[18] One of the main requirements of such a year was to restore social structures in a way that allowed disinherited people to recover their heritage and slaves to return to their family homes. The intent was to restore equality to all once again, as the Covenant demanded. Gnuse describes the Jubilee tradition and its import:

> The Jubilee legislation found in Leviticus 25 presents a vision of social and economic reform unsurpassed in the ancient Near East. The comprehensive scenario for economic reform encompassed slave release, interest free loans, debt release, and the restoration of land to the original owners. Exilic theologians of Israel (586-539 B.C.E.) articulated this vision of hope while in the throes of Babylonian captivity. Drawing upon ancient legal traditions they proclaimed a manifesto for reform which was an assault upon any understanding of society which justified the aggrandizement of wealth in the hands of a few.[19]

In Luke 4:16-21 Jesus describes his mission to his countrymen in line with the messianic expectation of Deutero-Isaiah. This quotation carries a direct reference to the Jubilee proclamation of liberation, release, and a year of favor for the poor. Some scholars have shown that Isaiah 61 was a passage selected for reading at the commencement of the Jubilee Year. The Jubilee images found in the text from Isaiah were understood by Jesus' contemporaries as referring to blessings promised to Israel particularly at the time of God's eschatological reign. Although the prophetic reading of that text within the Nazareth pericope challenged the assumption of privilege, it left the social revolutionary implications of the Jubilee imagery intact.[20]

It is accepted by a number of scholars that Luke offers here a rather fair account of how Jesus understood his ministry. The content of this preaching appears in two other traditions as well. In Matthew 11:1-6, Jesus gives a reply to John's question and places more stress on the blessings of the Kingdom than on the judgment that John was awaiting. This is evidenced in the dropping of the last phrase of Isaiah 61:2 in the Matthean pericope. More striking is the way Matthew emphasizes the poor as the addressee by concluding with the text of Isaiah, "And the poor have good news preached to them." In positioning the stress on the sixth clause Matthew wants his audience to understand that Jesus located the high point of his ministry here. As in Luke, here also the top priority of Jesus was the announcement of God's good news to the poor.

The other tradition is found in the Beatitudes. The first blessing is declared on the poor:

> "Blessed are you who are poor,
>   for yours is the Kingdom of God."
>   (Lk 6:20)

The point here is that in both Luke's and Matthew's list of Beatitudes, it is the pronouncement of blessing on the poor which has first place.

Jesus' first preaching in the synagogue at Nazareth was, therefore, well rooted in the earliest memories of the disciples, which imply that it was Jesus' own priority. Whatever ideas circulated concerning the Messiah, he was definitely seen as God's envoy who would restore justice and side with the poor and the weak against their oppressors.[21]

The question remains though: Did Jesus understand his mission in the setting of the Jubilee context? Luke for his part opens the public ministry of Jesus with a quotation from Isaiah 61 linking it with 58:6, "the clearest reference to any of the Jubilee texts in the Synoptic Gospels."[22] It is a very carefully staged introduction to the whole ministry of Jesus. What is peculiar to Luke is the specific connection of the Kingdom with the prophetic proclamation of the Jubilee Year, "the acceptable year of the Lord." In Luke this becomes Jesus' own mission. The eschatological aspect of *deror* in Isaiah 61:1-4 makes the connection of this text with Jesus' central message of the Kingdom even more plausible. Luke makes the connection even stronger by altering the quotation. His text differs from the Hebrew text. He eliminates one clause from the original text, "the day of vengeance to the Gentiles," and inserts another clause from Isaiah 58:6, "to let the oppressed go free" (literally, "to send the oppressed away liberated"). Many scholars either do not comment on this insertion or they dismiss it by saying that it adds nothing to the sense, and that it is hard to see why it was done.[23] Others maintain that this insertion makes the reference to the Jubilee legislation all the more obvious.[24]

Hanks, for example, concludes:

> This relationship makes it easy to appreciate the aptness of Jesus' insertion of a phrase from Isaiah 58:6 in his citation of Isaiah 61:1-2 in his sermon at Nazareth. By this method he was able to underscore the liberating dimension of his own ministry and his understanding of the Kingdom of God as involving the kind of socio-economic revolution envisioned in the Jubilee provision.[25]

Matthew's use of the text outlines Jesus' mission in the same way. Jesus' reply to the disciples of John the Baptist is nothing but the actualization of Isaiah 61:1-2 in the setting of a Jubilee proclamation. The Kingdom of God meant the transformation of all human structures in favor of justice and the rights of the poor. In this Jesus placed himself among the ranks of the great prophets and announced the "great year of God's favor" as the ultimate visitation of God on behalf of the people. Thus, the restoration of justice and the liberation of the oppressed belonged preeminently to his mission, whether or not the message of Jesus is to be understood in the context of the proclamation of the great eschatological Jubilee. The Kingdom of God required a renewal, which the Jubilee legislation envisioned at the end of history.[26]

If Jesus used the Jubilee Year idea, then his protest was definitely aimed at the current sociopolitical situation, which was irreconcilable with the breaking in of the Kingdom of God. Yahweh's great Jubilee Year demanded a radical restructuring of all present social structures on the basis of the Covenant. Jesus clashed with the authorities because they were not willing to accept his offer of social grace.[27]

Those exegetes who situate Jesus' message of the Kingdom in the context of the Sabbatical Jubilee tradition find here the best starting point to examine the political aspect of his message. His proclamation reveals a strong egalitarianism. Jesus was concerned with the restoration of Israel, as his prophetic and symbolic act of the election of the twelve disciples clearly indicates. He did then envision a Kingdom in which the nation of Israel, as a Covenant people, would be restored in all dimensions to being a truly faithful people.[28]

All the actions of Jesus point in this same direction: his constant concern for bringing the outcast and the marginalized back into the community; his demand for love of neighbor and enemy, which indicates his desire to make all into one community of brothers and sisters under the Fatherhood of God; his frequent reference to service; his desire not to be called rabbi or master, since we all have only one Father (see Mt 23:8-12). Furthermore, he demanded from those who would follow him equality by selling all they had and abandoning their social position. In so doing they would once again demonstrate that the Covenant was built on equality in all aspects of human life.[29]

If one can agree that Jesus envisioned the Kingdom in the setting of the restoration of Israel, then the Jubilee tradition was the best context for his message that he could have chosen. He saw the coming of God's reign in terms of a New People of God and of a new social order in this world. However, it also remains true that Jesus was absolutely convinced that this could not be brought about through armed struggle, but only through God's own direct intervention. We find in the preaching of Jesus quite a number of seemingly opposing views which are not easily reconcilable. The object of the Kingdom is this world, yet it is not of this world. Jesus claims the whole of Israel, yet he seems to be content with gathering only a small band, his disciples. He proclaims the Kingdom as salvation, yet he does not exclude judgment. The Kingdom is preached first to the sinner, yet the righteous are not excluded.[30]

This absolute confidence in God's activity alone to bring about the new order gave Jesus a kind of detachment from the type of activity of the revolutionists who made the final coming of God dependent on their strategy. In contrast, Jesus seems to have had no concrete plan of how the Kingdom would be realized. He left that to God, who would determine the time, as well as the way it would unfold. Jesus regarded himself as one who definitely had a role to play in the coming of this Kingdom, but it was the role of a humble servant (Mk 10:45) and not of a glorious leader marching as a triumphant conqueror into Jerusalem. His way of entering Jerusalem, riding on an ass and cleansing the Temple, were only prophetic and symbolic gestures. It is definitely unlikely that Jesus thought that these symbolic actions would convince the leaders that the Kingdom of God had now come or that they would convert the people en masse. He looked to God for the vindication of his message and his claim.[31]

Because of this ambiguity, the question of how, politically, Jesus understood his role in bringing about the Kingdom of God has found different answers in the history of the Christian faith. Those answers always seem relative to the speaker's own stand on social and political issues. It is, therefore, quite impossible to find among scholars a unified answer that will satisfy everyone's examination of this question.

One of the first considerations in attempting to develop an answer is an adequate analysis of the political-social situation of Palestine at the time of Jesus and a critical use of the social sciences to understand the historical Jesus within this setting.[32] The source-critical, reduction-critical, or literary-critical approach to the gospel has been the exclusive tool in scripture studies for the last fifty years. Few have used the social sciences and cultural anthropology to develop new understandings and new models of interpretation. Past studies which have utilized the social sciences seem too general and uncritical. Horsley makes the following assessment:

> Much of the earlier reconstruction of the social-political history of Palestine Jewish society, however, seriously underestimated the complexity of the society, particularly the potential differences in interest and outlook between the priestly aristocracy, who controlled the society as client rulers for the Romans, and the mass of peasants (90-95%) in any traditional agrarian society, who were taxed to support the aristocracy.[33]

The reasons for this insufficient understanding of the past are many, although they certainly have something to do with scholar's cultural and sociological background. The way the Zealots have been described in handbooks and dictionaries has been influenced by the way writers wanted to portray Jesus. By characterizing the Zealots as "bloody revolutionists" who advocated fanatical revolution against Rome, Jesus could easily be pictured as having nothing to do with any national-political movements that sought national-political liberation in the context of the coming Kingdom of God. Horsley's position certainly merits consideration when he writes:

> This view has served important functions, both theologically and politically. As the supposed fanatical advocates of violent revolution against the Romans, "the Zealots" served as a convenient foil over against which to portray Jesus of Nazareth as a sober prophet of a pacific love of one's enemies. Theologians and biblical scholars could then ward off any implication that Jesus had advocated any sort of active resistance to the established order.[34]

Recently a number of scholars have taken up the task of utilizing the social sciences in order to develop new interpretative models.[35] They start by describing first the social and political situation of the time that make up the background against which Jesus proclaimed his message of God's imminent Kingdom.

Israel's faith survived in Exile only insofar as and to the degree that the Israelites separated themselves from the influence of the pagan culture. Separation had become a question of religious survival. The common belief was that the Covenant people had been exiled by Yahweh because they had succumbed to paganism in the first place. Their survival now depended on not repeating the same mistake. The theological reasoning, however, for this separation was ultimately Israel's Covenant with Yahweh, which commanded the people: "You shall be holy, for I the Lord your God am holy" (Lev 19:2). God was holy, and therefore, Israel had to be holy. To be holy became equated with being faithful and being able to survive. The result was that the Jewish social world after the Exile became increasingly structured around the polarities of holiness and separation: clean and unclean, purity and defilement, sacred and profane, Jew and Gentile, righteous and sinner. Holiness became the paradigm by which the Torah was interpreted. The laws in the Torah which placed emphasis on Israel's uniqueness among all other nations and which stressed separation from everything impure became dominant and particularly important within Israel. In short, the hermeneutical key for understanding and interpreting the Torah had become the concepts of "holiness and purity." The test of who was a faithful Jew, loyal to the Covenant in the circumstances of the time, became a question of how far one lived up to the demands of holiness and purity.[36] All movements in the post-exilic time were deeply concerned and formed by these demands. The major known groups were the revolutionists, the Pharisees, and the Essenes.

The *revolutionists* believed that holiness could only be achieved by expelling Rome, the impure and idolatrous Gentile occupier. Implicitly, the resistance fighters radicalized the first commandment: "You shall have no other Lords besides God." Israel's only loyalty was to God and the Torah. It was against the Torah to pledge allegiance to the emperor and to pay taxes to Rome.

The *Pharisees*, which probably means "the separated ones," regarded the whole land of Israel as holy as the Temple itself. They, therefore, attempted to live on the level of holiness and purity required of priests in the Temple, wanting to share in the Temple's holiness.[37] Furthermore, they sought to spread their vision of the holiness of the land by transforming the Jewish people into a "Kingdom of priests." By doing so they intended to counteract the threat to the identity of the Jewish people. The laws regarding purity and tithing were the major focus of the pharisaic intensification of holiness. In particular, they were concerned with the greatest source of nonobservance of the Law, that which was created by the double system of taxation. People, mostly small farmers, were taxed 35 percent of their crop, 20 percent of which was to be paid to the Temple (also called "tithes"). The tithe was required by the Torah, and therefore, was understood to be divine Law. This tax, however, could not be enforced by legal sanctions. The additional 12-15 percent tax had to be paid to the Romans. The way these Roman taxes were collected made the amount even higher. Rome sold the privilege of collecting taxes to "tax farmers," who paid Rome a fixed amount and whose own profits depended on the percentage they added to the taxes. The taxes to Rome had to be paid, being enforced by legal sanctions. Farmers would lose their land if they could not pay. Since many farmers were unable to come up with the full amount of the double-taxation, they would skip the taxes that could not be forced on them, that is, the Temple tax or the tithes. But by so doing they would sin against a religious obligation and become so-called non-observant Jews.[38]

All tithes were to be paid, and one who would be holy could not eat untithed food. Loyalty to God meant giving to God what was God's—namely the tithes commanded by the Torah. This became a point of controversy particularly when it came to sharing a meal with others. How could they keep the purity of the meal table in a land where many did not care where the food came from?

The Pharisees had no police power to enforce the payment of the tithes. Their sanctions were of another kind: social and religious ostracism. They were the most visible manifestation of the politics of holiness. The Pharisees sought to preserve and shape the Jewish social world by intensifying the Torah precisely in the area in which the temptation to nonobservance was the greatest. They tried to provide the people in their present situation with a way of being faithful to God and the Torah without leaving secular society. They accepted the Roman occupation and taxation with an attitude of resigned acquiescence. Only when Roman practices violated the Torah would they protest publicly. Though constantly reminding themselves and the people that their first loyalty was to God, they were still permitted other loyalties, as long as the Torah was not violated. One should not forget that the Pharisees were a highly devoted people. Their absolute loyalty to God, love of neighbor, zeal for the Sabbath, intense prayer life, and fasting were a powerful witness of their deep commitment to Yahweh and the Covenant.[39]

The *Essenes* believed that a life of holiness in the Jewish society of their time was impossible. Consequently, they withdrew from society and went into the wilderness. They called themselves "men of holiness" and a "house of holiness." Holiness meant separation from impure society. They regarded themselves as "children of Light" and looked at the Romans and most Jewish people as "children of darkness," whom God would soon destroy.

In each case—the revolutionists, the Pharisees, and the Essenes—the zeal and dedication of the group were impressive. The consequence was that such groups regarded those outside of their own group as being sinners or even apostates. To disagree with their understanding and practice of the Law meant that one was a sinner, because one was disregarding the Law. The righteous were those who were members of the group, those who kept the Law as understood by the group. The major tool of social and religious ostracism meant that one would refuse table fellowship with all those outside of the group. To share a meal with a person was an expression of acceptance. Accordingly, the refusal to share a meal indicated open disapproval and rejection of the other's way of life. It was obvious then why the members of those movements would not share a meal with non-observants.

Jesus' quarrel and controversy with the different groups had their ultimate root here. He refused to accept their key for understanding and interpreting the Torah, namely holiness and purity. He saw his mission precisely to call those to the Kingdom of God whom the most zealous of Israel had rejected. Jesus objected vigorously against this kind of Torah-interpretation; it was in no way compatible with his own experience of God as an all-compassionate and loving Father. Jesus never opposed the Torah itself; rather, it was his interpretation of the Torah that put him at odds with his opponents.[40]

TWO VIEWS OF A POLITICALLY INVOLVED JESUS

The issue of a politically involved Jesus has found a particular echo by theologians in the developing countries. We will present two here, one from Latin America, Juan Luis Segundo, and the other from South Africa, Albert Nolan. Both authors affirm the above-presented theory; namely, that holiness and purity had become the key for understanding and interpreting the Torah at the time of Jesus. Each one, however, analyzes the effects of such an interpretation differently.

Segundo shows how such a view led to the marginalization and oppression of entire groups. Nolan, while agreeing with Segundo, places the emphasis on the suffering—which was caused because of such an interpretation of the Torah—imposed on these marginalized people. Both authors want to bring to light the reaction of Jesus to this marginalization and suffering brought about by a wrong understanding and application of the Torah and the tradition.

Juan Luis Segundo

Segundo starts his investigation by describing the sociopolitical situation in which Jesus lived and proclaimed the Kingdom. This description differs from the usual textbook presentation of how Jesus understood his message. Segundo claims that it was not the Roman domination but the Jewish theocracy of the time which accounted for the internal social structure of Israel in Jesus' time. These structures went back to the Babylonian Exile when the gap between the elite and the rural population came into focus. Only the religious and cultural elite of Israel were exported into Exile while the rural population remained largely in Palestine. Without their priests and cultural leaders, their faith as practiced in Yahwist orthodoxy deteriorated considerably. Thus, the elite in Exile referred to them pejoratively as the "poor of the land." After the return from Exile the elite took control of the land more on religious rather than political grounds. Their Yahwist orthodoxy, including their knowledge of the Law and the observance of its external obligations, made them the effective political power in Jewish society. It was, therefore, the Mosaic Law that organized the life of the Jewish citizens, determined their place in society, and fixed their rights and obligations. Legal purity and impurity became the decisive factor in the division of Jewish society into classes and groups.[41]

By means of a particular interpretation of the Mosaic Law, the elite Jews had managed to marginalize the poor as sinners and had allowed a religious elite to benefit from the sociopolitical situation. The "people of the land" were declared religiously impure. They were, therefore, not only poor economically but also poor morally, that is, sinners. The poor were impoverished because they were sinners, and they sinned because their poverty made it impossible for them to observe the Laws that would make them righteous. As Segundo puts it:

> The Poor themselves are sinners. If we view them in terms of their material situation and their marginalized place in society, they are poor. But if we view them in terms of alleged reason of their poverty and marginalization, they are sinners. In other words, declaring them sinners is a way of offering the ideological reason for their poverty, of hiding and justifying it. Here we find ourselves right in the middle of a political conflict, and the power of one of the groups lies in its interpretation of the law, in its religious conception.[42]

The prevalent theology at the time of Jesus not only explained, but also sanctioned and maintained the poverty of the poor through such an interpretation of the Torah. The Pharisees who lived among the people had no political power at all. Their prestige and authority rested on their interpretation of the Law. Wittingly or unwittingly, they actually provided the governing authority with a divine justification for their position in the existing sociopolitical situation. That authority was the Sanhedrin composed of the elders, high priests, and scribes. The last two were the officially constituted religious authority of Israel, while the Pharisees represented the most significant group of the Jewish laity. The dilemma was, as Horsley observes, that even the sacred tradition had been compromised in order to support the system:

> Certain sections of the sacred Torah itself were instrumental in maintaining the priestly aristocracy's privileged position and in holding the peasantry in conditions of worsening poverty.[43]

The sabbatical year itself was compromised in favor of the oppressive situation. The Torah stipulated that debts were to be cancelled every seventh year. But to circumvent such Covenantal law a legal device was created called "prosbul," which enabled the creditor to avoid the literal requirements of the sabbatical cancellation of debts. It was true that peasants could get easier loans on the basis of that law, but they no longer had sabbatical protection to cancel their debts.[44] Even though the Pharisees stood in general on the side of the peasantry, their interpretation of the Law was found by Jesus to be oppressive to ordinary people: "Woe also to you lawyers! For you load people with burdens hard to bear, and you yourselves do not lift a finger to ease them" (Lk 11:46; Mt 23:4).

What really oppressed people economically was the double burden of taxation. As we have already seen above, there were the many dues to be given for the cult and the priests, as well as the tribute to be paid to the Romans. Neither the Romans nor the Jewish aristocracy would forgo its share by reducing the tax demand. Instead they collaborated in the exploitation of the peasant population.

This was the social context in which Jesus preached the Kingdom of God. His message revolved around three key words: *Kingdom, poor,* and *good news*. It is properly expressed in the phrase: *The Kingdom of God is good news for the poor!* This message, as Segundo sees it, is simultaneously religious and political. Jesus showed a clear preference for the poor over the rich because of the inhuman nature of their situation. As such, Jesus' proclamation of the Kingdom aroused "profound interest and passionate enthusiasm among his contemporaries."[45] It became a divisive message, because it touched on the sociopolitical reality of his native land. Jesus' message of the Kingdom was directed against that interpretation of Israel's faith. It was not an attack on the "politics of the Roman occupation," since that had little influence on the simple people and their sociopolitical situation. Jesus struck at a much deeper level; he attacked the whole theocratic structure of Jewish society as it had been interpreted by the religious and political elite. He undermined the structure by revealing a new image of God, who is "humane and humanizing," one who cannot tolerate a situation which turns human beings into subhumans. Nor can God allow the justification of such a situation by appeal to divine will. To the God of Jesus, the human being constitutes a primary value. God's joy consists precisely in rescuing human beings from their misery and restoring their humanity to them. Therefore, by undermining the religious authority, Jesus exercised a much more subversive political activity than any direct political attack on the social structure of Israel. His discrediting of the Pharisees on religious grounds undermined the very basis of the power of the real authorities who dominated the social system. Consequently, Pharisees, priests, elders, and scribes had a common interest in getting rid of him; their status in society was at stake.[46] Walter Brueggemann reaches almost the same conclusion when he writes:

> The Law had become in his days a way for the managers of society, religious even more than civil, to effectively control not only morality but political-economic valuing that lay behind the morality. Thus his [Jesus'] criticism of the "law" is not to be dismissed as an attack on "legalism" in any moralistic sense, as is sometimes done in reductionist Pauline interpretation. Rather, his critique concerns the fundamental social valuing of his society. In practice Jesus has seen, as Marx later made clear, that the law can be a social convention to protect the current distribution of economic and political power. Jesus in the tradition of Jeremiah, dared to articulate the end of a consciousness that could not keep its promises but that in fact denied the humanness it purported to give.[47]

Albert Nolan

Nolan, in *God in South Africa*, contributes a similar social analysis of the setting in which Jesus proclaimed his message. However, Nolan is concerned with the sin and suffering caused by the sociopolitical situation. At the time of Jesus the system of purity and holiness determined the whole of society. The center of the world was the Holy of Holies in the Temple. From there everything was arranged outward in concentric circles toward diminishing degrees of holiness and purity: the sanctuary, the altar, the court of priests, the court of the Israelites, the court of the women, the Temple mount, Jerusalem, and the land of Israel. There were the feast days and fast days with the Sabbath as the holiest of holy days. Things were categorized as pure or impure; so were people, according to their status and their momentary state of purity or impurity. Socially, people were identified, classified, and separated according to their degree of purity and holiness, including racial purity. This system of purity and holiness determined the entire social structure of economic and political domination, ensuring that those who had privileges would not lose them. It was a total system and not merely a religious system.[48]

To act against the system or to rebel against it meant to commit sin. To be outside the system meant to be a sinner. Those who fell outside the boundaries of holiness and purity were sinners: pagans, lepers, prostitutes, tax-collectors, shepherds, people of mixed race, and all the lower classes of people who were dirty and ignorant of the Law. God was holy; God would have nothing to do with anyone or anything that was not pure, clean, and holy.

Jesus rejected this entire system. For him this had never been the intention of the Law and the prophets. Jesus broke the Sabbath laws, as well as the laws of fasting and ritual washing. He touched lepers, ate unclean food with unclean people, mixed with prostitutes and other impure people, declared all foods clean, and predicted the destruction of the Temple and all the holy places. The unclean and the impure became Jesus' friends: "Look, a glutton and a drunkard, a friend of tax collectors and sinners!" (Mt 11:19). But why this total rejection of the Law? In the eyes of Jesus the system of holiness and purity had became a system that caused a great deal of suffering and pain in that society. For Jesus the starting point for determining the nature of sin was suffering. Sin was about suffering, about making people suffer, allowing them to suffer, or ignoring their sufferings. In the last analysis sin was not a transgression of the Law but a transgression of love. No sin was harmless to anyone. At the very least, sin harms the sinner; at most, it harms millions of people (now and in the future). Sin becomes visible in suffering. The seriousness or gravity of a sin must be measured in terms of the amount of pain and suffering it causes.

SYNTHESIS

Judea in the time of Jesus was an oppressed country. All kinds of movements tried to envision the coming Reign of God and to help it come about. The most frequently mentioned movement by scholars is the group called the Zealots. The Zealots grew out of the peasant movements that sought reform in the name of Israel's Covenant tradition against the all-powerful aristocracy that had sold out to Rome. Although they fervently longed for the coming Kingdom of God, as all Jews did, they were fighting a class war against their own nobility as well as against the Roman oppressors. Their aim was the restoration of Israel's Covenant institutions: an egalitarian society free from the oppressive aristocratic ruling class who were oppressing its own people and betraying the state to the Romans.[49]

One has to understand this movement more from the perspective of the peasantry who in the grip and under the exploitation of the aristocracy had still preserved the "dangerous memory" of Israel's past when Israel had been a free and independent people with no ruling class. In the beginning Israel had established its independence as a peasantry free from any ruling class and had made a Covenant with Yahweh and one another to guarantee this freedom. The Covenant provided the overall social organization and the religious-political coherence, free from overlords and kings, independent of foreign occupation, living under the rule of God in a just and egalitarian order.[50]

This was the content of the "dangerous memory" preserved in the collective memory of the people. Horsley identifies its importance:

> It became a reference point for subsequent generations, an utopian ideal over against which later subjection to kings and foreign empires was measured and found contrary to the will of God.[51]

Jesus appeared in the midst of such turbulent times and situations. He was a peasant himself, and he addressed his message to peasants, which is obvious if one reads his parables and similes. Did he share his people's aspirations, as well as their clamoring for a social-political-economic restoration of Israel to its Covenant ideal? That is, how political was Jesus? Certainly, he was born a Jew at a particular time, and therefore understood Yahweh, the God of the Covenant, in the context of the colorful history of his people's failure and Yahweh's enduring fidelity. He shared with them the hope of the final visitation of God, which so fervently found its expression in the Kaddish prayer of the sabbatical liturgy:

> Exalted and hallowed be His great Name in the World which He created according to His will. May He establish His Kingdom in our lifetime and in your days and in the lifetime of the whole household of Israel, speedily and at a near time. May His great Name be praised forever and unto all eternity.

The final visitation of Yahweh was seen as the total restoration of Israel to its original luster and ideal. It was expected to be the great Jubilee of Yahweh. It meant the final liberation of Israel from all bondage and slavery and the ultimate restoration of the true Covenant, in which Israel would finally become his people and where he would be their God. Jesus came to understand his own mission to be the one sent to fulfill this age-old dream of his people and to be in his person God's ultimate coming and offer of salvation. His concern, therefore, was first and foremost the restoration of the Covenant and the return of Israel to its original ideal. The initial idea of the Covenant was of an egalitarian society in which everybody was equal and respected as a participatory member of the community based on possession and inheritance. What was left of this idea at the time of Jesus was almost unrecognizable. The divisions and marginalizations in the community had worsened over the centuries and had become the main concern of Jesus. The main target of his protest was the defense and even the theological justification of marginalization by the leading groups' peculiar interpretation of the Mosaic Law.

The message Jesus preached was the Kingdom of God, which by its very nature aimed at the conversion of the people to the Covenant idea. This in turn required the restructuring and transformation of the social-political structures and institutions. According to James D.G. Dunn there were three possible ways to actualize this Kingdom vision: the revolutionary, the sectarian, and the worldly.[52]

The revolutionists, with their battle cry "Let us take it," wanted to change the present by overthrowing those who ruled, bringing in God's reign by force. This option was open to Jesus, but he neither commanded it nor accepted it. The sectarians, following the motto "Let us create it," insisted on a total withdrawal from society and the creation of a new model of community in which the Covenant would be realized to the full. This was the option of the Qumran community. With this option the world is abandoned as being beyond all repair. Jesus did not choose this option either. He did not join the Qumran community but stayed where the people were and used their marketplaces for his preaching and actions. Jesus chose what Dunn called the "worldly option," with its command "Live it!" He showed that the Kingdom is taking place now in the midst of human affairs and that human actions may become the carrier of this Kingdom. To accept the Kingdom meant to celebrate its presence now, not in withdrawal but within this world. Jesus' option can be called "worldly" since it asks us to live wholly within this world by otherworldly values, challenging this world to allow itself to be transformed by the values of the Kingdom Jesus came to bring.

The following conclusion can now be drawn. Although, the gospels do not present us with a specific political program for all ages, they do offer criteria by which any particular program must be evaluated. The most fundamental criterion is precisely the Kingdom. Jesus made all authority relative by referring it to the Father and to the Kingdom. He took actions that had political consequences, the most radical of which was to deny all authority any claim of absolute power. The imminent Kingdom placed all authority and power into question since it demanded a total restructuring and reordering of all relationships. Steidl-Meier, referring to the question of how political Jesus was, offers an instructive response by first distinguishing between two kinds of politics. He writes:

> It is important to distinguish between politics as struggle over legitimate authority and politics as a precise social agenda. I think that in the former sense Jesus was decidedly political, whereas in the latter he was only partially so. His politics can thus be called normative politics rather than prescriptive politics with a precise agenda. Thus the gospel does not present a precise program

for all ages but suggests criteria by which any precise program may be evaluated.[53]

To the specific question of how political Jesus was, Steidl-Meier offers these three points. First, Jesus presents us with "normative politics," that is, all legitimate authority must be subjected to the breaking in of the Kingdom. Second, Jesus does not provide us with "prescriptive politics," that is, a precise agenda, although some of its elements might be found in the gospels. Third, the question we must ask today is, What is Jesus continuing to do now, and how do we become one with him in bringing it about? After all, in the risen Christ and the church after Pentecost the general imperatives of "normative politics" continue and will have to be translated into "prescriptive politics" for our time. The assertion that Jesus' message of the Kingdom was purely religious and had nothing to say about sociopolitical structures cannot be supported on the basis of scripture. It can be supported only on the basis of a dualistic worldview which denies any relevance of the gospel to inner-earthly realities.[54]

One needs to look carefully at Jesus and how the Kingdom becomes present among us in order to grasp what the gospel has to say to any given human situation. As was noted earlier, Jesus made the Kingdom present through his actions and his life. His actions in the form of miracles demonstrated that God wants to restore the brokenness of human existence and allow us to participate in the divine life. Healings and exorcisms demonstrate the presence of God's Kingdom in the world now. They indicate an "integral liberation" and not only a spiritual one. Against the Old Testament background, the miracles are directed at the eschatological gathering of Israel in whose midst no disease will be permitted. In the coming Kingdom no one will be excluded from salvation: neither outsiders, nor sinners, nor the sick.[55] In Jesus' life the criteria of the Kingdom became incarnate and visible. His living in history demonstrated what the Kingdom means here and now. With his coming the Kingdom is possible here and now. We can make it present by acting and living as he did, by being in union with him. It is only through such a commitment to him, to act and to live as he did, that we will come to see what the Kingdom is truly about and what it demands of us today.[56]

11

Salvation and the Kingdom of God

THE SALVATIONAL ASPECT

The message of John the Baptist was that the Kingdom of God is imminent, about to be inaugurated by one who is to come. God is about to visit God's people for judgment and salvation. The breaking in of the Kingdom is an act of God which will bring judgment on the present order. John flatly rejected any Jewish particularism and any ethical passivism. Jewish ancestry was no guarantee of salvation. He adopted "baptism"—a rite used for Jewish proselytes—thereby saying that in effect Jews stood on the same level as the Gentiles in light of the coming messianic visitation. John's view can be summarized in four points:

• John preached the Kingdom as imminent, and this future coming is for him the principal motive for acting now, the motive for *metanoia* (conversion).

• This future is seen primarily as a "future judgment" not as salvation.

• His message is eschatological in the sense that this absolutely certain judgment is coming soon.

• The future is seen negatively: one acts now in the present not because salvation is coming but in order to escape the terrible judgment that is imminent.[1]

It is important not to separate Jesus too radically from John. They had very much in common. Jesus, like John, probably baptized for some time in the Jordan region (Jn 3:22, 26; 4:1). This indicates that he was a disciple of the Baptist, or at least inwardly and outwardly was bound closely to the Baptist's movement.[2] Jesus never questioned the message of John, although he himself changed the emphasis without, however, endangering the primary aspects stressed by John. Some points of comparison and contrast include:

• The eschatological thrust is the same but the Kingdom is not just near, in the immediate future. It is already here, breaking into the present. Jesus stressed the Kingdom as a present reality.

141

• The Kingdom present is a time of salvation and must be seen in positive terms. It is a time of God's gracious offer of salvation and not of God's judgment.

• Its coming does not depend on us. There are no "ifs" or conditions which must be fulfilled on our part in order that the Kingdom might enter the world. It is God's doing and we can neither hasten nor hinder its coming.

The contrast between John and Jesus needs to be carefully drawn. For John, the one absolutely certain event is the impending judgment of God, which nothing can prevent from occurring soon. This announcement is apodictic in that God has decided it this way and no human interference can hinder it. John confronts people with the message of this imminent unavoidable judgment and challenges them to face it and amend their ways accordingly. For Jesus, the absolutely certain event which is happening at this very moment in his words and actions is that God is offering his final salvation to all in this precise hour. This is Jesus' apodictic announcement. This offer is absolutely unconditional and has only one aim: the salvation of all, but particularly of those with the least hope for it, the sinners and the outcasts. It does not depend on us; neither can we prevent its coming. The motive for action in the face of the breaking in of the Kingdom now is not the coming judgment but this unconditional offer of salvation. The function of the coming judgment is not as a threat of condemnation, but rather as a warning not to remain deaf and closed to the present offer of salvation. Jesus' view of the coming judgment, in contrast to John's view, is dependent on the reaction of human beings to the breaking in of the Kingdom. In the light of this final offer of salvation it should be obvious to the hearers of this message that they need to sell all and leave everything in order to gain this great treasure or this costly pearl (Mt 13:44-45).[3]

Luke makes this salvational aspect of Jesus' message very clear in the first sermon of Jesus in his home town (Lk 4:16-21). Here Jesus announces that the good news of God's year of favor as foretold by the prophet Isaiah (61:2b) is fulfilled now in their hearing. He stops just before the phrase of Isaiah "and the day of vengeance of our God." Jesus consciously proclaims a year of grace and the coming of God, not as judge but as One who comes to save, to heal, to forgive, and to create all things new. With this message he steered away from John's conception of the coming Kingdom.

In prison, John must have heard through his disciples that the one to whom he had given witness, Jesus, was not following his line. It must have upset John greatly. It must have seemed to John that Jesus had not understood the gravity of the situation. How could he preach a year of grace in the light of the coming wrath of God? John was afraid. One could not play with God's wrath. Yes, there would be a year of grace, but not before the day of judgment. This Jesus, his favorite disciple, was jeopardizing the whole message he had entrusted to him. In his distress he sent two of his disciples to Jesus to question him. When they came to Jesus, they said, "Are you the one who is to come, or are we to wait for another?" (Lk 7:18-20).

The question posed was hard and indicated the crisis between the two men caused by Jesus' preaching of a year of grace. John could no longer see his message in the message of Jesus. His whole endeavor to save his people seemed to be in jeopardy. John must have asked himself, Do I have to look for someone else who will represent my message and will shake up the people for the day of God's impending wrath?

In John's vision, what Jesus was preaching was for the day after the judgment, not before it. Jesus was offering the Kingdom for an undervalued price. The difference between the men was not merely one of method, of how to teach. Rather, it was in regard to their "God image," which shaped their message. John stood in line with prophets like Jeremiah and Amos, and sided with the apocalyptic thinkers of his time. They saw Yahweh first as the judge who would come to destroy and judge his enemies within Israel, and in particular, the foreign nations which had oppressed the chosen people. Jesus distanced himself from such a God image, taking the line expressed in prophets like Hosea and Isaiah. In these prophets a different God image emerges. God is compassionate, tender, and merciful toward a sinful people. He does not desire to destroy them or to take revenge against them for their transgressions. Jesus' response to John's inquiry makes it obvious that he embraced the salvific God image. By weaving together the different texts of Isaiah, Jesus communicates a God who comes to heal, set free, and announce good news to the people, instead of a God of judgment and condemnation.[4]

John needed to make an enormous mental adjustment and a fresh assessment of the scriptures in order to be able to recognize the eschatological Kingdom in such a man and in such deeds as Jesus was performing. In the spirit of Elijah, John thought of the coming of the eschatological event in terms of earthquakes, wind, and fire. But Jesus asked him to contemplate a different kind of coming, in terms of the "sound of a gentle breeze." He could not. John failed to recognize the Kingdom when it finally appeared on his horizon; it did not match his expectations. A new pair of glasses, a new epistemology was needed to recognize the dawn of the Kingdom in the deeds of Jesus. "Happy is the man who does not find me a stumbling block."[5]

For Jesus, the Kingdom is a message of peace and joy. It is good news, not bad news (Mk 1:14). Now is not the time to mourn and fast; this is a time of joy like a wedding feast (Mk 2:18ff.). Satan's reign is collapsing (Lk 10:18). Jesus sees himself as the messenger who brings the good news, the gospel of Deutero-Isaiah: "How beautiful upon the mountains are the feet of the messenger who announces peace, who brings good news, who announces salvation, who says to Zion, 'Your God reigns'" (Is 52:7). Jesus separated the original understanding that judgment and salvation would be one final event. He offers salvation now and leaves the separation of good from evil to the final judgment (Mt 13:24-30).[6]

It is important to regard the constant breaking in of the Kingdom of God as being *always* good news and never judgment or condemnation. Jesus did not abandon judgment (the word appears fifty times in his preaching); he postponed it. Only the one who does not heed the message of the Kingdom *now* will have to face judgment when the fullness of the Kingdom comes. In contrast to the belief and expectation of the time, and even of John the Baptist who saw the coming Kingdom first as judgment of the sinner and the pagan nations, Jesus stressed that the Kingdom was offering salvation for all now, at this very moment. Therefore, wherever the Kingdom is preached, judgment should not be anticipated by us. The gospel has always to remain good news and to be preached accordingly.

THE KINGDOM AS UNIVERSAL

For whom was Jesus' message of salvation meant? For the righteous and the Jews only, or also for the sinner and the Gentile? Jesus understood his mission primarily as a service to Israel and in Israel. He is conscious of the uniqueness of his people, accepts their scripture as authoritative and restricts his ministry to them. He came to gather and to restore this people of God. Within this community he saw himself sent first of all to look after the lost sheep: the poor, the sinners, the outcast, the marginalized, and all those who in the official theology of the time had hardly any chance of entering the Kingdom when the Messiah would come.

But who precisely were these people—called in scripture the poor, the sinners, and the outcasts?

The Poor

The poor are those who are (1) materially impoverished; (2) economically and politically powerless; and, (3) cognizant of their own weakness, looking to God for help they cannot find anywhere else. Theologically, it can be said that in the Old Testament the mere fact of poverty laid a heavy responsibility on the non-poor, an obligation which was demanded by the law and not left to the goodwill of the individual (Dt 24:10-15). The prophets especially made it clear that social responsibility for the poor and oppressed belonged to the Covenant and took priority over worship (Is 1:11-17). God had a particular love for the poor and disadvantaged in society; God would stand up for them.[7]

Jesus never did away with the Old Testament view on everyone's responsibility toward the poor in society. He only added a dimension to poverty which might be called the poverty of spirit. It means nothing can save us except total reliance on God's infinite love, which is now entering the world through Jesus. The things of this world cannot save and those who rely on their riches and possessions will perish (Mk 10:23-27). The poor in spirit are those who have found their security in the knowledge that God loves them and will save them, not because of what they have, but because of God's love. The Spirit of poverty means to live as Jesus himself lived: totally dependent on the Father and the Father's love for us, finding in this love our ultimate security and joy.

The Sinners and Outcast

A sinner in the Old Testament is not someone who "has committed an offense against God." Rather, to be a sinner means to be someone "who breaks or disregards the Law." The Law is the heart of the Jewish concept of sin and sinner. The Law was intrinsically linked to the Covenant, and keeping the Law meant living in the Covenant. Israel's privilege was that God had given to the chosen people the Law which marked them out from the rest of the world. The Law defined the boundaries of the People of God; breaching the Law meant living outside the boundary marked by the Law, outside the people who by definition are those who live within the Law. Sinners were, therefore, first of all Gentiles who lived outside the Covenant; and second, all those Jews who did not keep the Law.[8] Borg explains:

> The term "sinners" referred to an identifiable social group just as the term "righteous" did: those who did not follow the ways of the fathers as spelled out by the Torah wisdom of the sages. The worst of the sinners or non-observant were the outcasts. We do not know the exact extent of the class, though it included the notoriously "wicked" (murderers, extortioners, prostitutes, and the like), as well as members of certain occupational groups, membership in which made one a "non-Jew."[9]

Shepherds and the tax-collectors, frequently mentioned in the New Testament, belonged to this group. The outcasts had lost all civil and religious rights; they were deprived of the right to sit on local councils and lost their place as children of Abraham in the life of the age to come. They became "Gentiles."

Jesus' Example

Against this background we must place Jesus' words: "I have come to call not the righteous but sinners"(Mk 2:17). Jesus himself was regarded as a sinner because he did not follow the strict observance of the law which the elite demanded. Jesus accepted the criticism hurtled against him. He turned it around and made it a statement of positive intent, forcing his opponents to realize that he had come precisely for these groups whom they had ostracized. There are three areas where Jesus showed himself most at odds with his opponents: his table fellowship with "sinners," his view regarding the Sabbath, and his stand toward women.

Table Fellowship

A regular and important feature of Jesus' ministry was his eating with all kinds of people. It was his eating with "sinners" that became one of the main points of contention posed by his opponents. A meal had a quasi-sacred character. It was a religious act and those who shared it saw it as an expression of acceptance and friendship. The host would bless the bread, break it, and distribute it to those with him at table so that they might share in the blessing spoken over the bread. Members of a sect would naturally restrict table fellowship to those whom they regarded as worthy, that is, those who were not sinners.

In the Maccabean period, and thereafter, the laws on ritual purity had become litmus tests of Covenant loyalty. Many Israelites had been martyred in the Maccabean crisis (1 Mc 1:62-63) by refusing to eat unclean food and keeping to prescribed food laws. How could any devout Jew dare to ignore these food laws without dishonoring those who had died for their faith? It was particularly at table that the vowed Temple purity of the Pharisees was most at risk. Was the food from the marketplace kosher? Was it tithed? Were the utensils ritually clean? Who had been sitting on the couch at the meal table?

Qumran had similar restrictions. Meals were restricted to full members only. A novice could not eat with the community. Only after a long period of instruction in the Law as it was understood at Qumran could one be admitted to the table.

Jesus rebuked these false priorities in Mark 7:1-23. Borg notes: "What to many Pharisees was a sinful disregard for Covenant ideals was for Jesus an expression of the gospel itself."[10] Jesus proclaimed by his sharing of the table with sinners that they were the very ones whom God was inviting to the royal banquet.

Sabbath

The Law says: "To keep the Sabbath is to hold fast to the Covenant." Exodus 31:12-17 was the basis for strict observance of the Sabbath. Breach of the Sabbath was a breach of the Covenant itself. Nonobservance of the Sabbath was sufficient to exclude an Israelite from the Covenant people. The keeping of the Sabbath belonged to Israel's self-understanding. Jesus is accused twice of breaking the Sabbath: In Mark 2:23-28, his disciples pluck the ears of grain; while in Mark 3:1-5, Jesus heals the paralyzed man. Why did he have to heal this person on the Sabbath? Why could the man who had been paralysed for many years, not wait for a few hours more until the sun would have set and the Sabbath would be over? The Law permitted the rescue of a person or even of an animal on the Sabbath if life was threatened. But here, in the case of the paralyzed man, there was no urgency.

Women

The social status of women in the Old Testament is well known. Since blood played such an important role in terms of purity, a normal healthy woman of childbearing age was prevented from taking part in religious ceremonies for much of her life. There was always the danger that she might render others impure by social contact. Women were not allowed into the inner court where the sacrifices were offered.

Jesus overturned these regulations, disregarding the traditional taboos. Women were among his closest followers and friends (Mk 15:40-41; Lk 8:1-3; 10:38-42). In John 4:27 we find the disciples surprised when Jesus talks with a woman. His teaching on divorce applies to both partners (Mk 10:11-12). He was unconcerned about defilement from the woman with the hemorrhage (Mk 5:25-34) and fearless of contracting infections from those with contagious skin disease (Mk 1:40-41).

Summary

Borg summarizes well Jesus' example in all of these situations:

In all these cases Jesus was confronted by boundaries drawn within Israel, by Jews against Jews, boundaries drawn for religious reasons, drawn by those most admirable for the strength of their commitment in religious matters, those most concerned that their religious practice be what God wants. In each case Jesus called these boundaries in question, disregarded them, broke them down. And he did so in the name of God's Kingdom. He came to call sinners, not the righteous. God is for those whom men think to exclude in his name.[11]

Yet Jesus was not sent only for the Jews, but for the Gentiles as well. None of Jesus' statements about the Kingdom differentiates between the destiny of the Jew and the Gentile. The gospels, however, clearly show that he did not work for or proclaim his message to the Gentiles but rather restricted himself to the regions of his own people. Even so, the universality of the offer of salvation is implicitly present in his concept of the Kingdom of God. This is shown in the way Jesus foresaw the coming of the nations (Mt 8:11) in the image of the great pilgrimage of Isaiah 2:2-3.[12]

For Jesus, the coming of the nations is God's work and indicates the end-time. Nonetheless, he does envision their participation in the restoration of Israel. Jesus seems to have personally appropriated the prophetic interpretation of God's history. As the prophets saw it, God selected from the many peoples of the world a single people, Israel, to serve as a visible sign and carrier of salvation. But this offer of salvation is not meant for Israel alone. Because God's salvation for all is offered through this people, God's Kingdom in this world will always remain mediated by a visible community. Still, God is not necessarily bound to this one people. God can choose other people besides Israel, as Jesus tells us in Matthew 21:43: "The kingdom of God will be taken from you and given to a people that produces the fruits of the kingdom." Who are these people? Jesus seems to divide the human race between the haves and the have-nots according to Luke's version of the Beatitudes (6:20-26). In the parable of the Great Banquet (Lk 14:15-24) it is a division between those who decline the invitation and those brought in to take their place. In the parable of the Sower (Mk 4:3-9) it is a division between those who yield fruit and those who do not. Patrick Dale explains the dynamic as follows:

> Perhaps we could generalize to say that the promise of the Kingdom has been transferred from Israel to those who have been excluded from power and reward in this world and those who have renounced them.[13]

What matters is that a community remains a sacramental bearer of the Kingdom. It will place itself in the service of God's ultimate plan of salvation for all. Jesus entrusted the mission of spreading the Reign of God, previously the role of the people of Israel, to the community of his disciples. With this new election the purpose of the Old Testament people was transferred to this New People. It is now the active carrier of this salvation. It is called out of the nations in order to take up a mission for the nations.[14]

12

Salvation Outside the Church

If God has chosen to be bound to a visible community, the church, in order to dispense the saving grace wrought through Christ to all human beings, how can this grace of salvation reach the followers of other religious traditions?

There are three main theological positions in answer to this question: ecclesiocentrism, christocentrism, and theocentrism. While the first position has been generally abandoned, the discussion remains heated between the second and third. The theocentric approach seems to be gaining momentum, but it raises a host of theological problems concerning the role of Christ in the history of salvation and his personal role in the salvation of humankind. A brief survey of the history of the issue of salvation outside the church illuminates the direction for an insightful resolution.

BEFORE VATICAN II

Since the Patristic age the understanding of the relationship of the church to the salvation of followers of other religious traditions has been described as teeter-tottering between two fundamental beliefs: (1) God's universal love and desire to save all human beings. This view is well expressed by the Council of Arles (473): "God does not want anyone to perish, Christ died for all"; (2) The necessity of the church for the salvation of all. Cyprian (d. 258) formulates the traditional expression as, "Outside the church, there is no salvation." Cyprian's original intent was that for heretics, those who had been Christians but then rejected the faith, salvation was lost. Only later was it applied, through misinterpretation, to non-Catholics.

It has never been easy to balance these two beliefs. In the first three centuries the Fathers were more open. They held that an authentic offer and possibility of salvation was extended to all people. This was a "common opinion" which found its expression in phrases like "the

149

seminal Word" (*Logos spermaticos*) of which all humankind partake (Origen, Justin), or the "naturally Christian Soul" (Tertullian). Even Augustine held that true religion existed from the very beginning of humankind and that the saving grace of this religion had never been refused to anyone who was worthy of it.[1]

However, when Christianity moved from being a minority religion to becoming the official state religion under Theodosius (emperor, 379-395), the church became more secure and a change in position became noticeable. The balance tipped increasingly toward the "necessity of the church for salvation," gradually ruling out the first position. Islam and its threat to Christendom added further weight to the argument in favor of the necessity of the church.

The Fourth Lateran Council repeated Cyprian's formula and added: "Outside of the church, there is no salvation *at all*." Boniface VIII in *Unam Sanctam* (1303) clarified the term *church* and insisted that one had to accept papal authority in order to belong to the church and find salvation. The Council of Florence (1442) stated:

> There is no doubt that not only all heathens but all Jews and all heretics and schismatics who die outside the Church will go onto everlasting fire prepared for the devil and his angels. No persons, whatever almsgiving they have practiced even if they have shed blood for the name of Christ can be saved, unless they have remained in the bosom and unity of the Catholic Church (Denzinger-Schönmetzer, 1351).

All these exclusive statements were made in an age when it was generally held that the gospel had been preached throughout the whole world. After the discoveries of the New Worlds in the sixteenth and seventeenth centuries, the realization came quite suddenly that there were millions of people who had never heard of the name of Jesus. The question was: Are these people automatically designated for hell, through no fault of their own? The church had to take a different position. The Council of Trent, facing up to the new situation, proposed the famous distinction of baptism in *re* and baptism *in voto*. If such people followed their conscience and lived morally, they were implicitly expressing a desire to join the church and could thus pass through the doorway to salvation. The catch-phrase was *"implicit desire"* (Denzinger-Schönmetzer, 3870).

What really had happened over the centuries was a development from an *exclusive* to an *inclusive* understanding of the church as the sole channel of grace. But the problem remained that no one dared to say that this grace could reach the person *through* the practice of his or her religion. Other religions were still regarded not as carriers of grace but as instruments of the devil. The vexing question, therefore, was this: How does grace reach the followers of other religious traditions? It seemed that such people could be saved, but only by renouncing their own religion and making a decision for God through a grace that came like an inspiration from nowhere.

VATICAN II

Vatican II, in *The Declaration on the Relationship of the Church to Non-Christian Religions*, was the official turning point. First of all, the council strongly stressed the universality of grace available everywhere in the history of humankind. God's general will of salvation was placed in the forefront, as opposed to the prior emphasis on the necessity of the church. Second, other religions were regarded differently. Although the council did not state explicitly that non-Christian religions are ways of revelation, it taught that "authentic religious experiences" take place in and through these religions. Most Catholic theologians take this for granted. Their view could be expressed in these words: "Grace does reach the hearts of men and women through the visible, experiential signs of various religions." Still, the council also maintained the other axiom: "The church is necessary for salvation" or,

> It is through Christ's Catholic church alone, which is the all-embracing means of salvation, that the fullness of the means of salvation can be found (*Lumen Gentium*, 14).

The theologian who made this position of the council even remotely possible was Karl Rahner. In the 1960s he laid the foundation for this Catholic position, which is today the most advanced among the Christian churches. Rahner starts with the axiom that God wills the salvation of all. But since salvation is not possible without grace, grace must be offered to all human beings in an *effective way*. He explored first the "existential openness" of the human person to the supernatural with his theory of the "supernatural existential." To be human means there is a "supernatural horizon" which belongs to human nature itself and which makes every human person receptive to the supernatural once it appears on his or her horizon. The second point Rahner stresses very forcefully is that we are by nature sociohistorical beings. If grace is to be universally available it needs to be grounded in historical-social reality. It must become body, flesh, event, symbol. This happens in history, in the various religions which visibly contain the grace that leads to salvation. The conclusion is simple: God's saving grace reaches the person not from outside of his or her religion but from within it.

With such a view it is rather easy to overcome the theological position called ecclesiocentrism. Other religious traditions are acknowledged as bearers of God's saving grace, which in effect means that one does not have to be a member of the church in order to be saved.

The saving grace in other religious traditions is seen within the context of God's larger plan for the whole of creation, a plan expressed in the Bible with the symbol Kingdom of God. Since the Kingdom is not to be identified with the church now because the Kingdom is operative beyond the realm of the church as well, God's saving power is, therefore, available to all human beings inside and outside their respective religious traditions. The question is no longer how do world religions relate to the church but how do they relate to the Kingdom. Since the Kingdom aims at the transformation of the world and is already present, not only in the church, we have to regard followers of other religious tradition as members of the Kingdom already present as a historical reality. We still can maintain that the church on earth is the "universal sacrament" of the Kingdom, and yet affirm that other traditions mediate the same Kingdom for their followers, even if in a different and lesser way, which is difficult to determine theologically.[2] The church has no monopoly on the Kingdom of God. One of the chief temptations for the church in history is to claim the Kingdom for itself, to take over the management of the Kingdom, and even, at the limit, to present itself as the realized Kingdom of God over against other religious traditions and the world. The Kingdom of God is not the Kingdom of Christians.

If we accept the view that the church will itself dissolve into the Kingdom at the end—as a number of theologians hold—then members of other religions can share in the fullness of the Kingdom without a relationship to an eschatological church.

> One day the Church will have completed her earthly task and will be absorbed in the eschatological Kingdom of Christ or God.[3]

The Kingdom is not only the church's future but also the world's as well. In the words of Yves Congar:

> In God's unitary design the church and the world are both ordered to this Kingdom in the end, but by different ways and on different accounts. Church and world have the same end, but only the same ultimate end. That they should have the same end is due to God's unitary plan and the fact that the whole cosmos is united with man in a shared destiny. That they should have only the same ultimate end prevents a confusion that would be bad for the church, as raising a risk of dissolving her own proper mission in that of history, and bad for the world, as raising the

risk of misunderstanding and hindering its own proper development.[4]

If we focus on the Kingdom as already present and future we will
see easily that Christians and others belong together in the Kingdom
of God, already present in history. We have a common responsibility
to contribute to its growth and its final fulfillment in the end-time.
Wherever and whenever Christians and others stand up for human
rights or promote genuine human liberation, especially the rights of
the poor and the oppressed, or advocate religious and spiritual values,
the Kingdom of God is built up. We all have one common task: the
promotion of the Kingdom of God by promoting its basic values: justice, peace, and joy. All those who care for these values are fellow
travellers en route toward the fullness of the Kingdom which in its
content is the new humanity willed by God for the end-time.[5]

TODAY

The former ecclesiocentrism has been overcome in the Catholic
church. The question today is no longer whether the church is constitutive for salvation, but how constitutive is Christ for the salvation of
all, of Christians and of followers of other religious traditions?

Dupuis frames the issue succinctly when he asks: "If a Kingdom-
centered theological model helps us to overcome the ecclesiological
perspective which hindered for too long an open theology of religions
and of interreligious dialogue, can the same model help us also to
bypass the christocentric approach in order to reach a more theocentric
view of salvation for all?"[6] The theocentric approach puts all religions on an equal level. There are many mediators of salvation and
Jesus Christ is seen as one among many. Christianity is neither unique
nor so different from other religious traditions that it can claim to be
normative to other faith traditions.

The theological question in the Christian faith is how intimately
Christ is linked to the Kingdom. Is it possible to perceive the Kingdom
of God as detached from the person of Jesus of Nazareth? Most New
Testament scholars would say no. One cannot separate the Kingdom
of God as preached by Jesus from the person of Jesus. There is an
identification between the message and the messenger. The strongest
wording of this position is found in the encyclical *Redemptoris Missio*
of John Paul II, wherein he writes:

> The Kingdom of God is not a concept, a doctrine, or a program
> subject to free interpretation, but is before all else a person with
> a face and a name of Jesus of Nazareth, the image of the invis-

ible God. If the Kingdom is separated from Jesus, it is no longer the Kingdom of God which he revealed. The result is a distortion of the meaning of the Kingdom, which runs the risk of being transformed into a purely human or ideological goal, and a distortion of the identity of Christ, who no longer appears as the Lord to whom everything must one day be subjected (cf. 1 Cor 15:27) (*Redemptoris Missio* 18).

Dupuis has tried to overcome the strong Christic view by referring to the Holy Spirit, who now continues the mission of Christ. After the resurrection, Christ remains present in the power of the Holy Spirit. It is the Spirit who makes God's reign present in the church and outside the church. The members of other religious traditions share the Kingdom of God as already historically present through the combined activity of the risen Lord in the Holy Spirit. Dupuis concludes:

> The Kingdom of God as a historical reality is thus made up of all believers, Christians and otherwise, who in different ways and through varied mediations have heard the Word of God and received it in their hearts, and who responded to the promptings of the Spirit and opened themselves to his life-giving influence. It follows that the "elements of grace" contained in the religious traditions of the world, which mediate for their followers the entry into the Kingdom of God, have been sown in them by the Word of God and his spirit.[7]

Everything considered we can say that God wants the salvation of all human beings. God's saving grace will radiate effectively to all, in their respective religious traditions or otherwise. God's grace will reach all no matter what their faith or confession. But all saving grace is linked to Christ and his Spirit, regardless of how difficult it may be to explain it theologically.

13

Defining the Kingdom

OVERVIEW

As we have seen, Jesus never defined the Kingdom of God. He described the Kingdom in parables and similes (see Mt 13 and Mk 4) and in concepts like life, glory, joy, and light. Among theologians we still find a naive helplessness when it comes to defining the Kingdom of God. The best biblical description is given in Paul:

> For the kingdom of God is not food and drink but righteousness and peace and joy in the Holy Spirit (Rom 14:17).

Some authors regard this text as the only definition of the Kingdom ever attempted in the entire New Testament. The constant danger has been to interpret these words exclusively in a spiritual sense and overlook that its basic concepts like "righteousness, peace, and joy" are equally meant for the life of the Christian in the here and now. In the words of Viviano:

> Strangely, the closest the Bible ever comes to a definition is found where, by all rights, it should not be found, in Rom 14:17. This verse is usually misunderstood to refer exclusively to private, individual, interior, purely spiritual blessings such as a righteous standing of the individual before God, peace of mind and heart due to forgiveness of sins, the joy of the redeemed child. But, while those blessings are not to be excluded, they do not exhaust or even do full justice to the message of these words. After all, peace means primarily the opposite of war, the tranquillity of order, social order; justice means justice, the virtue proper to social relations; and joy, although it has an individual dimension to it, can mean a rejoicing precisely in the blessings brought by peace and justice.[1]

Although Paul uses the symbol *Kingdom of God* only fourteen times (Matthew uses it fifty-five times), the Kingdom remains of major importance in his entire preaching. His use of this symbol should be taken as basically the same as Jesus'. Paul usually translates and expresses the phrase *Kingdom of God* with the "dynamic equivalent" expression "Jesus is Lord."[2] This baptismal profession uniquely expresses the all-pervasive and dynamic sovereignty of Christ now present in the church and in the whole of creation. A number of scholars, therefore, maintain that the phrase, *Kingdom of God*, is not only the center of the synoptics but the center of the whole New Testament, despite the less frequent literal use of the expression.[3]

Concerning Paul's definition of the Kingdom in Romans 14:17, Albert Schweitzer called it "a creed for all times."[4] In his writings, Paul tends to reserve the phrase to refer to the Kingdom in its future aspect. Only here in Romans 14:17 and 1 Corinthians 4:20 does it refer to the present moment. The three qualities (righteousness or justice, peace, and joy) he lists are all important concepts for him. The concluding words, "in the Holy Spirit," are to be attached to all three words.[5] With righteousness (justice), peace, and joy, Paul describes the content of the Kingdom of God, which he sees as already concretely present in the eschatological community.[6] We might call these three characteristics the fundamental values of the Kingdom. The phrase could be seen as a rule of faith or Christian conduct. Black quite rightly says that the

> Kingdom of God is virtually here "regula dei" (like *regula fidei*), as in the rabbinical idea of taking on oneself the "yoke" of the Kingdom of God. In other words, it is here a spiritual absolute, though naturally also eschatologically conceived.[7]

With this brief background in mind, it should not be difficult to discover parallels in Jesus' message, although expressed in a different vocabulary. Some of these include the following: (1) Matthew 6:25-33 and Luke 12:22-31, "Do not worry about your life, what you will eat or what you will drink. . . . Strive first for the kingdom of God and his righteousness"; (2) The "yoke" theme as found in Matthew 11:29-30, "Take my yoke upon you, and learn from me . . . my yoke is easy, and my burden is light." This sentence brings to mind the rabbinical phrase, "to take upon oneself the yoke of the Kingdom of God"; (3) the last judgment (Mt 25) as examined in the light of the Kingdom values. Johnston sees the last verdict of Matthew 25:46 as related to the justice demands of the Kingdom now. He writes:

> The ethical imperative that imposes itself on the hearer is that the duty to be kind to the poor, the outcast, the prisoner, and the disadvantaged is for this present life.[8]

The Kingdom, defined in a brief formula, is nothing other than justice, peace, and joy in the Holy Spirit. These are not just feelings or sentiments but realities to be implemented in this world.[9] We might rightly call these three characteristics the fundamental values of the Kingdom. "Striving for the Kingdom of God" or "taking on the yoke," in the words of Paul means, therefore, nothing else than to commit oneself daily to the values of the Kingdom. Just as the pious in the Old Testament would commit themselves daily to the great Shema and in doing so would "take upon themselves the yoke of the Kingdom" so the disciple of Jesus is asked to commit himself or herself to the same Kingdom by living for the values of justice, peace, and joy.

JUSTICE

The literature on the issue of justice in recent years is overwhelming. Nonetheless, justice as a biblical concept could best be translated as *right relations*. These relations extend in four directions: to God, to oneself, to one's neighbor both as individual and as part of society, and to creation as a whole. To be just means first to respect all of one's relationships with others; namely, in the family, in the clan, in the land, in the world, and in nature. There is justice when everyone respects his or her commitment to others and when everyone is respected and treated fairly in society. Justice in the Bible is therefore primarily a matter of relationship:

> To live in Old Testament terms is to be open to relationships. For the Israelite death is not simply the cessation of life but the end of a relation to Yahweh, to fellow Israelites and to the land. In most general terms justice is fidelity to this threefold relationship by which life is maintained.[10]

Or, in other words:

> Justice in the Bible is preeminently a relational bond which links persons together in a community of mutual responsibility and mutual rights. It is the prime characteristic of the Covenant relationship which binds God to the people of Israel and the people to each other.[11]

The scale on which the justice of the whole society is weighed is the poor, the widows, the orphans, and the aliens. When they are exploited and oppressed, neither worship of God nor knowledge of God can be true religion.[12]

Justice and Worship

The issue of justice in the Old Testament is often linked with the question of true worship. The relationship of justice between the human being and neighbor, on the one hand, and between the human being and God, on the other, easily come into conflict within the context of worship. Worship of God can conceal deficiencies in relationships with fellow human beings. The prophets, in no way against worship as such, uncovered and attacked the discrepancy between the worshiper's devotion and his or her concrete behavior toward a neighbor in dire need. The only worship pleasing to Yahweh is one that is integrated into a cohesive whole, consisting of a just relationship with God, one that would affect social life globally.

The underlying argument runs like this. In worship one turns to a God whom one believes that one knows. To turn to Yahweh and to express one's devotion becomes a lie if this worship is carried out while ignoring the essential connection between knowing Yahweh and doing justice. How can anyone dare to turn to Yahweh in devotion and in search of help while oppressing and exploiting his or her neighbor? And what is worse, to believe that such exploitation will go unnoticed? This connection between knowing Yahweh and practicing justice is expressed in the famous text of Jeremiah 22:16, which equates knowledge of Yahweh with doing justice:

> He judged the cause of the poor and needy;
>   then it was well.
> Is not this to know me?
>   says the LORD.

The critique of the prophets is located here. It is directed precisely against elaborate liturgical feasts, the construction of altars and temples, the practice of fasting, and of pilgrimages to traditional shrines. These are no longer seen as expressing true religion. Rather, they are used to avoid the real issues and to soothe the conscience by believing that Yahweh might genuinely be pleased with this kind of relationship. Isaiah writes:

> What to me is the multitude of your sacrifices?
>   says the LORD;
> I have had enough of burnt offerings of rams
>   and the fat of fed beasts; . . .
> Bringing offerings is futile;
>   incense is an abomination to me. . . .
> Your new moons and your appointed festivals
>   my soul hates; . . .

> learn to do good;
> seek justice,
>   rescue the oppressed,
> defend the orphan,
>   plead for the widow (Is 1:11-17).

In summary, we could say that according to the prophets, knowledge of Yahweh depends on the practice of justice. God cannot be deceived by sacrifice and worship. Justice toward one's neighbor is the primary human responsibility and, therefore, of first importance, even before the duty of worship.[13]

W. Brueggemann, in his article "Voices of the Night—Against Justice," expresses it this way:

> In biblical faith, *the doing of justice* is the primary expectation of God. Everything else by way of ethical norm and Covenantal requirement derives from this, for God is indeed a "lover of justice" (Ps 99:4). Israel is here commanded to attend to the very thing which God most values, namely justice.[14]

Brueggemann, admitting that there are various definitions and conflicting understandings of justice, offers this biblical description of justice: "Justice is to sort out what belongs to whom, and to return it to them." Then he comments:

> Such an understanding implies that there is a right distribution of goods and access to the sources of life. There are certain elements that cannot be mocked. Yet through the uneven workings of the historical process, some come to have access to or control of what belongs to others. If we control what belongs to others long enough, we come to think of it as rightly ours, and to forget it belonged to someone else. So the work of liberation, redemption, salvation, is the work of *giving things back*. The Bible knows that when things are alienated from those to whom they belong, there can only be trouble, disorder and death. So God's justice at the outset has a dynamic, transformative quality. It causes things to change, and it expects that things must need change if there is to be abundant life.[15]

Justice as a Gift from God

It is important to realize that justice is a gift, something we as humans do not know. Only God is just, and in the measure we open ourselves and get to know God, we become just: "He judged the cause of the poor and needy; . . . Is not this to know me? says the LORD" (Jer 22:16).[16]

The Bible is not very interested in justice in the abstract. It gives concrete instances of justice and injustice in the lives of people. In consulting the scriptures about justice we need to ask: What relationship to particular persons or groups does scripture characterize as just or unjust? What relationships does scripture approve or disapprove so that we may apply them to our modern categories of justice? For what specific reason are these relationships endorsed or condemned?

The Jacob story in Genesis 25:19—33:20 serves as a beautiful illustration of the fact that justice is not something we know naturally, but something we need to learn by encountering God. The story is the history of an ambitious person so completely taken up with his own interests that he is ready to fight for them even with illegitimate means. The name *Jacob*, which literally means "cheat," perfectly characterizes that person.[17] Only after he has fought with Yahweh and has been given a new name, *Israel* (Gn 32:28), which means "God perseveres" or "prevails," is he ready to reconcile himself with his brother (Gn 33:1-17). For once, Jacob acts with generosity. The relationship of justice toward his brother, corrupted since their birth, is reestablished now, but only because of Jacob's wrestling with God.[18]

The same observation holds with regard to nature. God gave us this world and we must enter into the right relationship with it. To be master over all creation does not include the right to destroy it as a result of greed or lack of concern for life. Only a right relationship with God will enable us to find the right relationship to nature as well. Jean Louis Ska describes the task of human beings in God's creation as to "subdue" the earth, which means to "take possession."[19] But the word means also to "accompany," to "pasture," to "guide," and refers to the function of a shepherd. We are responsible for the animals like a shepherd for the flock. Our power is not absolute; we are God's representatives. We are called to "care for the living creatures." Thus, all violence is excluded. The issue of the environment and the integrity of creation so much talked about in our days is, therefore, ultimately an issue of justice.

Justice in the New Testament

In the New Testament the concept of justice is linked to the Kingdom theme insofar as justice refers to right relationships. The whole ministry of Jesus is geared toward reestablishing those relationships on which the Covenant was built. His image of God as the Compassionate One concerned with justice, his constant critique of his opponents for having ostracized whole groups, and his untiring effort to bring those marginalized back into the Covenant community indicate how Jesus understood his mission in terms of justice. In whatever way we may describe Jesus' challenge to his contemporaries, one element of his behavior and actions is most obvious: he was extremely sensitive to any kind of discrimination, be it religious, moral, social, cultural, racial, national, or sexual. Since he understood his mission to make all human beings children of our common Father and brothers and sisters among ourselves, he struck at anything that would not let this community come about. This is often, however, easily overlooked. It is not so much the individual acts of justice Jesus performed that we must consider here, but rather his whole character that would not tolerate injustice. Instead he demanded establishing God-willed relationships, worthy of the Kingdom which was coming with him.

This is what Jesus expected of his apostles. In Matthew 19:28 he outlined the mission of the Twelve as that of "judging" the twelve tribes of Israel. The Greek word *krinein* is not correctly translated with "to judge." That is too narrow. Its meaning has to be seen in the light of the prophetic announcements of Yahweh's final coming to "judge" the world. In the prophetic expectation, the phrase "God's coming to judge the nations" means that God will establish justice in the midst of the chosen people and through them among all the nations. God will bring the world into a new relationship of justice and peace. The mission of the Twelve, as described in Matthew 19:28 with the word *krinein*, therefore means "to establish God's eschatological justice in Israel and in all the nations." The mission of the church here is fundamentally geared to the Kingdom value of establishing the justice of the end-time.[20]

Dogmatic theology also supports viewing the Kingdom as relating to justice in the sense of "right relationships." The thinking goes like this: The Kingdom of God is ultimately the Kingdom that exists in God. It "reigns" in God, "among" the three Persons of the one God. But what is it that reigns in and "among" God? In the triune God there reigns a perfect exchange: The Father gives himself totally to the Son, and the Son on his part gives himself totally back to the Father. This personal reciprocal self-giving is the "Person" of the Holy Spirit. Thus the Holy Spirit is the love that reigns in God. The Father is totally related to the Son, and the Son is totally related to the Father. The Holy Spirit is this "right relationship" of self-giving love in the triune God. This life-creating and life-sustaining relationship is, par excellence, the Kingdom of God.

When our creed says "for us and for our salvation," it means that the love reigning in God has gone out toward us and the world, so that all of creation can have a part in God's glory. The whole history of the Old Testament, beginning with Abraham, was and is nothing else but God's unceasing attempt to self-communicate, turning to creation as a self-giving. This relationship is life-giving for us. Only where the divine relationship, the Spirit, reigns and grows among people and all of creation, can we say "all things are created anew and the face of the earth is renewed." God's Kingdom is present only where the relationship between humanity (and all things) is renewed in the pattern of the relationship that reigns in God. It is only then that we have a "New Heaven and a New Earth." The Kingdom is ultimately relationship. It is the relationship which exists in God between Father and Son. The Kingdom is the extension of this relationship into creation. It is the divine life, which God wants to share with creation by drawing all things in Christ to God.[21]

Justice and the Integrity of Creation

As mentioned earlier, the issue of justice includes ecology, which is moving rapidly into center stage as a question of planetary survival. The ecological crisis has its origin in the "mechanistic" way we symbolize the world process. This metaphor means viewing the environment simply as a source of raw material and as a dump for waste. Nature has value only if it can be forced into our mechanistic imagination. Many regard the mechanistic metaphor as the "culprit" of the ecological crisis. For example, the virgin forest, in the symbol of the mechanistic imagination, is "undeveloped." Yet in its own terms it is "richly developed"; it is full of life and variety.

Are there alternative symbolizations of the world process? The oldest known is what we might call the organic metaphor, which sees the whole world in terms of evolution. Most traditional cultures have lived for ages out of this metaphor. Its strength is in seeing all things as interrelated. Its drawback is in having no concept of development but only experiencing the world as a "cyclic process." Neither our mechanistic metaphor nor the organic metaphor suffices to deal with the crisis of the environment in which we find ourselves today. The hope was that the mechanistic metaphor would free us from the domination of nature. But the mechanistic metaphor places a few in control, treating the rest as mere cogs in the machine. The organic metaphor, on the other hand, makes humans the objects of fate. In other words, while the mechanistic metaphor makes nature the victim, the organic metaphor tends to make humankind the victim of nature.[22]

How can we strike a balance? Although there have already been various responses to this issue, a new cosmology is needed to achieve an integral synthesis. We need a new metaphor, a new symbol, or even a new vision of creation and the world process if all the efforts to save the planet are to get us anywhere. Some have suggested that we must gratefully accept our creative powers in order to comprehend how these powers may be models of cooperation and complementarity with nature rather than models of its domination and exploitation.

The search for a sustainable environment, one that will enable the world to maintain and enhance life on this earth now and for the future, has raised several issues that are amazingly close to the concerns of the Kingdom of God as well. Here are some insights that ecology and the Kingdom hold in common as essential for this world.[23]

1) Ecology, as well as the Bible, views the world in a long-range perspective. The world must be seen in terms of a time scheme that cannot be measured and approached in a short period. Life on this planet evolved over billions of years. The effects of the misuse of the environment, for example, are not immediately felt or seen but will definitely manifest themselves later. It is equally true that it will take considerable time before the damage done to the environment can be healed and the balance restored. The Bible in a similar way sees history as a long-range plan that God has with the world. Each human being is important, fitting into this long-range plan. Each human being can hinder or advance God's design for creation. The effects of human actions on nature and history are often not immediately visible but reveal themselves only over a long period of time.

2) Human beings of all times possess an inner respect for nature and know instinctively that they form part of an integrated life organism. This sense—partly lost in modern times because of technological thinking and consumerism—forces itself once again on us today. Natural sciences show us ever more clearly that all things are interrelated and are intrinsically interconnected. Ecology speaks of the web of life, of diversity and mutuality, of dynamism and change. The Bible grounds this interrelatedness of the world in the fact that all created things come from the hand of God and are good, even very good. All creatures have a right to live because God wants them to live. According to the Bible God did not make us "masters" of nature but appointed us "stewards" of creation. We do not have the right to determine which species of life are beneficial to us and which should be wiped out. We are part of creation, bonded together with all that lives. In scripture this view is presented in various ways but finds its most vivid expression in the psalms (e.g., Ps 8 and Ps 114). To interpret and to see everything in purely anthropocentric terms is unbiblical and can only lead to total destruction. At the present a profound shift is occurring from an anthropological view of theology toward a view which takes nature as a context for Christian theology. This shift is more apparent in less academic theology than in the writing of most scholarly theologians. The Bible, however, supports such a way of doing theology. Here the natural world is taken very seriously. Human beings are seen as part of creation, and creation is the context within which God's salvation and redemption is accomplished. Although the story of redemption focuses on human beings, it does not exclude the rest of creation.[24] The value of other creatures besides human beings is as-

serted in the first chapter of Genesis where God is said to *see* that they are good without any reference to human beings. Cobb explains the point as follows:

> When the creation is completed, God views the whole and sees that it is very good. The implication is not only that species and their members are of value in themselves individually, but also that the total creation with all its complex patterns of interdependence has a value greater that the sum of its individual members.[25]

The world is God's creation and not ours. We must substitute Descartes's pernicious words—that we are the masters of creation and therefore can use the world and its plants and animals at our convenience—with those of Albert Schweitzer: "We want to live together with all life that wants to live." Sharing our planet with all that lives restricts the pattern of our life and our use of land, air, water, and the natural resources. In the words of Chief Seattle, a Native American leader:

> This we know. The earth does not belong to people. People belong to the earth. This we know. *All things are connected.* Whatever befalls the earth, befalls the people of the earth. We did not weave the web of life. We are but a mere strand in it. Whatever we do to the web, we do to ourselves.[26]

Technological progress at all cost cannot remain the ultimate norm of human creativity. A commonly held anthropological view of theology, which sees everything as being subordinated to human beings, does not do justice to creation as a whole. This approach obscures or ignores those right relationships to nature that human beings must establish to respond to the biblical demand for justice. Nature as a whole, not humankind as set apart, must be taken as the context of theology.

3) The Bible gives particular significance to the idea of land. Land is a central theme of biblical faith. Human beings are regarded as deeply rooted in the land. In the Old Testament the People of God and the land are firmly joined. There is no way to choose one without the other: either they care for the land on which they live or they ruin it and with it themselves. To be human in biblical terms means to have one's feet firmly on the ground. This truth should prevent us from any excessive spiritualization of the human person. The yearning of people for land has always been a driving force in history. Land has given people the feeling of belonging and of power. The biblical ideal of a human being is one who lives on the land in an environment of balance, harmony, and mutual dependence. This ideal is found through-

out the whole Old Testament, though most vividly expressed in the prophet Micah, as we will see in the next section.

4) If there is anything that we have come to realize today, it is our limits. This world is limited, and we are required to work toward a human society that accepts limits and seeks a decent life for all within these limits. Humankind has reached ecological limits in society and politics. There are no unlimited resources available for the human race. The dream of lasting material growth proclaimed by short-term thinkers will not come true. This kind of utopia is unattainable. We are living on a finite planet with finite possibilities for material growth and with a finite resistance to abuse. Ecologists tell us in unison that we must live with less and use the available resources sparingly, prudently, and in a way that supports the environment. This means we have to live in balance with other species, and first and foremost, we must live on the renewable resources of the planet. The Bible reminds us in the creation story that God put limits to land and water. God gave humankind limits, saying: "Live by them according to my purpose, and you will live. Spurn them and you will die." As physical creatures, human beings live within limits to which they must adapt or perish.

5) All human behavior has consequences. Every breath breathed, every dollar spent, and every relationship created modifies the universe. Every person's behavior is ecologically significant in all its dimensions. This is an insight which, when taken to heart, will demand far-reaching changes in all sectors of human behavior. From the biblical view we can say that all human behavior has consequences because of the nature of the physical-spiritual universe in which God has placed us. The universe is subject to a moral order that cannot be disregarded without serious consequences. We will have to bear the effects of our actions because of the nature of the physical, spiritual, and moral universe God has created—which reflects, of course, the very character of God. The universe is ordered not just logically, psychologically, or sociologically, but also ecologically. The ecological perspective affirms and encompasses all other dimensions. The relationship between humanity and its environment is symbiotic—a mutually supportive, interdependent living with—rather than parasitic. Thus Snyder remarks:

> According to the Bible, we do not really understand the ecology of the world until we recognize its source, the Lord God and that the space-time physical world is interpreted and held together by a spiritual world and by spiritual energy that comes from God. From this standpoint, we really are not thinking ecologically—even from a scientific point of view—if we do not include the dimension of the Spirit.[27]

The Kingdom of God transcends all ecological concern since it aims at the transformation of the whole of creation. This world is the object of God's ultimate plan, and therefore, the search for an ecological balance of nature is at the very heart of the Kingdom of God as well. It is because of God's design and purpose that, according to Snyder,

> economics must recognize the finiteness and vulnerability of our ecosystem and the seriousness of environmental issues, seeking to preserve and protect the earth's biosphere. It must recognize the genius of human community as a key factor in economic policy and organization. This means, among other things, working to support and encourage human-scale economic arrangements that build neighborhoods, local communities, and families. . . . Economics must give special attention to the poor and oppressed recognizing that every person has moral, ecological, and economic significance and that all our lives are interdependent. Kingdom economics will demonstrate that, when the full ecology of our world is understood, caring for the poor and oppressed is actually economic wisdom as well as sense.[28]

What kind of a change is needed and how long the road to success will be is most vividly expressed in these words by Cobb:

> As long as we collectively suppose that meeting economic needs and having full employment require a growing economy, we will collectively support policies that put greater and greater pressure on an already overstressed environment. We will also continue to support policies whose results are greater and greater injustice, with the rich getting richer and the poor getting poorer both within each country and among the world's nations. Only when we see that our real economic needs can be met more adequately with quite a different economic practice will we make the changes needed to avoid worse and worse catastrophes. In this sense, showing that Christian theology opposes both injustice and ruthless exploitation of the earth is not enough. As Christians we are called to lead in envisioning a more livable world.[29]

To avoid despair, we need a realistic view of the world situation today and a firm belief that God's Kingdom is active, transforming creation into his final design. That is the source of the courage to work creatively for alternate solutions to the present crisis. Or, in the words of Cobb:

If we are to deal realistically and responsibly with our global situation, we need both spiritual deepening and a renewed sense of hope. If this hope is only a private or other-worldly one, it will not undergird wise policies. Hence, we need a vision of a possible hopeful future for the planet even if we cannot avoid catastrophes. The New Testament image of hope is the Kingdom of God. Throughout Christian history a great variety of meanings have been read into that image. We need to give it a content that is fashioned in the teeth of the fullest recognition of the limits of our human situation.[30]

The issue of ecology, with its concern of justice for the planet and the species of this earth, calls into question every theological topic dealt with in purely anthropocentric terms. If nature becomes the context of theology, a biblical basis for the issues of ecology can be easily developed.

PEACE

Peace in the Old Testament

Shalom is one of the words in scripture which cannot be translated literally. This word and its derivatives occur more than 350 times in the Old Testament. The root meaning of *shalom* in the Old Testament is "to be sound," "to be safe." It means "well-being" with a strong material emphasis.[31]

Fundamentally *shalom* refers to wholeness, total health, total welfare. Anything that contributes to wholeness can be expressed in terms of shalom. It covers the sum total of God's blessings on a person who belongs to the Covenant community. In a community where shalom reigns, harmony and opportunity for growth exist for every person. Von Rad describes shalom as follows:

We constrict the term shalom if we equate it with "peace." . . . In many instances shalom really signifies bodily health or well-being and the related satisfaction. More commonly shalom is referred to a group, e.g., a nation enjoying prosperity. . . . This brings us to the great number of passages in which shalom denotes a relationship rather than a state. The relationship may be that of a people. It may naturally exist between individuals too.[32]

In the Greco-Roman world peace does not denote primarily a relationship among several persons, but rather a state or a condition. It is a "time of peace" or a "state of peace" considered as an interval in a continuous state of war. In Greek thought peace means the absence of war. In Hebrew thought the opposite of shalom is not war but injustice.[33]

What the Old Testament means by shalom seems to be best expressed in a text that is found twice in the Old Testament, in Micah and Isaiah. The passage envisions what will happen when God comes to bring the Kingdom into this world and when people are willing to let this reality into their lives:

> They shall beat their swords into plowshares,
>   and their spears into pruning hooks;
> nation shall not lift up sword against nation,
>   neither shall they learn war any more;
> but they shall all sit under their own vines and
>   under their own fig trees,
>   and no one shall make them afraid;
> for the mouth of the LORD of hosts has
>   spoken (Mi 4:3-4; see Is 2:4).

Micah presents here a vision of what will be when the nations submit themselves to God's Kingdom. In a nutshell there are two fundamental changes that will take place in the individual and in the nations at large: (1) no war anymore and even no training for war and no war industry; and, (2) the return to a simple and peaceful lifestyle, concerned not with accumulating more and more but rather with fostering interpersonal relationships. According to the prophet, when that submission takes place, the whole war machine will be dismantled and a new social order will emerge. He envisions a transformed human consciousness and a new public policy. It is the age-old dream of every Israelite: to settle for a simple standard of living, content with vine and fig trees. The peace envisioned here demands a shift in priorities wherein greed will end, exploitation will cease, and an entirely new social order will take over. Brueggemann comments on the radicality of its vision:

> It anticipates nothing less than the dismantling of the presently-known world for the sake of an alternative world not yet embodied.[34]

The prophet Micah hints at what will be of concern for people when the Kingdom takes hold of them: They will be concerned with their fellow human beings, and they will be contented with a simple life and a peaceful environment around them. We might find this to be utopian and utterly otherworldly. If, however, we look closer at this prophecy, we can easily discover the two great human temptations which have always plagued humanity and our age and time in particular: a war mentality and a consumer mentality. In a rather strong way John Paul II addressed these two mentalities in his 1993 New Year Peace Message. The text is worth quoting:

> Nothing is solved by war; on the contrary, everything is placed in jeopardy by war. The results of this scourge are the suffering and death of innumerable individuals, the disintegration of human relations and the irreparable loss of an immense artistic and environmental patrimony. War worsens the suffering of the poor; indeed, it creates new poor by destroying means of subsistence, homes and property, and by eating away at the very fabric of social environment. Young people see their hopes for the future shattered and too often, as victims, they become irresponsible agents of conflicts. Women, children, the elderly, the sick and the wounded are forced to flee and become refugees who have no possessions beyond what they can carry with them. Helpless and defenseless, they seek refuge in other countries or regions often as poor and turbulent as their own. . . . After so many unnecessary massacres, it is in the final analysis of fundamental importance to recognize, once and for all, that *war never helps the human community*, that violence destroys and never builds up, that the wounds it causes remain long unhealed, and that as a result of conflicts the already grim condition of the poor deteriorates still further, and new forms of poverty appear (no. 4).

> In today's industrialized countries people are dominated by the frenzied race for possessing material goods. The consumer society makes the gap separating rich from poor even more obvious, and the uncontrolled search for a comfortable life risks blinding people to the needs of others. In order to promote the social, cultural, spiritual and also economic welfare of all members of society, it is therefore absolutely essential to stem the unrestrained consumption of earthly goods and to control the creation of artificial needs. *Moderation and simplicity ought to become the criteria of our daily lives*. The quantity of goods consumed by a tiny fraction of the world population produces a demand greater than available resources. A reduction of this demand constitutes a first step in alleviating poverty, provided that it is accompanied by effective measures to guarantee a fair distribution of the world's wealth (no. 5).

Isaiah 65:20-23 presents us with another vision of what should happen when the peace of the Kingdom of God is given a chance here on earth. It describes what God wants to see happen in the human community. This has been called the Isaiah agenda.[35] Its objectives are clear and specific:

> Children will not die.
> Old people will live in dignity.
> Those who build houses will live in them.
> Those who plant vineyards will eat their fruit.

The vision clearly expresses God's plan and hope for the human community. God desires that children not die, that old people live in dignity, and that those who work enjoy the fruit of their labor. Most astonishing is its seemingly immediate relevance for today. It is not about paradise or a world to come but about human history, about the here and now. In theological terms, the text does not offer what is most pleasing to God, the fully developed and happy person. Rather it insists on what is minimally acceptable to God concerning human behavior toward our brothers and sisters.

Of course, in this agenda we can find many manifestos of political parties and secular governments, but this does not make it less a biblical vision. If we believe that God's Kingdom makes itself felt anywhere, then we have here a clear indication—to use a parable of Jesus—that the "leaven of the Kingdom is penetrating the dough of this world." The beauty of the agenda is that we are assured of what God wants of us, what God's will for us is now. Here is something offered to which everyone can make a contribution and so make the Kingdom of God felt in our midst.

Peace in the New Testament

In the New Testament the word peace is used in at least five different ways:
1. as the absence of war or chaos;
2. as a right relationship with God or with Christ;
3. as a good relationship among people;
4. as an individual state, that is, tranquility or serenity;
5. as part of a greeting formula.

Two, three and four are of particular importance to our discussion. In the New Testament the word *eirene* (peace) occurs ninety-one times, and means, above all, well-being and eschatological salvation. According to the Jesus of the gospels peace means wholeness and comprises the physical, social, and spiritual elements. When Jesus heals a person he says, "Go in peace" (Mk 5:34; Lk 8:48). This peace is not only physical, but often social as well. When Jesus tells the woman with a hemorrhage, "Go in peace," he indicates that she has been newly reintegrated into society, that she is once again a full member of the community. The same can be observed when he says to the woman with the ointment, "Go in peace" (Lk 7:50). At that moment Jesus rebukes those who had ostracized her and restores her to society.[36]

Peace as right relationship with God or with Christ, the vertical dimension of peace, comes close to reconciliation and harmony. It is God's act which restores people to a right relationship with God (Rom 5:1; Acts 10:36). Peace as good relationships among people is a logical and natural extension of this meaning. The right relationship with God should result in good relationships among people. To live in peace means, positively, to live in harmony, and negatively, to avoid any action that would cause disharmony or contention (Mk 9:50; 2 Cor 13:11; Col 3:15).

The Christian meaning of peace, for example, "serenity," "tranquility," and "peace of mind," is not part of the meaning of the term in either the Hebrew or Greek secular worlds. The peace that Jesus leaves with us and gives to us (Jn 14:27) is clearly contrasted to worry and fear. The verse can be restructured in this way:

Peace of mind (or serenity) is what I leave with you. The peace of mind that comes from me—this is what I am giving you. Do not be afraid, worried, or upset.

A person who has entered into a right relationship with God and lives in good relationship with people will as a consequence experience peace of mind, serenity, and tranquility.[37]

In short, peace, or the Hebrew word *shalom,* means wholeness, reconciliation, the harmony of having come to full authenticity concerning our four basic relationships: with ourselves, our neighbor, nature, and God. Shalom is the ultimate state of fulfillment and the great gift of the end-time. It means not only the absence of war but the fullness of life.

The gospel of John sees Jesus' entire mission as related to bringing the eschatological peace announced by the prophets. Shalom in John is bound up with Jesus' passion and death. Unlike the synoptic gospels, it is only after the resurrection that Jesus will greet his disciples with the salutation, "Peace!" The shalom that he has gained for them through his suffering and death is the great gift of the risen Lord to his disciples on Easter morning. "Peace I leave with you; my peace I give to you" (14:27). "I have said this to you, so that in me you may have peace" (16:33).[38] It is the reconciliation of the world with God, the eschatological peace that Jesus was to bring to this world (20:19, 21, 26). Therefore, whatever concerns the Kingdom concerns peace.

JOY

The basic meaning of *joy*, *chara* (noun) and *charo* (verb), in the Bible is in reference to physical comfort and well-being. The word appears 133 times in the New Testament (including 20 times in Luke; 11 in Acts; 18 in John; 12 in Matthew; 14 in Philippians; 13 in 2 Corinthians; 7 in Romans; and 6 in 1 Thessalonians). It refers most often to the joy of the eschatological fulfillment of the end-time, in short, to the Kingdom that is experienced as already present now.[39]

Joy is a recurring refrain of the parables. It is used, for example, in relation to finding what was lost (Lk 15), a treasure in the field, and a pearl of great price (Mt 13:44-45).[40] Joy in the biblical sense means *life*. It is the expression of fullness, life, and love. The Kingdom of God is a matter of life and love in abundance. After all, *the* image of heaven in the Bible is the wedding feast where the happiness and joy of all are guaranteed.

In concrete terms *joy* means to give to each person the space to unfold and to become creative according to his or her abilities and gifts. Since it is to be understood in a holistic sense, that is, including all aspects of human existence, it refers in the present world to what we call "matters of human rights." Every creature has a right to life on this earth, which God has given us as a common heritage to enjoy and to share in its richness.

JUSTICE, PEACE, AND JOY IN THE HOLY SPIRIT

The phrase *in the Holy Spirit* refers to all three characteristics of the Kingdom: justice, peace, and joy.[41] It is the most important aspect of our present discussion. Since the Kingdom on earth is now an anticipation of the New Heaven and the New Earth, it can only be a creation of the Holy Spirit, the one who will bring forth the New Creation. Therefore, we can only possess the gifts of the Kingdom as a "foretaste" or a "foreshadowing" of what is to come. Nevertheless, they can be experienced and identified as the Kingdom present and operative now in the midst of our world.

How these three fundamental characteristics should determine any theological description of the Kingdom can be seen in the following definitions of the Kingdom by Edward Schillebeeckx:

• The Kingdom of God is the saving presence of God, active and encouraging, as it is affirmed or welcomed among men and women. It is a saving presence offered by God and freely accepted by men and women which takes concrete form above all in justice and peaceful relationships among individuals and peoples, in the disappearance of sickness, injustice and oppression in the restoration of life of all that was dead and dying.

• The Kingdom of God is a new world in which suffering is abolished, a world of completely whole or healed men and women in a society where peace reigns and there are no master-slave relationships— quite a different situation from that in the society of the time. As things are there, "not so with you" (Lk 22:24-27).

• The Kingdom of God is a changed new relationship (*metanoia*) of men and women to God, the tangible and visible side of which is a new type of liberating relationship among men and women within a reconciling society in a peaceful natural environment.[42]

14

The Challenge of the Kingdom

Jesus' Image of God

JESUS' VIEW OF REALITY: THE COMPASSION OF GOD

Jesus' vision teaches us how we should look at reality. Most of us envision reality as something indifferent, hostile, something we have to protect ourselves against, a judge that has to be appeased. Modern Western culture with its essentially "one-dimensional" understanding of reality continually supports and reinforces this image of reality as ultimately indifferent toward us. The result is a constant search for security on all levels of our life. This deeply affects our image of God. The widespread, infantile, and erroneous images that many people have about God have their roots mainly in the way they look at reality. God for them is someone who is angry, who is out to "get" them, a God who makes people feel guilty and worthless. These images are the demons that Jesus came to expel.

Jesus saw reality differently. For him reality was not threatening or hostile; rather, it was ultimately gracious and compassionate. Jesus expressed this experience in poetic imagery like Matthew 6:26-33 ("Look at the birds of the air; they neither sow nor reap. . . . Consider the lilies of the field . . . "). For Jesus, nature was filled with God's glory, cosmic generosity, and intensive care.[1] Behind all reality we find a God who cares, who is in love with creation, and who reaches out to creatures with compassionate solidarity.

The word Jesus used most often to identify these qualities of God— glory, generosity, care—was *compassion*. The word *compassion* belongs to a Hebrew word group that is normally translated in the English language with the word "mercy." The three Hebrew words for the English equivalent word *mercy* are: *hesed, hen/hanan,* and *rahamim.* These three words are used to define an essential truth in Old Testament theology, well expressed in Exodus 34:6:

"The LORD, the LORD,
a God merciful [*rahum*] and gracious
      [*hannun*],
slow to anger,
and abounding in steadfast love [*hesed*].

Hesed, normally translated as "faithfulness," refers to the kind of love which is mutual and dependable. This "mercy" is found between husband and wife; it is the bond of deep friendship. It both initiates and characterizes the Covenant bond between Yahweh and Yahweh's people. Thus, it becomes a way of defining the Covenant God (Ex 34:6-7) and the Covenant people (Mi 6:8).

The second Hebrew word for mercy *hen/hanan,* translated as "grace," is understood as a free gift, with no reciprocity implied or expected. It is not necessarily long-term or done among equals but depends solely on the good will of the giver. People seek it and Yahweh grants it.[2]

The third root word *rahamin* comes closest to what compassion means. In the Hebrew language the word is taken from the "womb of a woman." Thus the word *compassionate* bears the connotations of "wombishness," loving the way a mother loves the child of her womb, nourishing, giving life.[3] It implies a physical response in the sense that compassion for another is felt in the center of one's body. This "mercy" calls for and results in action. It is a feeling often expected of Yahweh who has mother-love (Is 49:15, Jer 31:20) or father-love (Ps 103:13; Is 63:15-16) for Israel. It is this "womb-love" of Yahweh which leads to forgiveness for God's wayward children.[4]

The word in the New Testament that comes closest to the Hebrew word *rahamin* is *splanchnizomai,* which implies the physical feeling of mercy. The word *splanchna* with its derivatives originally denoted inner organs, especially the heart, and lower kidneys. It means the emotions, which the ancients considered to be seated in the lower organs.[5]

In the synoptic gospels the Greek word *splanchnizomai* is used only for the behavior of Jesus when faced with human suffering. Furthermore, it determines the actions of the key persons in the three parables, the Unforgiving Servant, the Prodigal Son, and the Good Samaritan.

On the lips of Jesus the meaning of the word *splanchnizomai* goes beyond the literal sense. The word means "his heart contracted convulsively." To the sight of crying human needs Jesus reacts with a messianic compassion. The cases reported in the gospels are: a leper with his petitions (Mk 1:41); the people like sheep without a shepherd (Mk 6:34; Mt 14:14; cf. Mk 8:2; Mt 15:32: "I have compassion" in direct speech); the sight of the harassed and exhausted crowd shortly before the sending out of the Twelve (Mt 9:36); two blind men who besought him (Mt 20:34); and the widow of Nain mourning her only son (Lk 7:13). In Mark 9:22 it is used in the petition for driving out a demon.

The same word is found in the two parables, the Unforgiving Servant (Mt 18:23-35), and the Prodigal Son (Lk 15:11-32). Here again *splanchnizomai* expresses the strongest feeling of a compassionate (Mt 18:27) or loving (Lk 15:20) reaction which forms the central point of the stories. In both parables *splanchnizomai* makes the unconditional compassion of God visible. In the parable of the Good Samaritan (Lk 10:30-37) *splanchnizomai* in verse 33 expresses the attitude of complete willingness to use all means, time, strength, and life, for saving at the crucial moment.[6]

THE KINGDOM AS GOD'S UNCONDITIONAL LOVE

Jesus expressed his view of reality in the symbolic phrase *Kingdom of God*. What adequate description can we give to this multifaceted symbol?[7] Is there one? The best seems to be that the Kingdom of God in Jesus' message is God's unconditional love for creation. This love, revealed in Jesus Christ, has the sole purpose of leading all human beings and ultimately all of creation to participation in God's own life and love. Jesus revealed this intention of God in images and parables. The most vivid ones are most probably found in Luke 15. If we would have nothing of what Jesus said and did except the three stories of Luke 15—the Prodigal Son, the Lost Sheep, and the Lost Coin—we would still have the essence of his message.

What is the outstanding message of these parables? They reveal the true image of God that Jesus came to communicate to us: a God whose basis for dealing with us is unbelievable, compassionate love. The behavior in all three parables is the most unlikely that a reasonable human being would take. By human standards, was the older brother not right? Did the woman not spend more in celebrating with her neighbors than she had lost? What responsible shepherd would leave ninety-nine sheep in the desert and expose them to wolves and lions in order to run after a lost one? This is precisely the point Jesus wants to make in these parables: God acts out of love and not out of rationality or even common sense. Like any true lover God behaves foolishly because God's motive in dealing with us is love alone. This is the good news of God's Kingdom, to which Jesus wants us to be converted and in which we are called to believe.

Others have singled out the following three parables as the clearest demonstration of the image of God that Jesus came to reveal: The Laborers in the Vineyard or the parable of the Good Employer (Mt 20:1-16); the parable of the Unmerciful Servant or the parable of the

Merciful Master (Mt 18:23-35); and the parable of the Prodigal Son or the parable of the Unbelievably Merciful Father (Lk 15:11-32).

We find again this image of God in one of the most striking features of Jesus' ministry, his eating and drinking with the outcasts. Jesus' meals with outcasts are *the* central feature of Jesus' ministry. He portrays here an understanding of God as gracious and compassionate, embracing even the outcasts, those whose mode of life placed them outside the boundaries of respectability and acceptance in society. His table fellowship with outcasts was an action parable revealing the compassionate God, who desires to embrace all human beings in one great community of brothers and sisters.

The theological message in all these parables and actions is the same. They demonstrate the incomprehensible goodness and kindness of God toward all human beings when the Kingdom will come in its glory. A new order is starting now, based not just on justice but on God's goodness and kindness. Justice gets subordinated to this kindness and compassion of God. Jesus is demonstrating that all human beings stand in need of God's kindness and compassion and these will undoubtedly be given to each one at the end. Since this is the case, no one can be judge anymore over his or her fellow human being.[8] Commenting on the parable of the Laborers in the Vineyard, Joachim Jeremias concludes:

> God is depicted as acting like an employer who has compassion for the unemployed and their families. He gives to publicans and sinners a share, all undeserved, in his Kingdom. So will he deal with them on the Last Day. That, says Jesus, is what he is like; and because he is like that, so am I; since I am acting under his order and in his stead. Will you then murmur against God's goodness? That is the core of Jesus' vindication of the gospel: Look what God is like—all goodness.[9]

This was Jesus' vision that determined his whole life. For this vision he lived, suffered, and ultimately died. It has been called the agapeic vision of the New Testament. With this vision Jesus offended the just of his time. Jesus' proclamation of God as unconditional love was always upsetting. It upset all standards insofar as he saw salvation coming, not from what human beings would do, but from the acceptance of a "God who comes to love us first."

The real content of Jesus' message of the Kingdom consists, therefore, in his image of God: God loves every human being with *unconditional love*. Jesus teaches us three important lessons: God always loves us, God always forgives us, and God is always present with us. Conversion to the Kingdom message of Jesus means, first of all, a conversion to the image of God that Jesus came to proclaim not as a worldview, not as an idea—as brilliant as it may be—but as his vision of reality, something he lived for, worked for, suffered for, died for. Scripture reads:

> No one has ever seen God. It is God the only Son, who is close to the Father's heart, who has made him known (Jn 1:18).

What is the true nature of God?

> God is love. God's love was revealed among us in this way: God sent his only Son into the world so that we might live through him. In this is love, not that we loved God but that he loved us and sent his Son to be the atoning sacrifice for our sins (1 Jn 4:8-10).

This image of God, which Jesus came to reveal in its fullness, already runs like a thread through the entire Old Testament. After having examined the Old Testament under this aspect, one Old Testament exegete sums up his findings as follows:

> The most important of all the distinctive ideas of the Old Testament is God's steady and extraordinary persistence in continuing to love wayward Israel in spite of Israel's waywardness. It is His persistent love that will not let Israel go, a love that not all of man's weakness and sinfulness and stubbornness can destroy. His love never wavers, never ceases. This is an Old Testament truth of permanent force and validity, one that we cannot dispense with.[10]

A Jewish scholar who commented on the three parables of Luke 15 had this to say:

> The virtues of repentance are gloriously praised in the Rabbinical literature, but this direct search for and appeal to the sinner are *new* and moving notes of high importance and significance— Jesus is not passing on a commonplace idea of the teaching of his day. He is saying something of which his contemporaries knew nothing as he proclaims the truth that God is a seeking God, one who reaches out in love to the sinner and brings him home.[11]

THE KINGDOM AS A CALL TO CONVERSION

Jesus joined the indicative, that the Kingdom of God was a reality at hand, with an imperative, that conversion is needed to respond to

God's coming in him. This response to the Kingdom at hand is expressed with the words *repent* and *believe*.

The word *repentance* is a collective term used by the evangelists primarily to summarize the response Jesus sought from the people. Jesus gave concrete directions for the new life he was calling people to embrace. What Jesus was seeking from the people he expressed in two phrases; namely, "to follow in discipleship" and "to believe." However, the traditional term *repentance* used in the New Testament can easily cover a whole range of meanings. Once this term is seen against its Old Testament origins, it can mean becoming poor, giving up everything, following the Lord in total obedience. Goppelt remarks that the term *repentance*

> was quite suitable when the prophets were calling Israel back to its God and his covenant. But the coming kingdom required a forward, rather than a backward orientation. According to Mt. 11:3-6, he was coming to realize his promise. Therefore, turning to the reign of God was both the return to the God of Israel—the prodigal son comes home—and the return of creatures to their creator. Thus, the term "repentance" is able to express not only the vital link between Jesus' ministry and the coming kingdom but also between that ministry and the already existing relationship between God and Israel.[12]

Since the Kingdom is a dynamic power that constantly breaks into this world, the call for repentance is a permanent one directed to everyone, not only to the sinner, but also to the righteous who have committed no great sins. What does the phrase "repent," "be converted," mean in the proclamation of Jesus' Kingdom message? Using biblical images we could envision conversion in six terms.

1. Turn Around: "Let it into your life"

To *convert* does not mean, first of all, to return to the Law and to make amends for one's transgressions of the Law. To repent does not mean primarily to turn away, to leave one's way of life, to leave behind everything that is wrong and sin-permeated. No, to convert means first of all *to turn toward*, to respond to a call that reaches me from behind. One is asked to let this new unheard of message into one's life, to let oneself be overtaken by this great news. Of course, such a turn around toward the Kingdom will include a turning away, but what makes one turn is the actual breaking in of the Kingdom of God and not some demand to make oneself ready for its future coming. Real conversion is possible only if one can imagine such a God, if one can envision such a love as real and actual now. The question of conversion is: Are we willing to let this image of God into our life? Are we ready to let Jesus' vision of reality determine our actions and behavior?

2. Well Up: "Let it well up from within you"

In the gospel of John Jesus employs the image of a well that is within to symbolize the Holy Spirit (see Jn 4). Conversion here means to let the life-giving waters of the Holy Spirit well up from within us and bring us to life. In Luke 17:20-21 Jesus speaks about the Kingdom not as coming in signs and wonders but as the Kingdom "within us." The early Church Fathers understood this to mean the Kingdom is in our reach; it is so close and intimate that we can take hold of it if we really want it.

3. "Becoming a Child"

The parable of becoming a child (Mk 10:15; Lk 18:17) presents us with another way of understanding conversion:

Truly I tell you, whoever does not receive the kingdom of God as a little child will never enter it (Mk 10:15).

At the time of Jesus, children ranked very low on the social scale. Since children were not yet knowledgeable of the Torah, they had no merit before God. A. Stock summarizes the position of the child in Jesus' time:

The child was considered a person of no importance, meriting no attention or favors.[13]

This makes Jesus' attitude toward children all the more surprising. There are three groups of sayings in the gospels that relate children to the Kingdom. The first group insists that the "Kingdom belongs to them" (Mt 19:14; Mk 10:13-16; Lk 18:17); the second group states that only "in becoming like children can one enter the Kingdom" (Mt 18:3); and the third group explains that anyone who receives a child receives Christ himself (Mt 18:5; Mk 9:37; Lk 18:17).[14] In addition, there are two occasions where Jesus heals children (Mk 5:35-43; 7:24-30). Finally, he is "indignant" over the disciples' rebuke of those who brought children to him.[15]

By promising the Kingdom to children Jesus challenged contemporary theological thinking on merit, reward, and the entire patriarchal society by declaring that the child's incapacity for earning the Kingdom was its greatest asset.[16] Being "like a child" means one has nothing to give, nothing to show, in order to gain the Kingdom. It means this helplessness, this being without any claim of deserving or earning it.[17] Jesus does not advocate childishness nor does he have a naively romanticizing attitude toward children. It is the absolute gratuitousness of the Kingdom that is stressed. To say that God is gracious means that the relationship with God is not dependent upon performances and merits. God is gracious to each one of us prior to achievements on our part. Borg explains:

> Whenever one says that God's love depends upon having met requirements of any kind, one has abandoned grace as the dominant image of reality, no matter how much the language of grace remains.[18]

The child opens up a vast area of Kingdom qualities: trust, humility, obedience, a forgiving spirit, as well as helplessness and dependence.[19] C. S. Mann writes:

> The Kingdom "belongs" to the children in the sense that children appreciate a gift as an absolute, something which they are aware they cannot have worked to deserve. Children in this saying are at one and the same time in this sense symbolic and nonsymbolic. The children are rightful recipients because they are receptive. But they are symbolic in that the gift of salvation is something which cannot be earned.[20]

The precondition of entry into the Kingdom in the eyes of Jesus is "becoming a child." Jesus asks those who want to follow him for an immediate and all-important necessary step in order to enter the Kingdom. Adults are judged as being out of step with what it means to be human in the eyes of God. We are asked to abandon false values such as status seeking, power, and wealth. These values are signs of an unauthentic being and serve as barriers to entering the Kingdom of God.

Instead of seeking prestige and status, the Kingdom requires that we humble ourselves, get rid of our self-imposed importance measured in worldly values. We are asked to find our true vocation in obedient service to God. In doing so, we become one with Jesus. We become his disciples. "Being a child" indicates more than a change of direction. It implies new life and rebirth as expressed more explicitly in this Johannine imagery (Jn 3:3-5):

> Jesus answered him, "Very truly, I tell you, no one can see the kingdom of God without being born from above." Nicodemus said to him, "How can anyone be born after having grown old?

Can one enter a second time into the mother's womb and be born?" Jesus answered, "Very truly, I tell you, no one can enter the kingdom of God without being born of water and Spirit."

Jesus' demand of "becoming a child" expresses the necessity for adults to make a new beginning, to have a new responsiveness and openness to God and other people. We are asked to learn or relearn the ways of God. Only then will we rediscover lost potential and gain integrity and wholeness.[21]

4. To Become Christlike: "Let Christ make his home in you"

The Pauline perspective sees conversion happening when Christ is taking shape in us (Eph 3:14-19). Indwelling is the endpoint toward which all conversion must be directed. Conversion means a turning to Christ, accepting salvation from him. According to Colossians 1 all human beings are created in the image of Christ. They carry in themselves his image as their true "hidden self." Thus we read: "To them God chose to make known how great among the Gentiles are the riches of the glory of this mystery, which is Christ in you, the hope of glory" (Col 1:27). Conversion from this perspective means to let Christ take shape in us and to lead us from mere image into likeness.

5. Think Differently: "To look at reality with the eyes of Jesus"

According to the Greek word *metanoia,* conversion means to "think differently," to look at reality the way Jesus did. It means to accept his perspective and his frame of reference, to use his "eyeglasses" when looking at the world and human reality. The images are relative, but they all indicate a profound change in the person who opens himself or herself to the new reality, the breaking in of the Kingdom of God, allowing it to determine the direction of his or her life. One's whole attitude toward the Kingdom message will be different depending on whether the Kingdom is seen first as something beautiful that calls for full attention, or whether it is first of all a call to repentance to leave old ways of doing and living. Important is the continual awareness that Kingdom and conversion belong together. The preaching of the Kingdom is always connected with the call to turn toward it, to let its power into our life. Since the Kingdom of God is now a reality that constantly breaks into this world and radiates into our life, encompassing all creation, the call for conversion will always accompany this message. Conversion is, therefore, not something that happens once and for all, but a demand that asks for a response whenever the Kingdom is preached. Conversion belongs to the essence of Jesus' message.[22]

Sin must be judged in the light of the coming Kingdom of God. Sin means that we refuse to let the power of the Kingdom determine the direction of our lives. The Kingdom wants to free us from the constant temptation to be our own masters and to determine the world in our way. Only when God becomes the Lord of our whole life and the Lord of the whole universe will the fullness of the Kingdom be accomplished.

6. Commitment to the Values of the Kingdom

This model of conversion asks: What rule of conduct should determine the disciple's life? Jesus made it clear that the Pharisaic rulings could never be taken as a pattern for his disciples. As Dunn observes:

> It was not so much the law to which Jesus objected, as it was the way in which it was used. Not the law itself, but the use of the law as a barrier to exclude others, was what he reacted against; and particularly the overscrupulous interpretation of the law which resulted in a negative judgment against those who failed to conform, the over-definition of the will of God so that the channels of God's grace became ever more restricted, the attitude which assumed that only what was acceptable to one's own group was acceptable to God.[23]

Jesus' key for interpreting and understanding the law was "compassion and love" as we have observed. He saw love as the key factor in seeking to live in accordance with the law. Consequently, he summed up the law in the twin commandment of love of God and neighbor: "He set forth love of neighbor as a principle which showed how the law is to be observed in the light of circumstances, rather than a rule to be obeyed whatever the circumstances."[24]

Yet for Jesus, love of God and neighbor is not something a disciple can do on his or her own; it is a response to God's prior action. It is God's love, God's compassion and forgiveness, that in turn enables us to love and forgive. We can love God and neighbor because we have been forgiven and in this way express our gratitude. One follows from the other. This is clearly expressed in the parable of the Great Sinner (Lk 7:36-50). The love the woman showed toward Jesus is the result of God's forgiving love, which she has received and accepted:

> Therefore I tell you, her sins, which were many, have been forgiven; hence she has shown great love (Lk 7:47).

Only the experience of being loved to the utmost bears fruit in a love of neighbor which itself endures through all disillusionment and setbacks. This love expresses itself in two characteristic ways: forgiveness and service.

Readiness to forgive becomes then the ultimate measure of how far one has truly become a disciple of Jesus (see Mt 18:21-22; Lk 17:3-4; Mt 5:43-45). Yet the disciple cannot forgive except when he or she has experienced God's forgiving love first. It is only in the strength of the forgiveness received that we are enabled to forgive those who have wronged us. According to Matthew 6:14-15, those who do not forgive demonstrate that they have not received or have not accepted God's forgiveness. They have refused to allow God's forgiving love into their life and therefore are unable to forgive.

The second characteristic of Jesus' commandment of love is expressed through "service of neighbor." The disciple is not forbidden to think thoughts of greatness, but the greatness pointed to is that of service (Mk 10:35-45). The model is Jesus himself, who put concern for the neighbor's well-being above everything else, not just social conventions and taboos, but also above possibilities of social advancement, prestige, and even life itself.[25]

Moreover, forgiveness and service, as ultimate demands of discipleship, take concrete shape in one's life according to the values of the Kingdom: justice, peace, and joy in the Holy Spirit. The phrase "in the Holy Spirit" once again makes it clear that living for these values and making them our rule of conduct are a consequence of our having first allowed the Kingdom into our life. Here conversion means to begin to live out these new relationships of justice, peace, and joy, and, in doing so, to witness concretely to the presence of the Kingdom now. The acid test of true discipleship will always remain whether the community of Jesus' disciples lives the "creed for all times": righteousness and peace and joy in the Holy Spirit (Rom 14:17).

THE KINGDOM AS TRUST AND BELIEF

According to Mark, Jesus joins the phrase "and believe the good news" (1:15) to the word *convert*. *To believe* does not mean primarily to accept something as being true. It means, rather, "to trust," "to entrust oneself," "to find one's security in." Paul and John rarely use the words *convert* or *repent*; they prefer *believe*. In Hebrew, it is *amen*, which originally meant "I know where my security lies" or "to know, to be secure" (e.g., Is 7:9). What Jesus is asking for is trust in this message. There is no other security to be found than in the Kingdom he now offers. It is God's unconditional love for each one of us that is the rock on which we can stand. It is something never heard before, something most beautiful, something to which we can entrust our whole being. We are asked to accept that God has already accepted us with infinite love and compassion. It is our final salvation.

Conversion is a joyful occasion, good news, and not a terrible event of judgment and condemnation. The lost child has come home (Lk 15:25); the dead man has come alive again: "This son of mine was dead but he is alive; he was lost but now he has been found" (Lk 15:24,32). Conversion, therefore, is preceded by God's action to which we are called to respond. Only God's love makes a response possible at all. Conversion is a person's reaction to God's prior action.[26]

However, the Kingdom of God is not only a summons to conversion; it is at the same time a summons to faith. The disciple holds firm to the belief that now already the messianic future is operative. The promise invades our relationships and circumstances. The presence of the Kingdom robs the oppressive circumstances of this world of their seemingly ultimate validity. The faith in the Kingdom becomes a kind of resistance movement against fatalism. The world does not have to stay as it is. Our lives and the circumstances in which we live can be changed. Our task is patiently to dismantle the destructive structures and direct our steps toward the coming Kingdom. It makes all the difference if there are communities who pray for God's Kingdom to come, who advocate the cause of the poor and oppressed, and who proclaim the acceptable year of the Lord, God's liberating future.[27]

THE KINGDOM AS COMMITMENT TO THE PERSON OF JESUS

In whatever way we may try to describe or define the content of the symbol *Kingdom of God*, it ultimately reveals God's unconditional love for creation. This incomprehensible love (Eph 3:18-19) became visible and tangible in the person of Jesus of Nazareth. Therefore, we have to keep in mind that the Kingdom is not just a "grand design," a "utopian dream come true," "God's ultimate plan for creation"; it is in the last analysis a person: Jesus Christ. In the words of John Paul II:

> The Kingdom of God is not a concept, a doctrine or a program subject to free interpretation, but before all else a person with the face and name of Jesus of Nazareth, the image of the invisible God. If the Kingdom is separated from Jesus, it is no longer the Kingdom of God which he revealed (*Redemptoris Missio* 18).

The real nature of the Kingdom can only be sensed and imagined in a personal encounter with him "who loved me and gave himself for me" (Gal 2:20). In the measure we come to realize this personal aspect of the Kingdom, we will experience an urgency to let ourselves be grasped and swept away by the unheard of and unbelievable good news of the Kingdom that is offered to us at this very moment.

Conversion surely means a change of our life, attitudes, and behavior toward God and fellow human beings. But we must keep in mind that conversion does not mean primarily a change of something, or a conversion to something, it means to turn to *someone*. It means to welcome, to accept Jesus as the center of our whole life. For him and his gospel we subordinate everything else (Mk 10:28), even life itself (Mk 10:32). Prior to the question of the nature of the Kingdom, there is the question, "Who is Jesus for me?"[28] Conversion is, in the last analysis, a personal commitment to Jesus, an open declaration for him. The person of Jesus becomes the decisive factor for salvation, for acceptance or rejection in the Kingdom of God. This personal attachment is a new and unparalleled element in the claims of Jesus. It means adopting his way of life and living in close company with him. Only the one who commits himself or herself to fellowship with the Lord will ultimately come to see what the Kingdom is and who Jesus is, in whom the Kingdom makes itself present.

In the gospels we find a phrase that contains everything Jesus came to communicate. This one phrase that occurs frequently and emphatically is the simple demand: "Follow me." These two words embrace in a nutshell what God wants of each of us and what we should regard as the ultimate will of God for us in this life. The phrase appears twenty times in the gospels. In the Old Testament the essential vocation of a true Israelite was to adore the true God and to follow the prophets. In the New Testament these two words are combined, adoration and fellowship. The true adorers of God are those who have chosen to follow the Lord, in whom is revealed who God really wants to be for us.

Ultimately, the challenge of the gospel to us is revealed in questions such as these: Do we believe that the three parables of Luke—the Prodigal Son, the Lost Sheep, and the Lost Coin—convey the true nature of God's love for us in Christ? Do we believe that God searches for every human being in the same way as a shepherd does for the lost sheep? Do we believe that God is like a father who sees his lost son from afar and goes to meet him, and that this alone gives the son the strength to go ahead and meet his father? Can we accept such a God as the true one? Jesus had nothing to say to us except that God is deeply in love with the world. His whole mission consists in converting us to this God. Luke 15 sets the question that really matters before us: Do we really believe that God goes after every human being, day after day, with the sole intention of meeting and bringing him or her home?

SUMMARY

Briefly, then, the core message of Jesus contains an *indicative*, which epitomizes all of Christian theology, and an *imperative*, which sums up all of Christian ethics. The indicative is the proclamation of the Kingdom, that is, the revelation of God's unconditional love for everyone. The imperative is a call to turn toward this breaking in of the Kingdom and to let its power into our life. We could also use the image of John in which Jesus describes the Kingdom as something that is welling up from within us. Jesus talks about the Holy Spirit, that great gift of the end-time which will be given in such abundance that it is compared with a fountain within us leaping up to provide eternal life (Jn 4:14). We can therefore formulate the basic message of Jesus as follows:

Indicative	+	Imperative
(kingdom)		*(repentance)*
God loves us unconditionally.		Turn toward God's love; it is the only security we can trust.

15

The Kingdom of God—Already and Not Yet

INTERPRETATIONS

The Kingdom of God is, first of all, a dynamic concept, denoting the reign of God in action. Jesus proclaimed the Kingdom as present, but he also referred to the Kingdom as a reality that is still to come. So, how are the present and the future of the Kingdom related to each other? The correct understanding of this interrelationship is still one of the most problematic questions in the contemporary study of Jesus' teaching. Very different positions have been taken. Each position can be supported by following one of the lines of thought suggested by the synoptic kerygma of the Kingdom of God. The one strand is extracted and strengthened through interpretation to bolster the chosen position. Other passages are either rejected as being unauthentic, disregarded as unimportant, or even misconstrued in order to support the position pursued. What emerges then is an impressive, univocal, and consistent picture of Jesus. But how far does this picture square with reality?[1]

In the ongoing discussion of the proper relationship between the present and future of the Kingdom of God, three models of interpretation have emerged: otherworldly and future, this-worldly and present, this-worldly but future.[2]

Otherworldly and Future

The modern discussion of the Kingdom started with the publication of Johannes Weiss's *Jesus' Proclamation of the Kingdom of God* (1892),[3] and with the subsequent popularization of Weiss's views in Albert Schweitzer's *The Quest of the Historical Jesus* (1906).[4] Since then the Kingdom of God has been the subject of intense scholarly research and discussion. Eventually a consensus emerged saying that the Kingdom of God is the central concern of the teachings and works of Jesus.

In the school of thought of the "Konsequente Eschatologie," whose main proponents were Weiss and Schweitzer, the Kingdom in Jesus' preaching is considered as an object of imminent expectation, yet still to come. Statements that refer to the present are interpreted as prophetic visions. This means that future events are presented vividly so that the distance separating them from the present are so shortened that their occurrence seems immediate. This interpretation of Schweitzer is also called "thorough-going or consistent eschatology." Weiss summarized the Kingdom message of Jesus in six characteristics: (1) It is radically transcendent and supramundane; (2) it is radically future and in no way present; (3) Jesus did not inaugurate the Kingdom but waited for God to bring it about; (4) the Kingdom cannot be identified with the group of Jesus' disciples known as the church; (5) the Kingdom does not come gradually by growth or development; and, (6) the ethics encouraged by the Kingdom are negative and world denying.[5]

Schweitzer basically agreed with this view. The essence of Schweitzer's approach is the assumption that the whole life, work, and teaching of Jesus were dominated by the expectation that the Kingdom of God would come within a few months. Jesus regarded himself as its messenger. With this realization in mind, he preached its imminent coming, sending his disciples on their mission as recorded in Matthew 10. He did not expect them back before the Kingdom would come. The failure of the parousia of the Kingdom to take place immediately was the turning point of Jesus' ministry. Convinced that the pre-messianic tribulations were transferred by God to the suffering and death of the messenger of the Kingdom, Jesus realized that he had to take upon himself those tribulations expected for the end-time in order for the Kingdom to come. Schweitzer explains:

> The others are freed from the trial of suffering, Jesus suffers alone.
> . . . He suffers in their stead, for he gives his life as a ransom for
> many.[6]

Jesus suffered the violent death he foresaw and interpreted in connection with the coming of the Kingdom.[7] The Kingdom, however, did not come, at least not in the way he had expected.[8] Schweitzer's thesis has been opposed quite strongly, especially the assumption that Jesus was mistaken about the arrival of the Kingdom during his lifetime or at least with his death. In addition, Schweitzer's emphasis on Jesus as an "apocalyptic fanatic" is also considered excessive. Since he positioned Jesus' complete frame of reference within the expectation of Judaism, his theory has always held a fascination for those who want to interpret Jesus in the context of Judaism. The latest in this trend might be E. P. Sanders.[9] Sanders follows the basic thesis of

Schweitzer, explaining the whole life and mission of Jesus along those lines. Although his results are worth our consideration, if all the emphasis is placed on the future of the Kingdom, as he does, it is difficult to see how the Kingdom can be present at all.

This-Worldly and Present

Mainly in reaction to the apocalyptic Jesus of Weiss and Schweitzer, C. H. Dodd proposed his view of the Kingdom, which has become known as "realized eschatology." The Kingdom of God as preached by Jesus is a present reality. It is already here. History has become the vehicle of the eternal. This world has become the scene of a divine drama in which the eternal issues are laid bare. It is the hour of decision. The parables in particular present the Kingdom as an event that is happening now, in the present experience of the people.[10] Jesus, therefore, was not mistaken about the time when the Kingdom would come. The decisive texts for Dodd concern Jesus' practice of exorcism, as found in Matthew 12:28 and Luke 11:20. Here the sovereign power of God has come into effective operation. The Kingdom becomes a matter of present experience and not of the near future. Against this background Dodd interpreted the "engiken" of Mark 1:15 as "the time has reached fulfillment and the Kingdom of God has come upon you." From these Dodd concluded that the fundamental principle of Jesus' teaching is this presence of the Kingdom and not some future coming:

> It appears that while Jesus employed the traditional symbolism of apocalypse to indicate the "otherworldly" or absolute character of the Kingdom of God, he used parables to enforce and illustrate the idea that the Kingdom of God had come upon men there and then. The inconceivable had happened: history had become the vehicle of the eternal; the absolute was clothed with flesh and blood.[11]

Sayings that seem to indicate a future coming of the Kingdom were interpreted by Dodd as referring to those in the future who would come to share in the presence of the Kingdom. Or else those sayings were attributed to the early church, which expected an imminent coming.[12] However, Dodd later modified his view to allow for a real futurity of the Kingdom. This he did in response to the criticism of Joachim Jeremias, who regarded his "realized eschatology" as too one-sided and an unnecessary contraction of eschatology.[13]

Rudolf Bultmann, like Dodd, interpreted the Kingdom in the context of the background developed by Weiss and Schweitzer. His approach is known as "existential eschatology." He maintained the "wholly future" of Jesus' Kingdom message as Schweitzer had proposed it. According to Bultmann, Jesus did in fact appropriate his notion of the Kingdom from apocalypticism. Not once did Jesus speak about a present coming of the Kingdom. Thus, Bultmann rejected Dodd's realized eschatology as escape reasoning, arguing: "On the contrary, Jesus clearly expected the irruption of God's reign as a miraculous, world-transforming event."[14] Bultmann wanted to rescue the relevancy of Jesus' apocalyptic Kingdom message as a present reality by interpreting the future of the Kingdom in existential categories rather than in temporal ones. He undertook his famous demythologizing program in order to recover the essential understanding of existence contained in both Jesus' eschatological proclamation and the early church's eschatological outlook. Bultmann demonstrated that Jesus' expectation of the Kingdom was only his awareness of the absolute sovereignty of God. Jesus' proclamation of its imminent coming was an expression of the fact that in the face of the sovereignty of God all human beings stand in a crisis of decision.[15] In light of the eschatological proclamation of the Kingdom, human existence must be understood as always being challenged to a decision. God's word demands from each one confronted by the gospel a decision, here and now, against the world and for God:

> The one concern in this teaching was that man should conceive his immediate concrete situation as the decision to which he is constrained, and should decide in this moment for God and surrender his natural will. Just this is what we found to be the final significance of the eschatological message, that man now stands under the necessity of decision, that his "Now" is always for him the last hour, in which his decision against the world and for God is demanded, in which every claim of his own is to be silenced.[16]

Bultmann, as well as Dodd, wanted to make Jesus both intelligible to modern culture and relevant to contemporary Christian faith. They felt the central problem was that Jesus had apparently expected the Kingdom of God to come in the near future. If he was mistaken, how could he and his first-century message be relied on in the twentieth? In their interpretations they tried to show that the message of the Kingdom of God is essentially timeless and therefore relevant for all times.

For Dodd the eternal had come into present time through Jesus, who proclaimed that the Kingdom had already come. For Bultmann the apocalyptic Kingdom was already being inaugurated in that it determined the present and demanded an existential decision now. Thus, the apocalyptic Kingdom mythology was "demythologized" and interpreted for the present.

The "presentist" focus of both Dodd and Bultmann was challenged in the 1960s and 1970s, particularly by proponents of the "theology of hope" and the "new theology." In these later movements the future once again moves to center stage. The importance of the future for Jesus and the early Christians is newly recovered against a completely new view of humanity as the creator of its own destiny. To this view we now direct our attention.

This-Worldly but Future

Lastly, there is the school which tries to maintain a balance between the future and the present. This position can be summarized as follows:

> The relationship between the present and the future element in the teaching of Jesus concerning the Kingdom should be seen as a relationship between a present in which the long-promised eschatological salvation is known at a personal level and through the ministry of Jesus, and a future in which it will be manifested universally or cosmically through some climatic act of God.[17]

Or, as Jeremias describes it: "It is Eschatology that is in the process of realization."[18] This position is known as the "already and not yet." The differences among those who hold this position are often questions of emphasis; they stress either the "already" or the "not yet" of the Kingdom. We shall survey six scholars of this school.

For J. Jeremias the hour of fulfillment is here because the bearer of salvation is here; this is the basic message of the parables. The parables look forward to the future for the fulfillment of that which has begun in the present. There are two aspects in the parables: hope and crisis. While hope looks in expectation toward what is to come, crisis—understood as imminent catastrophe—calls for a decision now, either for or against the person of Jesus in whom the Kingdom is present. The present time of salvation is moving toward a time of catastrophe that will reach its climax in the eschatological triumph of God, the parousia. The person of Jesus binds present and future together.[19]

For R. Schnackenburg the presence of God's Kingdom is inextricably linked with the person of Jesus and his work. God "dynamically" effects salvation in the present through Jesus, although the consummation as judgment and final salvation remains in the future. We can best understand the Kingdom either as the presence of the messianic fulfillment of the promise of salvation, which is not yet consummated, or as the beginning of eschatological salvation, which is moving toward a new climax. Since Jesus' proclamation of the Kingdom as already breaking in, the fullness of the Kingdom has become tangible and certain in Jesus. It penetrates through him into "this aeon" and works within humankind. It is already present and yet awaits its manifestation in glory.[20]

O. Cullmann puts the stress on the tension between present and future. He phrased the now widely known distinction of the "already" and the "not yet." He uses a metaphor from warfare to explain the tension between present and future:

> The decisive battle in a war may have already occurred in a relatively early stage of the war, and yet the war still continues. Although the decisive effect of that battle is perhaps not recognized by all, it nevertheless already means victory. But the war must still be carried on for an undefined time.[21]

In the ministry of Jesus the decisive battle has been fought and won; Satan has fallen (Lk 10:18) and the power of the evil spirits is broken. Yet the battle still goes on: "The hope of the final victory is so much the more vivid because of the unshakably firm conviction that the battle that decides the victory has already taken place."[22]

N. Perrin stresses the experiential aspect of the Kingdom now present. The words *present* and *future* should be emphasized not as temporal concepts but as experiential ones. Of particular importance are the signs of the Kingdom (e.g., exorcisms, healings, and forgiveness of sin), in which the Kingdom can be experienced by the individual as a present reality. The consummation of that which has begun in the ministry of Jesus will be just as much a reality to be experienced as was the initial experience of the ministry of Jesus and of those who believed in him.[23]

W. Pannenberg explains the "already" and the "not yet" by using the two ideas of the "ontological priority of the future" and the "category of anticipation." The imminent Kingdom is a "proleptic reality," meaning that the finality of all human possibility is already anticipated. It is the future that has an imperative claim upon the present, and the present is the result of the future. This stands in marked contrast to the conventional assumption that past and present are the cause of the future. The Kingdom present is the key to history and to its final end. It anticipates the end of history "proleptically." It unlocks the meaning of history but at the same time constantly points to its final consummation. It is the future that makes the present understandable. In Jesus' message of the Kingdom the end of history has come into history itself. It reveals the meaning of history and the finality toward which it is moving. The content of the Kingdom is the final fulfillment of humankind's social destiny and the ultimate revelation of God and who God really is for us.[24]

J. Moltmann sees the already more in terms of a "hope" that makes the present dynamic. The reason for a life of hope in the future is the resurrection and appearances of Jesus. The resurrection should be seen as a seed with an imminent vitality and a definite tendency: "Faith is directed in hope and expectation toward the revelation of what has already been found hidden in Christ." Only in him who is the "mirror of our future" do we see toward what we are marching. Moltmann places significant emphasis on the future. The present situation cannot inspire hope. It is only through the promise given in Christ that "the hidden future already announces itself and exerts its influence on the present through the hope it awakens."[25]

The weakness of Moltmann's position lies in its overemphasis on a future which affects the present only in the form of a promise. A promise which is not grounded in an experiential present can easily turn the future into "pie in the sky." If the dynamics of the Kingdom do not affect human experience individually as well as socially, they are in danger of becoming "empty and ineffective" in transforming human reality.

THE CURRENT DISCUSSION

While almost all Catholic scholars maintain *both* the "already" and the "not yet" of the Kingdom as a biblical reality, there is still considerable difference of emphasis among them. Is it the already or the not yet of the Kingdom that should determine our understanding? Both positions can be found in the New Testament. It is argued by some that Matthew's gospel supports the not yet or apocalyptic view, while Luke seems to support the already position that emphasizes the here and now of the Kingdom, thus revealing a more positive view of present reality.[26]

It is tempting to take either position and carry it to the extreme. The one is to regard the Kingdom as totally other, a transcendent reality beyond this world. Such a view regards the Kingdom as having nothing to do with the labyrinth of the world, referring instead only to the paradise of the heart. Here the world becomes insignificant and ultimately meaningless, and thus not worth the struggle. Such a temptation comes easily when the complexities of the world become unbearable. Bonhoeffer comments: "Whenever life begins to become oppressive and troublesome a person just leaps into the air with a bold kick and soars relieved and unencumbered into so-called eternal fields."[27] Such a view reminds one of Karl Marx's definition of religion: "Religion is the sigh of the oppressed creature, the sentiment of a heartless world and the soul of soulless conditions. It is the opium of the people."[28]

The other temptation is to define the Kingdom of God in secular terms. This secularist temptation identifies the Kingdom consciously or unconsciously with some earthly goal. Here the Kingdom is no longer God's but ours. We build it and we are its architects. This is one of the main concerns of the Roman Catholic magisterium with liberation theology:

> Thus there is the tendency to identify the Kingdom of God and its growth with the human liberation movement, and to make history itself the object of its own development, as a process of the self-redemption of man by means of the class struggle.[29]

John Paul II in his encyclical on missionary activity made this remark:

> Nowadays the kingdom is much spoken of, but not always in a way consonant with the thinking of the church. In fact there are ideas about salvation and mission which can be called anthropocentric in the reductive sense of the word inasmuch as they are focused on man's earthly needs. In this view, the kingdom tends to become something completely human and secularized; what counts are programs and struggles for a liberation which is socioeconomic, political and even cultural, but within a horizon that is closed to the transcendent. Without denying that on this level too there are values to be promoted such a notion nevertheless remains within the confines of a kingdom of man deprived of its authentic and profound dimension. Such a view easily translates into one more ideology of purely earthly progress. The kingdom of God, however, "is not of this world . . . is not from the world" (Jn 18:36) (*Redemptoris Missio* 5).

The correct understanding of the relationship between the present and the future of Jesus' preaching about the Kingdom remains one of the most problematic issues in the contemporary scholarship. In stressing the imminence of the Kingdom, one already assumes the position that Jesus underscored the present impact of the imminent future. If, on the other hand, one stresses the future of the Kingdom, the danger emerges that the present impact of the Kingdom, while not denied, is minimized and confined to the personal and the spiritual arenas. Wherever one locates the emphasis will definitely mirror quite accurately the person's own view of reality and its accompanying spirituality.[30]

Theology will have to face this question: What is the connection between the future being created and the Christian hope of eschatological completion? The Second Vatican Council wanted to avoid a mistaken "flight from the world" mentality but failed to make the transition to a more integrated view.[31]

As far back as 1973 Schillebeeckx remarked that the relationship between a human future and an eschatological expectation allows for two types of Christianity. One will bear witness to this expectation (not yet); the other will prepare here and now for the Kingdom by building a better future on earth (already).[32]

The official church has never really clarified this relationship between the already and the not yet. Although Vatican II is regarded as the great turning point in the church's discernment of history in the light of the Kingdom, even *Gaudium et Spes* remains ambiguous. Human history is viewed as a struggle against the power of darkness, standing in need of purification. The document speaks about the New Earth and the New Heaven in such a way as to presuppose the complete disappearance of this earth to make way for something totally different. Yet at the same time it speaks of the growth here of a new body able to "give some kind of foreshadowing of the new age." This ambiguity can be recognized in the following text:

> Earthly progress must be carefully distinguished from the growth of Christ's Kingdom. Nevertheless, to the extent that the former can contribute to the better ordering of human society, it is of vital concern to the Kingdom of God. For after we have obeyed the Lord, and in His Spirit nurtured on earth the values of dignity, brotherhood and enterprise, we will find them again, but freed of stain, burnished and transfigured (*Gaudium et Spes* 39).

In Paul VI's "Profession of Faith" in 1968 we find a similar statement. The pope is eager to ensure that the Kingdom should never be mixed with inner earthly progress, and so he says:

> It [the Kingdom] consists in an ever more profound knowledge of the unfathomable riches of Christ, an ever stronger hope of eternal blessings, an evermore ardent response to the love of God, and finally in an ever more abundant diffusion of grace and holiness among men.

In the same statement the pope also urges that all

> contribute . . . to the welfare of their earthly city, to promote justice, peace and fraternal concord among men, to give their help generously to their brothers, especially to the poorest and most unfortunate.

Evangelii Nuntiandi speaks of people seeking the Kingdom, "building it up, and implementing it in their lives" (no. 13). *Gaudium et Spes* clearly expresses the value of human activity by saying:

> For man, created to God's image, received a mandate to subject to himself the earth and all that it contains, and to govern the world with justice and holiness. . . . Thus by the subjection of all things to man, the name of God would be wonderful in all the earth. . . . They can justly consider that by their labor they are unfolding the Creator's work, consulting the advantages of their brother men, and contributing by their personal industry to the realization of the divine plan (*Gaudium et Spes* 34).

Redemptoris Missio offers the following comment:

> The kingdom of God is the concern of everyone: individuals, society and the world. Working for the kingdom means acknowledging and promoting God's activity, which is present in human history and transforms it. Building the kingdom means working for liberation from evil in all its forms. In a word, the kingdom of God is the manifestation and the realization of God's plan of salvation in all its fullness (*Redemptoris Missio* 15).

One can quote one passage after another from the church's teaching in support of either side. The end result would still be a certain ambiguity. How does one, for example, interpret the terms used in these documents that refer to the Kingdom, such as "sign," "flowering," and "building up," as if to build a more just world is not a sign of the growth of the Kingdom? Once again, several more recent solutions have been proposed to resolve this ambiguity.

The "Not Yet" Position

Individualistic View of Salvation

At the risk of oversimplification this position could be described as follows: God creates all human beings in order to lead them to their final destiny, heaven. In order to prove himself or herself every one is to be put into this sin-permeated and dangerous world. If the person stands the test, the reward is eternal life on the New Earth and the New Heaven.

The New Earth and the New Heaven are created, therefore, from those who have proved themselves. In terms of the gnostic and mystery religions, the gods are busy trying to populate Olympus with a few select souls who have been rescued from the tumultuous sea of matter and human history.[33] The individual is regarded as a self-contained unit, a Robinson Crusoe. God's call is addressed as to someone on an island, and salvation takes place exclusively in terms of a private relationship with God.[34] The individual could be compared to a mosaic stone used in putting together a beautiful design. In such a picture, history does not make sense. The world is just a great testing ground without any meaning in itself. It is not important. The only thing that matters is that the individual pass the test in order to go to heaven. The Kingdom of God refers to the termination of this temporal world which is succeeded by a supernatural world. The otherworldliness of the Kingdom and its remoteness from time are continually underscored. Overlooked is the fact that no individual exists in isolation. It is not possible to speak of salvation without reference to the world of which one is a part. Such a picture is accompanied, of course, by a corresponding spirituality concerned only with the salvation of one's own soul.

Pessimistic View of the World

This next view, which stresses exclusively the not yet to the detriment of the already, has also been called "millenarian eschatology." According to R. Wall this position has four chief characteristics:

1) It reveals a decidedly pessimistic view of historical change; history and its corrupted institutions will only get worse. Only the inbreaking of the future Kingdom will be able to change the world. The structures of the fallen world cannot be transformed this side of the second coming of the Lord. The stress is constantly on the future coming and never really on the presence of the Kingdom. What counts is the not yet while the already of the Kingdom, though not denied, is totally spiritualized.

2) The emphasis must be placed on the transcendence of God who will intervene at the end of history to bring about the hoped-for, dramatic reversal of events by destroying and creating a lasting and perfect world. Historical existence as we know it does not really matter since the powers which transform it come at history's end and not before.

3) A distinction is made between the realities of the consummated Kingdom and any experience we might have of it in the present. In this interim period the community of faith experiences God's Kingdom "personally, inwardly, spiritually, and vertically."

4) God's transcendence is preserved without dilution. God is "the heavenly Father" who reigns now from a "heavenly Kingdom" in the hearts of God's disciples. The mission of the community of disciples is not to bring about structural changes in the prevailing sociology of

conflict. Their mission is to work for spiritual change and not to attempt to usurp God's work on God's future day. Christians should not forget that the most important result of being saved is not change of the structures of society and the practice of justice, but rather the persuasion of others to become followers of Jesus so that they too may be eternally saved.[35]

The "Already" Position

Outlook on History

This solution is concerned with creation as a whole and with the purpose of the human race as it has evolved, developed, and continues to develop throughout the centuries. It asks this question: "Do historical events and human activity in history in all its various dimensions have any meaningfulness with respect to the Kingdom that God is fashioning now and will establish in glory at the second coming of the Lord?"[36] Or, in other words, What should Christians hope for in human history? Is a world where justice, peace and joy have triumphed something we are *commanded* to work and pray for or only *permitted* to dream about? Or, is it perhaps *forbidden* by the gospel to entertain such a utopia as a real possibility? Can we support such a view from scripture if the gospel itself presents us with a more positive outlook concerning history and the presence of God's Kingdom?

Some authors have seen such a view in Luke. His emphasis is on the already. The now of salvation is intensified, with the power of the risen Lord being experienced as a power to set free those who most need liberation. The church's mission is within the world to help people and nations realize God's shalom, which Christ has already brought to earth. In a practical way, situating God's Kingdom and the blessings of salvation in the future of human history conceals an inability to take seriously and to work for actual radical change in humanity's present position. Futuristic eschatology, as outlined above, only postpones the triumph of God and effectively prevents salvation from being realized historically. In order to give meaning to the history of humankind a critical shift in the thinking of the church must be made from the second to the first coming of the Lord. God's righteousness, peace, and joy (Rom 14:17) have already broken into human history. The power and promise of God's triumph over evil structures are not beyond history but within it.[37]

Theologians themselves have no answer that integrates the two views. Even popes have had different views about the subject:

No more war, war never again. . . . If you want to be brothers, let the weapons fall from your hands. You cannot love with weapons in your hand. . . . This is the goal worthy of your efforts; that is what people of the world expect from you. This is what must be achieved (Paul VI at the United Nations in 1965).

In this world a totally and permanently peaceful human society is unfortunately a utopia, and . . . ideologies that hold up that prospect as easily attainable are based on hopes that cannot be realized, whatever the reason behind them (John Paul II on the Day of Peace in 1982).

At times it is argued that common sense and experience must say no to the emphasis on the already of the Kingdom. Personal and structural sin will make it impossible ever to create a world where justice and peace will triumph. On the other hand, advocates of a more positive view maintain that a new world is no mere utopian dream but a possibility for the realization of which we are all responsible.

Theological Foundation

The theological reasoning for the positive view begins with revelation concerning creation, Incarnation, and Resurrection. First, creation is basically good. The sin that permeates the world does not make it evil. History, humankind, and the world remain fundamentally good. They are meant not for destruction but for a restructuring according to the original design of God.

Second, the most distinctive New Testament concept of the universe is its Christological emphasis. The world was created by God through the Word (Jn 1:10), and without him nothing that has been made was made (Jn 1:3). The Christ whom the gospel proclaims as the agent of redemption is also the agent of God's creation:

He is at the same time the goal toward which all creation is directed (Col 1:16) and the principle of coherence of all reality, material and spiritual (Col 1:17). In the light of the universal significance of Jesus Christ, the Christian cannot be pessimistic concerning the final destiny of the world. In the midst of the changes of history, he knows that God has not abdicated his throne and that at the proper time all things will be placed under the rule of Christ (Ep 1:10; Col 3:15). The gospel implies the hope of "a new heaven and a new earth" (Rv 21:1; 2 Pt 3:13).[38]

Third, the resurrection of Christ affects the whole of creation. There is no basis in the gospel for limiting the fulfillment of the promise of a new creation inaugurated on the first Easter morning to the personal and private sphere of life. As God's Word assumed in the incarnation all that is human, earthly, and cosmic without exception, so God's Son has begun in the resurrection to transfigure the whole of creation. In the resurrection Christ has become the heart of the world. He is, therefore, the primary, imminent agent in the struggle for peace and justice. Since Pentecost the Spirit of the risen Lord has become the energizing force of creation that is at work as the ultimate world-transforming power.

This world will be transformed into the New Heaven and New Earth because the power of the Resurrection is now at hand. The emphasis is on the already of the Kingdom.[39] Bonino equates the continuity-discontinuity between the present life in history and the life of the Kingdom in fullness, to the comparison which Paul makes between the earthly body and the risen body. The transformation of this body does not "disfigure" or "denaturalize" bodily life; instead, it fulfills and perfects it, eliminating its frailty and corruptibility.[40]

Others have pointed out that the belief in the resurrection of the body carries with it the demands to care here and now for the hungry, the homeless, and the abused. The understanding of the end as a new order—the Kingdom of God, the New Jerusalem—means for us that God wills here, as well as hereafter, a just and peaceful society and habitable cities.[41]

These theological arguments lead readily to the implications that follow below. The ultimate goal of creation is for Christians the vantage point from which we understand ourselves and all of reality. It is the Christian vision, the horizon against which we locate everything.

Theological Implications

Four principal implications can now be drawn from the previous discussion.

1. The Kingdom is meant for this world. The most important implication is the realization that it is this sin-permeated and corrupted world—a world in which there is so much hatred, egoism, oppression, and hopelessness—which is the object of transformation into the New Heaven and the New Earth. This world is the arena where God's ultimate plan for creation unfolds. The Kingdom of God happens here, in the midst of our human affairs. It is meant for this world here and now, although its future fulfillment is still to come. Let us recall citations such as the following:

The seventh angel sounded his trumpet, and there were loud voices in heaven, which said: "The kingdom of the world has become the kingdom of the Lord and of his Christ, and he will reign for ever and ever" (Rv 11:15).

After we have obeyed the Lord, and in his Spirit nurtured on earth the values of human dignity, brotherhood and freedom, and indeed all the good fruits of our nature and enterprise, we will find them again but free of stain, burnished and transfigured. This will be so when Christ hands over to the Father a kingdom eternal and universal: "a kingdom of truth and life, of holiness and grace, of justice, love and peace." On this earth the kingdom is already present in mystery. When the Lord returns, it will be brought into full flower (*Gaudium et Spes* 39).

2. The Kingdom means the transformation of the whole of creation. Salvation for the individual does not consist in being taken out of this world like an isolated stone within a mosaic. The person will be saved insofar as he or she is part of the whole that will be transformed. Personal salvation is embedded in the transformation and salvation of the whole of creation. The salvation offered to us in Jesus Christ is universal in scope. God wants all people to be saved (1 Tim 2:4). Padilla writes:

> Jesus is not the savior of a sect but the "savior of the world" (Jn 4:42; 1 Jn 4:14; 1 Tm 4:10). The world is the object of God's love (Jn 3:16). Jesus Christ is the Lamb of God who takes away the sin of the world (Jn 1:29), he is the light of the world (Jn 1:9; 8:12; 9:5), the propitiation not only for the sins of his own people but also "for the sins of the whole world" (1 Jn 2:2; cf. 2 Co 5:19). To this end he was sent by the Father, not to condemn, but "that the world might be saved through him" (Jn 3:17).[42]

The biblical idea of redemption always includes the earth. There is an essential unity between human beings and nature. The earth is not merely an indifferent theater in which a person carries out the daily tasks of life. Rather, it is also the expression of the glory of God. As the earth took part in the sin of humanity, so it will also share in God's final redemption. God's final intervention is seen as a new creation of the sin-cursed creation of old:

> For I am about to create new heavens
> and a new earth (Is 65:17; 66:22).

Since the most general characteristic of human existence is being in the world, and the primary mode for human interaction is relationship, salvation for each person cannot be a deliverance from creaturehood or an escape from bodily existence. The resurrection of the body is an integral part of biblical hope. The world is not evil per se, and therefore not a realm from which a person must escape in order to find true life. There must be a total transformation of nature if we ourselves are to be transformed. This view can be found in Paul's writing once again: "The whole creation has been groaning in labor pains ... while we wait for adoption, the redemption of the body" (Rom 8:22-23).

3. The Kingdom demands transformation of the present reality. The Kingdom already present in the world demands that all reality be restructured now according to the principles of the Kingdom. Human history must be taken seriously since it is our world, the way we have made it, that will be transformed. With this conviction comes a particular spirituality. Being a Christian is a call (which means a privilege) to participate actively in this transformation of creation. It is not only a question of saving our own soul.

The Kingdom of God is a power that is constantly breaking into this world in order to transform it. This old, sin-permeated, corrupt world must be challenged by this message of the presence of the Kingdom in order for it to be transformed through the power and dynamism of its final destiny: the Kingdom of God in its fullness. In such a vision, the social ministry of the church becomes a constitutive element of evangelization. What happens to this world is not irrelevant. All the structures of this world must be subjected to the gospel judgment and be restructured according to the Kingdom principles. As Bonino puts it:

> In relation to the kingdom, history is not an enigma to be deciphered but a mission to be carried out. This mission, be it noted immediately, is not a mere ensemble of actions but a manifestation of a new reality—of the new life that is offered and communicated in Christ and his Spirit. The first fruits of the Spirit are the anticipation of the kingdom. They are the quality of personal and collective existence that has a future, an eschatological reality, and that concentrates authentic history around its center.[43]

4. The Kingdom as challenge to human freedom. Finally, the New Heaven and the New Earth do not have a predetermined content. Human freedom is respected to the highest degree. The transformed world will be formed from the interaction of human freedom and the breaking in of the Kingdom. No doubt, the New Heaven and the New Earth remain God's own doing. We cannot create or build the Kingdom of God. It is God's work and gracious gift, but our actions on earth make a difference. What will be transformed is our world as we have made it, at the time determined by God. The content, the color, the design, will have our imprint since it will be made out of our history. This is what Vatican II meant when it said that all that we have done here on earth to foster community, human dignity, and enterprise will be found again in the New Creation, although "freed of stain, burnished and transfigured" (*Gaudium et Spes* 39).

Three Kingdom Models of the "Already"

In *Models of the Kingdom* Snyder presents three models which put the predominant or even exclusive emphasis on the "already" of the Kingdom: the Kingdom as political state, the Kingdom as Christian culture, and the Kingdom as earthly utopia.

The Kingdom as political state is a model that served in many ways as the basis for empires and states. The best known examples are Byzantine Christianity, the Geneva of Calvin, Cromwell's England, and Colonial America. It remained a basic idea for the founding fathers of the United States as well.

Its main argument runs as follows: Since the Kingdom is the goal of all reality it provides the values and the methodology for the social, political, and economic organization of society. Theocracy is the primary metaphor for this model. Three characteristics are dominant here: (1) The emphasis is on law and the insistence that biblical morality ought to be the foundation for all civil law. (2) Stress is placed on the sovereign authority of God as judge and ruler. (3) Great optimism is placed on the church, the coming of the Kingdom, and the influence of the church on the world. God's Kingdom becomes visible in the political-social order. The church is seen as the custodian of God's rule on earth. God rules also through the political structures, which God has divinely ordained. Signs of the Kingdom are righteousness in society and God's blessing, including prosperity, on God's people. Enemies are the satanic forces, as well as all political, social, and economic forces opposed to God's rule. It has a popular appeal because of its confidence that the gospel can be applied to the present social order. The main line is that God's reign is a socially transforming reality and "that the Kingdom comes gradually now, not in some future cataclysm."[44]

The second model of the "already" is called the Kingdom as Christian culture. Here again the Kingdom is seen not merely as present or as the inward experience of believers, but as an active, dynamic principle of social reconstruction empowered by God's Spirit. The Kingdom is present, not just future; social, not just individual; material, not just spiritual. The metaphor of leaven might be adequate for describing this model because it sees the Kingdom as an active, transforming agent in society. Still more accurate would be the image of enlightenment. The Kingdom progressively illuminates humankind, overcoming fear and ignorance, bringing about a better world. The transformation unfolds gradually, not cataclysmically. Three key features of this model are: relevance, transformation, and optimism. (1) This model stresses the present social relevance of the Kingdom, often in conscious contrast to more otherworldly views. Kingdom is a present social reality broader than the church. God intends the redemption of the entire social order. (2) The accent is transformation through social, political, and economic realities. The Kingdom is a social program, the logical and necessary working out of the gospel in society. One cannot restrict the gospel to spiritual experience and the church. (3) This model reveals an optimism about the social transformation of the world. The power of the gospel can bring a world of peace, justice, and harmony now, within history. Human effort is stressed and human responsibility is seen as playing an important role in bringing about the fullness of the Kingdom.

The third model listed under the "already" is the Kingdom as earthly utopia. The Kingdom can be understood as an earthly utopia—a perfect society on earth rather than a "heavenly city." Three marks identify this model: (1) It has a strong visionary character, highly idealistic in its vision of earthly society and its optimism about what can be accomplished through human effort. (2) It embodies the ideal of the Golden Age to be experienced by humanity. (3) It attempts to build a utopian community or society as a prototype of the age to come.

In this Kingdom vision the final goal is a perfect, harmonious, balanced society on earth in which there is peace and economic justice. Those who now embody this vision are participants in the Kingdom, but potentially all of humanity and the whole earth may receive the Kingdom. The primary modern-day version of this vision has been Marxist communism, a secularized, materialistic version of the Christian hope of the Kingdom.

For all their legitimate stress on the Kingdom present and its world-transforming power, the danger of these three models is that they easily forget that the Kingdom remains God's work and cannot be achieved by human activity. We can only receive it as a gracious gift from God, and in response we may radiate God's Kingdom into the world in which we live. We are God's cooperators, but the Kingdom remains God's until its final coming.

CONCLUSION

We must continually orient our self-image and our worldview to Jesus' vision of reality if we want to call ourselves Christians. He came to convey a vision which outshines every utopian dream humankind has ever conceived or will ever conceive. He was obsessed by this vision. For it he lived, worked, suffered and died. He left behind a community of disciples whom he commissioned to carry on this vision and to make the Kingdom present wherever they lived and worked. Christ does not expect us to be successful in this task in the same way the world talks about success. Rather, we are to be faithful to the power of the Kingdom in us and around us. We are not the builders of the Kingdom; it is God who gives it. It will come to completion at the time and under the circumstances God finds appropriate. Our task is to witness to this presence of the Kingdom, to make it felt by our concern for "justice, peace, and joy" where we live and work, and to challenge every human society to restructure itself according to the Kingdom's principles. We will never build a perfect society where peace and justice are fully established. Our task is to set up signs on the way to the Kingdom; signs which radiate the vision of Christ into a world that looks, at times, so hopeless and doomed. By so doing we are called to provide a vision for which we can live, work, and die. Fackre expresses our task when he writes:

> The confidence that the End will truly consummate the purposes of God, as anticipated by Exodus and Easter, energizes the believing community to set up signs on the way to the kingdom and city. Hope mobilizes, while despair paralyzes. The content of the End—glorified bodies, the "holy City with the radiance of some priceless jewel" (Rv 21:11), crystal waters, and flourishing forests—renders unacceptable emancipated [emaciated] bodies, cities of the homeless and hapless, poisonous rivers, and decimated forests.
>
> Eschatology makes us pilgrims and strangers in the wilderness short of the New Creation and disturbers of the facile peace of the way things are.[45]

Both aspects of the Kingdom, the already and the not yet, must be held in dialectical tension. On the level of inner-earthly involvement in the name of the Kingdom present, the proponents of the not yet seem to maintain consciously or unconsciously a dualistic worldview, or at best acknowledge a duality of faith and history that is always on the verge of relapsing into dualism. Their concept of the Kingdom of God as being already present in history is rather barren. While not denying its presence, they constantly presume that this world and its structures cannot be transformed before the second coming of the Son of Man. To the extent that God's final shalom for the world and creation is postponed until the future coming of Christ, it is logical for them to speak of salvation in exclusively personal and apolitical ways.[46]

The temptation of the defender of the already is to identify the Kingdom consciously or unconsciously with one or another earthly goal. Maybe the tension cannot be solved completely. Could it be that we will have to settle with two types of Christianity as seen by

Schillebeeckx? The not yet type will constantly bear witness to the future fulfillment still to come. The already type will "prepare the matter for the Kingdom by building a better future on earth."[47] One could express it this way: Our hope in the final consummation of what is already at work makes us pilgrims and strangers (not yet) in the wilderness short of the New Creation and disturbers (already) of the facile peace of the way things are.[48]

Jesus had a vision for the whole of creation that he came to throw like fire into this world (Lk 12:49). He then entrusted this vision to his disciples. We who want to follow in his footsteps will never make this vision acceptable and attractive to anyone if we ourselves are not enthused by it and on fire with it. What the present world seems to be most in need of is people who can provide and radiate an inspiring vision. Paul VI put it this way:

And may this world of ours which is searching with anguish, sometimes with hope, be enabled to receive the Good News not from evangelizers who are dejected, discouraged, impatient or anxious, but from ministers of the Gospel whose lives glow with fervor, who have received the joy of Christ (*Evangelii Nuntiandi* 80).

Part 3

THE KINGDOM AND JESUS CHRIST

16

The Kingdom of God and the Person of Jesus

INTRODUCTION

What is the connection between the Kingdom of God, which Jesus preached as having arrived, and the preacher himself? Does the person of Jesus have anything to do with the message he preached? Is it the Kingdom that interprets the person of Jesus as well as his mission, or is it Jesus who interprets the Kingdom? There is a noticeable shift in the New Testament between the object of preaching before Easter and after Easter; Jesus the preacher of the Kingdom of God becomes after Easter the object of preaching, Jesus the Christ. Is this shift from the Kingdom to Jesus a legitimate transition or is it a distortion?

As we saw, there are six fundamental tension points or polarities that are central to the mystery of the Kingdom of God. It is of tantamount importance to recognize these polarities as biblical. They are the following: (1) present *vs.* future (already—not yet); (2) individual *vs.* social; (3) Spirit *vs.* matter (religious—political); (4) gradual *vs.* climactic (eschatological—apocalyptic); (5) divine action *vs.* human action (gift and task); and, (6) the church's relationship to the Kingdom; the tension seeing the church and the Kingdom as essentially the same and as clearly different. Any theology of the Kingdom that dissolves these tensions, opting wholly for one side or the other, is to that degree unbiblical. A true Kingdom theology will in some way maintain and live with these tensions.[1] The question is, How are these polarities related to the person of Jesus? In the Christian scriptures the picture of Jesus emerges more clearly than does the profile of the Kingdom. Consequently, the starting point for the ultimate understanding and interpretation of the Kingdom of God seems to be the person of Jesus himself. The Kingdom must be explained and comprehended in the light of Jesus Christ. Only in so doing can we also say that Jesus Christ is to be understood in the light of the Kingdom theme.[2] Or in the words of Jürgen Moltmann:

Whoever becomes involved with Jesus, becomes involved with the kingdom of God. This is unavoidably so, because the concern of Jesus—then and now—was and is the "kingdom of God." Whoever searches for God and asks about the kingdom wherein "righteousness and peace kiss each other" (Ps 85:10) must look to Jesus and immerse themselves in his story—the narration of events that took place in the past but still occur today through the spirit. This is self-evident and quite in our grasp, because the response to the question of who is Jesus is that he is none other than the kingdom of God in person. Jesus and the Kingdom of God, the Kingdom of God and Jesus, the two are inseparable. . . . If then, one wants to learn about the mysteries of the "kingdom of God," one must look to Jesus; and if one wants to understand who this Jesus is, one must first experience the kingdom of God.[3]

Whatever definition one wants to give to the symbol of the Kingdom, it definitely must center on its dimension as God's ultimate offer of *unconditional love*. The concrete form of God's "final visitation" was becoming man in Jesus of Nazareth. Only in him, then, can we come to understand the real meaning of the Kingdom he preached. This coming of God to redeem God's creatures must be considered within the total scheme of creation.

GOD'S DESIGN FOR CREATION

Creation and the Fall

There is an intentionality in the whole of creation, a "dynamis" (power) that will move humankind and all creation with it to its final goal. That goal is not to be understood as "destiny," as something that will come by necessity or by the forces of nature as predicted by historical and dialectic materialism. Christian faith understands this finality of all creation as a "love-gift" from God. It is an offer to enter into a relationship of love with God in which we remain free to accept or to reject this gift. The final goal of God for creation is, therefore, to give us a share in divine life and through us to lead the whole of creation into the New Heaven and the New Earth. Toward this goal "the creation waits with eager longing" that it may come to pass (Rom 8:19).

The realization of this divine intentionality for creation, even if only faint, can be detected in every culture and people of this earth. History as a whole, in spite of being permeated by sin, is to be understood as God's self-communication to humankind. However, history as such remains an ambiguous sign of this self-communication of God because of the ambiguity of the yes or no with which each person responds to God.[4]

This great offer of God's gift of love can only be accepted in freedom. We are respected as partners in the Covenant, and we can say no. Without our free acceptance of this love-gift the divine intentionality cannot become reality. The two words *free* and *creature* seem to stand in dialectical opposition to each other. The word *free* makes us divine and the word *creature* indicates that we can possess the divine only as a free gift from God. Humankind can find its final fulfillment and true authenticity only if it freely accepts God's offer as an unmerited gift of love. The last security, the only "rock and amen" on which we can ultimately stand, is God's unconditional love which we do not deserve but can accept in gratitude and joy. We must understand ourselves as being created by this love, held in existence by it, and called to find ourselves in it. The inexplicable mystery is that human beings can refuse to accept this final call. The constant temptation for a free human being is to create an alternative basis on which to stand. It is to deny that the only secure ground is that which comes as a gift from God. This temptation seems to be built into our nature since we are created as free beings and yet remain creatures whose vocation is to share in the divine life of God.

The story of the fall in Genesis is portrayed as a broken Covenant that God had made with Adam and Eve. The disastrous effect of the fall is that humankind has no more basis to stand on. Original sin is humankind's refusal to accept the ultimate basis for existence from God as a free gift. The only hope left is that God's love will not let humanity remain in this hopeless and desperate situation. Revelation shows that God has never abandoned us. Immediately after the fall he took Adam and Eve and "covered their shame." It is as if God took part of the blame for humanity's fall by defending them against the serpent, the great tempter (Gn 3:21).

God's Re-creation: The Covenant with Israel

God's divine intention is clearly visible and tangible in God's entrance into the history of the chosen people in the Old Testament. The "Covenant formula" has to be considered as the most suitable expression of God's intention for creation: "in order that he may establish you today as his people, and that he may be your God" (Dt 29:13). This phrase contains in a nutshell the meaning of revelation and shows God's ultimate intention for the whole of humankind:

> Then I saw a new heaven and a new earth. . . . And I saw the holy city, the new Jerusalem, coming down out of heaven from

God, prepared as a bride adorned for her husband. And I heard a loud voice from the throne saying,

> "See, the home of God is among mortals.
> He will dwell with them as their God;
> they will be his peoples,
> and God himself will be with them."
>
> (Rv 21:1-3)

God did not leave humanity on the road of total destruction but cared for us from the very beginning. The Covenant with Israel is the first historically visible step of God to effect the promise made to Adam after that initial rejection. From the viewpoint of revelation God steps into history by calling Abraham to be the Father of faith in order to bring about God's plan of salvation within human history. Through Abraham a whole people is called to bring about this intention and a special Covenant is established to make visible this design for the whole of creation. The Covenant is a concrete realization of and witness to a people living out of God's loving care. Their response to this new initiative of God was to demonstrate what is in store for the whole of humankind.

The Covenant, however, proved to be a failure with respect to Israel's response. The history of the Covenant people became a history of a broken Covenant; the people were unable to respond in a way that could have made the Covenant the new creation. The fundamental insight of the Old Testament is that we are unable to respond to God's loving self-communication in a way that would realize the final goal of humankind. It is from this insight that we must look to the emerging hope for a Messiah, who alone could make the Covenant come true. He would accomplish what we had been unable to achieve: the appropriate loving response to God's offer of salvation.

GOD'S INTENTION IN JESUS

Jesus in the Context of the Covenant

Jesus' whole life must be seen in the setting of Israel's history and its Covenant with God. Jesus makes sense only in this context.[5] He was sent to complete the Covenant. Theologically, Jesus is God's ultimate offer of unconditional love and our response (through Jesus) to that offer.

The two concepts of *identification* and *representation* are of great importance if we are to understand the mission of Christ at all. Jesus is the Covenant in his person; that is, he is not only God's self-communication to us (identification), but also the complete human response taken on our behalf (representation). Having assumed our nature—God's union and communion with us—he, as one of us now, represents us to God—our union with God. He is the fulfillment of God's intentionality for creation: God's final and unambiguous self-communication to humankind.

But this Covenant of God with humankind took place in the "condition of a broken Covenant," in a sin-permeated world, in the context of God's Covenant constantly broken by God's chosen people. The incarnation, life, and death of Jesus takes place in such a history. It is from this perspective that we must look at Jesus' Kingdom message and the mission he came to accomplish.

The Origin of Jesus' Message of the Kingdom

How did Jesus come to the image of the Kingdom of God as the center of his preaching? Nothing is said in the Bible about Jesus' earlier life, though he was known in his hometown. The notion of the Kingdom must have come to him before he actually started his ministry.

Scholars trace the origin of Jesus' use of this phrase to several sources: First, *social-historical*—from the preoccupation of his contemporaries with the idea of the immediate coming of the Kingdom for which various groups had dedicated themselves through prayer and lifestyle or through armed struggle. The general mood of the Jews at the time of Jesus was an expectancy that Yahweh would come soon to establish his rule forever. The coming Kingdom was the talk of the day. Some inspiration could have come to Jesus from these revolutionists, whose base of operation was Galilee. Jesus did not join them, although he shared their radicalism for God's sovereign rule over everything.

Second, *liturgical*—from the Kaddish-prayer used in the liturgy with its fervent petition for the coming of God's Rule. This request became, in the Our Father, the central petition of a disciple of Jesus.

Third, *personal*—from Jesus' own experience of Israel's God as Father, which was Jesus' own unique way of addressing God. It is this unusual use of the word *Abba* for God that seems to have been the ultimate source of Jesus' choice to center his preaching around the symbol Kingdom of God. [6]

Where did Jesus find this image? Attempts have been made to trace Jesus' *Abba* experience back to his childhood. Although theology does not easily take psychological reasoning into consideration, the following observations deserve attention unless one rejects all historical background concerning the infancy narratives in Luke and Matthew.[7]

We know better than other generations before us that the first years of our life are decisive. The way we look at reality, the way we perceive God, the way we relate to God are all fixed in childhood. Our images of human beings and of God are conditioned for the rest of our life by how we have experienced our mother and father. Our image of God is based on the God-image of our parents. Their image will remain with us throughout our life unless we try seriously to change it. Whether God has a loving face or not depends on whether we experienced a friendly and loving face in our parents. If we take incarnation seriously, we must ask what kind of God-image Jesus' parents had. Only thus can we get at the roots of Jesus' perception of God.

Luke introduces the parents of John the Baptist as belonging to the "just of Israel" and as "well versed" in the Torah:

> Both of them were righteous before God, living blamelessly according to all the commandments and regulations of the Lord (Lk 1:6).

Zechariah belonged to the priestly caste and Elizabeth to the tribe of Aaron. Mary, the mother of Jesus, was related to Elizabeth. Luke presents Elizabeth as well as Mary as being versed in the Torah. Both knew the tradition of their fathers and mothers, which can be seen in their respective hymns. At least this much we can say, Jesus seems to have grown up in an environment that knew the Torah and the tradition well.

This impression is reenforced when we look at the gospel of Matthew. Joseph is called just, which means he is observant of the Torah. *Just* meant to be one of those who kept the directions and the demands of God as revealed and laid down in the Law and the Prophets. To call Joseph a just man was to say that he had a sufficient knowledge of the Torah. In addition, Matthew tells us that Joseph was of the lineage of David. He was, therefore, a just one (*zadik*) and of Davidic descent, which meant he had a double obligation to keep the Torah.

But Matthew gives us another hint of the way Jesus will later deal with the Torah. Joseph, the just man, provides us with an unusual interpretation of the Torah.

> Joseph, being a righteous man and unwilling to expose her to public disgrace, planned to dismiss her quietly (Mt 1:19).

Joseph interprets the Law in terms of mercy and compassion, not in the strict sense which would denounce Mary publicly as an adulterous woman, leading in turn to her being stoned. The Law gave him not only the backing for doing so, but also actually demanded it. Joseph, however, acts differently. His behavior is unusual. He could only act as he did if his God-image "allowed" him such behavior. With the commonly held God-image, he would have been obliged to expose

Mary in public. But Joseph interpreted the Torah differently. His God knew compassion and mercy and wanted it to be applied to human beings accordingly.

We might therefore conclude that Jesus' unusual God-image had its roots in the faith of his parents. According to Luke, the maternal side of Jesus seems to have been shaped profoundly by the apocalyptic expectation of his time. The paternal side of Jesus seems to have conveyed to him an image of God that was compassionate and kind toward human beings. Joseph, the Torah-observing Jew, presents us with a God-image that was different from the common view. That image he communicated to Jesus. "Keep the Law but interpret it compassionately" seems to have been the teaching that Joseph transmitted to the Immanuel. It is possible that Joseph was the first one who taught Jesus to call God *Abba*.[8]

Joseph's view reaffirms what can be found in prophets like Hosea and Isaiah:

> When Israel was a child, I loved him,
>   and out of Egypt I called my son.
> The more I called them,
>   the more they went from me; . . .
> Yet it was I who taught Ephraim to walk,
>   I took them up in my arms; . . .
> I led them with cords of human kindness,
>   with band of love;
> I was to them like those
>   who lift infants to their cheeks.
>   I bent down to them and fed them.
>   (Hos 11:1-4)

> Look down from heaven and see,
>   from your holy and glorious habitation.
> Where are your zeal and your might?
>   The yearning of your heart and your
>   compassion?
>   They are withheld from me.
> For you are our father,
>   though Abraham does not know us
>   and Israel does not acknowledge us;
> you, O LORD, are our father;
>   our Redeemer from of old is your name.
>   (Is 63:15-16)

Jesus must have heard these texts in the synagogue of Nazareth and in his parents' house. It was this God-image that formed him. Yet, one day he would have to decide himself what image of God he would accept for the rest of his life.

Jesus decided one day to go to John at the Jordan. He let himself be baptized by John and joined the group of John's disciples.[9] How long Jesus spent with John is not easy to determine. Certainly he was a disciple long enough for some of John's disciples to transfer their allegiance to him. The Baptist himself might have directed some of his disciples to Jesus as the gospel of John suggests (Jn 1:29-35). He could have seen in Jesus an assistant as Elijah had Elisha (1 Kgs 19:16-21) and as Jeremiah had in Baruch (Jer 36). Since Jesus was a relative of the Baptist, the choice was, according to the Oriental mentality, all the more obvious. According to John 3:22 and 4:1-4 Jesus seems to have exercised at the beginning of his public life a ministry which was identical to that of John the Baptist, centered on the administration of the baptism of repentance in view of the eschatological judgment that would precede the coming of God's final Kingdom. At that stage Jesus' ministry was an extension of the Baptist's ministry.[10]

Two questions which may be raised almost immediately are: Why did Jesus change the ministry of John radically both in content and lifestyle? What brought about this change? The answers vary. A number of exegetes suggest it was Jesus' personal experience of being bestowed with the power of the Spirit which convinced him, that not the demand for repentance sealed by baptism as the Baptist had seen it could save, but only the Kingdom of God that was already working in him through the power of the Holy Spirit (Mt 12:28). For James G.D. Dunn it was Jesus' consciousness of having the eschatological Spirit working in him and his sense of sonship that caused him to move away from the Baptist's message of repentance and impending judgment. Dunn explains:

> Jesus thought of himself as God's son and as anointed by the eschatological Spirit, because in prayer he experienced God as Father and in his ministry he experienced a power to heal which he could only understand as the power of the end-time and an inspiration to proclaim a message which he could only understand as the gospel of the end-time.[11]

Bruners sees the conversion that made Jesus change from being a disciple of John in their opposing God-images.[12] The message of the Baptist aimed at leading people back to Yahweh and preparing them for the terrible judgment that was imminent before the Kingdom would come. This message of John seems to have first appealed to Jesus; he was familiar with this kind of thinking, at least as far as his mother's side was concerned.

At first Jesus might have been attracted by John's image of God, which insisted that only the just had a chance to enter the Kingdom. Although John opened the door of conversion for all, his God-image remained austere and stern. Jesus must have realized that he could not share this image of God. Soon he left John's view behind and chose the God who was kind and compassionate with people. He decided for a motherly-fatherly face of God. His view of reality had become different: God was gracious and compassionate and so was reality as a whole. Without this basic trust in a God who is gracious and compassionate, Jesus' love and compassion for all human beings is not understandable.

When John had been put into prison Jesus started his own preaching. But he does not take up any of the catch phrases of John in his proclamation of the Kingdom. The message of Jesus is not composed of stern warnings and threats of an impending judgment; rather, it is a message of consolation and great joy. Jesus tells his audience that God is coming in love and forgiveness, not in anger and wrath.

The gospels suggest that the breakthrough of this motherly-fatherly image of God happened in connection with Jesus' baptism by John. Here Jesus was affirmed in his God-image and was told that he was both infinitely loved and the "beloved son." This gave Jesus a self-confidence that never left him. He was not only the son, but it was also made known to him that he was "the one." This affirmation was given to him once again in the transfiguration story: "This is my beloved son, listen to him" (Mk 9:7). In the gospel of John, Jesus lives totally from this reality and his mission consists in conveying this message to his disciples.[13]

J. Jeremias sees the real origin of Jesus' Kingdom message in his *Abba* Experience, which Jesus received and expressed in his prayer.[14] H. Schürmann agrees with this view. For him, the Kingdom message was "sent" to Jesus in his prayer and therefore is intimately tied to his personal experience of God as *Abba*. Jesus experienced God as one coming as unconditional love, entering human history in a way and to a degree not known by the prophets. This experience of God, which Jesus realized and which determined his whole life, is the real core of the Kingdom message. It led Jesus away from his family to the Jordan. If Jesus lived unmarried among his peers, then the Kingdom message of the Father's incomprehensible love for humankind came early to him. Matthew 19:12 gives us the reason why he remained unmarried: "For the Kingdom's sake."[15]

In the same way, some parables point to an overwhelming, personal experience early in Jesus' life; for example, the Costly Pearl and the Treasure in the Field (Mt 13:44-46). Some exegetes have said that these two parables are a key that unlocks the other parables and, with that, the whole mystery of Jesus' proclamation.[16] The ultimate root of Jesus' Kingdom message should be regarded then as his *Abba* experience, which formed the heart of his entire message.

God's Ultimate Offer of Salvation

The earthly life of Jesus can be outlined briefly from the above perspective. The starting point is the statement in Philippians 2:7 that he was human in every aspect except sin. Jesus was born into the culture and religion of the Jewish people. There he learned about Yahweh who had elected the chosen people and had promised them through the prophets a "final visitation"—soon to come—which would complete all prior promises. Jesus, who from early childhood on experienced such an intense love relationship with Yahweh that he came to call him *Abba*, realized at some stage of his life that Yahweh wanted to lead Israel and ultimately all human beings into that intimacy and love which he himself experienced. This is expressed most explicitly in the Lord's Prayer. Here Jesus authorized his disciples to follow him in addressing God as *Abba*. By doing so he allowed them to participate in his own communion with God. Only those who can say this childlike *Abba* will be able to enter the Kingdom of God.[17] However, Jesus also sensed that his own relationship with God was distinctive. He realized that the relationship he wanted to offer to all was dependent on his own.[18]

In Jesus the Father wanted to establish the Covenant. Jesus perceived this as the Kingdom of God, which was to come through him into the world as God's unconditional love, a love that knows no limits in fulfilling the age-old promise of salvation for every person and the whole of creation.

Jesus started to preach *his* message of the Kingdom, God's ultimate offer of love, as the new basis for finding salvation once again. This offer of love would be accessible only through him. Anyone who would come in contact with Jesus would be in contact with God's unconditional love for creation. The demand for conversion consists then in turning to Jesus and in accepting in him God's salvific love. This offer is made to those who know that they have no claim on God through their religious practices and good works, nor any claim on society through their prestige, power, or wealth. They are asked only to let God's gracious gift enter their lives and to allow themselves to be transformed in the process.

Since Jesus himself is God's ultimate offer to us, then he is God's Kingdom present in the world. Jesus is the Kingdom in person, the "auto-*Basileia*," or, as Origen put it: "Jesus is the Kingdom of God realized in a self." John Paul II speaks in the following terms:

The proclamation and establishment of God's Kingdom are the purpose of Jesus' mission: "I was sent for this purpose" (Lk 4:43). But that is not all. Jesus himself is the "good news," as he declares at the very beginning of his mission in the synagogue of Nazareth when he applies to himself the words of Isaiah about the Anointed One sent by the Spirit of the Lord (cf. Lk 4:14-21). Since the "good news" is Christ, there is an identification between the message and the messenger, between saying, doing and being. His power, the secret of the effectiveness of his actions, lies in his total identification with the message he announces: He proclaims the "good news" not just by what he says or does, but by what he is (*Redemptoris Missio* 13).

The breaking-in of the Kingdom takes place through the ministry of Jesus, in which the newness of the Kingdom visibly manifests itself. Here the Kingdom becomes a present experience and so no longer remains only a hope. The activity of Jesus during his earthly ministry can be defined as a *sacrament*, because it makes the fullness and finality of the Kingdom visible on the horizon of human history. The Kingdom as a present reality becomes visible on two levels: Jesus' activity, and his life.

On the level of *activity*, Jesus' miracles demonstrate that God wants to repair the brokenness of human existence and allow us to participate in the divine life. Healings, as well as exorcisms, demonstrate the presence of God's Kingdom in the world now. They indicate the kind of world the Kingdom ushers in. When the Kingdom of God arrives, sickness and disease simply must disappear.[19]

On the level of *life*, the criterion of the Kingdom becomes incarnate and is made visible. In the presence of God, Jesus lives as the Son with a total dedication to the Father who is everything to him. In the presence of other human beings he lives as one who welcomes sinners, acts like a servant, puts brotherhood above religious cult, subordinates the Law and sacred institutions—like the Sabbath—to the physical welfare of persons in need, disregards all qualifications arising from social status or past history, and demonstrates that every human being can look forward to a future.

The earthly and historical ministry of Jesus as the sacrament of God's reign present in history rectifies and demystifies all superficial presentations of the inner nature of the Kingdom of God as the goal of history. In him the Kingdom manifested itself to a degree never yet seen. Jesus' lifestyle in history demonstrated in a sacramental way, that is, in an anticipatory way, the fullness of the Kingdom. Since his coming the Kingdom becomes an initial possibility for all through faith in him. Through commitment to Jesus it is possible to make the

Kingdom present as he did, through activity and life. Only that commitment to act and to live as he did will clarify for us who he is and who acted through him.[20]

Jesus embodies in his person all the Kingdom polarities mentioned earlier. He introduces the Kingdom in a twofold way. He proclaims it as present *now*, not as utopia for the end of the world. And he offers a vision of a future completeness. That vision keeps us from frustration in the face of history's ambiguities and helps us to avoid the incoherence of immediate responses that presume we can build the Kingdom in its fullness now.[21] Furthermore, in Jesus all the earthly, this-worldly promises of the Kingdom so much stressed in the Old Testament will find their fulfillment. Jesus shows us clearly in his incarnation, life and death that God intends to save us with our environment, not without it.[22]

The Death of Jesus and the Final Coming of the Kingdom

Theologically we could say that in the incarnation Jesus identified with us. Although without sin (Phil 2), he took upon himself our "situation in its state of broken existence." He entered a world of people who had no ground on which to stand, who were cut off from God and from each other.

Jesus not only identified himself with us. He also represented us to the Father; he would give the ultimate response on our behalf (Heb 8-10) so that the Covenant of humankind with God might finally come true. His life was ruled by two principles. First, he was totally dedicated to his Father: "My food is to do the will of him who sent me" (Jn 4:34). From the Father Jesus drew his life; God was the "rock" on which Jesus stood, his Amen. To God he dedicated his whole life. Second, he was totally dedicated to his mission, that is, to us: "No one has greater love than this, to lay down one's life for one's friends" (Jn 15:13).

Jesus preached his message of God's love with great enthusiasm, hoping that Israel as a whole would respond spontaneously and generously to his offer. But very quickly Jesus came to realize that Israel would not listen to his message. What ought he to do next? What is the connection between the Kingdom that Jesus preached and his death on the cross? Was Jesus' death necessary for the Kingdom in its fullness to come?

Historical Reasons for Jesus' Death

With historical certainty most scholars agree that Jesus was condemned on two charges. First, he was condemned as a political agitator, as "King of the Jews" according to the inscription on the cross.

This was the Roman version. The Romans at least must have thought him dangerous for exciting the hopes and dreams of the Jews. At the same time, however, they must have regarded his movement as harmless, because they left his disciples unmolested.[23]

Second, Jesus was put to death by his own people on charges of being a false prophet and a blasphemer. Was it Jesus' stand toward Judaism that finally brought him the death sentence, or was his death the plot of the Temple aristocracy, as some scholars would have it? Each side has its arguments. Those who plead for Jesus' opposition to Judaism present the following arguments: (1) Jesus placed himself in direct opposition to Jewish religious practices: his demand to let the dead bury their dead in Matthew 8:22 was seen as a violation of something holy to all religions; his attitude toward women was at the least very unusual; his rejection of fasting in Mark 2:18ff. was disqualifying behavior for a religious teacher. (2) Jesus' attitude to the outcasts of society was unacceptable: his association with tax-gatherers was an outrageous provocation from the Jewish point of view. It was scandalous to take into one's company those who had separated themselves from the true Israel; Jesus' fundamental openness to Gentiles and half-pagan Samaritans was incredible; and (3) Jesus' stand toward the Torah, the final dispensation of the divine purpose of God, was untraditional: he continually broke the Sabbath Law which was punishable in the Torah by death (Mk 2:27; 3:4); he continually violated the cultic purity laws that were so important to the Pharisees as well to the Qumran community. Mark 7:15 is a radical criticism of the whole concept of purity laws; he denied the possibility of divorce (Mk 10:6-8), which was against the Torah (Dt 24:1ff).

These arguments lead to the conclusion that

> for Jesus the Torah no longer formed the focus and ultimate standard. Jesus—unlike the whole body of his Jewish contemporaries—stood not *under* but *above* the Torah received by Moses at Sinai. This is the deepest reason why there could be no understanding between Jesus and a Jew of Qumran or of Pharisaic practice.[24]

All the above-mentioned reasons about Jesus being in opposition to Judaism and the Torah can also be explained in the way we outlined earlier. Jesus was not against the Torah but against the way his opponents interpreted it. For them the key to interpretation was holiness and purity; for Jesus it was justice and compassion. A careful reading of the gospels shows that in almost all instances where Jesus seems to break the Law, he does it out of concern for people and their well-being. He does not break the Law because he feels above it, but because it had been wrongly understood and interpreted. What his

opponents could not tolerate was Jesus's claim that the correct interpretation of the Law had nothing to do with holiness and purity but
everything to do with compassion and justice.

Other scholars see the hostility against Jesus explained not by his
opposition to Judaism but to the Temple aristocracy—the priests and
the Temple nobility whose status was dependent on the Temple and
its economy. As G. V. Pixley sees it: "The Jesus movement saw the
principal obstacle to the realization of God's Kingdom in Palestine to
be the Temple and the class structure that it supported." Pixley regards the strategy of Jesus as one of ideological attack. Jesus suppos-
edly regarded the Temple domination as more oppressive than the
Roman occupation forces, and so he intended to do away with the
Temple structures first. Pixley, however, sees Jesus' chief enemies as
being the Pharisees in Galilee and the priests in Jerusalem. He regards
both groups as the principal beneficiaries of the class system. The Pharisees are the ones who taught the religious ideology that supported the
priestly class.[25]

The symbolic actions of Jesus—like his threat against the Temple
and his entry into Jerusalem on an ass as a would-be king—demonstrated the nearness of a new order which had to be seen as a challenge to the existing order. Jesus is understood to have regarded the
Temple economy, guaranteed by the Temple aristocracy, as directly
opposed to the Kingdom he was proclaiming.

According to Lohfink, the last straw, which provoked Jesus' condemnation by the leaders of Israel, was his cleansing of the Temple
and his prophecy about it. Lohfink concludes:

> The factor that most deeply determined their position was Jesus'
> criticism of Temple practices. In a situation that is no longer
> reconstructible, Jesus must have openly taken position against
> the Sadducean-priestly Temple ideology. Certainly he spoke
> through a prophetically barbed utterance about the final destruc-
> tion of the Temple, but also of its miraculous new foundation by
> God. He might have expressed a prediction such as the follow-
> ing: "The Temple will be destroyed and in three days again be
> rebuilt" (cf. Mk 13:2ff.; Jn 2:19). In connection with this pro-
> vocative utterance there certainly followed a prophetic symbolic
> action, the so-called cleansing of the Temple (cf. Mk 11:15-19,
> 27ff.). By so acting Jesus called into question what for the
> Saddcuees was absolutely the central institution which guaran-
> teed the country's welfare.[26]

Israel, whose Covenant was based on an egalitarian society, had become a class society where the wealthy and influential lived at the

expense of the poor and outcast. The Temple economy was the sign of this deterioration.

Once again the Covenant community had reverted to a society of oppression and slavery as in the days of Solomon and Jeremiah. Moses' vision of a "contrast society" of justice and compassion over against Pharaoh's society of oppression and slavery had effectively been dismantled. The aristocracy of Israel had once again managed to create a society of security and oppression of which the Temple and its socio-economic base were the most obvious signs.

Israel's security had become the Temple and no longer the free God of the Exodus, who could not be manipulated as a mouthpiece of the powerful and who would not "sanction" their understanding and interpretation of the Covenant and the tradition.

Jesus, like Jeremiah in his days, saw destruction coming. This he expressed openly in his threat against the Temple, as Jeremiah had done in his time:

> Here you are, trusting in deceptive words to no avail. Will you steal, murder, commit adultery, swear falsely, make offerings to Baal, and go after other gods that you have not known, and then come and stand before me in this house, which is called by my name, and say, "We are safe!"—only to go on doing all these abominations? Has this house, which is called by my name, become a den of robbers in your sight? You know I too am watching, says the LORD. Go now to my place that was in Shiloh, where I made my name dwell at first, and see what I did to it for the wickedness of my people Israel. And now, because you have done all these things, says the LORD, and when I spoke to you persistently, you did not listen, and when I called you, you did not answer, therefore I will do to the house that is called by my name, in which you trust, and to the place that I gave to you and to your ancestors, just what I did to Shiloh. And I will cast you out of my sight, just as I cast out all your kinsfolk, all the offspring of Ephraim (Jer 7:8-15).

Jesus' attitude toward the Temple (Mk 11:15-19) was correctly understood by his opponents as a prophetic criticism like that of Jeremiah, indicating the end of the present regime, announcing the coming of a new age. Brueggemann explains:

> This was the most ominous threat because there he spoke directly about the destruction. He quotes Jeremiah 7:11 and with it mobilizes the painful memory of dismantling criticism and in fact radically replicating it.[27]

But there is no joy or pleasure on Jesus' part in foreseeing the down-fall of his people and its institutions. Like Jeremiah, there was only room for lament and grief. Jesus could only weep for his people and the city he loved so much and whose salvation he had sought so earnestly. They had failed to recognize in him the one whom God had sent for the final restoration of the Covenant and the coming of God's Kingdom for the salvation of all.

> "Jerusalem, Jerusalem, the city that kills the prophets and stones those who are sent to it! How often have I desired to gather your children together as a hen gathers her brood under her wings, and you were not willing! See, your house is left to you. And I tell you, you will not see me until the time comes when you say, 'Blessed is the one who comes in the name of the Lord!'" (Lk 13:34-35).

> As he came near and saw the city, he wept over it, saying, "If you, even you, had only recognized on this day the things that make for peace! But now they are hidden from your eyes" (Lk 19:41-42).

There was nothing further Jesus could do but to take upon himself the "perversion," the "numbness" of his people and suffer in compassion the coming catastrophe in his own body so that the new humanity might finally be born and God's ultimate plan be achieved.

The Temple nobility, therefore, had a vested interest in getting rid of this troublemaker who challenged the present social and political order with its respective power and property relations expressed in the Temple economy. By proclaiming its imminent dissolution through the breaking-in of the Kingdom, Jesus touched a very sensitive nerve. This is especially true since he associated that Kingdom with his person. Although Jesus' actions were in no way a direct political threat to the establishment, the Jewish authority found them too dangerous to ignore.[28]

But the real question remains: How did Jesus understand his death? How did he interpret his failure? Numerous solutions have been offered. It is not easy to discover Jesus' own understanding. The only source, the gospels themselves, present Jesus' death and his interpretation of it from the post-Easter perspective. That makes it almost impossible to say which sayings are authentic.[29]

The Fate of Prophets in Israel

Jesus, standing in the prophetic tradition of Israel, could foresee quite early a fatal end to his mission. In Mark 2:7 he is immediately accused of blasphemy, a crime that carried the death penalty. The hostility of the leaders started at the beginning and increased throughout his whole public ministry. The fate of John the Baptist was a clear indication of what could happen to him. Jesus was familiar with the widespread tradition of late Judaism that Israel had murdered most of its prophets. He who saw himself in line with the great prophets had to expect a similar fate. Texts like Luke 13:32-33 and Matthew 23:31-39 seem to be biographical:

> Yet today, tomorrow, and the next day I must be on my way, because it is impossible for a prophet to be killed outside of Jerusalem (Lk 13:33).

> Thus you testify against yourselves that you are descendants of those who murdered the prophets. Fill up, then the measure of your ancestors (Mt 23:31-32).

The Trials Linked to the Coming of the Kingdom

Albert Schweitzer proposed a solution which has been accepted by a number of scholars. He argued that the arrival of the eschatological Kingdom of God could never have been proclaimed by Jesus without his knowledge of the trials and sufferings this apocalyptic phrase evoked. Schweitzer explains:

> The reference to the Passion belonged as a matter of course to the eschatological prediction. A time of unheard of affliction must precede the coming of the Kingdom. Out of these woes the Messiah will be brought to birth. That was a view prevalent far and wide: in no other ways could the events of the last times be imagined. According to this view Jesus' words must be interpreted. It will appear then that in his preaching of the Kingdom he brought into sharp prominence the thought of the affliction of the last times.[30]

If Jesus proclaimed the Kingdom of God as imminent, then the thought of suffering had to come to him quite naturally. It was not possible to separate the eschatological Kingdom from the thought of eschatological trial, the coming Messiah from the suffering in the age that would immediately precede the arrival of the Kingdom. Suffering had to be proclaimed as necessary for the final coming of the Kingdom of God. Although this teaching of a period of great tribulation marking the transition between the present time and the age to come was widespread in Judaism, it has to be admitted that most of these sayings occur in later rabbinic sources.[31]

The numerous references to suffering and eschatological trials in the proclamation of Jesus should be seen from this perspective. In particular, the gospel of Mark makes this connection quite obvious. Before the Galilean crisis these references are only implicit, but after the crisis the necessity of suffering and its relation to the Kingdom are openly proclaimed. Jesus, who clearly understood his connection with the coming Kingdom, realized that he had to undergo suffering and death as a necessary prerequisite for the Kingdom finally to break into this age.[32] Kasper, making Schweitzer's view his own, concludes:

> Jesus certainly saw the trials of suffering and persecution as part of the lowly and hidden character of the Kingdom of God, and as such they passed into the mainstream of his preaching. There is, therefore, a more or less straight line from Jesus' eschatological message of the *Basileia*, the Kingdom, to the mystery of his passion.[33]

The arguments about his person were connected with his message of the passing of the old and the coming of the new. Jesus accepted this conflict as part of his message and interpreted his death accordingly. Ultimately, it was the will of the Father that Jesus felt he had to fulfill at all costs. By allowing himself to be condemned by the existing order Jesus revealed the sin and the corruption of the present system as an order of death centered around the Temple. Only through his death could the corruption and alienation of the present system be overcome and the Kingdom make its final entry into human history as the only power able to set humankind free from all enslavement. Brueggemann writes:

> The crucifixion, then, is not an odd event in the history of faith, although it is the decisive event. It is, rather, the full expression of dismantling that has been practiced and insisted upon in the prophetic tradition since Moses confronted Pharaoh. As with Moses, so Jesus' ministry and death opposed the politics of oppression with the politics of justice and compassion. As with Moses, so Jesus' ministry as death resisted the economics of affluence and called for the economics of shared humanity. As with Moses, so Jesus' ministry and death contradicted the religion of God's captivity with the freedom of God to bring life where he wills, even in the face of death. The cross is the ultimate metaphor of prophetic criticism because it means the end of the old consciousness that brings death to everyone.[34]

The Last Supper and the Kingdom

The eschatological perspective of Jesus' death is evident in the passages dealing with the Last Supper (Mk 14:17-25 and 1 Cor 11:23-

25). Prior gatherings at table—that had provoked such scandal because Jesus excluded no one, not even public sinners, and which thus
expressed the heart of his message—were types of the feast to come in
the time of salvation (Mk 2:18-20). The Last Supper, as all gatherings
at table, is an anticipation or "anti-donation" or foreshadowing of
the consummation of the Kingdom. It is an "already" of the "not
yet," the advent of the perfect reign of God, the fulfillment of the
great banquet, everything that can only become a full reality after his
death. The final gathering presupposes this giving of himself for the
many:

> "Truly I tell you, I will never again drink of the fruit of the vine
> until that day when I drink it new [Mt: with you] in the kingdom
> of God."

This sentence is found in Mark 14:25 and Matthew 26:29 at the
conclusion of the eucharistic account; in Luke 22:16, on the other
hand, it is before the account. It has been shown that the wording of
Mark is closest to the original, but Luke's arrangement is preferable.
The eschatological reference has the following meaning: Jesus will no
longer sit at table with the disciples on earth but will do so again for a
new meal in the coming Kingdom of God. For this to happen his death,
which he awaits, is a necessary condition. The disciples can partake of
the final eschatological banquet only if Jesus first lays down his life
for them (Lk 22:20).[35]

To partake in the Kingdom of God is only possible after Jesus has
fulfilled its precondition, after he "has drunk the cup and has been
baptized with the baptism" (Mk 10:35-40).[36] The true nature of the
task that Jesus has to undertake in order to bring in the fullness of the
Kingdom is expressed in the words regarding the bread and wine. He
must surrender his life so that men and women may share the feast of
the Kingdom with him:

> His resolution to complete the mission that God had given him
> in relation to the Kingdom and his confidence that he would
> soon be participating in its joy sound the keynote of his last
> meal with his disciples. The Last Supper is framed in affirmation
> of the death of Jesus in prospect of the Kingdom of God.[37]

THE DEATH OF JESUS: GOD'S ULTIMATE REVELATION

At some point in his life Jesus must have come to realize that the
only way left to fulfill his mission was to demonstrate the immensity
of God's love for us to the very end (Jn 13:1). The cross and his death
appear as the only way that remained to prove God's redeeming love

in the sin-permeated history of humankind. The "Galilean crisis" is regarded by many as this turning point in Jesus' life. From then on his attention is focused on his death and suffering in Jerusalem (Mk 8:31; 9:31; 10:33; 10:45).

Even when Jesus came to realize that the will of the Father was leading him to the cross in order to prove God's love for humankind, he did not run fanatically toward the cross and his own death. Rather, Jesus was afraid and even horrified when he thought of what was to come:

> "I have a baptism with which to be baptized, and what stress I am under until is it completed!" (Lk 12:50).

> "Now my soul is troubled. And what should I say—'Father, save me from this hour?' No, it was for this reason that I have come to this hour" (Jn 12:27).

> In the days of his flesh, Jesus offered up prayers and supplications, with loud cries and tears, to the one able to save him from death (Heb 5:7).

> His sweat became like great drops of blood falling down on the ground (Lk 22:44).

> At three o' clock Jesus cried out with a loud voice: " . . . My God, my God, why have you forsaken me?" (Mk 15:34).

What do these passages tell us? Was Jesus afraid of physical death? What horrified him when he thought of his coming suffering and death? Did he break down at the end as Bultmann thinks? Did he only experience the darkness and distress of death more deeply than any other man or woman? Many solutions from one extreme to the other have been offered. Some see in the cry on the cross a cry of despair; others regard it as a cry of victory.[38] If Jesus consciously took upon himself the "eschatological tribulations and sufferings," the question remains as to the nature of these tribulations that make the final coming of the Kingdom possible. A solution could be developed along the following lines. In the life of Jesus there is a tension between his intimate life with the Father and his "living our life to the very end." Nevertheless, he remains faithful to his mission most adequately expressed in the words *identification* and *representation*. It seems Jesus felt that the more he identified with us, the more he would experience our sinfulness, our forlorn situation, our insecurity as those who had rejected God's gift of love, the only real security for a creature. He came to realize that if he carried his mission through to the very end—taking upon himself our hollow existence—he would have to experience the full reality of what it means for a creature to be "cut off" from God. For Jesus it would mean to experience being cut off from the Father, who meant everything to him, from whom he drew life, and whose will he had come to do. The thought that this moment was coming horrified him. The Father would regard him as "humankind in its God-forsaken, abandoned state." Jesus would have to experience his being completely *identified* with us in our sinfulness and being dealt with as our *representative* before God. Rosse explains:

> The Son of God has thus passed through the entire gamut of human anguish. He experienced death in all the tragic religious meaning acquired as a consequence of sin: estrangement from God. He became, as Paul will say, "sin," a "curse" (2 Co 5:21; Ga 3:13), and that to the extreme consequence of sin: death. The theological dimension of abandonment now comes to light: Jesus, the incarnate Son, has completely assumed the human condition of estrangement from God.[39]

The cry on the cross is the moment when Jesus most identified with our God-forsakenness (Mk 15:34). In this moment it seemed as if the love of the Father from whom he drew life had stopped flowing.

Jesus entered into the abyss of lovelessness and consumed it from within, so that, in his dying, death and sin are no more. What appeared to be God-forsakenness thus turns out to be the purest expression of love between Father and Son.[40]

The "eschatological tribulations" are precisely this experience of our true state without God: forsaken, condemned, without hope. In this light we have to see the death of Jesus as Mark portrays it (Mk 15:34). On the cross Jesus experienced God as the one who withdrew and left him abandoned. This was the real trial of the coming Kingdom, which was to overcome sin, condemnation, and death.[41]

Walter Brueggemann sees Jesus' death on the cross in the context of prophetic criticism:

> It is the crucifixion of Jesus that is the decisive criticism of the royal consciousness. The crucifixion of Jesus is not to be understood simply in good liberal fashion as the sacrifice of a noble man, nor should we too quickly assign a cultic, priestly theory of atonement to the event. Rather, we might see in the crucifixion of Jesus the ultimate act of prophetic criticism in which Jesus announces the end of a world of death (the same announcement as that of Jeremiah) and takes that death into his person. Therefore we say that the ultimate criticism is that God himself embraces the death that his people must die. The criticism consists

not in standing over against but in standing with; the ultimate criticism is not one of triumphant indignation but one of passion and compassion that completely and irresistibly undermines the world of competence and competition. The contrast is stark and total: the passionate man set in the midst of numbed Jerusalem. And only the passion can finally penetrate the numbness.[42]

God's unconditional love reaches its ultimate climax here. Paul has expressed this in different ways:

For God has done what the law, weakened by the flesh, could not do: by sending his own Son in the likeness of sinful flesh, and to deal with sin, he condemned sin in the flesh (Rom 8:3).

Christ redeemed us from the curse of the law by becoming a curse for us (Gal 3:13).

So if anyone is in Christ, there is a new creation: everything old has passed away (2 Cor 5:17).

The cross is not the revelation of a revengeful God. On the contrary, it reveals two essential realities. First, it manifests the immensity and incomprehensibility of God's love as compassionate love. Compassionate love means that God did not redeem the world by reaching down from on high and pulling us up to heaven. Rather, God "came down from heaven," entering into our human misery by experiencing it to the ultimate limits. In experiencing the effect of sin as condemnation God, in Jesus Christ, took on the destiny of a humankind alienated from its own being. "He descended into hell!" These are the "eschatological tribulations" which had to be endured for the Kingdom finally to come in full glory. Second, the cross reveals the utter hopelessness of our human condition as sinners who have rejected God's love. The cross tells us what sin really is. God redeemed the world in Jesus by taking on all the consequences of our free decisions against God; God suffered our state. By going to the limit God went ahead of us and caught us in our fall before we would smash to pieces. Moltmann observes:

Only if all destruction, all abandonment by God, absolute death, and immersion into nothingness are found in God himself will union with God be eternal salvation, never ending joy, sure election, and divine life.[43]

Among Catholic theologians Hans Urs von Balthasar has dealt most profoundly with Jesus' abandonment by the Father and his descent into "hell." He writes:

Jesus becomes the true possessor, through his own experience, of what "Hell" means in the New Testament; he becomes the judge who has measured out all the dimensions of man in his own experience, and now can assign to each his lot eschatologically. And thus it is from this point that we see the emergence of concepts of Hell, Purgatory and Heaven, which for the first time are theologically meaningful. [44]

Rosse concludes his findings as follows:

But in order that salvation may be offered to all, Jesus, in his journey to the dead, in his experience of death, not only bears the pain of the impious—in the loss of all spiritual light of faith, hope and love (Urs von Balthasar)—in order to reach even those who will refuse. He thus runs through all the dimensions of hell so that every man in his estrangement from God will have the possibility of recognizing himself in Christ.[45]

Mark presents the death of Jesus against the background of three signs which serve to interpret it in the form of visual theology: the darkness, the torn curtain, and the centurion's confession of faith.[46] The first sign is darkness: "When it was noon, darkness came over the whole land until three in the afternoon" (Mk 15:33). In prophetic and apocalyptic language darkness is part of the "day of the Lord," that is, the day of the great judgment at the end of time. By using this language Mark expresses the universal and eschatological meaning of the death of Christ, which inaugurates the judgment of the world. Thus we read in the scriptures:

> On that day, says the Lord GOD,
>   I will make the sun go down at noon,
>   and darken the earth in broad daylight.
>   (Am 8:9)

Some exegetes compare the darkness before Jesus' death to the penultimate plague of Egypt:

So Moses stretched out his hand toward heaven, and there was dense darkness in all the land of Egypt for three days" (Ex 10:22).

The darkness which precedes the death of Jesus presents the "new exodus," that is, the passage to glory through the death of the cross.[47]

The torn curtain and the centurion's confession ask a few perennial questions: Where can God be found? In the Holy of Holies? Mark tells us that the moment Jesus died the huge curtain which hung before the Holy of Holies was torn in two from top to bottom. What is Mark telling us? According to Jewish belief God touched the earth with his foot in the Holy of Holies. Here one could be sure of finding God. From the moment Jesus died, God could no longer be found in the Temple.

There are, of course, different explanations given to the torn curtain. According to Rosse there were two curtains in the Temple, one situated before the Holy of Holies, the innermost part of the Temple where only the high priest could enter once a year. It is possible to see in this sign the fact that in the death of Jesus access to God became free for all, Jews and Gentiles; or again in the crucified Jesus the curtain has fallen that prevented one until then "from seeing God in the splendor of his weakness." If the indication concerns the external curtain, which closed the entrance of the Temple and was visible to all, one could see there a reference to the future destruction of the Temple "made by human hands" and, more generally, to the surpassing of the Jewish cult. In the letter to the Hebrews Jesus is seen as the one who opens up for us a new path through the veil of his flesh. The author of the epistle identifies the body of the crucified Jesus with the curtain. The crucified Jesus, who dies "with a loud cry," thus becomes the tear in the vault of heaven, the opening that puts God and man into contact with one another.[48]

In the cry of this dying Jesus of Nazareth, God's very nature is revealed: unconditional, compassionate love. How incomprehensible is God's love for us! (Eph 3:14-19). The cross becomes the climax of God's self-revelation in the history of humankind.

The second question Mark asks is, Who recognized Jesus on the cross as Son of God? The theologians? No! The pagan centurion! The centurion "looking at the crucified" represents all those who believe in Christ, especially the Gentiles. As Rosse observes: "Before the crucified, and through the mouth of the centurion, the Christian community expresses its faith in the crucified Jesus, the Son of God."[49] Thus in scripture we read:

No one has ever seen God. It is God the only Son, who is close to the Father's heart, who has made him known (Jn 1:18).

For God so loved the world that he gave his only Son. . . . Indeed, God did not send the Son into the world to condemn the world, but in order that the world might be saved through him (Jn 3:16-17).

The cross remains *the* revelation of God's unconditional compassionate love. Now it is possible to point to a visible, historical fact, located in space and time, and say: Here is God's ultimate self-communication to us. God can never withdraw again.[50]

SUMMARY

How is the Kingdom of God connected with the person of Jesus? The Kingdom is not a thing, not just a gift from God; it is ultimately God's self-communication to us in love. Its meaning has been made visible in sacramental form in the person of Jesus of Nazareth. It is the incomprehensible and compassionate love of God, who did not spare God's only Son but gave him up for our sake so that we may have life and have it in abundance (Rom 8:32; Jn 10:10).

17

The Kingdom and the Holy Spirit

How is the Kingdom of God present in the world since the resurrection of Jesus? The answer is that the Kingdom is present in the Holy Spirit. To understand this simple response we need to look briefly at the role of the Holy Spirit in the history of salvation.

THE MESSIANIC GIFT OF THE END-TIME

Just as the "true Israel" was expected to emerge only at the end-time, so also the outpouring of the messianic Spirit was anticipated as an eschatological event. This outpouring was regarded as the distinctive mark of the latter days of the final period in history, the "golden age of the Spirit." Tappeiner writes:

> In this final age of God's glory (Is 11:9; Hab 2:14) and the glory of his people the Spirit really comes into His own, because that age is uniquely characterized as the age of the Spirit.[1]

The Spirit's Link to Creation and Life

The Old Testament combined the phrase *ruah-elohim* with the notion of a creative and life-giving force.[2] The Spirit is seen as the "divine breath" which guarantees the life of every human being and of everything that exists. To live means to participate in the life of the life-giving Spirit. As long as the Spirit is active in a person he or she lives. But when God withdraws the Spirit, life comes to an end. The basic scriptural text for this view is Genesis 1:2. It is the "*ruah elohim*" that brings forth the world out of the inchoate primeval waste and creates the world. Nothing comes into existence except through the power of God's creative Spirit; the Spirit is the agent of creation as well as of life.[3] As Genesis 2:7 tells us, life is found in the human person because God "breathed into his nostrils the breath of life; and the man became a living being." The spirit in human beings is God's Spirit in the sense that God is its creator. The Spirit's role in all creatures is most explicitly and beautifully expressed in Psalm 104:29-30:

> When you hide your face, they are dismayed;
>   when you take away their breath, they die
>   and return to their dust.
> When you send forth your spirit, they are
>   created;
>   and you renew the face of the ground.

What strikes home most in this passage is the dynamic aspect of this creative power of God. It is God's Spirit who not only creates all things but who holds all things constantly in existence. Anything new that might emerge has its origin in this creative power of God. The Spirit is seen in these passages as the "ground of life," the "power of life," in short, "the origin of life."[4] This realization of God's all-pervasive presence in whatever exists and lives provides us with the theological basis for any discussion concerning the care for nature and life on this planet. Issues of ecology for Christians should be approached from the biblical insight that God has created everything and sustains everything with the creative power of love. Things are valuable because God created them and declared them good. Human beings do not give value to created things. Rather, they have value because of having been created and being loved by God's Spirit of love.

When the prophets announced a "new creation" (Is 43:19: "I am about to do a new thing"), it is the Spirit who is linked immediately to this innovative activity as the Spirit of the new creation and the Spirit of life everlasting. The prophet Ezekiel, in particular, sees the final coming of Yahweh linked with a superior activity of the Holy Spirit (Ez 36:27; 37:1-14). But Isaiah 44:3; Zechariah 6:1-8, and Joel 2:23-30; 3:1-3 also promise the outpouring of the creative and life-giving Spirit in abundance on "all flesh" at the eschatological time. The end-time will be the "golden age of the Spirit." The Spirit of God is seen as the consummating power of the New Age."[5] Pannenberg describes the situation in the following passage:

> For Israel the distinction between the eschatological and the present working of the Spirit consists in the fact that in the eschaton, the Spirit . . . will be completely given to men. Therefore, we can expect that life in the eschaton will be a higher life in comparison to the earthly condition in which men do not really have the Spirit of God but can only be driven by him.[6]

The age to come will be distinguished as the age of the Spirit in a threefold way. First, the "One who comes" is One upon whom "the spirit of the LORD shall rest" (Is 11:2; 42:1; 61:1). Second, the age to come is inaugurated by the outpouring of the Spirit on all flesh (Is 32:15; 44:3; Ez 39:29; Jl 2:28). Third, this age of the Spirit is marked by a deeper, inward spirituality; a new Covenant (Is 59:21; Jer 31:31-34; 32:37-40) will emerge and a new heart will be given through the abiding presence of God's Spirit (Ez 36:27).[7]

The Spirit of Prophecy and Revelation

Besides the creative and life-giving power promised for the end-time, the Spirit, especially in later Judaism, is seen preeminently as the *Spirit of prophecy and revelation.* The prophets are the bearers of the Spirit of God par excellence. Through the medium of prophets the Spirit imparts Yahweh's will and instructions for Israel, giving divine directions for the religious and political guidance of the people (Ez 2:2f; 3:24; 11:4-5). The prophetic spirit rests predominantly upon Moses, the prototype of the leader of the people and of the prophets (Nm 11:17,25; Is 63:11).[8] The idea of the Spirit as prophetic Spirit became so dominant in Judaism that the Spirit as creative and life-giving power was almost lost. Particularly in the intertestamental development the Spirit is regarded as the prophetic Spirit, active in the golden age of Israel's history but now quiescent (Sir 48:12; 1 Mc 9:27).[9]

In the messianic age this prophetic Spirit will be poured out upon all of Israel and all will receive prophetic insight, not only prophets but even slave girls, the bottom of the social scale in ancient society (Jl 3:1-2). Here the Spirit becomes that divine power that sets us apart, cleanses us, and impels us in our innermost being to obedience to the will of Yahweh (Jer 31:31-34). The indwelling Spirit of Yahweh becomes the agent and guarantee of divine human fellowship (Ez 36:24-28). The Spirit becomes the law itself in us (2 Cor 3:3-6; Rom 8:2).[10] This means two things. First, the Spirit will reveal the will of God (the Law) not only to the prophets but to everyone (Jl 3:1-2). Second, the Spirit will create in us the "divine human fellowship" that links us to God's own life and is the final fulfillment of the eschatological expectation—human beings in union with God. In the eschatological time, therefore, the Spirit not only reveals to us what God wants us to do (1 Jn 2:27), but also gives us the power to do it. The Spirit enables us to respond to God's offer of divine life. The Spirit makes us "sons in the Son," enabling us to address God as Father. The Spirit draws us into God's own life (Rom 8:15; Gal 4:6). Although the Spirit as prophetic Spirit was dominant in Judaism, both views can still be found, especially in Ezekiel, where it is written that God will renew us as a people (Ez 37). God will fill our new hearts with the power of the Spirit, enabling us to lead holy lives because the Spirit will be our law and guide (Ez 36:26-27).[11]

The Spirit and the Messiah

Although the evidence for the expectation that the Messiah would be equipped with the Spirit of God is not extensive, there are enough passages to support this idea.[12] The Messiah is perceived as prophetic (Dt 18:15: "The LORD your God will raise up for you a prophet like me from among your own people; you shall heed such a prophet"), as kingly, as a charismatic leader (Is 11:1-10) and as a glorious supernatural person of divine qualities (Dn 7:13ff). Isaiah 11:1ff. presents a masterly portrayal of the future ideal ruler, who is to be endowed permanently with the Spirit of the Lord. On the messianic King "rests" all the fullness of God's Spirit (the sevenfold gifts in which this fullness consists). It is first the Messiah who will receive the Spirit and through him all who join the new community.

There are three texts from Isaiah that attest to one outstanding activity expected from the messianic bearer of the Spirit: the practice of compassion, concern for justice and for the rights of the poor, the lowly, the weak, and the marginalized.[13] What is at stake is the creation of a community without exploitation of and discrimination against the weakest in its midst. It is the establishment of a true society of Yahweh in which all are respected and possess equal rights:

> A shoot shall come out from the stump of Jesse,
>   and a branch shall grow out of his roots.
> The spirit of the Lord shall rest on him, . . .
> He shall not judge by what his eyes see,
>   or decide by what his ears hear,
> but with righteousness he shall judge the poor,
>   and decide with equity for the meek of the
>   earth (Is 11:1-2,3-4).

The same connection is found in Isaiah 42:1-3:

> Here is my servant, whom I uphold,
>   my chosen, in whom my soul delights;
> I have put my spirit upon him;
>   he will bring forth justice to the nations.
>   . . .
> a bruised reed he will not break,
>   and a dimly burning wick he will not
>   quench;
>   he will faithfully bring forth justice.

The servant protects the endangered and the vulnerable. His mission is a universal one. He will extend his judgment to the peoples of the whole world.

The third text is Isaiah 61:1-4, which speaks of the Spirit of Yahweh resting upon the one who is sent to bring good news to the poor and to proclaim a year of liberation for those in captivity and slavery. It is this text that Jesus applied to himself in Luke 4:16ff. Matthew 12:18ff. explicitly connects Isaiah 42 to Jesus and his activity. Jesus is the one on whom the Spirit of Yahweh rests and remains. He will bring "justice to victory" for all the nations.

These three texts of Isaiah affirm the three basic attitudes about God revealed in the history with the chosen people. First, Yahweh is a God who hears the cry of the poor and comes to liberate them from their oppression (Ex 3:7-9). Second, God is a "lover of justice" (Ps 99:4); "He judged the cause of the poor and needy. . . . Is not this to know me?" (Jer 22:16). Third, the God of Israel is moved by compassion toward the weak and the downtrodden. The Messiah is portrayed in these texts as the one who will be filled with these divine attitudes and whose mission consists in accomplishing final salvation for all by living according to these attitudes.

Certain apocryphal writings, which influenced Christian literature and helped to form the baptism stories, associate the messianic office with a particular bestowal of the Spirit. The Messiah is regarded as filled with the Holy Spirit. The outpouring of the Holy Spirit upon the eschatological community is intimately linked with the Messiah, who receives the Spirit first and then gives it to the messianic community which is intimately linked to the Messiah.

JESUS AND THE HOLY SPIRIT

Generally it can be said that the New Testament understanding of Spirit corresponds to the wide range of the word *ruah* in the Old Testament.[14] In particular, the major aspect of the Spirit in the Old Testament as the experience of God powerfully present and active in the midst of the people remains one of the main characteristics of the Spirit in the New Testament. A shift, however, occurs in the New Testament to the effect that this experience of the Spirit is intrinsically bound up with the historical Jesus.[15]

The Earthly Jesus and the Holy Spirit

The gospel of Luke reveals a particular interest in the Holy Spirit. Tappeiner writes:

To Luke must go the title "Historian of the Holy Spirit," even as Paul and John must share the title "Theologians of the Holy Spirit." This is not to say that Luke is not theological in his treatment of the Church's experience of the Holy Spirit. Rather it is because he uses the vehicle of history preeminently to provide an external framework large enough to contain the full significance of the experience of the Holy Spirit. . . . Luke focuses on the movement of salvation history, on the leadership of the Holy Spirit in the missionary task of the Church, and on the manifestation of the Holy Spirit in the external frame of history.[16]

The Annunciation Story

For Luke the whole life of Jesus is closely related to the Holy Spirit. From the very beginning Jesus is the work of the Spirit. As the Spirit of God was active at the creation of the world, so that same Spirit could be expected at its renewal. The entry of the redeemer into history was regarded as the work of the Spirit. The activity of the Spirit in the infancy narratives introduces the messianic-eschatological age. The part played by the Holy Spirit in those narratives is the fulfillment of God's promised redemption in a new act of creation, comparable with that of Genesis 1. As the Spirit hovered over the "chaos at the beginning" to bring forth the world of creation, so he hovers now over a virgin to bring forth the *new* creation.[17]

The phrase "power of the Most High" (Lk 1:35) indicates that Jesus is not just another pneumatic figure in the Old Testament tradition. Rather, he is from the very beginning uniquely a man of the Spirit, even by origin, so that he is holy, the Son of God (1:35). John the Baptist, in contrast, though "even before his birth he will be filled with the Holy Spirit" (Lk 1:15), is not conceived of the Holy Spirit.[18]

The Baptism of Jesus

Here, as in the birth narratives, the Spirit is the creative activity of God that calls into being the messianic era. The Spirit, descending as a dove from heaven, hovers over Jesus to bring forth in him the new creation as in the classic Old Testament paradigms. Koch writes:

Just as on the morning of the first creation, the ruah-elohim flew to and fro like a bird above the primordial waters as a power of fruitfulness and life, or as after the flood the dove bore a fresh olive branch in its beak as a sign of peace for the new humanity embodied in the Messiah (Gn 8:11).[19]

All four evangelists testify to the Baptism of Jesus as a special bestowal of the Holy Spirit at the beginning of Jesus' public ministry. In addition, John stresses that the Spirit not only comes upon Jesus but "it remained there," thus characterizing him as "baptizer" with the Holy Spirit (Jn 1:32). Although Jesus already possessed the Spirit by virtue of his unique conception this special bestowal of the Holy Spirit is necessary if Jesus is to fulfill his role as initiator of the age to come. The account of the baptism of Jesus by John shows further that Jesus experienced a new consciousness of his sonship and of the Spirit. It was the awareness of the Spirit in him that made Jesus realize that the end-time had come and that John's ministry was over. The decisive indication for Jesus that the Kingdom had arrived was the presence of the Spirit working in and through him. Associated with that descent of the Spirit is the realization of sonship. Jesus is declared to be the "beloved Son."[20]

A new relationship is established between Jesus as the representative of the new messianic community and God. The Spirit provokes the end-time by leading humankind through Jesus into that final relationship that God had promised as the great gift of the last days. In the baptism story, the life of the Trinity is extended into this world since Jesus "as one of us" already lives that "divine-human fellowship" which is promised as the great gift of the end-time. It is the fulfillment of God's saving plan for humankind.

The Public Ministry of Jesus

To the eschatological Kingdom of God belongs the eschatological activity of the Spirit. They cannot be separated. The final coming of the Kingdom was present for Jesus because the Spirit of the eschatological age was active in and through him. He was so filled with the Holy Spirit that "the Spirit immediately drove him out into the wilderness" (Mk 1:12) where the struggle between the Kingdom of God and the anti-kingdom of the evil one was initiated. The exorcisms, the miracles, and the forgiveness of sins that Jesus performed are all signs of the "new age." They are clear signs of the eschatological Spirit in whose power he drove out demons (Lk 4:36; Mt 12:28), healed the sick and infirm, and raised the dead to life (Lk 5:17; 6:19; 8:54; 13:32). He prayed in the Holy Spirit (Lk 3:21; 5:16; 6:12; 9:18; 11:1; 22:32) and he overflowed with joy in the Holy Spirit.[21] It was this manifestation of the power of God which was the sign of the Kingdom.[22]

Particularly important is Matthew 12:28: "But if it is by the Holy Spirit of God that I cast out demons, then the kingdom of God has come to you." The emphasis should be focused on the two phrases, "Spirit of God" and "Kingdom of God." The phrases are intimately linked together. The significance of the saying is twofold. First, the Kingdom is present now because of the effective power of the Spirit, which shows itself in the work of conquering the demonic powers. Second, Jesus claims to have in himself the end-time Spirit in contrast to all others who drove out evil spirits. Their work can be compared with his being empowered by God to begin the final battle with Satan. Jesus' self-understanding and his Kingdom message are deeply linked with his being conscious of having the eschatological Spirit.[23]

The link between Jesus and the Spirit is so intimate that it could be said that Jesus did not just have the Spirit, but he *was* the Spirit in human form.[24] Yet, the gospel avoids direct emphasis on the Spirit for the following reason:

> Jesus acted under the necessity of a divine constraint. Lack of glory and a cup of suffering were the messianic vocation, and part of his poverty was the absence of the signs of the Spirit of God. They would have been inconsistent with the office of a humiliated Messiah.[25]

Or, in the words of John's gospel: "As yet there was no Spirit, because Jesus was not yet glorified" (Jn 7:39).

The Glorified Christ and the Holy Spirit

The cross is the climax of God's love for us in the human form of the incarnate Son. Easter, from this perspective should be seen as the "eternalization" of that love. This love becomes the "dynamis" (power) that will ultimately transform this old creation and bring it into the new creation. Jesus' death was necessary in order that the Kingdom could become a "transforming power" for the whole of creation. The power of the new creation is the Holy Spirit, the principle of life and love itself. The first fruit of Jesus' death out of love for us is the transformation of his earthly body into the new creation. The resurrection of the crucified Jesus is seen in scripture as the work of the Holy Spirit, the life-giving power of God:

> It was the Father—in response to Jesus' faithfulness until death— who raised Jesus to glory through the Spirit who gives life (Rom 8:11; Eph 1:19-20; 1 Cor 6:14; 2 Cor 13:4).

According to Acts 2:33 it is Christ himself who first receives the Spirit from the Father; the Spirit causes the raising up of his body and his exaltation at the right hand of the Father. Christ became such a spiritual being in the resurrection that from then on he pulsates with the overflowing and life-giving power of the divine Pneuma. He became life-giving Spirit (2 Cor 3:17). In his humanity Christ is in solidarity with us in the condition of sinful flesh (Phil 2:7; Rom 8:3; Gal 3:13; 2 Cor 5:21). As such he is first the "recipient" of the Holy Spirit who transforms Jesus' humanity into the new creation that he might become "the first born from the dead." Flesh—the old sin-permeated world—has been created anew, and in Christ the Kingdom of God in its final form has become a reality. As our representative now, the risen Lord is in himself already the final fulfillment of our future "in advance."

Jesus' resurrection is the fulfillment of the promise that God will pour out the Spirit upon all flesh at the end-time. For John the mission of Jesus is seen as "releasing the Spirit." In John 19:30 the last breath of Jesus is seen as the breathing forth of the Spirit. The death of Jesus is necessary for the coming of the great eschatological gift—the Holy Spirit. Koch explains:

> From the wound in his side when he was crucified (Jn 19:34; see also 1 Jn 5:6ff.), from the glorified body of Christ as the messianic temple (see Jn 2:19; Ez 47), the Spirit was indeed to be poured out over all the earth and to the end of time.[26]

On the evening of the day of his resurrection the risen Lord imparted to his disciples his great Easter gift, the Holy Spirit: "He breathed on them and said to them, 'Receive the Holy Spirit'" (Jn 20:22). Again the image from the creation story comes to mind. As God created the first Adam into a living creature by "blowing his breath into his nostrils" so the new Adam, the eschatological community, comes into existence through the life-giving Spirit going forth from the mouth of the risen Lord. It is God's life-giving Spirit who brings forth the new creation, the end-time community.

Luke presents the same view, only in different images. First, he makes sure that the connection between the Jesus who proclaimed the Kingdom and the risen Lord is maintained: "After his suffering he presented himself alive to them by many convincing proofs, appearing to them during forty days and speaking about the kingdom of God" (Acts 1:3). Second, they, the disciples of the Lord, will soon be empowered by the Holy Spirit whom Jesus will send from the Father. Endowed with that power from on high they will continue Jesus' mission: proclaiming the Kingdom as present by driving out demons, healing people, and forgiving sins. In short, they will be enabled to perform the same signs of the Kingdom as Jesus had done in the power of the eschatological Spirit. The Kingdom will remain present because the eschatological Spirit is present, the end-time has arrived. The outpouring of the Spirit upon the eschatological community, however, must be understood as the result of Jesus' life, death, and resurrection. It is the great gift of salvation, the endowment of creation with the life of the Trinity.

The resurrection of Jesus must be seen in connection with his proclamation of the Kingdom of God. His claim that in him the eschatological Kingdom was present needed confirmation from the coming Kingdom. In raising Jesus from the dead the Father confirms the claim that Jesus had made. In him the ultimate self-revelation of God has taken place. In as far as he is now our "representative" in the parousia, it is correct to say that in him alone the final fulfillment of humankind's social destiny has been achieved "proleptically," that is, in advance.[27]

The Present Kingdom and the Holy Spirit

Christ has gone into the new creation completely. How then does his saving work continue? Jesus promised: "I will not leave you orphans; I will come back in the power of the Holy Spirit (Jn 14:18)." At the juncture between the ministry of Jesus and the life of the church stands the event of Pentecost, the decisive imparting of the Holy Spirit to believers. The experience of the early church is the outpouring of the eschatological Spirit who brings to life this "new entity," the new community. The Spirit who was at work at the beginning of the world, who "hovered over the chaos" to bring forth the world of creation (Gn 1:1), now hovers over the small group of Jesus' disciples (Acts 2:1-4) and brings forth the new creation, the eschatological community. The church is created by this event. It is the sphere in which Christ makes himself constantly present through the power of his Spirit. To have received the Holy Spirit means to be in contact with the risen Lord, and to be in contact with him means to be living *already* in the sphere of the new creation: "If anyone is in Christ, there is a new creation" (2 Cor 5:17).

The community knows that part of the future hope is already realized in its midst. But it knows equally well that another part still remains in the future. It does experience—at least dimly, as a foretaste—the justice, peace and joy of the Kingdom in the power of the Holy Spirit (Rom 14:17). However, it also still experiences itself and the world as permeated by sin.

The experience of those who allow the power of the Kingdom into their lives has been described in many ways. The Spirit of Jesus the risen One has given us a new way of life: "We were enslaved to the elemental spirits of the world" (Gal 4:3), but "for freedom Christ has set us free" (Gal 5:1). Now we are called to a new life in community where there is "no longer Jew or Greek, there is no longer slave or free, there is no longer male and female; for all of you are one in Christ Jesus" (Gal 3:28). "We know that we have passed from death to life because we love one another" (1 Jn 3:14). The true sign of whether we have been open to the power of the risen Lord is our willingness to create "just relationships" with our fellow human beings. The power of the Kingdom is focused on creating that ultimate community where there will be no more division. Here the ultimate goal of God's intentionality with creation will come to completion: union and communion with him. "They will be his peoples, and God himself will be with them" (Rv 21:3). Christ has already drawn us into this new union with the Father and each other. An absolutely new intimacy is now offered which we cannot verbalize, but to which the Spirit gives expression:

> When we cry, "Abba! Father!" it is that very Spirit bearing witness with our spirit that we are children of God (Rom 8:15-16; Gal 4:6).

The possession of the eschatological Spirit does not lead to a withdrawal from the world. We have the "first fruits of the Spirit," received not for our own selfish needs. These fruits of the Spirit should open our eyes and hands to the whole of creation that groans and eagerly awaits the final transformation by the Spirit already operative in us. In the words of E. Schweizer:

> The new creation of man by the Spirit is not a flight of faith into heaven or an abandonment of this imperfect world. On the contrary, the new creation means beginning to see the world as it is, suffering with it and taking its suffering to heart. The work of the Spirit is to make us aware of our solidarity with the world.[28]

In the light of the Kingdom we come to see that creation is one. It is the possession of the Holy Spirit that leads us into solidarity with the whole of creation in its destiny and its hope. This is well expressed by Bonhoeffer:

> The hour when the Church today prays for the coming of God's Kingdom drives it for better or for worse into the company of the earthlings and worldlings, into a compact to be faithful to the earth, to its distress, its hunger, and its dying.[29]

CONCLUSION

The initial question of our previous chapter asked: What is the connection between Jesus the preacher of the Kingdom of God and the message he preached? We answered by saying that since the Kingdom is God's unconditional love for humankind made visible in the person of Jesus Christ, then Jesus is the Kingdom in person. God's redeeming love made itself visible and thus accessible to us in the life, death, and resurrection of the Son. The love of Jesus, which reached its climax in his death on the cross, became in the resurrection the all-pervasive power of the Holy Spirit. That power will transform all human creation and lead it into God's eternal design. The Kingdom makes itself present now in the power of the Holy Spirit, who is the great gift of the risen Lord. Since Jesus is risen and lives as our representative in the new creation, nothing can prevent the realization of God's final plan for creation—the New Heaven and the New Earth. Indeed, the eschatological struggle will go on. Some battles will be lost; some will be won. But the final outcome of this war is clear. As dark as the world may seem, as hopeless as the times may appear, the Christian should always heed Paul's battle cry: "Christ has been raised from the dead" (1 Cor 15:20).

18

The Kingdom and the Church

INTRODUCTION

What exactly is the relationship between the Kingdom that Jesus preached and the church he intended? Are they essentially distinct or the same? Answers vary. Some authors sharply distinguish between church and Kingdom. Others make them identical, seeing the church as the present form of the Kingdom. Still others do not raise the question at all. The commonly held position in the past was often something similar to the following. The Kingdom of God is identical now with the visible church. The present form of the Kingdom is the church. God reigns now on earth through the church and particularly through the structures of authority. The visible church is sign, symbol, and representative of God's invisible reign over all things.

The problem with this model, however, is that whenever the church is closely linked or identified with the Kingdom we find a tendency toward triumphalism and lack of self-criticism. The church becomes blind to its own faults and intolerant of its critics. Not only the church as a whole, but also the structures in particular, become sacralized so that proposals for fundamental renewal may be seen as rebellion against God's reign. The church is primarily conceived as a sacrament and regarded as the present imperfect form of the future Kingdom. In the words of Snyder:

> In sum, the Ecclesiastical Kingdom model is marked by a close identification of Church and Kingdom, yielding a conception of God's reign that tends to be sacramental, conservative, hierarchical, and often authoritarian. The Church easily drifts into this model through the gradual force of traditionalism and institutionalism and through its own success within a given cultural context.[1]

The only biblical text in which the concepts church and Kingdom appear side by side in the teaching of Jesus is in Matthew 16:18-19:

248

"And I tell you, you are Peter, and on this rock I will build my church. . . . I will give you the keys of the kingdom of heaven, and whatever you bind on earth will be bound in heaven, and whatever you loose on earth will be loosed in heaven."

Many exegetes hold that this saying is not authentic, but a later ecclesiastical addition. There are 114 occurrences of *church* in the New Testament referring to the Christian community, but the word *church* occurs only twice on the lips of Jesus. Can we conclude from here that the central teaching of Jesus was the Kingdom while the church occupied no significant place in Jesus' thought? Did the early church substitute the church for the Kingdom because the parousia did not come? It would be dangerous in theology to measure everything by the range of the names applied to it. The word *church* may not appear often in Jesus' teaching, but the very concept of the messianic community intrinsically bound up with the Kingdom implies what is meant by the concept church. It is therefore correct to say that

the Kingdom of God and the Church are two key New Testament concepts, both are crucial for the understanding of God's plan for humanity. They are central to the fulfillment of his redemptive purpose. While the Church cannot be identified with the Kingdom, for the latter is a larger and more comprehensive term, the two are nevertheless in such close correlation that they cannot be separated either.[2]

The following observations should not be overlooked. In the New Testament we find two sets of ideas connected with the Kingdom of God which might be helpful in order to understand better the tension that exists between the Kingdom and the church.

First, the Kingdom is understood in spatial terms, as a territorial reality. This is expressed in sayings like these. One can enter the Kingdom (Mt 5:20; 7:21; 18:3) and one can be thrown out of it (Mt 8:12). There are keys to the Kingdom, as mentioned above. The Kingdom is also compared with a house into which people are invited. The spatial terms of the message of Jesus are largely new but are pervasively present in his Kingdom message.

Second, the Kingdom is understood as God's sovereignty or kingly rule. It is a dynamic concept, signifying God's active rule over all reality, particularly at the end of time. It is all-embracing, yet provisional in the sense that the fullness is still to come.

Theses two strands create a tension that is fundamental in the New Testament.[3] While they help us to understand better the world in relation to the Kingdom, they may help us also to clarify the tension between church and Kingdom. They indicate that while the Kingdom is a reality that embraces all of creation, God still has situated the Kingdom in a concrete mode, within a particular group in space and time now.

We have previously described the Kingdom as the vision of reality, creation, God, and humankind which Jesus came to communicate. This faith-vision is the most grandiose vision the world has ever known. It is something we should be inspired to live for, work for, suffer for, and even, if necessary, die for.

Jesus entrusted this vision to his community of disciples. We in turn have received the Kingdom vision of Jesus. It has come to us through the faith community into which we were born, the church, not as a sudden bolt from heaven. This faith community, the church, has given this vision its own frame and shape, which it has consequently communicated to us. The Kingdom-vision is inextricably tied up with the frame and shape given to it by the church. Since we are members of this community—and most of us even highly engaged members as priests, religious, or laypeople—we must ask how this community, called church, understands itself vis-à-vis Jesus and his Kingdom.

Since Jesus' vision is always communicated to people in some concrete shape, in this case through the preaching and teaching of the church, the question is ultimately this: What image do we have of the church as the true bearer and carrier of Jesus' own vision? Do we have an image of the church which can inspire people and provide them with an ideal with which they can identify and to which they can commit themselves with enthusiasm and lasting zeal? For this we need a vision that explains the raison d'etre of the church and clearly indicates the goal toward which it is moving. We need a vision that corresponds to the faith experience of the individual member, as well as of the community; one which presents a set of values and priorities and explains the relationship between the church to which we belong and the world in which we live today. Finally, we need a vision that can be a guiding star, and yet one which is within our reach, so that it can also give us a clear mandate for action.

Do we have such a vision, and if not, can we provide one? Some scholars claim that the ineffectiveness of the church in many sectors of its apostolate today is due to the fact that we have no adequate image of the church "into which people can plausibly fit what they think they ought to be doing." They claim that "if we could fashion an inspiring and realistic image of the church, we might be able to act confidently, and in such a way that our self-understanding would be reinforced by feedback from others."[4]

The present prevailing image of the church in many parts of the world is still that of organized religion with laws, rules, and structures. The church is seen as an institution in society which fulfills expected functions along with other institutions like business, government, labor, and entertainment. Society has allotted a role to religion and expects it to fulfill it without interference in any other institutions and their respective functions. In allowing itself to be integrated totally into society, the church loses its world-transforming power. Jesus gave the keys to the Kingdom to his church, but to many today it appears that the church has lost them. The result is the constantly heard refrain, "Jesus yes, church no." The need for a prophetic ministry to rekindle the fire that Jesus came to throw into the world is obvious. Brueggemann expresses what many think when he writes:

> The time may be ripe in the Church for serious consideration of prophecy as a crucial element in ministry.[5]

What Brueggemann is asking for is the exercise of a prophetic ministry that can create a new consciousness in the church. Its task is to evoke an alternative to the consciousness and perception of the dominant culture around us with its overpowering ethos of consumerism. This alternative consciousness would engage in dismantling the present order, which is legitimized by the dominant consciousness. But criticism alone is not enough. The new alternative consciousness must at the same time energize the faithful and the communities by its promise that there are alternative ways of Christian community living to those contemporary society offers. It must lead the church to form or reform itself into an alternative community in order "to live (once again) in fervent anticipation of the newness that God has promised and will surely give"[6]

It has become a commonplace truth to declare that the church is sick today and needs serious attention. The cure, of course, depends largely on the right diagnosis. Many experts diagnose the sickness precisely as a lack of a comprehensive vision. Could a return to the fundamental vision of Jesus, the Kingdom of God, be the best starting point for the necessary cure? There is no better way to start than to go back and to regain for ourselves the memory of that vision that Jesus came to throw like fire into this world (Lk 12:49). The critical importance of this task is correctly noted by Brueggemann:

> The Church will not have power to act or believe until it recovers its tradition of faith and permits that tradition to be the primal way out of enculturation. This is not a cry for traditionalism but rather a judgment that the Church has no business more pressing than the reappropriation of its memory in its full power and authenticity.[7]

Christ entrusted the keys of the Kingdom to his church (Mt 16:19). With it he gave the church not only the medicine for the whole world, but also the medicine for its own sicknesses. The cure for the church is the return to the Kingdom vision of Jesus. People looking at the church today might say: Physician heal yourself before you offer your medicine to us. The symbol, Kingdom of God, offers the church a horizon of transcendence that will save it from enclosing itself again and again in stifling structures. Only the Kingdom of God has the dynamic power that can create new images and visions of what the church is to be and has to do in the concrete situations of human history on its way toward its final goal.

THE IMAGE OF THE CHURCH IN VATICAN II

In our century we have seen an enormous interest in the church, particularly in the years prior to Vatican II. The highlight of this ecclesial interest was the Council itself with two important documents on the church: *Lumen Gentium* and *Gaudium et Spes*. One should also include the first encyclical of Pope Paul VI, *Ecclesiam Suam*. The Council was very much concerned about presenting us with an image of the church which could serve as a kind of reference point in order to grasp the church's identity and mission in the world today. It wanted to express a vision of the church which would elicit new enthusiasm among the faithful and offer a new alternative to the way the world perceived reality. What was that vision, and did the Council succeed?

The Council did not define the church in clear concepts. However, the Council Fathers were very much concerned to correct a church image that was conceived generally as being too rigid and in many ways out of touch with the reality of the present world. The first concern was to go beyond any purely apologetical approaches to a self-understanding of the church that were so common in the time after the Reformation and in the wake of the Enlightenment.

As a result we find in the documents on the church a refreshing return to the biblical understanding of church and the rich heritage of the Church Fathers, particularly St. Augustine. In addition the theological and spiritual insights of our century are taken seriously into consideration in working out a new self-understanding of the church. Meriting special mention are the liturgical and biblical movements in the church prior to Vatican II, the return to a more universal view of salvation as seen by the Greek Fathers, and the awakening of the self-consciousness of the mission churches. All these aspects were employed in order to arrive at a church image that would be more credible for our age and time.[8]

If we consider the opening phrases of the two main Council documents on the church, knowing how ecclesial documents express their main concern and thrust in their opening words, we can sense how the Council wanted to define and see the church for today. *Lumen Gentium* (meaning "Light for the Nations," although this metaphor refers here to Christ) envisions the church as light to all nations. Here the church could be compared with a ship that is equipped with enormous lights moving through the centuries, indicating to the other ships on the ocean which way they should move in order to reach the shores of salvation. If we compare this picture with the older one, this is indeed a change. The older ecclesiology, taking the scriptural image of the great dragnet Jesus used in his Kingdom parables and applying it to the church, saw the church as a ship that was moving through the ocean of the centuries dragging an enormous net behind it and trying to catch as many fish as it could. Only those actually caught in this net could be saved. Today we would say there are as many ships as there are religions that can carry people to salvation. The church's mission is here perceived not as taking the people from their ship into the "bark of St. Peter," but rather to indicate to them which way to stir their boats.

The document *Gaudium et Spes* ("Joy and Hope") aims to define the church's relation to the world. It describes the church basically as a community whose mission is to give joy and hope to a world which often looks gloomy and desperate, lacking real joy and real knowledge of which way to move. This is all well and good. However, the question is: Did the Council succeed? Did the renewed church become a "light for the nations" and a community that radiates "hope and joy" into the world today?

In his encyclical *Ecclesiam Suam* ("His Church") Paul VI attempted to show the real origin of the church, its Trinitarian dimension. The church is not merely a human reality but a divine mystery which ultimately escapes complete definition. Without the realization of this element of the church we would by necessity despair because of the church's all-too-human appearance and sinfulness down through the ages.

In working out in more detail a new vision of the church the Council employs biblical images and symbols from Patristic literature which describe and portray the mystery and the mission of the church. (*Lumen Gentium* 6, footnote 12, lists a whole range of images found in scripture.) The Bible itself employs ninety-five images and symbols which refer to the entity we call church. Vatican II took some of these images as a kind of reference point to indicate the perspective from which we should look at the church in order to grasp its identity and mission in the world today.

The best way to start describing the church theologically is to conceive of it as the end-time community in the "here and now," as the final fulfillment of the eschatological Kingdom anticipated in space and history. The church is the historical anticipation or the historical concretization of God's ultimate plan with humankind and creation as a whole. It is the "already of the not yet," meant to be the concrete realization of God's Kingdom now and sent for the witnessing of the Kingdom present and the proclamation of it to all nations and the whole world.

In making this vision concrete, the Council chose from the ninety-five images and symbols of church in scripture the following images as basic for our time: the new People of God (Paul's concept of church); the body of Christ (Christological dimension); the sacrament of salvation (the real mystery of the church); and the creation of the Holy Spirit (the influence of the East).

Theologically, these images may adequately describe the essence and the function of the church, and as such, they will always remain of importance as points of reference in looking for an image of the church. Nevertheless, the question remains: How adequate are these images in spelling out a vision within which we can express our own faith experience today with conviction and enthusiasm? By answering this question we will obtain an answer to the basic questions posed above: Did the Council succeed? Did the renewed church become a "light for the nations" and a community that radiates "hope and joy" into the world today?

The New People of God

The favorite image the Council employed was the Pauline image of the church as the new People of God. In taking the Jewish idea of Israel as the People of God, Paul sees the Christian community as the new People of God, profoundly linked with the Old Testament. For Paul, the history of salvation is only one (Rom 9-11). The *berit* (covenant formula), paraphrased in many ways and summarized in the biblical statement "You are my people and I am your God," finds its eschatological fulfillment in the new *berit* in Christ's blood. But this New Covenant can only be understood and explained in terms of its origin: the Old Covenant.

With this image, the Council wanted to counter-balance the too hierarchically perceived image of the church. It was to restore to the People of God their legitimate right to participate in the governing power of the church since all are equal before God. The image was thought to break with the unegalitarian and anti-democratic ideology of the earlier ecclesiology. By using this image for the church, the Council, furthermore, wanted to stress that the church has to be seen as a growing community, involved in history, and therefore, affected by the weaknesses and infidelities of its members, who constantly stand in need of God's mercy and forgiveness. This notion serves as a corrective and a warning against all triumphalism. It is this definition of church that we find most frequently in the New Testament.

By stating that the church is the People of God, the Council affirmed that prior to all individuality and every individual calling the church is a people founded by divine calling, into which the individual is incorporated. The individual's relationship to God is not primary, independent of all socialization. The divine calling is aimed at constituting humanity as a people by reason of its common eschatological destiny, the Kingdom.[9]

The idea of the People of God should, however, remind us that although God has bound the offer of salvation to a concrete community in history, God is not necessarily bound to this one people. God can choose other people besides Israel as Jesus says in Matthew 21:43: "The kingdom of God will be taken away from you and given to a people that produces the fruits of the kingdom."

By analyzing the biblical origin of the people of Israel, Norbert and Gerhard Lohfink have concluded that Yahweh's intention was to create this nation as a "counter society." In the Exodus story we are told that Yahweh takes the people out of a social system that produced their misery, suffering, and oppression. The people are removed from Pharaoh's oppressive system, and God creates out of them the miracle of a new society in contrast to all previous societies. A "Yahweh society" emerges in which there is no more oppression and slavery by one to another. In that society all are free and regarded as God's children among whom justice and peace will reign. Here we have the beginning of a divine counter society which Yahweh creates in order to accomplish the divine plan for the whole of creation.[10]

Walter Brueggemann shares the same view. For him the break of Moses and Israel from imperial reality is a break from both the religion of static triumphalism and the politics of oppression and exploitation. What emerges is an alternative religion of the freedom of God, with the politics of oppression and exploitation being replaced with a politics of justice and compassion. This is a counter community with a counter-consciousness that matches the vision of God's freedom. Thus, he writes:

Israel can only be understood in terms of the new call of God and his assertion of an alternative social reality.[11]

The early church communities seem to have understood themselves precisely in this way: God's counter society or alternative community where all are equal and no class distinctions exist anymore:

There is no longer Jew or Greek, there is no longer slave or free, there is no longer male and female; for all of you are one in Christ Jesus (Gal 3:28).

> Now the whole group of those who believed were of one heart and soul, and no one claimed private ownership of any possessions, but everything they owned was held in common (Acts 4:32).

It was a society with a whole new value system: the values of the Kingdom experienced as concretely present in their midst. The attractiveness of such a view is obvious, particularly to Christian communities which find themselves in situations of oppression and dependence.

In Lohfink's view what matters most is that the Kingdom will remain linked to a community which must see itself then in the service of God's ultimate plan of salvation for all. Jesus tied the Reign of God, previously belonging to the people of Israel, to the community of his disciples. With this new election of a community, God's purpose for the Old Testament people was transferred to this new people. They are now to become a "visible sign of God's intention for the world" and the active carrier of God's salvation. They are called out of the nations in order to take up a mission for the nations. They will fulfill this mission precisely as a "counter society" in the midst of human societies.[12]

From this perspective the church is vital for the continuance of the Kingdom in the world. As L. Newbigin puts it:

> It is the community which has begun to taste (even only in foretaste) the reality of the Kingdom which alone can provide the hermeneutic of the message . . . without the hermeneutic of such a living community, the message of the Kingdom can only become an ideology and a program, it will not be a gospel.[13]

Snyder has called this view of the church with regard to the Kingdom, the "Counter-system." The Kingdom is seen as a "Counter-system," that is, a way of conceiving and organizing society that is counter to its dominant form at present. This model could also be called the subversive Kingdom, since it consciously seeks to replace society's dominant values and structures with those of the Kingdom of God. The Kingdom is a reality and a set of values to be lived out now, in the present order, in radical obedience to the gospel and in opposition to the powers of the present age. This model sees the Kingdom as a call to justice in society according to the values of the Kingdom. It shows particular concern for the poor and oppressed, the victims of society. It reminds the church of God's special care for the widow, the orphan, and the alien. This view is strongly christocentric in the sense that Jesus' life and his call to discipleship become the focus of attention. The church's mission is to be a counterculture in faithfulness to Jesus Christ. In the words of H. Yoder:

The alternative community discharges a modeling mission. The church is called to be now what the world is called to be ultimately. . . . The church is therefore not chaplain or priest for the powers running the world: she is called to be a microcosm of the wider society, not only as an idea but also in her function.[14]

Fidelity to Christ is the most important sign of the Kingdom now. To the degree that the values of the Kingdom (Rom 14:17), justice, peace, and joy, are realized here on earth now, the Kingdom makes itself felt here and now. The final goal of the Kingdom is peace and justice on earth and in all creation. This commences now but will be fully manifested only when God's Reign comes in glory. Snyder articulates the strength of this model when he writes:

The genius of this model is its affirmation of God's Kingdom as both present and future and as both individual and social without compromising either the power or the gentleness of the Kingdom. The image is the Lamb and the Lion (Rv 5:5-6).[15]

For some time after the Council this image of the People of God was in vogue. It is still used, but its popularity has declined. It seems that the faithful in many parts of the world cannot easily identify themselves as "people" in the sense that the Old Testament people could, since religious affiliation today does not correspond to ethnic and political identity. The image might remain appealing to minority groups, which would regard themselves like Israel as an oppressed and dependent group struggling for identity and freedom, finding in this image the vision that could lead and guide them in their struggle and search. In general, however, the image of the People of God did not become the kind of image of the church which could provide an inspiring vision, able to facilitate the desired reform of the church.

Body of Christ

In order to complement the image of the People of God, the Council felt obliged to take over another biblical image for the church, the body of Christ. The Council felt that the notion People of God could not express adequately the overwhelming change brought about by Christ. The notion body of Christ expresses the intimate union of the church with the risen and glorified Lord as his continuing presence in the world. It reveals the innermost center of the church—dependence on and union with Christ. Some hold this understanding of the church as the most mature result of the New Testament thinking of the church.

As beautiful as this image might be, it never really enjoyed a deep appreciation among the faithful. It seemed to be connected too much with collectivism and to identify the church too closely with its divine Head, not offering enough allowance for sin and infidelity on the part of its members, corporately as well as individually. Some see this image as limiting the church too much to being the physical body of Christ on earth. It is argued that just as the body has various members and diverse functions, so also does the church have many members with diverse functions. One should keep in mind that the church is the body of the risen Lord, who is now free from the limitations of earthly existence. Through the resurrection the limits of the earthly Jesus fell away, bringing forth a global relationship to all of reality. The body of the risen and spiritual Christ can no longer be considered as a physically definable entity from which we can deduce the limits of the church, the body of Christ. Any definition of the church as body of Christ must be carefully worked out.[16] So, as with the image of the People of God, the image of the body of Christ did not become an image of the church for our time.

Church as Sacrament

The notion of the church as sacrament was hailed by ecclesiologists as *the* achievement of the Council concerning a definition of the church in theological terms. Schmaus articulates this position:

> The statement of the Second Vatican with regard to the total sacramentality of the Church is probably the most important pronouncement it made concerning the Church. . . . All the council's other statements about the Church are affected by this insight. The key to the new understanding of the Church reached by the council is the teaching of the christocentric character of the Church.[17]

As Christ is the sacrament of God so the church is seen as the sacrament of Christ. The church makes him present and tangible in this world until he comes again. The church here signifies and effects the unity of all humankind with one another and with God in Jesus Christ, because it is a "sign and instrument" that really contain the grace they confer.[18]

This lofty image, however, contrasted with the harsh reality of the church. Many asked whether the church is really the sign of unity, love, justice and hope in the final Kingdom as this notion claims. Also, this image, as theological as it may be, did not inspire the mirroring of the vision in reality.

Creation of the Holy Spirit

The image of the church as creation of the Holy Spirit came more from the Orthodox churches, which have a much better developed view in this regard than the Western church. The Christian community at its earliest stage regarded itself as the fulfillment of the eschatological expectation promised through the prophets and brought about by Christ. The realization and understanding of who they were came to the early community through the experience of the outpouring of the Holy Spirit who was seen as *the* gift of the risen Lord. The Holy Spirit was so powerfully experienced that they regarded their new existence as a creation of the Holy Spirit. Since the church came into existence through the outpouring of the Holy Spirit, it would be better to start with this fact and to unfold any ecclesiology from the Holy Spirit. Such a procedure would lead more easily to the realization that the church is ultimately grounded in the Trinity itself.

If we look back at the Council after twenty-five years it seems that the leitmotif for the Council's idea of the church could best be described with the word *communio*, although this might not have been recognized immediately. Kehl defines the self-understanding of the Catholic church as it emerged in Vatican II as "sacrament of communion with God." The church is the communion of the faithful: united by the Holy Spirit, joined to Christ, called together with the whole creation to the Kingdom of God the Father. The church is seen as expressing here and now in a sacramental way the mystery of the communion of the Trinity.[19] Or in the words of Walter Kasper:

> The mystery of the church consists in the access we have to the Father in the Holy Spirit through Jesus Christ, so that we may share in God's divine nature. This communion of the church is made possible and sustained through the trinitarian communion of Father, Son and Holy Spirit. Finally, the church as communion, as Vatican II said following up what the martyr bishop Cyprian said, is participation in the trinitarian communion itself. The Church is in the same way the icon of the community of Father, Son and Holy Spirit.[20]

The notion of the church as a creation of the Holy Spirit has been further developed in the theology after the Council due particularly to the charismatic renewal. Some theologians in search of a deeper appreciation of the Holy Spirit in relation to the church have advanced this thesis: The church is a sacrament of the Holy Spirit, that is, as the "already" of the "not yet," the church signifies the new creation, the world to come which is the work of the Holy Spirit.[21]

The church's mission is to release the end-time Spirit, who is operative in the church as the future of the world, with the intention of leading creation into its final destiny. This aspect brings out the universality of the church's mission: to lead the world into the *new* creation, to discover where the Spirit is operative in the world, and to be open to the signs of the times.

Boff stresses this aspect very heavily. By delineating the way in which the church came into existence after the Easter event, Boff relies on the Pauline view that the risen Lord is the Spirit who creates the church and makes Christ constantly present. This view opens us up to the possibility that the Spirit, and that means ultimately the risen Lord, is not bound to the church alone, but moves where it wills.[22]

The church, perceived as a "creation of the Holy Spirit," opens a new way of conceiving the church as a charismatic community in which every member has a function. Each member has received a charism for the building up of the whole community. The well-being of the eschatological community depends on the exercise of these gifts. These charisms are given to the individual person by the Spirit directly. They do not need empowerment through delegation by the hierarchy.

In spite of these hopeful beginnings, this view suffered from the underdeveloped theology of the Holy Spirit with regard to the church. This is not surprising, since pneumatology remains rather undeveloped in the Catholic church. Therefore, the church as a creation of the Holy Spirit also did not become *the* image for the church.

It can be argued, however, that together with the image of the church as People of God, this image of the church as creation of the Holy Spirit offers a foundation for the ecclesiology of the emerging base ecclesial communities.

H. Küng calls three of these images—People of God, body of Christ, and creation of the Holy Spirit—"the fundamental structure" of the church.[23] As such they will remain forever reference points for any accurate and correct understanding of that entity we call the church. Theologically, they express the essence of the church and its true nature. We cannot dispense with them. They reveal the real mystery of the church: the Holy Trinity. This trinitarian and pneumatic view of the church, thanks to the Eastern churches, runs through all sixteen documents of the Council. However, the images which the Council employed did not really find the response that many hoped they would among the faithful. The main reason for this phenomenon seems to be located in the diverse situations and surroundings in which people must live their faith today. Their faith experience does not correspond with the "modes of faith-expressions" the church offers them in these images.[24]

Many scholars think that the ineffectiveness of these images and the general ecclesiological void which emerged after the Council stem from the fact that the official ecclesiologies expressed in these images correspond more to the development of a certain idea of the church rather than to the historical mode of existence. Thus, they do not actually reflect the concrete shape which the church takes or has taken in reality. To proclaim beautiful images is one thing; to study and to reflect seriously on how these images are concretely unfolded on the grassroots level is something else. For example, the church proclaims that all are equal before God and are members of the Christian communities. Yet, in fact, only male celibates are allowed to participate actively in the governing power of the church. If some participation in this power is granted to the laity, it is done only through delegation by the hierarchy and not because the laity has a natural right to participate. The basis for authority and government in the Catholic church is the sacrament of orders. Authority here is legitimated neither by the majority nor by consensus, but symbolically by Christ, who instituted the sacrament of orders. It is very difficult to see how more participatory ways of government could be introduced into such an understanding of authority.[25]

THE CHURCH IN THE CONTEXT OF THE KINGDOM OF GOD

After the Council, different concepts and descriptions of the church emerged. Some have been the result of the Council's own deliberation; others emerged out of the concrete situations in which the church finds itself today. These new circumstances have given rise to various understandings of the church's essence and mission. Theologians have analyzed these different approaches and views and have tried to synthesize them in order to come to grips with at least the main ones. The best known synthesis may be A. Dulles's *Models of the Church*, wherein he presents five descriptions of the church as the most prevailing ones in the post-conciliar church. They are church as institution, communion, sacrament, herald, and servant. Other scholars, like J. Theisen,[26] have come up with nine models or descriptions of the church, while R. McBrien[27] holds to three basic models. However, it becomes clear that whatever model of description one might propose for the church, the church must be seen first and foremost in the context of the Kingdom of God.

From the five models proposed by Dulles the one that explicitly sees the church in the context of the Kingdom is the servant model. In all the other models, the church is seen as the active subject, while the world is the object that the church acts upon or influences. These models focus on the internal reality of the church affirming its self-sufficiency in relation to the world. The question asked and answered by these models, as in former times, is, What can the world do to build up the church? However the question today is, What can the church do to make the world a better place in which to live?

The servant model is based theologically on the insight that the Kingdom of God is meant for the world and that the church must see itself and its mission in the service of the Kingdom. For the Kingdom is not only the future of the church, but also the future of the world. In the plan of God's salvation we cannot separate the church from the world. In the words of Yves Congar:

> In God's unitary design the Church and the world are both ordered to this Kingdom in the end, but by different ways and on different account. Church and world have the same end, but only the same ultimate end. That they should have the same end is due to God's unitary plan and the fact that the whole cosmos is united with man in a shared destiny. That they should have only the same ultimate end prevents a confusion that would be bad for the Church, as raising a risk of dissolving her own proper mission in that of history, and bad for the world, as raising the risk of misunderstanding and hindering its own proper development.[28]

Clearly, Jesus' mission is addressed primarily to his disciples. To them the Kingdom belongs, they will celebrate it, be in it. But this special proximity of the disciples to the Kingdom does not turn them into a closed society. The church has no monopoly on the Kingdom of God. Citizenship in the Kingdom never means a privilege; rather, it is always a summons to solidarity with people, particularly with the excluded and discriminated ones of society.[29]

One of the chief temptations for the church in history is to claim the Kingdom for itself, to take over the management of the Kingdom, and even, at the limit, to present itself as the realized Kingdom of God over against the world. The Kingdom of God is not the Kingdom of the Christians.

Gaudium et Spes presents this new understanding of the relationship between the church and the world. After recognizing the world's legitimate autonomy, the Council asserts that the church must consider itself as part of the total human family, sharing the same concerns as the rest of humankind. In articles 3 and 92 the constitution says that just as Christ came into the world not to be served but to serve, so the church, carrying on the mission of Christ, seeks to serve the world by fostering unity among all people.

The advantage of such an image for the church lies in these points: First, it helps the church to turn away from an over concern about its own internal affairs and to look at the world for which the Kingdom is meant. The important thing for the church is not to withdraw into itself and reduce itself to a small group which keeps its distance from the world. The church must take part in constructive action and liberation. Second, the church, as understood in this model, can give hope to a world stricken by war, injustice, and hatred by pointing continually to the coming Kingdom as having appeared already in Jesus Christ. It can give meaning to the small services everyone can do for a better world of justice, peace, and unity. Third, this model underlines the principle that *diakonia*—which includes the struggle for a new social order—is as essential to and even as constitutive of the mission of the church as are proclamation and sacramental celebration. The Kingdom demands the transformation of all human reality and the church must be an "agent" of this transformation.

The Church Is Not the Kingdom of God Now

In *Lumen Gentium* the Council begins by describing the church as the mystery of Christ. In the church is realized the "eternal plan of the Father, manifested in Jesus Christ, to bring humankind to its eternal glory." Here the church is seen in connection with the "bringing about of the secret hidden for ages in God" (Col 1:16; Eph 3:3-9; 1 Cor 2:6-10). Therefore, the church has to be seen in this broad perspective of God's plan of salvation, which includes all human beings and creation as a whole (1 Tim 2:4; Rom 8:22 ff). The most comprehensive symbol for God's plan with creation is the biblical phrase, Kingdom of God. The correct alignment of these terms is highly important: Kingdom—world—church.

The Kingdom aims at the transformation of the whole of creation into its eternal glory, and the church must be seen and understood in the context of this divine intentionality. The church's essence and mission make sense only in this setting. Its mission is to reveal through the ages the hidden plan of God to lead all humankind toward its final destiny. The church must see itself entirely in the service of this divine plan meant for the salvation of all creation.[30]

Nowhere in the gospels is the group of the disciples around Jesus identified with the Kingdom of God. The text that is often used for such identification is the parable of the Tares and the Wheat (Mt 13:24-30). But the "field" in this parable is not the church, but the world, as the interpretation of the parable clearly states: "The field is the world" (Mt 13:38). The teaching of the parable is about the Kingdom that invades history without a visible interruption of the present structure of this world. Good and evil will exist side by side and only in the future, when the Kingdom will come in fullness will there be a separation of both.

The distinction of the Kingdom in its eschatological fullness and the Kingdom of God present in history, the "already" and "not yet," has generally been accepted by all theologians.

God has inaugurated the Kingdom in the world and in history in two stages. First, the Kingdom was inaugurated through the earthly life of Jesus, his words and works, being fully inaugurated only through the Paschal mystery of his death and resurrection. Second, this Kingdom present in history must now grow through history in order to reach its eschatological fullness at the end of time.

The Council clearly accepted this distinction between the Kingdom present in history now and the eschatological fullness still to come (*Lumen Gentium* 5, 9). But did the Council also clearly distinguish between Kingdom and church?

There are two questions to be asked. First, did the Council identify the Kingdom of God in history with the pilgrim church, or did it consider the Kingdom of God in history as a reality that is broader than the church? Second, is the Kingdom of God in its final fulfillment identical with the church in its eschatological fullness, or does it again extend beyond her while embracing her?

A number of theologians still hold that a close analysis of the relevant texts of *Lumen Gentium* (3, 5, 9, 48) show that in Vatican II the Kingdom of God remains identical with the church, with the historical reality of the Kingdom now or with the eschatological fulfillment where it will find its fulfillment as well.

The same view can be found in the Final Document of the International Theological Commission in 1985. Once again the distinction between the pilgrim church in history and the heavenly church in its eschatological fullness is made, but the document continues to identify, on the one hand, the Kingdom of God in history with the pilgrim church, and, on the other hand, the eschatological fullness of the Kingdom with the heavenly church.

Only in the encyclical *Redemptoris Missio* can we find a clear distinction. In the words of Dupuis:

> An analysis of the recent document of the central teaching authority would show that the encyclical *Redemptoris Missio* is the first to distinguish clearly—while uniting them—the Church and the Reign of God in their pilgrimage through history: the Kingdom present in history is a broader reality than the Church; it extends beyond her boundaries to embrace the members of the other religious traditions.[31]

Did Jesus identify the Kingdom with the group of disciples or did he see the Kingdom as being broader than the group that became the church after his resurrection?

Jesus saw his mission as limited to the "house of Israel." Yet, there are instances in the gospel where Jesus oversteps the boundaries of Israel. Jesus made the Kingdom present through his miracles (Mt 12:25-

28; Lk 4:16-22). The gospels tell us that he healed those who did not belong to the people of Israel (Mk 7:24-30; Mt 15:21-28). These miracles signify, therefore, that the Kingdom is operative and present among others as well. Thus, it seems that Jesus did not exclusively identify the Kingdom with the "movement" created by him and destined to become the church.[32]

In later theology the Kingdom of God is seen under a new form, that of the kingship of the risen Christ in which it is realized. But this kingship (Col 2:10 and Eph 1:10) is not limited to the church; it extends to the entire world. Christ is the head of the world and of the church, but only the church is his body (Col 1:18; Eph 1:22; 4:15; 5:23). Church and world should be seen as two concentric circles, whose common center is Christ. The kingship of Christ as the presence of the Kingdom in history extends to the whole world, visible and invisible. Schnackenburg explains the dynamic between the two:

> The Kingdom of Christ is . . . a more comprehensive term than "Church." In the Christian's present existence on earth his share in Christ's Kingdom and his claim to the eschatological Kingdom . . . find their fulfillment in the Church, the domain in which the grace of the heavenly Christ are operative. . . . But Christ's rule extends beyond the Church . . . and one day the Church will have completed her earthly task and will be absorbed in the eschatological Kingdom of Christ or of God.[33]

Theologians who argue that the Catholic church in Vatican II distanced itself from any identification with the Kingdom in history base this view on their understanding that the Council saw the church as a sacrament of the Kingdom. Since God's saving grace can never be bound exclusively to a sacrament, one has to accept that the Kingdom is still broader than the church. They maintain such a separation is indirectly expressed in article 5 of *Lumen Gentium* and again in article 45 in *Gaudium et Spes*.

McBrien represents this position:

> It replaces what was perhaps the most serious pre-Vatican II ecclesiological misunderstanding, namely, that the Church is identical with the Kingdom of God here on earth. If it is, then it is beyond all need for institutional reform, and its mission is to bring everyone inside lest salvation elude them.[34]

Or, in the words of Karl Rahner:

> The Church is not identified with the Kingdom of God. It is the sacrament of the Kingdom of God in the eschatological phase of

sacred history which began with Christ, the phase which brings about the Kingdom of God. As long as history lasts, the Church will not be identical with the Kingdom of God, for the latter is only definitely present when history ends with the coming of Christ and the last judgment. Yet the Kingdom of God is not simply something due to come later, which later will replace the world, its history and the outcome of history. The Kingdom of God itself is coming to be in the history of the world (not only in that of the Church) whenever obedience to God occurs in grace as the acceptance of God's self-communication. . . . For the Kingdom of God in the world, which of course can never simply be identified with any particular objective secular phenomenon, the Church is a part, because of course the Church itself is in the world and in its members makes world history. Above all, however, the Church is precisely its special fundamental sacrament, i.e., the eschatological and efficacious manifestation, etc., of the world, the Kingdom of God at hand. Even here, therefore, as in the various individual sacraments, sign and thing signified can never be separated or identified (cf. *LG*, 9).[35]

According to Boff the church is only necessary because the Kingdom which Jesus preached was not accepted by the Jewish people. If the Kingdom preached by Jesus had been realized, there would have been no need for the church. Boff writes:

Essentially, the Church substitutes for the Kingdom and must, theologically, define itself as an instrument for the full realization of the Kingdom and as the sign of a true yet still imperfect realization of his Kingdom in the world.[36]

The church is, therefore, not the Kingdom now, because the Kingdom makes itself felt outside the church as well. The church's mission is to serve the Kingdom, not to take its place.

There are three dangers of which we must be aware. First, the church and Kingdom may seem so closely connected that an identification takes place. The result is an abstract and idealistic image of the church cut off from real history and its traumas. Second, the church and world may be identified, with the result that the image of the church is secular and mundane, and constant conflict with the powers of the world cannot be avoided. This has been called "the 'secularist temptation' when the Kingdom of God is consciously or unconsciously identified with some earthly goal or other, and the goal of the Kingdom of God entrusted to the care of the church."[37] Third, a church totally centered on itself, out of touch with the world and the Kingdom, risks becoming a self-sufficient, triumphal, and perfect society, not recognizing the relative autonomy of the secular.

According to Boff,

> these dangers are theological "pathologies" that cry out for treatment; ecclesiological health depends on the right relationship between Kingdom—World—church, in such a way that the church is always seen as a concrete and historical sign (of the Kingdom and Salvation), and as its instrument (mediation) in salvific service to the world.[38]

How can we say that the Kingdom of God—which Jesus brought through his life, death, and resurrection irrevocably into this world—is now also found outside the church? The theological reasoning for this view is based on the incarnation but ultimately on the resurrection of Jesus. In the resurrection the limitations of Jesus' earthly existence are gone. In him matter has been transformed into the state of the new creation. Christ is in his risen body the world to come. He, therefore, assumes a new global relationship with reality as a whole: he is present in creation in a new way.[39] As the future of the present world Christ relates to creation in a new way. The whole world belongs to him not only on the basis of creation (Col 1:1-15; Jn 1:1-14) but now on the basis of its transformation in the resurrection of his body into the new creation. We cannot limit the presence of the new creation to the church. This all-pervasive presence of the Kingdom of Christ in the world makes itself visible not only in the church, but also in historical movements outside of the church. This was expressed by the International Ecumenical Congress of Theology in São Paulo (Brazil, 1980) in these words:

> The coming Kingdom as God's final design for his creation is experienced in the historical process of human liberation. On the one hand, the Kingdom has a utopian character, for it can never be completely achieved in history; on the other hand, it is foreshadowed and given concrete expression in historical liberations. The Kingdom pervades human liberations; it manifests itself in terms, but it is not identical with them. Historical liberations, by the very fact that they are historical, are limited, but are open to something greater. The Kingdom transformed them. Therefore, it is the object of our hope and thus we can pray to the Father: "Thy Kingdom come." Historical liberations incarnate the Kingdom to the degree that they humanize life and generate social relationships of greater fraternity, participation and justice.

The encyclical *Redemptoris Missio* acknowledges the difference between the Kingdom and the church clearly but is very much concerned that the church not be seen and treated as separated from the Kingdom:

> One may not separate the Kingdom from the Church. It is true that the church is not an end unto herself, since she is ordered toward the Kingdom of God of which she is the seed, sign and instrument. Yet while remaining distinct from Christ and the Kingdom, the church is indissolubly united with both (*Redemptoris Missio* 18).

The Kingdom of God as Present in the Church

It is the Kingdom present now that creates the Church and keeps it constantly in existence. The Church is, therefore, the result of the Spirit, who names God's final saving intentionality effectively present as the true source of the community called Church.

Although the Kingdom cannot be identified with the Church that does not mean that the Kingdom is not present in the church. First, it makes itself present in a particular way. We can say that the church is an "initial realization" or a "proleptic anticipation" of the plan of God for humankind; or, in the words of Vatican II, "She becomes on earth the initial budding forth of the Kingdom" (*Lumen Gentium* 5).

Second, the church is a means or sacrament through which this plan of God with the world realizes itself in history (*Lumen Gentium* 8 and 48). As G. E. Ladd explains:

> The Kingdom creates the Church, works through the Church, and is proclaimed in the world by the Church. There can be no Kingdom without the Church—those who have acknowledged God's rule—and there can be no Church without the Kingdom; but they remain two distinguishable concepts: the Rule of God and the fellowship of men.[40]

This view of the Kingdom as present in the church in a preeminent way and the church as an anticipation of the final destiny of humankind creates a series of difficulties and problems that needs to be addressed. First, how can the absolute and final reconciliation of the whole history "already"—although initially—be realized in a particular phenomenon of history? Second, how can the already realized reconciliation of history be mediated through the church in the face of human freedom and in view of the constantly open future of history? And third, in what sense does the church, as a social entity of salvation, occupy a middle position concerning the question of individual fulfillment and the final universal fulfillment of humankind's social destiny in the universal resurrection of the dead?

The Kingdom in its final fullness will reconcile the two seemingly dialectically opposed dimensions of human personality: the individual (every human being is unique and unrepeatable) and the social (every human being is also communitarian and belongs to the species). The coming Kingdom can and will solve this apparent dichotomy, because it will reveal fully the image after which we are created: the triune God whose very essence is one in three. The apparent conflict exists only in this present condition of humankind. Only in a sinful and untransformed world does the constant conflict arise between the rights of individuals and the structures of society. This conflict becomes more intense in the measure that modern society is becoming increasingly complex and in need of more sophisticated structuring. The instinctive aversion of many people to all institutionalization will not make it easier for the church to present itself as the model of human society.

One more difficulty is the growing awareness that the church itself, as a reality in history, easily falls prey to class-consciousness, and yet, it pretends not to be affected by such prejudices. The church refuses to submit to the ideological critique which alone could unmask such class biases.[41]

In the light of such difficulties, it is all the more important that the church presents itself as an "honest institution"[42] or as "God's counter society,"[43] in order to witness to the whole of society its ultimate destiny. The church's essence and mission are to offer itself as a "test case,"[44] showing that individual rights of persons and a society of justice, peace, and joy are reconcilable and liveable in the present world with the understanding, of course, that they are only signs of what is to come. A perfect society in this world is not possible. But the church can offer in an "initial and anticipatory way" the fulfillment of humankind's social destiny, because the Kingdom of God has already broken into this world. Thus, the church can indicate the direction toward which all history must move and be transformed. Ladd expresses this view as follows:

> It is therefore the Church's duty to display in an evil age of self-seeking, pride, and animosity, the life and fellowship of the Kingdom of God and of the age to come. This display is an essential element in the witness of the Church to the Kingdom of God.[45]

We know that God's Kingdom is present. Even if the hoped-for future never comes in our lifetime, the choice of living for it may not be wrong. The Kingdom releases energies that affect the course of history deeply in often unintended ways. "To live for the future will mean concretely that we cease to try to succeed and establish our security in the present socio-economic order."[46]

The Threefold Mission of the Church

The church's mission today could be described as threefold. First, it is to *proclaim in word and sacrament* that the Kingdom of God has come in the person of Jesus of Nazareth. Sacrament means that in its symbolic order the church opens up the everyday world to the ultimate, the Kingdom of God. But in doing so the church is also forced to accept its provisional character. In the words of Schillebeeckx:

> The Church is not the Kingdom of God, but it bears symbolic witness to the Kingdom through its word and sacrament, and its praxis effectively anticipates that Kingdom. It does so by doing for men and women here and now, in new situations (different from those in Jesus' time), what Jesus did in his time: raising them up for the coming Kingdom of God, opening up communication among them, caring for the poor and outcast, establishing communal ties within the household of faith and serving all men and women in solidarity.[47]

Second, the church is *to offer its own life* as a test case that demonstrates that the Kingdom is present and operative in the world today. This should reveal itself in the church's own life, where justice, peace, freedom, and respect for human rights are made concrete. The church should offer itself as a "contrast society" to society at large.[48]

Third, the church is *to challenge society as a whole* to transform itself along the basic principles of the Kingdom now present: justice, peace, community, and human rights. This is a "constitutive element of proclaiming the gospel" since the ultimate goal of the Kingdom is the transformation of the whole of creation. The church must, therefore, understand its mission in the service of the imminent Kingdom.[49]

This threefold mission of the church is also called evangelization. At least among current Catholic authors the words *mission, evangelization*, and *witness* are often used as synonyms. Although each of these words has its own meaning and history they are all used to designate in a comprehensive way the one complex mission of the church. This threefold mission found its expression in *Redemptoris Missio* in the following way:

> The Church is effectively and concretely at the service of the Kingdom. This is seen especially in her preaching, which is a call to conversion. Preaching constitutes the Church's first and fun-

damental way of serving the coming of the Kingdom in individuals and in human society. . . .

The Church, then, serves the Kingdom by establishing communities and founding new particular Churches and by guiding them to mature faith and charity in openness toward others, in service to individuals and society, and in understanding and esteem for human institutions.

The Church serves the Kingdom by spreading throughout the world the "Gospel values" which are an expression of the Kingdom and which help people to accept God's plan. It is true that the inchoate reality of the Kingdom can also be found beyond the confines of the Church among peoples everywhere to the extent that they live "Gospel values" and are open to the working of the Spirit, who breathes when and where he wills (cf. Jn 3:8) (*Redemptoris Missio* 20).

Because the coming Kingdom of God in the present world always remains a "preliminary or proleptic" anticipation of the Kingdom, there will never emerge an "ideal community." Human societies, and the church itself, need structures which will always reveal the preliminary aspect and most often the "sinfulness" of all human endeavors. Only when the fullness of the Kingdom comes will all structures of the community be done away with, because the Kingdom in glory is "anarchy," that is, a community or society that no longer needs structures because perfect love has become the guiding rule. As Pannenberg writes:

> The Kingdom is not yet the way among men; it is not the present reality. Our present world, with its injustices, brutalities, and wars, demonstrates the gap between itself and the Kingdom. . . . But the future of the Kingdom releases a dynamic factor into the present that kindles again and again the vision of man and gives meaning to his fervent quest for the political forms of justice and love. . . . The function of the Church is a preliminary function. By this we mean that the existence of the Church is justified only in view of the fact that the present political forms of society do not provide the ultimate human satisfaction for individual or corporate life. If the present social structures were adequate, there would be no need for the Church. For then the Kingdom of God would be present in its completeness.[50]

Or, in the words of Jürgen Moltmann:

> The Church in the power of the Spirit is not yet the Kingdom of God, but it is its anticipation in history. Christianity is not yet the new creation, but it is the working of the Spirit of the new

creation. Christianity is not yet the new humankind but it is its vanguard, in resistance to deadly introversion and in self-giving and representation for man's future.[51]

The identity of the church depends ultimately on its Kingdom consciousness based on scripture. It would reveal this in its sensitivity to the priority of the Kingdom. According to Snyder such Kingdom consciousness includes the following five essentials:

1. Kingdom consciousness means living and working in the firm hope of the final triumph of God's reign. In the face of contrary evidence Kingdom Christians hold on to the conviction that God will eventually swallow up all evil, hate, and injustice. It is the firm belief that the leaven of the Kingdom is already at work in the dough of creation, to use Jesus' own parable. This gives Christians an unworldly, audacious confidence that enables them to go right on doing what others say is impossible or futile.

2. Understanding God's Kingdom means that the line between sacred and secular does not exist in concrete reality. God's Kingdom means that all things are in the sphere of God's sovereignty, and therefore, of God's concern. All spheres of life are Kingdom topics.

3. Kingdom awareness means that ministry is much broader than church work. Christians who understand the meaning of God's Reign know they are in the Kingdom business, not the church business. They see all activity as ultimately having Kingdom significance.

4. In Kingdom perspective, concern for justice and concrete commitment to the word of God are necessarily held together. An awareness of God's Kingdom, biblically understood, resolves the tension between the two vital concerns. Those committed to the Kingdom want to win people to personal faith in Jesus Christ, for the Kingdom is the ultimate longing of every human heart. They are also committed to peace, justice, and righteousness at every level of society because the Kingdom includes "all things in heaven and on earth" (Eph 1:10) and the welfare of every person and everything God has made.

5. The reality of the Kingdom of God can be experienced now through the Spirit who gives the believer the first fruits of the fullness of the Kingdom in the here and now. Particularly in their liturgy Kingdom people anticipate the joy of the Kingdom. The different charisms given by the Holy Spirit witness concretely to the Kingdom present and are appreciated by all as clear manifestations of the powerful presence of the Kingdom in the midst of their daily life.[52]

19

The Lord's Prayer as a Summary of the Kingdom Message

INTRODUCTION

Jesus proclaimed the Kingdom of God as having arrived with him. It had become a present reality, not a far distant hope anymore. It was in the reach of everyone who wanted to enter it. To the question of how to enter it, Jesus demanded conversion, a turning toward him and the message he proclaimed. A more concrete question, however, would have to be asked by those who had let the Kingdom into their lives and had heeded the call to conversion: What should be the norm by which we, your disciples, have to live now that we have responded to the Kingdom present? Jesus' answer is found in the Sermon on the Mount (Mt 5-7). Here we have the "Magna Carta" of all Christian behavior and the norm for all Christian action.

In the Sermon on the Mount we also find an answer to a question deeply linked to Christian living: How should we as disciples of Jesus pray? To this Jesus replied: "Pray then in this way: 'Our Father in heaven . . . '" (Mt 6:9). The Lord's prayer is, therefore, the norm that should guide and direct all our prayers. But as we will see, the Lord's Prayer is more than a guide to prayer. It contains, in brief, all that Jesus came to bring. It is a summary of Jesus' whole Kingdom message.

A JEWISH PRAYER

Where did Jesus get this prayer? Did he formulate it himself or did he take it over from his Jewish heritage? Jesus was a Jew of the first century. As a boy and young man he attended the synagogue every Sabbath—and perhaps Monday and Thursday as well—to listen to the scriptures and to pray. As a faithful Jew, he would have recited the

Shema upon rising and retiring each day, the heart of which affirmed: "Hear, O Israel: The Lord God is one Lord; and you shall love the Lord your God with all your heart, and with all your soul, and with all your might." Presumably Jesus participated in the Jewish festivals and went on pilgrimages to Jerusalem. He was obviously very familiar with the scriptures, the Hebrew Bible. He may have known it from memory, a feat not uncommon among the learned. The psalms were probably his "prayer book."[1]

Jesus probably took the basic material for the Our Father from Jewish sources, as he did for his parables. The structure of the Lord's Prayer corresponds to the ideal structure of Jewish prayer. It begins with praise of God and ends with thanksgiving if we add the doxology found in the *Didache:* "For yours is the Kingdom, the power, and the glory for ever and ever. Amen."

AN ESCHATOLOGICAL PRAYER

The Lord's Prayer is the most prayed prayer among all Christians, individually and communally. It has been analyzed and explained in many ways. Literature about it is immense: more than twenty-five hundred articles and books over the years. Most of them present meditations rather than exegetical or theological treatises on the prayer. What is presented in this short treatise on the Lord's Prayer is based on the analysis given by J. Jeremias, who treats the Lord's Prayer as an eschatological prayer.[2]

There are, of course, other ways to interpret this prayer. An eschatological interpretation takes the Our Father as a prayer of those who experience the Kingdom of God as a present reality—the already— and who wait for and cry out for its final consummation—the not yet.

Jesus' message centered on the imminent Kingdom of God. What people of this time considered one event—the decisive intervention of God in history—Jesus split into two related but separate events. He did this by bringing the beginning of the eschatological time into the "now" and postponing the consummation as a future event. This creates the classic problem of the already and the not yet.

The Christian community is, therefore, living in a peculiar state of affairs. On the one hand, it experiences the future fulfillment of the Kingdom already, in a "proleptic" or anticipatory way. It already possesses the eschatological gift, that is, the Holy Spirit, who creates that intimate union with God the Father (Rom 8:14; Gal 4:6) and enables us to create communion among ourselves (Gal 3:28; 1 Jn 3:14). This is a reality that belongs to the New Heaven and the New Earth at the end of time. On the other hand, this community is still in this world, circumscribed by all the restrictions of being in the flesh. Day after day this community experiences sinfulness—its own and that of the world around it—and the stunning power of evil at work. This is the backdrop for praying the Lord's Prayer. It is a prayer for the in-between time, the time of the church. We should not forget it is the only prayer Jesus gave us.

DIFFICULTIES WITH THE LORD'S PRAYER

The common ways people use the Lord's Prayer often create difficulties. It easily becomes a prayer for all occasions: for good weather, the poor souls, peace in the world, better health, and so on. In addition it often has been a penance in confession and a means for indulgences. In short, it becomes a way out when we do not know what to pray. The effect of such overuse is that we no longer know, experience, and appreciate its real meaning.

A more recent problem is that some find difficulty with the opening address, "Father," as the name for God. It seems too much of a male, chauvinistic approach to God. To address God as Father no longer seems to have an experiential correlation in all lives.[3]

The only real answer to these problems seems to lie in a continual effort to explain the depth of this prayer. Frequent preaching about it can unlock its treasures and the great concerns Jesus wants us to have. It is an excellent text for meditation. Repeating it should not be a problem for those who feel themselves drawn into exploring its real depth and meaning.

At a time when people are asking, "How should I pray" and "What should I pray," it is even more important to go back to what Jesus himself taught as a pattern of how and what his disciples should be concerned with when praying.

The Sermon on the Mount is the norm for all Christian action. It is understandable only in the setting of Jesus' eschatological message of the Kingdom as a present reality. In other words, Jesus' ethical requirements presuppose the proclamation and concretization of the Kingdom in the corporal dimension.[4]

THE LORD'S PRAYER IN THE ANCIENT CHURCH

In the beginning of the early church the Lord's Prayer seems to have been mainly a prayer of the individual Christian. *Didache* 8:2 (written around the year 110) tells us to pray it three times a day. Other sources say the Christian should pray it with the Symbol (creed) after rising in the morning and before going to bed in the evening.

Very soon, however, the prayer became the prayer of the community. According to Cyril of Jerusalem (350), the Lord's Prayer was part of the liturgical service before holy communion and prayed only by the baptized, the full members of the Christian community. It was an expression of their identity as Christians. Together with the Lord's Supper, it became one of the most holy treasures of the church, reserved for the full members only, and not disclosed to those who stood outside (*disciplina arcanum*). In short it was a privilege to pray it.[5]

The awe and reverence with which the early church looked at this prayer can be seen by the way it was introduced:

> Make us worthy, O Lord, that we joyously and without presumption may make bold to invoke Thee, the heavenly God, as Father and to say: Our Father.

In the revised Liturgy of the Hours we find almost twenty different introductions to the Lord's Prayer.

The Earliest Texts of the Lord's Prayer

We have two versions of the Lord's Prayer: Luke 11:2-4 and Matthew 6:9-13. We normally use the Matthean version with seven petitions and no doxology. Luke has only five petitions. The *Didache* adds the doxology to the Matthean version. Mark does not have it. Some exegetes conclude that it was the early Christian community that composed this prayer, based on Jesus' own prayer life as depicted in Mark 14:36, 39, but this theory is generally not accepted. The two forms are normally explained by the different audiences that the evangelists had to address. Matthew presented a catechism on prayer to Jewish-Christians. They had learned to pray in childhood, but their prayer was in danger of becoming routine. The Lucan catechism is addressed to people who are learning to pray. These Gentile-Christians had to be encouraged to pray constantly.

What Is the Original Form?

There is no agreement among scholars about the original form of the Lord's Prayer. A growing number, however, take Luke's version as the more original. It seems closer to the style of Jesus' own prayer, especially the use of the simple "Father" as the opening address. This preference of Luke fits well with his constant attention to and interest in Jesus' life of prayer. Matthew, whose gospel became the gospel of the church, presents the prayer in the form the community had made its own: Our Father who are in heaven.[6] For some scholars, the material added by Matthew has the effect of making the prayer more suitable for use in worship without adding anything new to the prayer. Others, who argue for the originality of the Matthean version, point out that Matthew would never have dared to add anything to a prayer of Jesus so treasured in the early community.

Philip Harner lists six reasons in favor of Matthew's version as the original, but does not find them convincing. He himself regards Luke's version as closest to the original. His reason: "There does not seem to be any adequate reason why Luke, or the early Christians before him, would have wanted to abridge the Lord's Prayer. It is much more likely that Matthew, or the early Christians before him, expanded each section of the prayer to make it more suitable for the use in worship and more similar in terminology and poetic structure to the Jewish prayers that they were familiar with."[7]

Careful analysis of both versions shows that they are really much more alike than may be apparent at first sight. To understand the prayer's essentials, it does not really matter which version one takes. After consulting about forty commentaries, I have concluded that Luke's form is probably closer to the form that Jesus gave to the prayer.

Scholars have reconstructed the Our Father in Aramaic. This is what it sounded like in Jesus own words:

Abba!	Father
Yitquaddash shemâk	May be sanctified name yours.
Têtê Malkûtâk	May come kingdom yours.
Lachmân de limchâr	Bread ours of tomorrow
hab lân yômâ dên	give to us day this.
u shebôq lân chôbênan	And forgive to us debts ours
kedi shebaqnân le chayyâbênan	as herewith forgive we to debtors ours
we lâ ta'êlinnan le nisyôn.	and not let fall us into trial.[8]

After a careful text-critical analysis, Jeremias proposes this wording as the original, based on the above Aramaic version:

Address:	**Dear Father**
First "thou petition":	**hallowed be thy name**
Second "thou petition":	**thy kingdom come**
First "we petition":	**our bread of tomorrow give us today**
Second "we petition":	**and forgive us our debts as we herewith forgive our debtors**
Concluding Request:	**and let us not succumb to temptation**

The Meaning of the Lord's Prayer

In Jesus' time various religious groups like the Pharisees, Essenes, and disciples of John all had prayers that distinguished them from other groups. The disciples in Luke 11:1 asked Jesus for an "identification prayer," something that would bind them together, identify them, and bring to expression their chief concerns. They asked for a prayer that would be their badge, their distinctive symbol. Jesus answered by giving them a prayer that is "the clearest and, in spite of its terseness, the richest summary of his proclamation we possess."[9] The Lord's Prayer is not just a prayer; it is the manifesto of our Christian faith.

The Address: "Dear Father (Abba)"

Fatherhood of God in the Old Testament and Judaism. Other ancient religions knew the word *Father* for God as well as the Jews of the Old Testament. Homer, for example, calls Zeus "the father of men and gods." In the Old Testament God is called Father only fourteen times. Many of these passages, however, are very important. God's fatherhood in the Old Testament is never linked to mythological motifs but always to the events of salvation history. God is revealed as father by acts of saving power in the history of the chosen people.

Absolute authority and tenderness are the two important aspects of fatherhood in the Old Testament. *Tenderness* is a word we normally associate more with a mother. The concept of Father for God in the Old Testament is, therefore, not to be understood in authoritarian categories and definitely not to be construed in male-chauvinistic terms. Attributes that our culture attaches to the concept of mother also belong to the biblical image of God as Father. By calling God Father, the Old Testament stresses the tenderness, mercy, care, and love of God for the chosen people. Fuerst explains the Old Testament nuances at length:

> The social meaning for "father" in Israel had to do with authority, care, discipline, protection, and dignity. It represented a role in a society that is harshly judged and incompletely understood today. It makes no sense to wish that Israel's God might not have been called father or king. At least when God's work is compared to that of a parent, the language is warm, gentle, affectionate, nurturing, caring, and at the very least and by any account respectful. When God is called father the texts are talking about creation, leading, and affection. "Father" was a social assumption, part of the social and cultural mold into which the faith of the Old Testament was poured. Like "king," it had a rightful and necessary place in the mold; to remove it is not an

editor's job, because it would require an operation with an incision three thousand years old.[10]

The prophets in particular reveal the depth of Yahweh's relationship to the chosen people expressed in his fatherly care in contrast with the people's constant ingratitude. The final word about divine fatherhood is God's incomprehensible mercy and forgiveness:

> For I have become a father to Israel,
>   and Ephraim is my firstborn (Jer 31:9).

> Is Ephraim my dear son?
>   Is he the child I delight in? . . .
> Therefore I am deeply moved for him;
>   I will surely have mercy on him.
>   (Jer 31:20)

> And I thought you would call me, My Father,
>   and would not turn from following me.
>   (Jer 3:19)

> When Israel was a child, I loved him,
>   and out of Egypt I called my son. . . .
> Yet it was I who taught Ephraim to walk,
>   I took them up in my arms;
>   but they did not know that I healed them.
> I led them with cords of human kindness,
>   with bands of love.
> I was to them like those
>   who lift infants to their cheeks.
>   I bent down to them and fed them.
>   (Hos 11:1, 3-4)

> Look down from heaven and see, . . .
> For you are our Father,
>   though Abraham does not know us
>   and Israel does not acknowledge us;
> you, O Lord, are our father;
>   our Redeemer from of old is your name.
>   (Is 63:15, 16)

However, according to Jeremias, the invocation of God as "my Father" or "our Father" never occurs directly in any prayer in the Old

Testament. The language is always indirect, as though implying a promise of what would be fulfilled someday.

In contrast, in the rabbinic literature the expression "heavenly Father" is used for God. Even the two words "our Father" are found in Jewish prayers used in liturgy. It occurs three times in the Eighteen Benedictions (Amidah): "Make us return, our Father, to your Torah"; or, "Forgive us, our Father, for we have sinned"; and again, "Bless us all, our Father . . . " The same could be said about the services for the New Year and the Day of Atonement. The invocation of God as "Our Father" expresses the trust and confidence, the security and mutual love, between God and God's people.[11]

Matthew seems to have taken over this Rabbinic tradition. The meaning is expressed in two convictions: first, one has to obey God, which is equal to following the Torah; second, God is the one who helps in time of need, particularly when no one else can or will help. A development away from the prophets can be seen however in later Judaism, where God is spoken of as the "Father of the individual Israelite," the one who cares for the individual personally:

> Thou art he whose mercy toward us is greater than that of a father toward his son. On whom can we depend? Only on our heavenly Father. My son, if you return, will it not be a return to your Father?[12]

The rabbinical teaching always distinguished between paternity and fatherhood. Paternity denotes the person who is responsible for the birth of a child. There is no necessary connection between father and child. Fatherhood describes a relationship of love and intimacy, of confidence and trust between parent and child.

Father as a Title for God in the Sayings of Jesus. The New Testament refers 421 times to God. Of these, 183 (43 percent) call him Father absolutely or the Father of Jesus or the believer. It is, therefore, the dominant model. Sixty-five percent of the references in John and 56 percent of those in Matthew use this same mode.[13] In the gospels we find the word "Father" for God on the lips of Jesus 170 times. "Father" was evidently the designation for God in Jesus' preaching. Mark uses it 4 times, Luke 15, Matthew 42, and John 108. There is a definite increase in the use of the word, particularly in Matthew in respect to Luke and Mark. Kreutz explains this development:

> Matthew's striking and frequent use of "Father" for God marks his most significant departure from Markan and Lukan patterns. He uses the term over forty times in a variety of expressions. . . . He presents the most vivid interpretation of the father idea among

the four Gospels. . . . God is a Father who rewards the modest, hears those of a few words and forgives us when we are forgiving toward others.[14]

In John "Father" becomes *the* title for God; it usually denotes the special relationship of Jesus to God. After a thorough analysis of the gospel passages closest to the actual words of Jesus, Jeremias concludes:

> The important thing is that we have discovered that all four gospel traditions report unanimously and without any hesitation that Jesus constantly addressed God as "My Father" (except Mk 15:34), and show that in so doing he used the Aramaic form "Abba." To call God Abba is one of the most outstanding characteristics of the historical Jesus.[15]

Abba belongs to the language of childhood and the home, a diminutive of endearment also used by adults for their own fathers. For the Jewish mind, *Abba* expressed accurately the most intimate and personal relationship anyone could think of. It was, therefore, inconceivable for a Jew to address God as *Abba*. Such an address would not indicate adequate respect for Yahweh, causing scandal to godly persons.

Jews would normally begin a prayer with a phrase of praise and thanksgiving; for example, "Blessed are you, Lord, God of the universe." They would be hesitant to address God directly but would first express the distance between them by praising and exalting the greatness and majesty of God. A personal dialogue with God could only take place after such praise. If Jews ever would address God as "Father," they would qualify the expression by saying "Our Father" or "Father in heaven," but never just "Father." "Father" standing on its own, as we find it in the prayer of Jesus, is most unusual and exceptional.[16]

Jesus, in his prayers, leaves us with a different style of praying. He addresses God directly with the word "Father": "I thank you, Father, Lord of heaven and earth . . . "(Lk 10:21). "Father, I thank you . . . " (Jn 11:41). Wijngaards discusses this point:

> It is a truism that Jesus called God by the Aramaic term "Abba." The term occurs three times in the New Testament: Mk 14:36; Rom 8:15; and Ga 4:6. Only the first is on Jesus' lips. In each case the Greek translation "the father," "ho pater," is immediately added. . . . In Gethsemane, Jesus expressed the conviction that his actions were the direct outcome of the will of God. Abba expresses closeness to God because it is an intimate familiar term. Jesus lived in the conviction that the Father knew

him, that he knew the Father and that through him God as Father is close to the disciples and known by them as God of mercy. This unusual term survived in the church in Aramaic, even though it needed translation (Rom 8:15; Ga 4:6). The force of this tradition indicates that the term expressed something prized by the church. . . . The term is inserted into a new and fitting context because of what Jesus himself had done and taught.[17]

If we accept the arguments of J. Jeremias, there is no parallel in Jewish literature where the pious would have dared to address God as *Abba*:

We are thus confronted with a fact of utmost significance. Whereas there is not one instance of God being addressed as "*Abba*" in the literature of Jewish prayers, Jesus always addressed him in this way (except for the cry from the cross, Mk 15:34).[18]

By using this word Jesus reveals the heart of his relationship with God: the simple trust and confidence with which a little child comes to a father who is known, loved, and trusted. Jesus, therefore, spoke with God as a child speaks with his or her father—simply, intimately, securely.

The word *Abba* encompasses the whole message and claim of Jesus: He came to lead us into a relationship with God that would be most adequately expressed with the word *Abba*. The astonishing point is that Jesus authorized his disciples to repeat the word *Abba* after him. We are called to share in this sonship and empowered to speak with our heavenly Father in the familiar and trusting way as a child would to a father. This is the new relationship which opens the door to God's Kingdom. Jesus leads his disciples into an intimacy with God expressed most adequately by being able to address God as *Abba*. What this means in reality is expressed very well in Galatians 4:6 and Romans 8:15. Both remarks show us that the cry of *Abba* is beyond all human capabilities and is only possible within the new relationship with God given by his Son. Lochman concludes:

The simple name "Father," then, carries with it the whole revolution in the concept of God which is linked to the message and especially to the destiny of Jesus Christ: Immanuel, the God of faithful nearness in the deepest, most binding, and truly unconditional sense, in the sense of incarnation, his identification with sons and daughters in life and death and to all eternity, God not merely in the height of his heavenly but also in the depth of his earthly course.[19]

It is *the* gift of the New Age we are entering now—a totally new relationship with God—a relationship that only the Holy Spirit can adequately express in us. Jeremias remarks:

> Perhaps at this point we get some inkling why the use of the Lord's Prayer was not commonplace in the early Church and why it was spoken with such reverence and awe.[20]

Barclay, in his commentary on the Lord's Prayer, stresses the importance of the "our" in the exposition of Matthew. The prayer is not an "I" prayer but a "we" prayer. We come before God not as individuals but as community. The opening address settles once and for all not only our relationship with God but also with our fellow human beings. If God is our Father, then our fellow human beings are our brothers and sisters. All discrimination, racism, exploitation stand condemned in the two words that open the Lord's Prayer.[21]

A serious analysis of "Father" as used by Jesus should make it clear that any patriarchal understanding of "Father" was always a serious misunderstanding. The Father of Jesus Christ is a wholly non-patriarchal Father. The best proof is the parable of the Prodigal Son, where the father behaves in a totally non-patriarchal and previously unknown manner. Lochman explains:

> We have only to note the figure of the father in the story. Against all prevailing laws and customs he does not stand in his son's way but lets him go, even though it is a highly risky and misconceived freedom that the younger son chooses. And when the prodigal returns crushed, the father does not count up and expect repayment but runs to meet him. The father runs: an unheard-of action in the patriarchal code. But this unheard-of feature in the father's attitude characterizes the New Testament concept. It cuts right across all pagan and pseudo-Christian ideas of God.[22]

Before we take up the individual petitions of the Lord's Prayer, it is most important to emphasize that we must see every petition in the light of the opening address. How should we address God? Who is God? To whom do we want to speak? The creator of the universe, the omnipotent, ever present, almighty, never changing Lord of heaven and earth? No, for us the God to whom Jesus directs us to pray is *Abba*. The address is, therefore, not just an introduction to the prayer but indicates what makes this prayer possible at all. This point is vividly expressed by Lochman:

> One cannot emphasize enough that the very first word of the Lord's Prayer is a decisive one that points the way. It is the word

284 THE KINGDOM AND JESUS CHRIST

"Father." Whether we follow Luke and take it in all its simplic-
ity, or Matthew with his liturgical expanded form ("our Father,
who art in heaven"), the first word is one that we cannot exchange: "Father." It sets the stage for our whole exposition of
the individual petitions. In the history of exposition it has rightly
been observed repeatedly that one's understanding of the whole
prayer depends upon one's understanding of this first word.[23]

The Two "Thou Petitions"

As the old Jewish form reveals, the two "Thou petitions" are
eschatological. They ask for the revelation of God's eschatological
Kingdom. The oldest form of the Kaddish prayer, which concluded
the service of the synagogue, runs like this:

> Exalted and hallowed be His great Name in the World that he
> created according to His will. May He establish His Kingdom in
> our lifetime and in your days and in the lifetime of the whole
> household of Israel, speedily and at a near time. May His great
> Name be praised forever and unto all eternity.

The two "Thou petitions" of Jesus can be regarded as a powerful
shortened version of the Kaddish. Yet in spite of all the similarities
between the Kaddish prayer and the two "Thou petitions" of the Lord's
Prayer, we should not overlook the great difference: With Jesus the
Kingdom has come; it is a reality now.[24]

Hallowed Be Thy Name. Although the word *hallow* means "praise,"
"bless," "glorify," this is not an expression of praise or respect for
God but a real petition. The mood in "hallowed be" has the same
force as in "come" and "be done"; therefore, petition, not praise, is
expressed. What then does it mean to pray that God's name may be
hallowed? To know the name means to know the reality behind the
name. Name is an expression of innermost being, essential nature,
and personal identity. To know God's name is to know God's self-
revelation and offer of salvation. The name here signifies God. It refers to God's innermost nature, especially self-revelation and actions
on our behalf. Here, it refers to the address of the prayer, "*Abba*." It
expresses the new relationship with God that the disciples receive as
followers of Jesus: "Righteous Father, the world does not know you,
but I know you; and these know that you have sent me. I made your
name know to them" (Jn 17:25-26). In this sense the word *Abba* gov-
erns all the petitions in the prayer.[25]
Hallowed has many meanings. It is important, as stated above, to
regard it as a petition, a request directed to God, asking for some-

thing. What is it that God should do? Some scholars translate it negatively: Knowing that we can never adequately "vindicate God's honor," the petition refers to the fact that only God can and will do it. By hallowing God's name, God creates Israel anew and in so doing, the Kingdom of God breaks into the world. That was the eschatological expectation connected with this petition. In this petition we pray: "Father, let the world come to know your name through your final revelation. We know who you are, what you are like, because your Son has revealed your name to us, your being *Abba*. Now let us see it in action." It is a petition for God to manifest and realize universally the unconditional love and care for the world as revealed in Jesus Christ. In it we seek the hour in which God's profaned and misused name will be glorified and God's Reign revealed according to the divine promise: "I will sanctify my great name, which has been profaned among the nations, and which you have profaned among them; and the nations shall know that I am the LORD, says the Lord GOD, when through you I display my holiness before their eyes (Ez 36:23).[26]

This petition is a missionary petition—it contains the whole mission of the church. We are called to make known God's name to the world, to let all people know who God really is: *Abba*. We know it, but we also know that most people do not really know who God is. Therefore we cry out in this petition: "Father may the world get to know who you really are!" The petition contains three different elements: First, "let us come to know more and more who you are and let us celebrate it in praise, thanksgiving, and adoration." Second, "may the whole human race come to know through our proclamation and witness of community living that you are our Father and we are all brothers and sisters." Third, "let the day come soon, when you will reveal in fullness to all creation your true name and being." It is a petition for the final consummation of the Kingdom, the day of the parousia.

Thy Kingdom Come. The central theme of Jesus' ministry was the proclamation that the Kingdom of God was imminent (Mk 1:15). One might have expected that this would be the first petition. But the first and the second petitions are intimately connected. The name of God refers to God's own innermost nature. The Kingdom of God refers to the divine activity. Since God's innermost nature finds expression in God's activity, it is appropriate for the petition concerning God's name to precede the petition concerning the Kingdom. The entreaty is a petition for the final consummation. We are praying God to establish the Kingdom of God completely, just as it was begun in the life and ministry of Jesus. The petition refers to the future aspect of the Kingdom, but this in turn is grounded in the fact that the Kingdom is already partially present. We find this same phrase expressed in the early church in the phrase, *"Maranatha*, Come, Lord Jesus!" (1 Cor 16:22; Rv 22:20), which concludes certain liturgical services. Having experienced the in-breaking of the Kingdom into the present and cel-ebrated it in the liturgy, the community cries out for the final consum-mation.

Matthew's third petition, "Thy will be done on earth as it is in heaven," says the same thing in another way. Since God's will and rule are identical, this petition means: God's rule should be established here on earth. May God, who reigns in heaven, finally establish God's rule here on earth too. This will be the sign that God's Kingdom has already come into this world. These petitions are like a cry from the depth of distress. The rule of evil is experienced, a world enslaved by sin and misery. Yet disciples know that the rule of God is already operative in this world. They know that the turning point has already come because God's saving work has already begun. They, therefore, ask for the full revelation of what has already been granted.

The Lord's Prayer is a prayer for the "in between time," for the "already" of the "not yet." It is for those who experience two "ages" and stand with one foot already in the New Age and the other still in the Old.

Some may see in this petition a cry to God for those who do not find God's will easy and ask help to fulfill it. Here too we can still maintain the above interpretation. After all, to do God's will means in practice to let the Kingdom, which is already present, rule our life. The petition would then mean: "Lord, let nothing except the presence of your Kingdom rule and determine all my actions and my life." This petition should be interpreted then in the light of Jesus' own struggle with the will of the Father. Particularly important here is the Gethsemane story (Mt 26:36-46; Mk 14:32-42; Lk 22:40-46). This is an authentic commentary on Jesus' understanding of the petition. At the heart of this prayer we find the same request twice: "Thy will be done, not as I will, but as you will." Jesus trembles before the suffer-ings he must undergo to make the Kingdom come true. There will be no cup of salvation without the cup of eschatological suffering.[27]

The disciples will have to keep in mind that promoting the King-dom here on earth and placing their lives under God's Kingdom will not spare them from struggling with God's will the way their master had to struggle.

The Two "We Petitions"

In the Jewish prayer called the Kaddish, the two "Thou petitions" can be found but not the "We petitions." The "Thou petitions" lead to the "We petitions." They form the heart of the Lord's Prayer. If the two "Thou petitions" seem to cry out for the coming of the Kingdom in its fullness, the two "We petitions" stress the now, the today. They seem to say: "Lord, if we have to stay in this sin-permeated world to carry on your work, please, give us now, today, something from the future so that we can go on witnessing to your Kingdom in our time and situations."

Our Bread for Tomorrow Give Us Today. Some scholars regard this petition as the heart and center of the Lord's Prayer. Up to now the center of attention was God's cause: thy name, thy kingdom, thy will. But now our cause enters into the foreground: our bread, our debts, our temptation, our being menaced by evil. Yet most surprising is that the first petition concerns our daily bread. Many have wondered in the history of interpretation of the Lord's prayer what connection there is between the eternal Kingdom and

> this almost petty attention to transitory and unimportant everyday things, and even more surprisingly to the paltry daily ration that we need to eke out life from today to tomorrow.[28]

The difficulty here is the Greek word *epiousios,* which is usually translated "daily." There are four major meanings for this term: (1) necessary for existence, (2) for today, (3) for the coming day, and (4) for the future.

Since the word *epiousios* is not used elsewhere in the New Testament, it is impossible to say for sure which of the four meanings is correct. The word has puzzled translators and interpreters since the early Church Fathers. References to bread and meals in the Old Testament, Judaism, and Jesus' own ministry are most helpful, particularly Jesus' own understanding of food and meals. This alone would suggest that we begin with a literal understanding of bread in trying to interpret this petition of the Lord's Prayer. Eating bread together always meant more than sustaining life. It provided, for example, an opportunity for creating and refreshing human relationships. There are also enough passages in the Old Testament and Judaism from which we could conclude that *epiousios* in the Lord's Prayer carries an eschatological sense, meaning "for the future." When the disciples pray, "Give us this day our bread for the future," they ask God to grant them, here and now, some gifts of the wonderful time of salvation that is still to come in its fullness. This view is supported by the Church Father Jerome, who writes in his commentary on Matthew 6:11:

> In the Hebrew Gospel according to Matthew it is thus: Our bread of the morrow give us this day; that is, the bread which Thou will give us in Thy Kingdom, give us this day.

In the Gospel called according to the Hebrews for "super-substantial" bread I found "mahar," which means "of the morrow"; so that the sense is: our bread of the morrow, that is, of the future, give us this day.

Many scholars agree that there is enough proof to conclude with Jerome that the translation should read: "Our bread for tomorrow give us today."[29] "Tomorrow" meant the "great tomorrow," the age of salvation, the final consummation. The "bread of tomorrow" is, therefore, the "bread of the age of salvation," the "heavenly manna." In this way the bread petition is seen as an eschatological petition. But is that not too much spiritualization? Does the petition not simply ask for what we need daily to stay alive, bread that fills the stomachs of the hungry? Yet food and meals are not just a means for staying alive. In Jesus' society every table fellowship is a guarantee of peace, of trust, of fellowship. Jesus' eating and sitting at table with sinners and outcasts was correctly understood by his opponents: "This fellow welcomes sinners and eats with them" (Lk 15:2; Mk 2:15-17).

Jesus, by having table-fellowship with outcasts, placed sinners on the same level as the righteous. Jesus understood his meals with the outcasts as "God sitting with man at table," a sign of reconciliation and an anticipation of the heavenly banquet in the consummation of the Kingdom. Every meal with Jesus was for his followers a symbol, a pre-representation, indeed, an actual anticipation of the meal of consummation. The continuation of the daily table-fellowship as a sacred rite after Jesus' death must be understood within this framework. Whenever the disciples, in the future, would eat their meals, they would recall their meals with Jesus, who had understood meal-sharing as an anticipation of the heavenly banquet. Every meal for disciples of Jesus would become a sign of the Kingdom present. Whenever they come together to share a meal, they make the Kingdom present in anticipation of the final table-fellowship of humankind with God. In this petition we pray: give us the necessary food today so that we will be able to make the sign of the Kingdom present now. How can we preach and make the Kingdom present if we do not have the means to create table-fellowship, which is for us the sign of Jesus' presence in our midst?

The stress is on *today*. We live in a world enslaved by evil, in a world where God seems to be remote, in a world of hunger and thirst. And yet we cry out: Let us experience today, now, here, the great tomorrow—give us the "bread of tomorrow." This petition has, therefore, a definite reference to the bread that we eat day by day. At the same time it places the bread within a broader context that has as its basis Jesus' proclamation of the Kingdom of God.

The eucharist, where God sits with us at table and gives us the "bread of tomorrow," is, to be sure, *the* anticipation of the great tomorrow. But as we have seen, the bread petition is not exclusively a eucharistic petition. The petition for the bread includes material and spiritual needs without making one more important than the other. Jeremias concludes: "We can fetch down the 'great tomorrow,' the Kingdom, believe it down, pray it down, right into our poor lives, even now, even here today."[30] There remain two little words in this fourth petition which we must not overlook. They are the pronouns "us" and "our." In the light of the Kingdom present my bread is never my bread alone. The bread of the fourth petition is bread that must be shared. It is here that the question of justice enters the Lord's Prayer. Lochman—referring to Isaiah 58:7, "Share your bread with the hungry," and Psalm 146:7, where the psalmist praises God as the one "who executes justice for the oppressed, who gives food for the hungry"—comments:

> The impressive reference to the hungry and oppressed, and the emphatic word "justice," cannot be excluded from any theologically responsible discussion of the petition for bread, and certainly not in any circumstances today. For the nub of the problem is that there are hungry people in our world, masses of them. This is true at a time when, as noted, in vast areas of the world the question of bread is to a large extent detached from the context of physical hunger.[31]

Or in the words of St. Basil the Great (fourth century):

> The bread that is spoiling in your house belongs to the hungry. The shoes that are mildewing under your bed belong to those who have none. The clothes stored away in your trunk belong to those who are naked. The money that depreciates in your treasury belongs to the poor![32]

In such circumstances any extravagance in food and eating becomes a real sin against our needy brothers and sisters and against God. In a consumer society the petition for bread becomes a demand for conversion not only on the individual level but on the social level as well. We ask for a change in the modern social order. It means: "O God, to those who have hunger give bread; and to those who have bread the hunger for justice."[33]

And Forgive Us Our Debts as We Also Herewith Forgive Our Debtors. The great gift of the eschatological age is forgiveness. Jesus, to the

surprise of his audience (Mk 2:5-7; Mt 9:2; Lk 5:20), understood forgiveness of sins within the framework of the imminent Kingdom. The
new time of salvation was understood as a time of forgiveness. Then
human beings would live in the presence of God, knowing that God
had forgiven them and created a new communion with them. Jesus is
telling his audience that this time of great forgiveness is already beginning, is reality at this moment. God's forgiving love and mercy, to be
expected as boundless in the end-time, is already offered now. Since
we are living in this end-time, we already pray in this petition: Grant
us, dear Father, this great gift of the messianic time on this day and in
this place. Although we know that we live in this great time of forgiveness, we also know full well that we are still imperfect, sin-permeated, and in constant need of forgiveness. We can ask for this forgiveness because we know that in Jesus the Kingdom has become a present
reality and its power is available to us.[34]

The problem here is how to interpret the ὡς καὶ (*hos kai*) of Matthew and the καὶ γαρ (*kai gar*) of Luke. In short, how is God's
forgiveness related to human forgiveness? Almost all scholars agree
that the phrase "as we forgive" should not be taken as a comparison,
as if God would forgive us in the measure that we forgive. The parable of the Unmerciful Servant (Mt 18:23-35) suggests quite clearly
that God's forgiveness precedes human forgiveness. God first forgives
us and then expects us to forgive one another. The parable implies
that human forgiveness is a consequence of God's prior action. We
have no excuse for being unforgiving. We can and must forgive one
another because we have first been forgiven. The magnitude of God's
forgiveness makes it ridiculous for us not to forgive one another.

The parable indicates that God's forgiveness becomes real for us
only when we accept this forgiving love as happening to us. It becomes part of our lives to such an extent that we are willing to forgive
our fellow human beings wherever and in whatever way they have
wronged us. If we do not forgive one another, we are actually showing
that we have not really accepted the great forgiveness of God's love
that is offered to us in this eschatological time. Our forgiveness of one
another, therefore, becomes the sign of how far we have accepted God's
great gift of forgiveness and love that is offered to us now.

Matthew 6:14-15, however, seems to be inconsistent with our interpretation:

> For if you forgive others their trespasses, your heavenly Father
> will also forgive you; but if you do not forgive others, neither
> will your Father forgive your trespasses.

This passage once again looks like a comparison, meaning human
forgiveness precedes God's forgiveness; only human forgiveness makes

God's forgiveness possible. The passage seems to be totally inconsistent with the parable of the Unmerciful Servant. Can it be reconciled? Yes, if we keep in mind that God's forgiveness always precedes human forgiveness, human forgiveness is a consequence of God's forgiveness, and God's forgiveness can become real for us only when we are willing to forgive one another.

Matthew 6:14-15 in vivid, forceful language demonstrates the third point. It says that God's forgiveness can become real for us only if we receive it graciously and let it change our life. In that way we can really forgive others in the power of the forgiving love of God that is here and now present in its eschatological fullness.[35]

The address *Abba* signifies that we are accepted and brought into a new relationship with God. This new relationship enables us to practice a forgiveness toward others which we could and would never be capable of by relying only on our own human resources. To be able to forgive is not a purely human capacity, for human beings have a tendency to desire revenge and a chance to get even. Being forgiving toward others is a gift from God and a true sign that a person has let the power of the Kingdom present into his or her life.

J. Jeremias translates Luke's words back into Aramaic: "As we also herewith forgive our debtors." The meaning then is: "We are ready to pass on to others the forgiveness which we have received. Grant us, dear Father, the gift of the age of salvation, thy forgiveness, so that, in the strength of received forgiveness we might forgive those who have wronged us."[36] How God's forgiveness precedes our ability to forgive and to love is most clearly expressed, according to Jeremias, in Luke's parable of the Great Sinner (Lk 7:36-50). Jeremias translates verse 47 as follows: "I tell you then the great love she has shown proves that her many sins have been forgiven." The woman's love for Jesus is the result of the forgiveness received that has given her the strength to love in such a way. It is, therefore, not her love that causes the forgiveness Jesus passes on to her, but the other way around.[37]

The Conclusion: "And Let Us Not Succumb to Temptation"

This is the only negatively formulated petition, and it stands out harshly. God does not tempt anyone, but we know also that "no one can obtain the Kingdom of God who has not passed through testing." We cannot escape testing, but we can ask not to succumb to the test. All we ask is to stand firm in the midst of temptation. What is promised is the overcoming of temptation. The petition is not a request to be spared temptation but rather that God will help overcome it.

What does *temptation* mean here? There are three possible interpretations: (1) We ask the Father to help us to avoid anything that is wrong or sinful. This is what a Jew would pray for when faced with temptations; (2) We ask that we will not deny our faith in times of suffering or persecution. This meaning refers to Matthew 26:41; Mark 14:38; and Luke 22:40,46: "Pray that you may not enter temptation"; and (3) A more eschatological interpretation: Jesus, using apocalyptic imagery, sees the Kingdom that enters this world with him engaged in a battle with evil forces.

The synoptic gospels portray the mission of Jesus as overthrowing the demonic power structure. "Have you come to destroy us?" (Mk 1:24). Since the "evil one" is not going to let his kingdom be plundered without resistance, the end-time is regarded as the time of Satan's final assault (Rv 3:10). The disciple, who lives in the end-time and who has sided with Jesus in the great eschatological battle, will have to experience the force of the "hour of trial." The temptation for the apostle is apostasy or falling away. More precisely it is the constant temptation to lose faith that the Kingdom is already in the world; it is the temptation to regard the experience of the Kingdom present in our world as an illusion, to give in to despair. It means to give up believing that the Kingdom, which is present only in the form of a tiny seed (Mt 13:31ff.), will ultimately grow into a large tree. It is the ever-present temptation to lose hope that God can bring about a glorious end from of a tiny beginning as we experience it in the present. This "apostasy" does not have to be a dramatic event. It is a temptation to which we can all easily succumb without even realizing it. It is often a gradual process. It is the temptation to give in to doubts and finally to despair, frustration, and bitterness. In short, it is to lose our faith that God's Kingdom is already in this world and will lead this world to its final destiny in the fullness of the Kingdom.

Jesus tells his disciples to ask God for the consummation of the Kingdom. He encourages them in their petitions to "pray down" the gift of the age of salvation into their own poor lives even here and now. But in this last petition he warns them against any false enthusiasm. Remember, you are engaged in the eschatological battle, watch out! We pray: Dear Father, this one request grant us: preserve us from falling away from Thee. Matthew also understood this petition in this way when he added the petition: "And deliver us from the evil (One)."

The Lucan and Matthean version of the Lord's Prayer do not conclude with a doxology. Only the *Didache* added a doxology, which we use today in the liturgy. Such a doxology is proper, for no biblical prayer ends without some closing words of praise to God.[38]

CONCLUSION

The Lord's Prayer must be seen in the context of Jesus' proclamation of the imminent Kingdom of God. The hallowing of God's name, the coming of the Kingdom, and the petitions of the bread of tomorrow and forgiveness are all petitions that sound quite different when prayed in this context—which the Old Testament could not provide at all. It is the prayer of those who already experience the Kingdom of God becoming actualized in their present lives and who in the power of the Kingdom present cry out for its final consummation. They pray that what they now experience dimly, may soon be theirs in all its fullness. Teresa of Avila commenting on the Lord's Prayer had this thought to offer:

> The sublimity and the perfection of this evangelical prayer is something for which we should give great praise to the Lord. So well composed by the good master was it, daughters, that each of us may use it in her own way. I am astonished when I consider that, in its few words are enshrined all contemplation and perfection, so that if we study it, no other book seems necessary. For thus far in the Lord's Prayer, the Lord has taught us the whole method of prayer and of high contemplation from the very beginning of mental prayer to Quiet and Union.[39]

Clement of Alexandria has preserved a saying of Jesus which is not written in the gospels. It says:

> Ask ye for the great things, so will God add to you the little things. You are praying falsely, says the Lord. Your prayers are always moving in a circle around your own small "I," your own needs and troubles and desires. Ask for the great things—for God's almighty glory and kingdom, and that God's great gifts, the bread of life and the endless mercy of God, may be granted to you—even here, even now, already today. That does not mean that you may not bring your small personal needs before God, but they must not govern your prayer, for you are praying to your Father. He knows all. He knows what things his children have need of before they ask him, and he adds them to his great gifts. Jesus says: Ask ye for the great things, so God will grant you all the little things. The Lord's Prayer teaches us how to ask for the great things.[40]

Notes

INTRODUCTION

1. John Fuellenbach, *Hermeneutics, Marxism and Liberation Theology* (Manila: Divine Word Publications, 1989), pp. 83-84.

2. Walter Brueggemann, *Prophetic Imagination* (London: SCM Press, 1992 [original, 1978]), p. 14.

3. Brueggemann, *Prophetic Imagination*, p. 13.

4. Brueggemann, *Prophetic Imagination*, p. 11.

5. "Unsere Hoffnung. Ein Bekenntnis zum Glauben in dieser Zeit," *Herder Korrespondenz* 30 (1976), 200-211 at pp. 208-209.

6. Marcus J. Borg, *Jesus, a New Vision: Spirit, Culture and Life of Discipleship* (San Francisco: Harper & Row, 1987), pp. 1-17.

7. K. Rahner and W. Thüssing, *Christologie systematisch und exegetisch* (Freiburg: Herder, 1972), p. 29.

8. G. C. Beasley-Murray, *Jesus and the Kingdom of God* (Grand Rapids, Michigan: Eerdmans Publishing Company, 1986), p. 269.

9. Jon Sobrino, "Jesús el Reino de Dios significado y objetivos últimos de su vida," *Christus* 45 (1980), 17-23 at p. 18.

10. A. Loisy, *L'evangile et l'eglise* (Paris, 1902), p. iii.

11. G. G. Soares-Prabhu, "The Kingdom of God: Jesus' Vision of a New Society," in *The Indian Church: The Struggle for a New Society*, ed. D.S. Amolorpavadass (Bangalore: NBCLC, 1981), 579-608 at p. 584.

12. Rudolf Bultmann, *Theology of the New Testament*, vol. 1 (New York: Scribner's, 1951), p. 33.

13. Helmut Wenz, *Theologie des Reiches Gottes: Hat Jesus sich geirrt?* (Hamburg: Herbert Reich Verlag, 1975), p. 21.

14. John Pairman Brown, "Kingdom of God," in *The Encyclopedia of Religion*, vol. 8 (New York: Macmillan, 1978), 304-312 at p. 304.

15. Albert Schweitzer, "Die Idee des Reiches Gottes im Verlauf der Umbildung des eschatologischen Glaubens in den uneschatologischen," *Schweizerische Theol. Umschau* 23 (1953), 2-20 at p. 20.

16. Wolfhart Pannenberg, "The Kingdom of God and the Church," in *Theology and the Kingdom of God* (Philadelphia: Westminster Press, 1977), pp. 52-53.

17. Mikhail Gorbachev in an address to the United Nations, 7 December 1988.

18. Leonardo Boff, *Jesus Christ Liberator: A Critical Christology for Our Time* (Maryknoll, New York: Orbis Books, 1978), p. 50.

19. Robin Green, "God Is Doing a New Thing: A Theological Reflection on the Practice of Partnership," *International Review of Mission* 80 (1991), 219-226 at p. 219.

20. Albert Nolan, *God in South Africa, The Challenge of the Gospel* (Grand Rapids, Michigan: Eerdmans Publishing Company, 1988), pp. 187-188.

21. Leonardo Boff, *Teología del cautivero y de la liberación* (Madrid: Ediciones Paulinas, 1978), pp. 13-33.

22. M. M. Thomas, "The South Needs a New Vision of Modernization," *Media Development* 39 (1992), 33-35 at p. 34.

23. Vaclav Havel, *Living in Truth* (Faber, 1989), p. 54, as quoted in "After the Day of the Lie," Editorial comment, *The Month* (April 1990), 128-133 at p. 130.

24. Havel, as quoted in "After the Day of the Lie," p. 130.

25. Havel, as quoted in "After the Day of the Lie," p. 130.

26. Havel, as quoted in "After the Day of the Lie," p. 130.

27. Brueggemann, *Prophetic Imagination*, p. 45.

28. Green, "God Is Doing a New Thing," p. 220.

29. Benedict T. Viviano, *The Kingdom of God in History* (Wilmington, Delaware: Michael Glazier, 1988), pp. 28-29.

30. Boff, *Jesus Christ Liberator*, p. 56.

31. Charles Elliott, *Praying the Kingdom: Towards a Political Spirituality* (London: Darton, Longman and Todd, 1985), p. 1.

32. Clodovis and Leonardo Boff, *Salvation and Liberation: In Search of a Balance between Faith and Politics* (Maryknoll, New York: Orbis Books, 1985), p. 83.

33. Gustavo Gutiérrez, *A Theology of Liberation* (Maryknoll, New York: Orbis Books, 1973), pp. 149-153.

34. Pannenberg, "The Kingdom of God and the Church," pp. 72-75.

35. Howard A. Snyder, *Models of the Kingdom* (Nashville: Abingdon Press, 1991), p. 153.

36. K. E. Skydsgaard, "Kingdom of God and the Church," *Scottish Journal of Theology* 6 (1959), p. 386.

37. Richard P. McBrien, *Catholicism* (London: Geoffrey Chapman, 1981), p. 686.

38. Felix Wilfred, "Once Again . . . Church and Kingdom," *Vidyajyoti* 57 (1993), 6-24 at p. 10.

39. John B. Cobb, Jr., *Sustainability: Economics, Ecology, and Justice* (Maryknoll, New York: Orbis Books, 1992), p. 21.

40. Michael Amaladoss, "Secularization and India: Modernization and Religion in an Eastern Country," *Exchange* 21 (1992), 34-48 at p. 36.

41. Thomas, "The South Needs a New Vision," p. 33.

42. Bryan R. Wilson, "Secularization," in *Encyclopedia of Religion*, vol. 13 (New York: Macmillan, 1978), 159-165 at p. 160.

43. Amaladoss, "Secularization and India," p. 37.

44. Thomas, "The South Needs a New Vision," pp. 33-35.

45. Michael Amaladoss, quoted in Ton Crijnen, "Secularization Seems to Be a Typical (Western) European Phenomenon," *Exchange* 21 (1992), 29-33 at p. 33.

46. Amaladoss, "Secularization and India," pp. 45-46.

PART 1: THE KINGDOM BEFORE JESUS—INTRODUCTION

1. John Bright, *The Kingdom of God: The Biblical Concept and Its Meaning for the Church* (Nashville: Abingdon Press, 1953), pp. 17-18.

2. P. Dale, "The Kingdom of God in the Old Testament," in *The Kingdom of God in 20th-Century Interpretation*, ed. Wendell Willis (Peabody, Massachusetts: Hendrickson, 1987), pp. 66-67.

1   THE NATIONAL-POLITICAL EXPECTATION

1. D. Senior, "Reign of God," in *The New Dictionary of Theology*, ed. J. A. Komonchak, M. Collins, D. A. Lane (Dublin: Gill and Macmillan, 1988), pp. 851-861.

2. Rudolf Schnackenburg, *God's Rule and Kingdom* (New York: Herder and Herder, 1963), pp. 11-40. In all the treatises of the last thirty years on the Kingdom this book has become a classic.

3.Norbert Lohfink, "Der Begriff des Reiches Gottes vom Alten Testament her gesehen," in *Unterwegs zur Kirche,* ed. Josef Schreider (Freiburg: Herder, 1987), pp. 43-54.

4.Bruce Chilton and J.I.H. McDonald, *Jesus and the Ethics of the Kingdom* (Cambridge: University Press, 1987), pp. 49-50.

5.Jean Louis Ska, "Creazione e Liberazione nel Pentateuco," in *Creazione e Liberazione nei libri del' Antico Testamento* (Torino: Editrice Elle Di Ci, Leumann, 1989), pp. 15-31.

6.Schnackenburg, *God's Rule and Kingdom*, pp. 29-30.

7.Wesley J. Fuerst, "How Israel Conceived of and Addressed God," in *Our Naming of God: Problems and Prospects of God-Talk Today*, ed. Carl Braaten (Minneapolis: Fortress Press, 1989), pp. 61-74.

8.Senior, "Reign of God," pp. 851-852.

9.Norbert Lohfink, *Option for the Poor: The Basic Principle of Liberation Theology in the Light of the Bible* (Berkeley, California: BIBAL Press, 1987), p. 36.

10. Norbert Lohfink, *Option for the Poor*, pp. 35-47.

11. Brueggemann, *Prophetic Imagination*, pp. 16-17.

12. Norbert Lohfink, "Der Begriff des Reiches Gottes vom Alten Testament her gesehen," pp. 43-54.

13. Norbert Lohfink, "Der Begriff des Reiches Gottes vom Alten Testament," pp. 55-66.

14. Senior, "Reign of God," p. 854.

15. Brueggemann, *Prophetic Imagination*, p. 37.

16. Schnackenburg, *God's Rule and Kingdom*, p. 30. He quotes here Sigmund Mowinckel (*He That Cometh* [Oxford: Blackwell, 1956], p. 143) and Walther Eichrodt (*Theologie des Alten Testamentes I* [Göttingen: ⁵1957], pp. 326 seq.).

17. Norbert Lohfink, "Der Begriff des Reiches Gottes vom Alten Testament," pp. 66-77.

18. Norbert Lohfink, "Der Begriff des Reiches Gottes vom Alten Testament," pp. 77-80. Lohfink contests the findings of Schnackenburg that the expectation of the coming Kingdom at the end of the Old Testament had become a "purely religious notion."

19. C. W. Kaiser, Jr., "Kingdom Promises as Spiritual and National," in *Continuity and Discontinuity*, ed. J. Feinberg (1988), 289-307 at p. 293.

20. Kaiser, "Kingdom Promises as Spiritual and National," pp. 303-307.

21. Schnackenburg, *God's Rule and Kingdom*, pp. 41-42. He admits that this national-political expectation represented the thoughts and sentiments of the broad mass of the Jewish people, but he emphasizes that this expectation does not lose its religious character.

22. Ben F. Meyer, *The Aims of Jesus* (London: SCM Press, 1979), p. 137. Meyer does not deny the universal-eschatological stress in Jesus' Kingdom message, but, as he writes: "Two conditions were always understood. The post-historical restoration of humankind would hinge on the historically rooted restoration of Israel. And Israel's restoration would not be realized without a willed act of acceptance."

23. H. Merklein, *Gottesherrschaft als Handlungsprinzip* (Würzburg: Echter Verlag, 1978), pp. 110-114.

24. What do we mean by Apocryphal literature? The word *apocryphal* often carries with it the sense of "false," but its origin and meaning are different. It means "outside books" and refers to books which lie outside the canon of scripture. Its exact sense varies depending upon the religious denomination using the term.

For Protestants it refers to certain books found in the Greek and Latin Bibles (Septuagint and Vulgate) but not in the Hebrew Bible. Catholics would call most of these "deutero-canonical." They were officially regarded as belonging to the canon at Trent (1546) and at Vatican I (1870). The Deutero-canonical books are the following: Tobit, Judith, Esther (certain additions), Wisdom of Solomon, Wisdom of Jesus Son of Sirach (Ecclesiasticus), Baruch (addition of the Letter of Jeremiah), Daniel (certain additions), 1 and 2 Maccabees. These books were composed during the last two centuries in Palestine.

Pseudepigrapha (also called Apocrypha by Roman Catholics) are those books "outside" the Apocryphal/Deutero-canonical literature. Most of these are apocalyptical literature. Some are Enoch, Book of Jubilees, Testament of the Twelve Patriarchs (140-110 B.C.), Psalms of Solomon (50 B.C.), Assumption of Moses, The Apocalypse of Abraham (A.D. 1-50), Apocalypse of Baruch (A.D. 50-100), Apocalypse of Moses (A.D. 80-100), The Sibylline Oracles (Greek, 150-120 B.C.). These books were very popular among the Qumran community and some of them were most probably written there. On this latter subject see D. S. Russell, *Between the Testaments* (London: SCM Press, Ninth Printing 1986), pp. 75-88.

25. John J. Collins, "The Kingdom of God in the Apocrypha and Pseudepigrapha," in *The Kingdom of God in 20th-Century Interpretation*, 81-95 at p. 95.

26. R. A. Horsley and John S. Hanson, *Bandits, Prophets, and Messiahs: Popular Movements at the Times of Jesus* (San Francisco: Harper & Row, 1985), pp. 23-29.

27. R. Horsley, *Jesus and the Spiral of Violence: Popular Jewish Resistance in Roman Palestine* (San Francisco: Harper & Row, 1987), pp. 178-180. Referring to the Qumran regulation that each meal had to be celebrated as if the Messiah were already here, Horsley concludes: "The Qumranites were thus celebrating their regular community meals as if the messiah were already there, i.e. were celebrating in anticipation of the future consummation" (p. 180).

28. Horsley, *Jesus and the Spiral of Violence*, pp. 200-201.

29. Norman Perrin, *The Kingdom of God in the Teaching of Jesus* (London: SCM Press, 1963), p. 171. Perrin quotes five instances in the apocryphal writings and Qumran of *Kingdom of God* being used to express the expectation of God's decisive, eschatological intervention in history and human experience.

30. B. T. Viviano, "The Kingdom of God in the Qumran Literature," in *The Kingdom of God in 20th-Century Interpretation*, 97-107 at p. 107.

31. Kaiser, "Kingdom Promises as Spiritual and National," p. 291.

32. O. Loretz, *The Truth of the Bible* (Freiburg: Herder and Herder, 1968), p. 58.

33. John L. Topel, *The Way to Peace: Liberation Through the Bible* (Maryknoll, New York: Orbis Books, 1979), pp. 3-5.

34. N. Flüglister, "Strukturen der alttestamentlichen Ekklesiologie," in *Mysterium Salutis* 6, 4 (Einsiedeln: Benzinger Verlag, 1972), pp. 77-90.

35. B. W. Anderson, "The New Covenant and the Old," in *The Old Testament and Christian Faith: A Theological Discussion* (New York: Harper & Row, 1963), 225-245 at pp. 231-234.

2   THE APOCALYPTIC EXPECTATION

1. Horsley, *Bandits, Prophets, and Messiahs*, pp. 16-20.
2. Horsley, *Bandits, Prophets, and Messiahs*, p. 152.
3. Russell, *Between the Testaments*, p. 95.
4. R. C. Dentan, "The Kingdom of God in the Old Testament," in *Interpreter's One-Volume Commentary on the Bible,* ed. Ch. M. Layman (London: Collins, 1971), 1159-1166 at p. 1164.

5.P. Sacchi, "Jewish Apocalyptic," *SIDIC* 18 (1985), 4-9 at pp. 5-7.

6.A. Abecassis, "Jewish Apocalyptic: Its Meaning and Message," *SIDIC* 18 (1985), 10-11 at p. 10.

7.Sacchi, "Jewish Apocalyptic," p. 9.

8.Russell, *Between the Testaments*, pp. 104-106.

9.Russell, *Between the Testaments*, pp. 97-100.

10. G. E. Ladd, *The Presence of the Future: A Revised and Updated Version of Jesus and the Kingdom* (Grand Rapids, Michigan: Eerdmans Publishing Company, 1974), p. 101.

11. Russell, *Between the Testaments*, p. 111.

12. Russell, *Between the Testaments*, pp. 119-142.

3   THE ETHICAL EXPECTATION

1.Abecassis, "Jewish Apocalyptic," p. 10. See also, Solomon Schechter, *Aspects of Rabbinic Theology: Major Concepts of the Talmud* (New York: Schocken Books, 1961), pp. 65-79, although most of the material presented there is of a later date.

2.Schechter, *Aspects of Rabbinic Theology*, pp. 71-72.

3.As quoted in Jacob Neusner, "There Has Never Been a Judaeo-Christian Dialogue—But There Can Be One," *Cross Currents* 42 (1992), 3-25 at p. 22.

4.Schechter, *Aspects of Rabbinic Theology*, 72ff. It is interesting that the idea of seeing Jesus as the one who by fulfilling the great Shema perfectly brought the Kingdom into the world has seldom been developed in Christology.

4   THE EMERGING CONTENT OF THE KINGDOM

1.R. Cabello, "El Reino de Dios," *Christus* 50 (1985), 16-22 at pp. 16-18.

2.Areas Mortimer, "Mission and Liberation: The Jubilee: Paradigm for Mission Today," *International Review of Mission* 73 (1984), 34-48 at pp. 35-36.

3.R. Gnuse, "Jubilee Legislation in Leviticus: Israel's Vision of Social Reform," *Biblical Theology Bulletin* 15 (1989), pp. 43-48.

4.Paul Hollenbach, "Liberating Jesus for Social Involvement," *Biblical Theology Bulletin* 15 (1985), 151-157 at p. 153.

5.G. W. Buchanan, *The Consequences of the Covenant* (Leiden, 1970), pp. 9-18.

6.Schnackenburg, *God's Rule and Kingdom*, pp. 41-74.

7.Dentan, "The Kingdom of God in the Old Testament," p. 1159.

5   THE KINGDOM OF GOD IN CONTEMPORARY EXEGESIS

1.A. M. Pernia, *God's Kingdom and Human Liberation: A Study of G. Gutiérrez, L. Boff and J. L. Segundo* (Manila: Divine Word Publications, 1990), pp. 7-28.

2.On how deeply Augustine's *City of God* influenced the conception of the Kingdom of God up to recent times, see Viviano, *The Kingdom of God in History*, pp. 55-56.

3.See Viviano, *The Kingdom of God in History*.

4.Norman Perrin, *Jesus and the Language of the Kingdom* (Philadelphia: Fortress Press, 1975), pp. 30-33. Using the language of symbol Perrin has introduced a distinction between "a steno and a tensive" symbol. There can be a "steno-symbol," like the mathematical symbol π, having a "one-to-one relationship" to what it represents. It then refers to only one anticipated concrete event, such as the dramatic interruption of God in history. No doubt many Jews saw the symbol of the kingdom in that way. But there is also a second kind of symbol, a "tensive symbol," having a "set of meanings which can neither be exhausted nor adequately expressed by any one referent." Perrin then views the kingdom as a tensive symbol.

5.B. Scott, *Jesus, Symbol-Maker for the Kingdom* (Philadelphia: Fortress Press, 1981), p. 11.

6.Pernia, *God's Kingdom and Human Liberation*, pp. 21-28.

7.Rene Coste, *Marxist Analysis and Christian Faith* (Maryknoll, New York: Orbis Books, 1985), p. 72.

8.Nicholas Berdyaev, *Christianisme, Marxisme* (Paris: Centurion, 1975), p. 35.

9.Rene Coste, "World History and the Coming of the Kingdom of God," in *Marxist Analysis and Christian Faith*, pp. 64-101.

10. Jon Sobrino, *Christology at the Crossroads* (Maryknoll, New York: Orbis Books, 1978), p. 348.

11. G. Gutiérrez, *The Power of the Poor in History* (Maryknoll, New York: Orbis Books, 1983), p. 66.

12. G. Gutiérrez, "Liberation Theology and Proclamation," in *Concilium*, New Series, vol. 6, no. 10 (1974), p. 69.

13. Theo Witvliet, *A Place in the Sun: An Introduction to Liberation Theology in the Third World* (Maryknoll, New York: Orbis Books, 1985), p. 26.

14. E. Schillebeeckx, quoted by Gutiérrez, *A Theology of Liberation*, p. 13.

15. Fuellenbach, *Hermeneutics, Marxism and Liberation Theology*, pp. 39-46.

16. R. Vidales, "Methodological Issues in Liberation Theology," in *Frontiers of Theology in Latin America*, ed. R. Gibellini (Maryknoll, New York: Orbis Books, 1979), p. 49.

17. G. M. Soares-Prabhu, *Commitment and Conversion: A Biblical Hermeneutics for India Today—A Proposal for Discussion*, unpublished manuscript, 1985, p. 5.

18. J. S. Croatto, "Biblical Hermeneutics in the Theology of Liberation," in *The Bible and Liberation*, ed. N. K. Gottwald (Maryknoll, New York: Orbis Books, 1983), pp. 140-167.

19. Sandra Schneiders, "Faith, Hermeneutics and the Literal Sense of Scripture," *Theological Studies* 39 (1978), 719-736 at p. 734.

20. Robert McAfee Brown, *Theology in a New Key* (Philadelphia: Westminster Press, 1978), pp. 97-98.

21. Gutiérrez, *The Power of the Poor in History*, p. 4.

22. Congregation for the Doctrine of the Faith, *Instruction on Christian Freedom* (Vatican City: Libreria Editrice Vaticana, 1986), no. 5.

23. Pernia, *God's Kingdom and Human Liberation*, p. 27.

24. Bernard Lonergan, "Theology in Its New Context," in *Conversion*, ed. W. E. Conn (New York: Alba House, 1978), 3-21 at p. 6.

25. Antonio B. Lambino, "A New Theological Model: Theology of Liberation," in *Towards Doing Theology in the Philippine Context* (Manila: Loyola Papers 9, 1977), 2-25 at p. 6.

26. Snyder, *Models of the Kingdom*, p. 20.

27. Avery Dulles, *Models of the Church* (London: Macmillan, 1974), pp. 22-24.

28. Lambino, "A New Theological Model," pp. 6-7.

29. Snyder, *Models of the Kingdom*, pp. 128-129.

30. Snyder, *Models of the Kingdom*, p. 18.

31. Snyder, *Models of the Kingdom*, pp. 16-18.

32. Snyder, *Models of the Kingdom*, pp. 127-128.

33. Avery Dulles, "The Meaning of Faith Considered in Relationship to Justice," in *The Faith That Does Justice*, ed. John Haughey (Maryknoll, New York: Orbis Books, 1977), pp. 10-46.

PART 2: THE KINGDOM MESSAGE OF JESUS

1. Sobrino, *Christology at the Crossroads*, p. 42.
2. Borg, *Jesus, a New Vision*, pp. 150-170.
3. Borg, *Jesus, a New Vision*, pp. 43-44.
4. Horsley, *Jesus and the Spiral of Violence*, pp. 167-177.
5. Horsley, *Jesus and the Spiral of Violence*, pp. 193-194.
6. Beasley-Murray, *Jesus and the Kingdom of God*, pp. 85-89.

6   THE LANGUAGE OF THE KINGDOM

1. Claus Westermann, *The Parables of Jesus in the Light of the Old Testament*, trans. and ed. by F. W. Golka and A. H. B. Logan (Edinburgh: T&T Clark, 1990).
2. Clement Thoma and M. Wyschogrod, eds., *Parables and Story in Judaism and Christianity* (New York: Paulist Press, 1989). In particular, see David Stern, "Jesus' Parables From the Perspective of Rabbinic Literature: The Example of the Wicked Husbandmen," pp. 42-80.
3. As quoted by Joseph Fichtner, *Many Things in Parables: Reflection for Life* (Makati, Philippines: St. Paul Publications, 1990), pp. 4-5.
4. Eamonn Bredin, *Rediscovering Jesus: Challenge of Discipleship* (Quezon City, Manila: Claretian Publication, 1990; originally published Dublin: Columba Press, 1985), p. 36.
5. Horsley, *Bandits, Prophets, and Messiahs*, p. 1.
6. Dermot Lane, "Jesus and the Kingdom of God," *Living Light* 19 (1982) 103-114 at pp. 106-108.
7. Scott, *Jesus, Symbol-Maker for the Kingdom*, p. 11.
8. M. Hunter, *The Parables Then and Now* (Philadelphia: Fortress Press, 1971), p. 10.
9. Neal F. Fisher, *The Parables of Jesus: Glimpses of God's Reign*, rev. ed. (New York: Crossroad, 1990), pp. 23-24.
10. M. I. Boucher, *The Parables*, New Testament Message 7 (Dublin, 1971), pp. 26-27.
11. Boucher, *The Parables*, pp. 16-17.
12. Bredin, *Rediscovering Jesus*, p. 38.
13. Herman Hendrickx, *The Parables of Jesus: Studies in the Synoptic Gospels* (Makati, Manila: St. Paul Publications, 1987), pp. 3-15.
14. Bredin, *Rediscovering Jesus*, p. 40.
15. William J. Bausch, *Storytelling: Imagination and Faith* (Mystic, Connecticut: Twenty-Third Publications, 1991), pp. 121-123.
16. Bredin, *Rediscovering Jesus*, pp. 42-44.
17. J. D. Crossan, *In Parables: The Challenge of the Historical Jesus* (San Francisco: Harper & Row, 1973), pp. 51-52.
18. Crossan, *In Parables*, pp. 30-31.
19. Crossan, *In Parables*, pp. 35-36, 82, 113.
20. A. M. Hunter, "The Interpreter and the Parables," in *New Testament Issues*, ed. R. Bates (London: SCM Press, 1970), pp. 71-87.
21. Joachim Jeremias, *Parables of Jesus* (London: SCM Press, 1963), p. 150.
22. Cabello, "El Reino de Dios," p. 17.

7   THE BASIC CHARACTERISTICS OF JESUS'
KINGDOM MESSAGE

1.Rudolf Schnackenburg in his work *God's Rule and Reign* (pp. 77-104) presents Jesus' Kingdom message under the following basic characteristics: the
Eschatological Character; the Saving Character; the Purely Religious and Universal Character; the Challenge of the Reign of God.

2.Snyder, *Models of the Kingdom*, pp. 16-17.

3.Beasley-Murray, *Jesus and the Kingdom of God*, pp. 3-5.

4.Beasley-Murray, *Jesus and the Kingdom of God*, pp. 71-75.

5.Soares-Prabhu, "The Kingdom of God," pp. 590-591.

6.Beasley-Murray, *Jesus and the Kingdom of God*, pp. 71-75. Similar to this is
the position of Scaria Kuthirakkattel, *The Beginning of Jesus' Ministry According
to Mark's Gospel (1:14-3:6): A Redaction Critical Study, Analecta Biblica* 123
(Roma: Editrice Pontificio Instituto Biblico, 1990), p. 94. He concludes his investigation of the phrase "the time is fulfilled" by saying: "To sum up, the time of
preparation and promises have come to an end; the long-awaited eschatological
time is definitely fulfilled in the commencement of Jesus' ministry inaugurating
the inbreaking of the kingdom of God himself. Yet it is Jesus who announces the
definite fulfillment of the Messianic time determined by God."

7.Beasley-Murray, *Jesus and the Kingdom of God*, p. 89.

8.Viviano, *The Kingdom of God in History*, p. 26.

9.Horsley, *Jesus and the Spiral of Violence*, p. 178.

10.Horsley, *Jesus and the Spiral of Violence*, pp. 178-180. He sees this in
connection with the practice of the Qumran community. He comments, "Since
the discovery of the Dead Sea Scrolls the recognition that the Qumran Community celebrated a similar 'messianic banquet' has given us a greater appreciation of Jesus' anticipatory celebration of the Kingdom of God" (p. 178).

11.Ladd, *The Presence of the Future*, p. 218.

12.R. Bultmann, "Zur eschatologischen Verleundigung Jesu," *Theologische
Literaturezeitung* 72 (1947), cols. 271-74 at p. 272.

13. Gerhard Lohfink, "The Exegetical Predicament Concerning Jesus' Kingdom of God Proclamation," *Theology Digest* 36 (1989), 103-110 at p. 104. Original text: "Die Not der Exegese mit der Reich-Gottes Verkündigung Jesu,"
Theologische Quartalschrift 168 (1988), 1-15.

14. Gerhard Lohfink, "The Exegetical Predicament," p. 106.

15. W. Kelber, *The Kingdom in Mark. A New Place and a New Time* (Philadelphia: Fortress Press, 1974), pp. 15-18.

16.Ladd, *The Presence of the Future*, p. 154. Ladd goes to some length to
explain the passages in scripture which refer to the overthrowing of Satan, particularly Luke 10:18 and Matthew 12:28, wherein Satan is attacked by Jesus. The
following mission of the Seventy is then seen by Jesus as evidence of the defeat of
Satan (pp. 154-158).

17. Rene W. Padilla, *Mission Between the Times: Essays on the Kingdom* (Grand
Rapids, Michigan: Eerdmans Publishing Company, 1985), p. 7.

18.Horsley, *Jesus and the Spiral of Violence*, pp. 186-187.

19. See Albert Nolan, *God in South Africa,* chap. 2, "Sin in the Bible," pp. 31-
48 at pp. 43-44.

20. See Delwin Brown, *To Set at Liberty: Christian Faith and Human Freedom*
(Maryknoll, New York: Orbis Books, 1981), especially chap. 4, "The Denial of
Freedom: An Understanding of Sin," 64-87 at pp. 78-81.

21. A. Moser, "Sin as Negation of the Kingdom," *Theology Digest* 30 (1982),
27-30.

22. Moser, "Sin as Negation of the Kingdom," p. 29.

23. Edward Schillebeeckx, *Church: The Human Story of God* (New York: Crossroad, 1990), p. 132.

24. Ladd, *The Presence of the Future*, pp. 333-334.

25. Kelber, *The Kingdom in Mark*, p. 18.

26. As quoted in Martyn, "From Paul to Flannery O'Connor with the Power of Grace," *Katallagete* 7 (1981), 10-17 at p. 11.

27. Neusner, "There Has Never Been a Judaeo-Christian Dialogue—But There Can Be One," pp. 3-13.

28. Martyn, "From Paul to Flannery O'Connor," p. 13.

29. As cited in J. C. Rottenberg, *The Promise and the Presence: Towards a Theology of the Kingdom of God* (Grand Rapids, Michigan: Eerdmans Publishing Company, 1980), p. 55.

30. Cobb, *Sustainability*, pp. 10-11.

31. As quoted by Martyn, "From Paul to Flannery O'Connor," pp. 12-13.

32. Perrin, *The Kingdom of God in the Teaching of Jesus*, pp. 158-206. Perrin writes: "The experience of the individual has become the arena of the eschatological conflict. Within this arena the Kingdom has come in the sense that the sovereign power of God is now being manifested in this aspect of the decisive battle against the arch-enemy" (p. 171).

33. Lane, "Jesus and the Kingdom of God," p. 110.

34. Joachim Jeremias, *Theology of the New Testament* (London: SCM Press, 1971), pp. 100-101.

35. Adolf Harnack, *What Is Christianity?* (New York: Harper & Row, 1957), p. 62.

36. Viviano, *The Kingdom of God in History*, p. 27.

37. Cyril of Alexandria, as quoted by Beasley-Murray, *Jesus and the Kingdom of God*, p. 102.

38. Beasley-Murray, *Jesus and the Kingdom of God*, pp. 97-103.

39. Norman Perrin, *Rediscovering the Teaching of Jesus* (London: SCM Press, 1967), pp. 70-74.

40. Edward Schillebeeckx, *Interim Report on the Book Jesus Christ* (New York: Crossroad Publications, 1981), p. 124.

41. Boff, *Jesus Christ Liberator*, pp. 282-286.

42. Elizabeth A. Johnson, *Consider Jesus: Waves of Renewal in Christology* (New York: Crossroad, 1990), pp. 54-56.

43. Ladd, *The Presence of the Future*, p. 331.

44. Ladd, *The Presence of the Future*, p. 53.

45. Schillebeeckx, *Church: The Human Story of God*, pp. 130-133.

46. Gerhard Lohfink, *Jesus and Community* (London: SPCK Press, 1985), p. 9.

47. E. P. Sanders, *Jesus and Judaism* (London: SCM Press, 1985), pp. 228-237.

48. Ladd, *The Presence of the Future*, pp. 171-194.

49. Gerhard Lohfink, "The Exegetical Predicament," p. 104.

50. Viviano, *The Kingdom of God in History*, p. 29.

51. Jürgen Moltmann, "First the Kingdom of God," *Tripod* 11 (May-June, 1991), 6-27 at pp. 20-21.

52. Moltmann, "First the Kingdom of God," p. 21.

53. Gerhard Lohfink, "The Exegetical Predicament," pp. 106-108.

54. Sobrino, *Christology at the Crossroads*, pp. 45-46.

55. Pernia, *God's Kingdom and Human Liberation*, pp. 28-58. Pernia entitles the chapter in which he treats Gutiérrez's understanding of the Kingdom of God "Divine Filiation and Human Fellowship," indicating Gutiérrez's precise conception of the Kingdom in these categories. See particularly pages 49-51 entitled "Gift and Task; Grace and Demand."

**8   THE FUTURE OF EVIL AND THE QUESTION
OF ETERNAL PUNISHMENT**

1.Ladd, *The Presence of the Future*, p. 333.

2.Ladd, *The Presence of the Future*, p. 334.

3.Joseph Ratzinger, *Eschatology, Death and Eternal Life: Dogmatic Theology*, vol. 9, ed. J. Auer and J. Ratzinger (Washington D.C.: Catholic University Press, 1988), p. 215.

4.L. Lochert, *Die Hölle gehört zur Frohbotschaft* (München: Herold Press, 1981).

5.J.N.D. Kelly, *Early Christian Creed*, rev. ed. (New York: Harper & Row, 1978), pp. 479-485. Also, Harold O.J. Brown, "Will the Lost Suffer Forever?," *Criswell Theological Review* 4 (1990), pp. 267-270. Brown argues strongly for the traditional view maintaining that Augustine's view is the one most Church Fathers shared to various degrees.

6.For a detailed comment on this chapter 21, see H. Urs von Balthasar, *Dare We Hope, "That All Men Be Saved"?* (San Francisco: Ignatius Press, 1988), pp. 47-72, especially pp. 65-72.

7."Preface: Not Interesting, Merely Terrible," Editor's Note, *New Blackfriars* 69 (1988), 467-471 at 469.

8.John Bowker, "The Human Imagination of Hell," *Theology* 85 (1982), pp. 403-410.

9.Von Balthasar, *Dare We Hope*, pp. 29-46.

10. Karl Barth, *Kirchliche Dogmatik* II/1 (Zollikon-Zürich: Evangelischer Verlag A.G., 1957), p. 551.

11. Gordan Graham, "The Goodness of God and the Conception of Hell," *New Blackfriars* 69 (1988), 477-487 at p. 478.

12. Clark H. Pinnock, "The Destruction of the Finally Impenitent," *Criswell Theological Review* 4 (1990), 243-259 at p. 254.

13. Pinnock, "The Destruction of the Finally Impenitent," pp. 245-246. The whole article is a strong critique and challenge to all traditional views which maintain that there is no other way to think of hell than in terms of eternal physical and mental punishment.

14. As quoted by Schillebeeckx, *Church: The Human Story of God*, p. 135.

15. Catherine of Siena as quoted by von Balthasar, in *Dare We Hope*, pp. 214-215. Normally, it is the saints' desire to do everything to prevent anyone from going to hell. "I would desire that there no longer be hell, or at least that no soul would go there. If I could remain united with you in love while, at the same time, placing myself before the entrance to hell and blocking it off in such a way that no one could enter again, then that would be the greatest of joys for me, for all those whom I love would then be saved" (p. 215).

16. J. Maritain, *The Range of Reason* (London: Geoffrey Bles, 1953), p. 60.

17. Pinnock, "The Destruction of the Finally Impenitent," pp. 252-253.

18. Edward Fudge, "The Final End of the Wicked," *Journal of the Evangelical Theological Society* 27 (1984), pp. 325-334. The article is a summary of Fudge's book, *The Fire That Consumes: A Biblical and Historical Study of Final Punishment* (Providential Press, 1982).

19. Fudge, "The Final End of the Wicked," pp. 325-326.

20. This is not only the view of Fudge but of Pinnock as well. See Pinnock, "The Destruction of the Finally Impenitent," p. 251.

21. Fudge, "The Final End of the Wicked," p. 330.

22. Fudge, "The Final End of the Wicked," pp. 329-330.

23. Fudge, "The Final End of the Wicked," p. 333.

24. G. Graham, "The Goodness of God and the Conception of Hell," pp. 480-484. Graham weighs here what is valid in this psychological argument with what remains questionable.

25. T. Davis Stephen, "Universalism, Hell and the Fate of the Ignorant," *Modern Theology* 6 (1990), 173-186 at p. 175.

26. Stephen, "Universalism, Hell and the Fate of the Ignorant," p. 184.

27. Stephen, "Universalism, Hell and the Fate of the Ignorant," p. 185.

28. Schillebeeckx, *Church: The Human Story of God*, p. 137.

29. Graham, "The Goodness of God and the Conception of Hell," p. 486.

30. Schillebeeckx, *Church: The Human Story of God*, pp. 137-138.

31. Karl Rahner, *Foundation of Christian Faith: An Introduction to the Idea of Christianity* (New York: Seabury Press, 1978), p. 443.

32. Fudge, "The Final End of the Wicked," p. 334.

33. Pinnock, "The Destruction of the Finally Impenitent," p. 252.

34. On the questionableness of this verdict on Origen see von Balthasar, *Dare We Hope*, pp. 47-64.

35. H. Urs von Balthasar, *Die Gottesfrage des heutigen Menschen* (München—Wien: Herold, 1956), p. 185.

36. H. Urs von Balthasar, *The Glory of the Lord: A Theological Aesthetics*, vol. 7, *Theology: The New Covenant* (Edinburgh: T & T Clark, 1989), pp. 202-235.

37. For a more detailed interpretation of this passage see Gerard Rosse, *The Cry of Jesus on the Cross: A Biblical and Theological Study* (New York: Paulist Press, 1987), pp. 88-95.

38. W. Pannenberg, *The Apostles' Creed in the Light of Today's Questions* (Philadelphia: Westminster Press, 1972), pp. 92-93.

39. Pannenberg, *The Apostles' Creed*, p. 95.

40. Lochert, *Die Hölle gehört zur Frohbotschaft*, pp. 125-33.

41. Stephen, "Universalism, Hell and the Fate of the Ignorant," pp. 174-175. Davis quotes these scriptural arguments as supporting universalism. He himself does not hold this position. Our own position differs from universalism in that we do not deny the possibility of hell.

42. R. Nordsieck, *Reich Gottes Hoffnung der Welt* (Neunkirchen: Neunkirchener Verlag, 1980), pp. 197-205.

43. Edith Stein, *Welt und Person: Beiträge zum christlichen Wahrheitsstreben*, ed. L. Gelber and Romaeus Leuven (Freiburg: Herder, 1962), pp. 158-160. Text as quoted by von Balthasar, *Dare We Hope*, pp. 218-221.

44. Newton, Andover, "I Believe in the Resurrection of the Body," *Interpretation* 46 (1992) pp. 42-52. He comments: "The majority opinion over the centuries, with an arsenal of texts, opts for the former. God will 'separate people one from another as a shepherd separates the sheep from the goats . . .' (Mt 25:32-33)." For him the universalists are claiming to know too much about the final will and way of God. But that could be said about the majority opinion as well. As he expresses it: "The homecoming of all is an article of *hope* and not an article of *faith*" (p. 48).

45. Pinnock, "The Destruction of the Finally Impenitent," p. 256.

46. Brown, "Will the Lost Suffer Forever?," pp. 277-278.

47. The key principle which any position on hell must affirm is clearly articulated in the *Catechism of the Catholic Church*: "Le peine principale de l'enfer consiste en la séparation éternelle d'avec Dieu en qui seul l'homme peut avoir la vie et le bonheur pour lesquels il a été crée et auxquels il aspire." [Translation: "The principal pain of hell consists in the eternal separation from God in whom alone a person is able to have the life and happiness for which he or she has been created and to which he or she aspires."] Certainly, all three positions, including annihilation, fulfill this requirement.

9   THE SERMON ON THE MOUNT . . .

1. W. D. Davies, and S. C. Allison, "Reflection on the Sermon on the Mount," *Scottish Journal of Theology* 44 (1991), pp. 283-309. The two authors, after

giving an excellent summary of the historical interpretations of the Sermon on the Mount in seven theses (see below), present their own view. Their conclusion is similar to that of Joachim Jeremias: The Sermon on the Mount presupposes the proclamation of the Kingdom and is meant for those who have answered to this challenge. In their own words: "How does one, in the briefest manner, character- ize the Sermon on the Mount, the Messiah's eschatological Torah? The answer is twofold. Mt. 5-7 has end in view and sets forth the means towards that end. The end, the ultimate end, is divine sonship (5:9, 45), which means firstly being like God, both in this world and the world to come (5:48). The means to this end, given by grace, are certain moral qualities, fully embodied by God's Son (cf. chap- ter 8-28), and the loving, kenotic, radical acts they engender, all of which may be summed up as dikaiosune and its fruits: poverty of spirit, purity of heart, love of enemy. In short, the Sermon on the Mount proclaims likeness to the God of Israel through the virtues of Jesus Christ" (pp. 308-309).

2.Joachim Jeremias, *The Sermon on the Mount* (Philadelphia: Fortress Press, 1963).

3.Jeremias, *The Sermon on the Mount*, p. 17.

4.Davies and Allison, "Reflection on the Sermon on the Mount," p. 297.

5.Lapide Pinchas, *The Sermon on the Mount: Utopia or Program for Action?* (Maryknoll, New York: Orbis Books, 1986).

6.Jeremias, *Sermon on the Mount*, p. 9.

7.Jeremias, *Sermon on the Mount*, p. 23.

8.Davies and Allison, "Reflection on the Sermon on the Mount," p. 304.

10   THE RELIGIOUS AND POLITICAL CHARACTER OF THE KINGDOM

1.Schnackenburg, *God's Rule and Kingdom*, p. 95.

2.Kaiser, "Kingdom Promise as Spiritual and National," p. 305. The first part of Jesus' ministry is depicted in the chapters up to Matthew 12. At Matthew 12:14-15 the shift between the two parts takes place. Kaiser himself does not agree with this view.

3.Robert L. Saucy, "The Presence of the Kingdom and the Life of the Church," *Bibliotheca Sacra* 145 (1988), 30-46 at p. 34.

4.Saucy, "The Presence of the Kingdom and the Life of the Church," pp. 44-45.

5.Saucy, "The Presence of the Kingdom and the Life of the Church," p. 46.

6.Norbert Lohfink, "Religious Orders: God's Therapy for the Church," *The- ology Digest* 33 (1986), 203-212 at p. 205. Lohfink is concerned with the reper- cussions such a view has on the understanding of the mission of the church today.

7.J. M. Bonino, ed., *Faces of Jesus: Latin American Christologies* (Maryknoll, New York: Orbis Books, 1983), p. 5.

8.Paul Hollenbach, "The Historical Jesus Question in North America Today," *Biblical Theology Bulletin* 19 (1989), 12-22.

9.Norbert Lohfink, "The Exegetical Predicament," p. 105.

10. Pannenberg, *Theology and the Kingdom of God*, p. 120.

11. John H. Yoder, *The Politics of Jesus* (Grand Rapids, Michigan: Eerdmans Publishing Company, 1972), pp. 16-19.

12. Pannenberg, *Theology and the Kingdom of God*, p. 80.

13. Oscar Cullmann, *Jesus and the Revolutionaries* (New York: Herder, 1970), pp. 29-30.

14. Martin Hengel, *Was Jesus a Revolutionist?* (Philadelphia: Fortress Press, Facet Books, 1971).

15. Gerhard Theissen, *The First Followers of Jesus* (London: SCM Press, 1978), p. 64.

16. Fuellenbach, *Hermeneutics, Marxism and Liberation Theology*, pp. 37-76.

17. William J. Doorly, *Prophet of Love: Understanding the Book of Hosea* (Mahwah, New Jersey: Paulist Press, 1991), pp. 123-128.

18. J. Kavunkal, "Jubilee the Framework of Evangelization," *Vidyajyoti* 52 (1988), pp. 181-190.

19. Gnuse, "Jubilee Legislation in Leviticus," p. 43.

20. Sharon H. Ringe, *Jesus, Liberation, and the Biblical Jubilee: Images for Ethics and Christology* (Philadelphia: Fortress Press, 1985), p. 44. This book is a thorough investigation into the Jubilee imagery found in the synoptic gospels.

21. James D.G. Dunn, *Jesus' Call to Discipleship* (Cambridge University Press, 1992), pp. 32-36.

22. Ringe, *Jesus, Liberation, and the Biblical Jubilee*, p. 36.

23. Thomas D. Hanks, *God So Loved the Third World* (Maryknoll, New York: Orbis Books, 1983), pp. 98-99.

24. Yoder, *The Politics of Jesus*, chapter 3: The Implications of the Jubilee, pp. 64-77. Yoder, like Ringe, is fully aware that the discourse at Nazareth alone is not sufficient to prove that Jesus understood his message as the inauguration of the year of Jubilee. For this a more complete reading of the whole gospel is necessary.

25. Hanks, *God So Loved the Third World*, p. 103.

26. Gnuse, "Jubilee Legislation in Leviticus," p. 47.

27. Paul Hollenbach, "Liberating Jesus for Social Involvement," pp. 154-55.

28. Hollenbach, "Liberating Jesus for Social Involvement," p. 152.

29. G. Pixley, *God's Kingdom: A Guide for Biblical Study* (Maryknoll, New York: Orbis Books, 1977). pp. 76-77.

30. Sanders, *Jesus and Judaism*, p. 231.

31. Sanders, *Jesus and Judaism*, p. 235.

32. There are quite a number of books written already about this issue. Here special reference is made to Marcus J. Borg, *Jesus, a New Vision: Spirit, Culture and Life of Discipleship*; Horsley, *Jesus and the Spiral of Violence*; and, Horsley, *Bandits, Prophets, and Messiahs*. By attempting to understand Jesus first and foremost in the setting of the social-political and economic situation of the time the authors challenge many cherished positions about Jesus, his vision, and his aims, which traditionally consider only the cultural and the religious dimensions. By ignoring the social-political-economic realities, the emerging picture of Jesus is too narrowly portrayed.

33. Horsley, *Jesus and the Spiral of Violence*, p. ix.

34. Horsley, *Jesus and the Spiral of Violence*, p. x.

35. Hollenbach, "The Historical Jesus Question in North America Today," offers an excellent overview on the current thought about this issue in the North American scene.

36. Borg, *Jesus, a New Vision*, pp. 86-87.

37. Dunn, *Jesus' Call to Discipleship*, p. 69.

38. Borg, *Jesus, a New Vision*, pp. 84-85.

39. Borg, *Jesus, a New Vision*, pp. 88-90.

40. Dunn, *Jesus' Call to Discipleship*, pp. 83-85.

41. Juan Luis Segundo, *The Historical Jesus of the Synoptics* (Maryknoll, New York: Orbis Books, 1985), pp. 93-94.

42. Segundo, *The Historical Jesus of the Synoptics*, p. 90.

43. Horsley, *Jesus and the Spiral of Violence*, p. 30. Horsley refers here to Exodus 28-29,39; Leviticus 8-10; Numbers 16-18; and Nehemiah 10:32-39.

44. Horsley, *Jesus and the Spiral of Violence*, p. 31.

45. Segundo, *The Historical Jesus of the Synoptics*, p. 71.

46. For a summary of Segundo's view see Pernia, *God's Kingdom and Human Liberation*, pp. 124-129.

47. Brueggemann, *Prophetic Imagination*, pp. 84-85.
48. Nolan, *God in South Africa*, p. 36.
49. Horsley, *Bandits, Prophets, and Messiahs*, pp. 223-241.
50. Horsley, *Bandits, Prophets, and Messiahs*, pp. 1-10.
51. Horsley, *Bandits, Prophets, and Messiahs*, p. 6.
52. Dunn, *Jesus' Call to Discipleship*, pp. 44-52.
53. P. Steidl-Meier, *Social Justice Ministry, Foundation and Concerns* (New York: Le Jacq Publishing Inc., 1984), p. 15.
54. Steidl-Meier, *Social Justice Ministry, Foundation and Concerns*, pp. 14-18.
55. Gerhard Lohfink, *Jesus and Community*, p. 14.
56. Sobrino, *Christology at the Crossroads*, p. 60.

11   SALVATION AND THE KINGDOM OF GOD

1. H. Merklein, *Die Gottesherrschaft als Handlungsprinzip*, pp. 146-147.
2. Gerhard Lohfink, *Jesus and Community*, p. 7.
3. Merklein, *Die Gottesherrschaft als Handlungsprinzip*, pp. 148-149.
4. Wilhelm Bruners, *Wie Jesus Glauben Lernte* (Freiburg: Christophorus Verlag, 1989), pp. 38-43.
5. Beasley-Murray, *Jesus and the Kingdom of God*, pp. 80-83.
6. P. Wolf, "Gericht und Reich Gottes bei Johannes und Jesus," *Gegenwart und Kommendes Reich*, ed. P. Fiedler and D. Zeller (Stuttgart: Katholisches Bibelwerk, 1975), pp. 47-49.
7. James D. G. Dunn, *Jesus and the Spirit: A Study of the Religious and Charismatic Experience of Jesus and the First Christians as Reflected in the New Testament* (Philadelphia: Westminster, 1975), pp. 33-44.
8. Dunn, *Jesus and the Spirit*, pp. 63-70.
9. Borg, *Jesus, a New Vision*, p. 92.
10. Borg, *Jesus, a New Vision*, p. 76.
11. Borg, *Jesus, a New Vision*, p. 82.
12. Joachim Jeremias, *Jesus' Promise to the Nations* (London: SCM Press, 1968), pp. 55-73.
13. Dale, *The Kingdom of God in the Old Testament*, pp. 77-78.
14. Gerhard Lohfink, *Jesus and Community*, pp. 17-29.

12   SALVATION OUTSIDE THE CHURCH

1. Paul Knitter, *No Other Name? A Critical Survey of Christian Attitudes Towards The World Religions* (Maryknoll, New York: Orbis Books, 1974), pp. 120-144.
2. Jacques Dupuis, "The Kingdom of God and World Religions," *Vidyajyoti* (November 1987), 530-544 at pp. 532-533.
3. Schnackenburg, *God's Rule and Kingdom*, p. 301.
4. Congar, *Lay People in the Church*, 2d rev. ed. (Westminster, Maryland: Newman Press, 1965), p. 88.
5. Dupuis, "The Kingdom of God and World Religions," p. 534.
6. Dupuis, "The Kingdom of God and World Religions," p. 535.
7. Dupuis, "The Kingdom of God and World Religions," p. 542.

13   DEFINING THE KINGDOM

1. Viviano, *The Kingdom of God in History*, p. 18.

2. Peter Kuzmić, "The Church and the Kingdom of God," in *The Church: God's Agent for Change*, ed. Bruce J. Nicholls (Cape Town: Oxford University Press, 1986), 49-81 at p. 61.

3. H. Wenz, "II. Die zentrale Bedeutung des Reiches Gottes in der Verkündigung des Neuen Testamentes," *Theologie des Reiches Gottes* (Hamburg: Reich Verlag, 1975), pp. 16-31.

4. Albert Schweitzer, *The Kingdom of God and Primitive Christianity* (New York: Harper & Row, 1968), p. 187ff.

5. Leon Morris, *The Epistle to the Romans* (Grand Rapids, Michigan: Eerdmans Publishing Company, 1988), pp. 488-489.

6. U. Wilckens, *Evangelisch-Katholischer Kommentar zum Neuen Testament VI/3 Der Brief an die Römer (Röm 12-17)* (Neunkirchen: Benzinger/Neunkirchener Verlag, 1982), p. 94.

7. M. Black, *Romans* (London: NCB, 1973), pp. 168-169. The recital of the great Shema ("Hear, O Israel!") at the beginning of a day was described as "taking upon oneself the yoke of Kingdom of God." It meant that the pious Jew would try to live the whole day before the Lord as if the Kingdom had already arrived. See Schechter, *Aspects of Rabbinic Theology*, pp. 65-79.

8. George Johnston, "Kingdom of God Sayings in Paul's Letters," *From Jesus to Paul, Studies in Honor of Francis Beare*, ed. P. Richardson and John C. Hurd (Waterloo: Laurier University, 1984), 143-156 at p. 154.

9. Wenz, *Theologie des Reiches*, p. 23.

10. John R. Donahue, "Biblical Perspectives on Justice," *The Faith That Does Justice*, ed. John C. Haughey (New York: Paulist Press, 1977), p. 77.

11. David Hollenbach, "The Church in the World: The Politics of Justice," *Theology Today* 38 (1981/82), p. 489. Hollenbach lists four biblical characteristics of justice: relational, creative, liberating, and vindicating. These characteristics are interconnected and inseparable, never to be pitted against each other. They are to be brought to the poor, the outcast, and the oppressed (p. 491).

12. John T. Topel, *The Way to Peace, Liberation Through the Bible* (Maryknoll, New York: Orbis Books, 1979), p. 53.

13. Fuellenbach, *Hermeneutics, Marxism and Liberation Theology*, pp. 68-69.

14. W. Brueggemann, Sharon Parks, Thomas H. Groome, *To Act Justly, Love Tenderly, Walk Humbly: An Agenda for Ministers* (New York: Paulist Press, 1986), p. 5.

15. Brueggemann, *To Act Justly, Love Tenderly, Walk Humbly*, pp. 5-6.

16. J. L. Mays, "Justice, Perspectives from the Prophetic Tradition," *Interpretation* 37 (1983), pp. 5-17.

17. Doorly, *Prophet of Love*, pp. 81-82. Doorly shows how Hosea's original interpretation of Jacob differs from the reinterpretation given to him later. Hosea described Jacob as a deceitful, wealth-seeking, egoistic person. Hosea then used the behavior of Jacob as a metaphorical comparison of the leaders of Israel in his time.

18. H. Simian-Yofre, "Justice," *Biblical Themes in Religious Education*, ed. J. S. Marino (Birmingham, Alabama: REP, 1983), pp. 200-202.

19. See Ska, "Creazione e Liberazione nel Pentateuco," chap. 1-2.

20. Horsley, *Jesus and the Spiral of Violence*, pp. 199-208.

21. Christoph Wrembek, "Der Heilige Geist und das Reich Gottes," *Geist und Leben* 64 (1991), 167-183 at pp. 173-175.

22. Neil Ormerod, "Renewing the Earth—Renewing Theology," *Pacifica, Australian Theological Studies* 4 (1991), pp. 296-306. The thoughts presented here are taken from this article and the references made there.

23. Snyder, *Models of the Kingdom*, pp. 136-141.

24. Cobb, *Sustainability*, pp. 94-95.

25. Cobb, *Sustainability*, p. 108.

26. Chief Seattle, quoted in Janet Morley, *Bread of Tomorrow* (Maryknoll, New York: Orbis Book, 1992), p. 65.

27. Snyder, *Models of the Kingdom*, p. 140.

28. Snyder, *Models of the Kingdom*, pp. 140-141.

29. Cobb, *Sustainability*, p. 5.

30. Cobb, *Sustainability*, p. 31

31. Herman Hendrickx, *Peace, Anyone? Biblical Reflection on Peace and Violence* (Quezon City: Claretian Publications, 1986), pp. 1-10.

32. G. von Rad, "eirene," *Theological Dictionary of the New Testament Vol. II*, ed. G. Kittel (Grand Rapids: Eerdmans Pubishing Company, 1964), pp. 402-403.

33. Hendrickx, *Peace, Anyone?*, p. 10.

34. Brueggemann, *To Act Justly, Love Tenderly, Walk Humbly*, p. 11. See also his "Vine and Fig Tree: A Case Study in Imagination and Criticism," *Catholic Biblical Quarterly* 43 (1981), 188-204.

35. Raymond Fung, *The Isaiah Vision* (Geneva: Risk Books Series, WCC Publication, 1992), pp. 5-11.

36. Lamar Williamson, "Jesus of the Gospels and the Christian Vision of Shalom," *Horizons in Biblical Theology* 6 (1984), 49-66 at pp. 58-64. He lists five aspects of shalom that can be found in the gospels: (1) physical wholeness; (2) spiritual wholeness; (3) shalom as harmony among disciples; (4) shalom as non-violence; and, (5) shalom as eschatological salvation.

37. D. C. Arichea, "Peace in the New Testament," *The Bible Translator* 38 (1987), pp. 201-206.

38. J. Massyngbaerde Ford, "Shalom in the Johannine Corpus," *Horizons in Biblical Theology* 6 (December, 1984), 67-89 at pp. 81-82.

39. E. Beyreuther and G. Finenrath, "Joy," *The New International Dictionary of New Testament Theology*, vol. 2, ed. Colin Brown (Exeter: Paternoster Press, 1976), pp. 352-561.

40. Johnston, "Kingdom of God," p. 155.

41. Not all exegetes will agree to this. Some hold that the phrase "in the Holy Spirit" only belongs to joy. Others, like W. Barclay, see the Kingdom here as consisting "in justice and peace and joy—and all in the atmosphere of the Holy Spirit." See Johnston, "Kingdom of God," p. 153.

42. Schillebeeckx, *Church: The Human Story of God*, pp. 116-133.

14   THE CHALLENGE OF THE KINGDOM

1. Borg, *Jesus, a New Vision*, pp. 99-101.

2. Irene Nowell, "Mercy," *The New Dictionary of Theology*, ed. J. A. Komonchak, Mary Collins, Dermont Lane (Dublin: Gill and Macmillan, 1990), 650-652 at p. 650.

3. Borg, *Jesus, a New Vision*, p. 102.

4. Nowell, "Mercy," p. 650.

5. Nowell, "Mercy," p. 651.

6. H. H. Esser, "Mercy," *The New International Dictionary of New Testament Theology*, vol. 2, pp. 599-600.

7. Every scholar dealing with the subject will define the Kingdom in his or her own terms without claiming to be exhaustive. Schillebeeckx, in *Church: The Human Story of God*, gives more then ten such descriptions.

8. Joachim Gnilka, *Jesus von Nazareth: Botschaft und Geschichte* (Freiburg: Herder, 1990), pp. 98-118.

9. Jeremias, *Parables of Jesus*, p. 139.

10. Leon Morris, *Testament of Love: A Study of Love in the Bible* (Grand Rapids, Michigan: Eerdmans Publishing Company, 1981), p. 84.

11. C. G. Montefiore, as quoted in Morris, *Testament of Love,* p. 157.

12. Leonhard Goppelt, *Theology of the New Testament,* vol. 1 (Grand Rapids, Michigan: Eerdmans Publishing Company, 1981), pp. 77-78.

13. A. Stock, *The Method and the Message of Mark* (Wilmington, Delaware: M. Glazier, 1985), p. 256.

14. Colin Brown, "Child," *The New International Dictionary of New Testament Theology,* vol. 1, pp. 284-285.

15. Hugh Anderson, *The Gospel of Mark* (Greenwood, South Carolina: Attic Press, 1976), p. 245. He remarks that "only here in the gospels is Jesus said to be indignant."

16. Joachim Gnilka, *Evangelisch-Katholischer Kommentar zum Neuen Testament: Das Evangelium nach Markus (Mk 8:27-16:20)* (Neukirchen: Benzinger/ Neukirchener Verlag, 1979), p. 81.

17. Anderson, *The Gospel of Mark,* p. 246.

18. Borg, *Jesus, a New Vision,* p. 102.

19. H. Herschel Hobbs, *The Exposition of the Gospel of Mark* (Grand Rapids, Michigan: Baker Book House, 1970), p. 155.

20. C. S. Mann, *Mark: A New Translation with Introduction and Commentary,* Anchor Bible Series (New York: Doubleday, 1986), p. 396.

21. Chilton and McDonald, *Jesus and the Ethics of the Kingdom,* pp. 87-88.

22. Joachim Jeremias, *Theology of the New Testament* (London: SCM Press, 1971), pp. 151-58.

23. Dunn, *Jesus' Call to Discipleship,* p. 84.

24. Dunn, *Jesus' Call to Discipleship,* p. 84.

25. Dunn, *Jesus' Call to Discipleship,* pp. 85-91.

26. Dunn, *Jesus' Call to Discipleship,* p. 152.

27. Jan Milic Lochman, "Church and World in the Light of the Kingdom of God," in *Church, Kingdom, World: The Church as Mystery and Prophetic Sign,* ed. Gennadios Limouris (Geneva: WCC Publications, Faith and Order Paper No. 130, 1986), 58-72 at pp. 70-71.

28. Cabello, "El Reino de Dios," p. 22.

15   THE KINGDOM OF GOD—ALREADY AND NOT YET

1. Hans Küng, *The Church* (New York: Sheed and Ward, 1967), pp. 54-55.

2. Günther Klein, "The Biblical Understanding of the Kingdom of God," *Interpretation* 26 (1972), p. 393.

3. Johannes Weiss, *Jesus' Proclamation of the Kingdom of God,* trans. and ed. with an introduction by Richard Hiers and David Holland (Philadelphia: Fortress Press, 1971).

4. Albert Schweitzer, *The Quest of the Historical Jesus,* trans. W. Montgomery with an introduction by James M. Robinson (New York: Macmillan, 1968).

5. Wendel Willis, "The Discovery of the Eschatological Kingdom," *The Kingdom of God in the 20th Century,* pp. 4-5.

6. Albert Schweitzer, *The Quest of the Historical Jesus,* p. 229. Schweitzer holds that Jesus found in Isaiah 52-64 the interpretation of his death as a "ransom for the many": "Jesus' idea of the Passion is in the end completely absorbed in that of Deutero-Isaiah." See also Albert Schweitzer, *The Mystery of the Kingdom of God: The Secret of Jesus' Messiahship and Passion,* trans. W. Lowrie (Buffalo, New York: Prometheus Books, 1985), p. 150.

7. Albert Schweitzer, *The Mystery of the Kingdom of God*, p. 137. Schweitzer is quite emphatic about this presumption, for there is no Kingdom without the messianic affliction: "A time of unheard of affliction must precede the coming of the Kingdom. Out of these woes the Messiah will be brought to birth. That was a view prevalent far and wide: in no other way could the events of the last times be imagined."

8. Albert Schweitzer, *The Kingdom of God and Primitive Christianity* (New York, 1968), pp. 221-223.

9. E. P. Sanders, *Jesus and Judaism* (London: SCM Press, 1985).

10. C. H. Dodd, *The Parables of the Kingdom* (New York: Scribner's, 1961), p. 159.

11. Dodd, *The Parables of the Kingdom*, p. 159.

12. C. H. Dodd, *The Apostolic Preaching and Its Development* (London: Hodder and Stoughton, 1936), pp. 58-59.

13. Jeremias, *Parables of Jesus*, p. 21.

14. Rudolf Bultmann, *Theology of New Testament*, vol. 1 (New York: Scribner's, 1954), p. 22.

15. Rudolf Bultmann, *Jesus and the Word* (New York: Scribner's, 1958), p. 51.

16. Bultmann, *Jesus and the Word*, p. 131.

17. Perrin, *The Kingdom of God in the Teaching of Jesus*, p. 88.

18. Jeremias, *Parables of Jesus*, p. 230.

19. Jeremias, *Theology of the New Testament*, p. 129.

20. Schnackenburg, *God's Rule and Kingdom*, pp. 213-14. Very close to Schnackenburg is Ladd, *The Presence of the Future*. Ladd admits his closeness to Schnackenburg, but states that his findings are independent from Schnackenburg (see p. 34, footnote 145).

21. Oscar Cullmann, *Christ and Time: The Primitive Christian Conception of Time and History*, rev. ed. (Philadelphia: Westminster Press, 1964), p. 84.

22. Cullmann, *Christ and Time*, p. 87.

23. Perrin, *The Kingdom of God in the Teaching of Jesus*, pp. 154-206. Perrin seems to put too much stress on the experience of the Kingdom now in the individual, as if the presence of the Kingdom of God could be divorced from the person of Jesus and be limited to human experience. See Ladd, *The Presence of the Future*, pp. 37-38.

24. Pannenberg, *Theology and the Kingdom of God*, p. 62ff.

25. Jürgen Moltmann, *Theology of Hope* (London: SCM Press, 1964), p. 16. Moltmann's book has had an enormous influence on a whole range of theologies that emerged in the 1960s.

26. Robert W. Wall, "The Eschatologies of the Peace Movement," *Biblical Theology Bulletin* 25 (1985), pp. 3-11.

27. Dietrich Bonhoeffer, "Thy Kingdom Come," in *Preface to Bonhoeffer*, D. Godsey, (Philadelphia: Fortress Press, 1965), p. 28.

28. Quoted in C. Rene Padilla, *Mission between the Times: Essays on the Kingdom* (Grand Rapids, Michigan: Eerdmans Publishing Company, 1985), p. 22.

29. Cardinal Josef Ratzinger, "Instruction on Certain Aspects of 'Theology of Liberation,'" IX, 3.

30. Fuellenbach, *Hermeneutics, Marxism and Liberation Theology*, pp. 118-125.

31. Elizabeth Lord, "Human History and the Kingdom of God: Past Perspectives and Those of J. L. Segundo," *Heythrop Journal* 30 (1989), pp. 293-303.

32. E. Schillebeeckx, *The Mission of the Church* (London: Sheed and Ward, 1973), p. 84.

33. J. M. Bonino, "Historical Praxis and Christian Identity," *Frontiers of Theology in Latin America*, ed. G. Gibellini (London: SCM Press, 1979), p. 271.

34. C. Rene Padilla, *Mission between the Times*, p. 1.

35. Wall, "The Eschatologies of the Peace Movement," p. 4.

36. J. M. Bonino, "Historical Praxis and Christian Identity," p. 272.

37. Wall, "The Eschatologies the Peace Movement," p. 7.

38. Padilla, *Mission between the Times*, p. 2.

39. Th. E. Clarke, "The Kingdom of Justice," *The Way* (July 1984), pp. 212-214.

40. Bonino, "Historical Praxis and Christian Identity," p. 272.

41. Gabriel Fackre, "I Believe in the Resurrection of the Body," *Interpretation* 46/1 (1992), 42-52 at p. 46.

42. Padilla, *Mission between the Times*, p. 4.

43. Bonino, "Historical Praxis and Christian Identity," p. 274.

44. Snyder, *Models of the Kingdom*, p. 100.

45. Fackre, "I Believe in the Resurrection of the Body," p. 46.

46. Wall, "Eschatology of the Peace Movement," p.3.

47. See Schillebeeckx, *The Mission of the Church*, p. 84.

48. Fackre, "I Believe in the Resurrection of the Body," p. 46.

16   THE KINGDOM OF GOD AND THE PERSON OF JESUS

1. Snyder, *Models of the Kingdom*, pp. 16-17.

2. Snyder, *Models of the Kingdom*, p. 128.

3. Jürgen Moltmann, "First the Kingdom of God," 6-27 at p. 6.

4. Karl Rahner, *The Church and the Sacraments* (London: Burns & Oates, 1979), pp. 11-19.

5. Gerhard Lohfink, *Jesus and Community*, pp. 7-29.

6. Heinz Schürmann, *Reich Gottes—Jesu Geschick* (Freiburg: Herder, 1983), pp. 24-26.

7. The following view is presented by Wilhelm Bruners, *Wie Jesus Glauben Lernte*.

8. Wilhelm Bruners, *Wie Jesus Glauben Lernte*, pp. 11-24.

9. Gerhard Lohfink, *Jesus and Community*, p. 7.

10. Jerome Murphy-O'Connor, "John the Baptist and Jesus: History and Hypotheses," *New Testament Studies* 36 (1990), 359-374.

11. Dunn, *Jesus and the Spirit*, pp. 67.

12. Bruners, *Wie Jesus Glauben Lernte*, pp. 33-44

13. Bruners, *Wie Jesus Glauben Lernte*, pp. 25-43.

14. Joachim Jeremias, *The Prayers of Jesus* (London: SCM Press, 1977), pp. 54-65.

15. Heinz Schürmann, *Reich Gottes—Jesu Geschick*, pp. 27-30.

16. Crossan, *In Parables*, pp. 33-36.

17. Jeremias, *Theology of the New Testament*, pp. 28-29.

18. Dunn, *Jesus and the Spirit*, p. 26.

19. Gerhard Lohfink, *Jesus and Community*, p. 13.

20. Beltram M. Villegas, "Bienaventuranzas y Theologia de la Liberacion," *Dialogo en Torno a la Teologia de la Liberacion* (Santiago de Chile: Editorial Salesiana, Instituto ILADES, 1986), pp. 37-57.

21. Boff, *Jesus Christ Liberator*, p. 282.

22. Howard A. Snyder, *A Kingdom Manifesto* (Downers Grove, Illinois: InterVarsity Press, 1985), pp. 74-75.

23. Sanders, *Jesus and Judaism*, p. 295.

24. H. Mekkel, "The Opposition between Jesus and Judaism," *Jesus and the Politics of His Day*, ed. E. Bammel and C. F. D. Moule (London: Cambridge

University Press, 1984), p. 143. Similar also is Gerhard Lohfink, *The Last Day of Jesus: An Enriching Portrayal of the Passion* (Notre Dame, Indiana: Ave Maria Press, 1984), pp. 11-13.

25. G. V. Pixley, *God's Kingdom*, pp. 64-87.

26. Gerhard Lohfink, *The Last Day of Jesus*, pp. 15-16.

27. Brueggemann, *Prophetic Imagination*, p. 84.

28. Sanders, *Jesus and Judaism*, pp. 305-306.

29. Walter Kasper, *Jesus the Christ* (London: SCM Press, 1976), p. 114.

30. Albert Schweitzer, *The Mystery of the Kingdom of God: The Secret of Jesus' Messiahship and Passion* (Buffalo, New York: Prometheus Books, 1984; original in German, 1914), p. 137.

31. Mwarinus De Jonge, *Jesus, The Servant-Messiah* (New Haven and London: Yale University Press, 1991), p. 59.

32. Albert Schweitzer, *Ausgewählte Werke in Fünf Bänden*, Band 5 (Berlin: Union Verlag, 1971), pp. 205-246.

33. Kasper, *Jesus the Christ*, p. 116.

34. Brueggemann, *Prophetic Imagination*, pp. 94-95.

35. Jeremias, *Theology of the New Testament*, p. 299.

36. Schnackenburg, *God's Rule and Kingdom*, p. 193.

37. Beasley-Murray, *Jesus and the Kingdom of God*, p. 263.

38. Gerard Rosse, *The Cry of Jesus on the Cross*, pp. 73-114.

39. Rosse, *The Cry of Jesus on the Cross*, p. 67.

40. John O'Donnell, "God's Justice and Mercy: What Can We Hope For?," *Pacifica* 5 (1992), 84-93 at p. 93.

41. Kasper, *Jesus the Christ*, p. 118.

42. Brueggemann, *Prophetic Imagination*, p. 91.

43. Jürgen Moltmann, *The Crucified God: The Cross of Christ as the Foundation and Criticism of Christian Theology* (New York: Harper & Row, 1974), p. 287.

44. Urs von Balthasar, *The Glory of the Lord*, p. 233.

45. Rosse, *The Cry of Jesus on the Cross*, p. 93.

46. These three phenomena are not to be treated as historical facts but rather as giving a theological explanation of the death of Jesus. See Rosse, *The Cry of Jesus on the Cross*, p. 19.

47. Rosse, *The Cry of Jesus on the Cross*, p. 16.

48. See Rosse, *The Cry of Jesus on the Cross*, pp. 19-20.

49. Rosse, *The Cry of Jesus on the Cross*, pp. 21-22.

50. Rahner, *The Spirit in the Church* (London: Burns & Oates, 1979), pp. 7-8.

17   THE KINGDOM AND THE HOLY SPIRIT

1. D. A. Tappeiner, "Holy Spirit," *The International Standard Bible Encyclopedia*, vol. 2, G. B. Bromiley, ed., fully revised (Grand Rapids, Michigan: Eerdmans Publishing Company, 1982), p. 732.

2. The word *ruah* (= wind) appears 380 times in the Old Testament. Its meaning covers a great range. However, to describe this force as "creative and life-giving" seems to sum up best the various activities. See R. Koch, "Spirit," *Encyclopedia of Biblical Theology: The Complete* Sacramentum Verbi, ed. Johannes Bauer (New York: Crossroad, 1981), pp. 869-889.

3. Walter Eichrodt, *Theology of the Old Testament II* (Philadelphia: Westminster Press, 1967), chap. 13, "The Cosmic Power of God," pp. 46-68.

4. W. Pannenberg, "Doctrine of the Holy Spirit and the Task of a Theology of Nature," *Theology* 75 (1972), p. 9. Pannenberg starts his treatise on the Holy

Spirit with the description given in the Creed: "I believe in the Holy Spirit, the giver of life." For him all discussion of the Spirit must begin here.

5. Eichrodt, *Theology of the Old Testament* I, 57-60: "The Spirit of God as the Consummating Power of the New Age."

6. W. Pannenberg, *Jesus-God and Man* (Philadelphia: Westminster Press, 1968), p. 171.

7. Tappeiner, "Holy Spirit," p. 732.

8. Koch, "Spirit," p. 873.

9. Tappeiner, "Holy Spirit," p. 732.

10. B. Schneider, "Kata Pneuma agiosunes," *Biblica* 48 (1967), 359-387 at p. 378.

11. Koch, "Spirit," p. 876.

12. C. K. Barret, *The Holy Spirit and the Gospel Tradition* (London: SPCK, 1947; reprint 1958), p. 120.

13. Michael Welker, "The Holy Spirit," *Theology Today* 46 (1989), pp. 5-11.

14. Koch, "Spirit," p. 877. According to Koch the word is found 375 times in the New Testament and exhibits the same range of meaning, though with a notable shift of emphasis.

15. Tappeiner points out that it is important to keep in mind that "the whole New Testament teaching regarding the Holy Spirit is radically conditioned by the experience of the Spirit in the early Church" ("Holy Spirit," p. 732).

16. Tappeiner, "Holy Spirit," p. 732.

17. Barret, *The Holy Spirit and the Gospel Tradition*, p. 24.

18. Tappeiner, "Holy Spirit," p. 773. See also Edward Schweizer, *The Holy Spirit* (Philadelphia: Fortress Press, 1978), p. 53. Schweizer points out correctly that the virgin birth is not the important issue here, but that with Jesus born of the virgin and the Holy Spirit something absolutely new is entering history.

19. Koch, "Spirit," p. 879.

20. Dunn, *Jesus and the Spirit*, pp. 64-65.

21. Koch, "Spirit," p. 879.

22. Dunn, *Jesus and the Spirit*, pp. 44-53.

23. James D. G. Dunn, "Spirit", *The New International Dictionary of New Testament Theology*, vol. 3, ed. Colin Brown (Exeter: Paternoster Press, 1978), 693-707 at p. 696.

24. L. Boff, *Church Charism and Power: Liberation Theology and the Institutional Church* (London: SCM Press, 1985), pp. 147-148.

25. Barret, *The Holy Spirit and the Gospel Tradition*, pp. 158-159.

26. Koch, "Spirit," p. 881.

27. Pannenberg, *Jesus, God and Man*, pp. 67-68.

28. Edward Schweizer, *The Holy Spirit*, pp. 109-110.

29. D. Bonhoeffer, *Gesammelte Schriften*, vol. 3 (München: Kaiser Verlag, 1958), p. 274.

18   THE KINGDOM AND THE CHURCH

1. Snyder, *Models of the Kingdom*, pp. 75-76.

2. Peter Kuzmić, "The Church and the Kingdom of God: A Theological Reflection," *The Church: God's Agent for Change*, ed. Bruce J. Nicholls (Australia: Paternoster Press, 1986), 49-81 at p. 49.

3. Kuzmić, "The Church and the Kingdom of God," pp. 61-63.

4. A. Dulles, *A Church to Believe In: Discipleship and the Dynamics of Freedom* (New York: Crossroad, 1982), pp. 1-18.

5. Brueggemann, *Prophetic Imagination*, p. 9.

6. Brueggemann, *Prophetic Imagination*, pp. 11-14.

7.Brueggemann, *Prophetic Imagination*, p. 12. By *enculturation* Brueggemann means the way the church has succumbed to the ethos of consumerism.

8.Medard Kehl, *Die Kirche: Eine katholische Ekklesiologie* (Würzburg: Echter Verlag, 1992), pp. 48-49.

9.Christian Duquoc, *Provisional Churches: An Essay in Ecumenical Ecclesiology* (London: SCM Press, 1986), p. 39.

10. Norbert Lohfink, *Option for the Poor*, pp. 48-52.

11. Brueggemann, *Prophetic Imagination*, p. 16.

12. Gerhard Lohfink, *Jesus and Community*, pp. 17-29.

13. L. Newbigin, *Sign of the Kingdom* (Grand Rapids: Eerdmans Publishing Company, 1980), p.19.

14. Howard J. Yoder, *The Priestly Kingdom: Social Ethics as Gospel* (Notre Dame, Indiana: University of Notre Dame Press, 1984), pp. 124-125.

15. Snyder, *Models of the Kingdom*, p. 84.

16. Boff, *Church Charism and Power*, p. 145.

17. M. Schmaus, *The Church as Sacrament* (London: Sheed & Ward, 1975), p. 5. See also W. Kasper, *Theology and Church* (London: SCM Press, 1989), pp. 111-147.

18. After Vatican II the image of the Church as sacrament gained momentum even in Protestant churches, although the terminology preferred was "instrument and sign" rather than sacrament. See Guenther Grassman, "The Church as Sacrament, Sign and Instrument," *Church Kingdom World*, ed. G. Limouris (Geneva: World Council, 1986), pp. 1-16.

19. Kehl, *Die Kirche*, pp. 51-52.

20. Walter Kasper, "The Church as Communion," *New Blackfriars* 74 (1993), 232-244 at p. 235.

21. W. Kasper and Gerhard Sauter, *Kirche Ort des Geistes* (Freiburg: Herder, 1976), particularly Part One, "Kirche als Sakrament des Geistes" by W. Kasper, pp. 13-55.

22. Boff, *Church Charism and Power*, pp. 144-153.

23. H. Küng, *The Church*, pp. 107-260.

24. Dulles, *A Church to Believe In*, pp. 1-4.

25. Duquoc, *Provisional Churches*, pp. 17-19, 99-100.

26. Jerome P. Theisen, *The Ultimate Church and the Promise of Salvation* (Collegeville, Minnesota: St. John's University Press, 1976).

27. Richard P. McBrien, *Catholicism*, pp. 710-721.

28. Congar, *Lay People in the Church*, p. 88.

29. Jan Milic Lochman, "Church and World in the Light of the Kingdom of God," 58-72 at p. 69.

30. Pannenberg, *Theology of the Kingdom of God*, pp. 72-75.

31. Jacques Dupuis, "Evangelization and Kingdom Values: The Church and the 'Others,'" *Indian Missiological Review* 14 (1992), pp. 4-21 at p. 8.

32. Dupuis, "Evangelization and Kingdom Values," p. 8.

33. Schnackenburg, *God's Rule and Kingdom*, p. 11.

34. McBrien, *Catholicism*, p. 686.

35. Karl Rahner, "Church and World," in Rahner et al., eds., *Sacramentum Mundi*, vol. 1 (London: Burns & Oates, 1968), p. 348.

36. Boff, *Church Charism and Power*, p. 146.

37. Jan Milic Lochman, "Church and World in the Light of the Kingdom of God," p. 59.

38. Boff, *Church Charism and Power*, pp. 1-2.

39. Boff, *Church Charism and Power*, pp. 145-146.

40. Ladd, *The Presence of the Future*, p. 277.

41. Boff, *Church Charism and Power*, pp. 108-110.

42. Pannenberg, "The Kingdom of God and the Church," pp. 82-84.

43. Gerhard Lohfink, *Jesus and Community*, 122-132.

44. McBrien, *Catholicism*, p. 716.

45. Ladd, *The Presence of the Future*, p. 269.

46. Cobb, *Sustainability*, p. 14.

47. Schillebeeckx, *Church: The Human Story of God*, p. 157.

48. Gerhard Lohfink, *Jesus and Community*, pp. 150-180.

49. McBrien, *Catholicism*, p. 717.

50. Pannenberg, "The Kingdom and the Church," pp. 80-82.

51. Jürgen Moltmann, *The Church in the Power of the Spirit* (New York: Harper & Row, 1977), p. 196.

52. Snyder, *Models of the Kingdom*, pp. 154-155.

19   THE LORD'S PRAYER AS A SUMMARY
OF THE KINGDOM MESSAGE

1. Borg, *Jesus, a New Vision*, pp. 39-40.

2. J. Jeremias, *The Lord's Prayer in the Light of Recent Research* (London: SCM Press, 1977).

3. Walter Strolz, "Fatherhood of God in Modern Interpretation," *The Lord's Prayer and Jewish Liturgy*, ed. J. Petuchoswski and M. Brocke (London: Burns & Oates, 1978), pp. 191-200.

4. Gerhard Lohfink, *Jesus and Community*, p. 33.

5. Jeremias, *The Prayers of Jesus*, pp. 82-85.

6. Krister Stendahl, "Your Kingdom Come," *Cross Current* 32 (1982), p. 263.

7. Philip B. Harner, *Understanding the Lord's Prayer* (Philadelphia: Fortress Press, 1975), 12-17 at p. 16.

8. John Wijngaards, *My Galilee: My People Walking on Water* (London: Housetop Publication, 1990), p. 90.

9. Jeremias, *The Lord's Prayer*, p. 12.

10. Wesley J. Fuerst, "How Israel Conceived and Addressed God," *Our Naming of God*, ed. Carl E. Braaten (Minneapolis: Fortress Press, 1989), p. 73.

11. *The Prayers of Jesus in Their Contemporary Setting*, no. 17 (London: The Study Center for Christian-Jewish Relations, Chepstow Villas, n.d.), pp. 9-10.

12. Jeremias, *The Prayers of Jesus*, pp. 29, 52, 96-98.

13. Edgar M. Kreutz, "God in the New Testament," *Our Naming of God*, p. 87.

14. Kreutz, "God in the New Testament," pp. 85-86.

15. Jeremias, *The Prayers of Jesus*, p. 57.

16. Wijngaards, *My Galilee: My People Walking on Water*, p. 89.

17. Wijngaards, *My Galilee: My People Walking on Water*, pp. 88-89.

18. Jeremias, *The Prayers of Jesus*, p. 57. Other scholars have questioned Jeremias's thesis by insisting that his research does not warrant the conclusion. First, the word *Abba* could be used as meaning simply "Father" and not only just as "the chatter of a small child," as Jeremias suggests. Second, there are instances in Hasidic piety where God is addressed as *Abba* meaning simply "Father." See Geza Vermes, *Jesus and the World of Judaism* (London: SCM Press, 1983), pp. 30-43, particularly pp. 41-43.

19. Jan Milic Lochman, *The Lord's Prayer* (Grand Rapids, Michigan: Eerdmans Publishing Company, 1990), p. 20.

20. Jeremias, *The Prayers of Jesus*, p. 98.

21. W. Barclay, *Beatitudes and the Lord's Prayer for Everyone* (New York: Harper & Row, 1963), pp. 157-173.

22. Lochman, *The Lord's Prayer*, p. 21.

23. Lochman, *The Lord's Prayer*, p. 16.

24. Perrin, *Rediscovering the Teaching of Jesus*, pp. 57-59.

25. Harner, *Understanding the Lord's Prayer*, p. 63.

26. Jeremias, *The Lord's Prayer*, p. 22.

27. Lochman, *The Lord's Prayer*, pp. 75-77.

28. Lochman, *The Lord's Prayer*, p. 84. He refers here to G. Ebeling, *On Prayer: The Lord's Prayer in Today's World* (Philadelphia: Fortress Press, 1978), p. 52.

29. Jeremias, *The Lord's Prayer*, pp. 23-27. See also Lochman, *The Lord's Prayer*, page 90, although he insists strongly that all interpretations of this petition must start with the literal meaning of the phrase first.

30. Jeremias, *The Lord's Prayer*, p. 27.

31. Lochman, *The Lord's Prayer*, p. 96.

32. As quoted by Leonardo Boff, *The Lord's Prayer: The Prayer of Integral Liberation* (Maryknoll, New York: Orbis Books, 1979), p. 84.

33. Stendahl, "Your Kingdom Come," p. 263. He quotes here a Latin American prayer.

34. Harner, *Understanding the Lord's Prayer*, p. 103.

35. Harner, *Understanding the Lord's Prayer*, pp. 104-106.

36. Jeremias, *The Lord's Prayer*, pp. 27-28.

37. Jeremias, *The Lord's Prayer*, pp. 214-218.

38. Harner, *Understanding The Lord's Prayer*, pp. 114-119.

39. As quoted in B. Basset, *Let's Start Praying Again* (New York: Herder and Herder, 1972), pp. 51-52.

40. As quoted in Jeremias, *The Lord's Prayer*, p. 33.

Bibliography

"After the Day of the Lie," Editorial Comment, *The Month* (April 1990), pp. 128-133.
"Preface: Not Interesting, Merely Terrible," Editor's Note, *New Blackfriars* 69 (1988), pp. 467-471.
"Unsere Hoffnung: Ein Bekenntnis zum Glauben in dieser Zeit," *Herder Korrespondenz* 30 (1976), pp. 200-211.

Abecassis, A., "Jewish Apocalyptic: Its Meaning and Message," *SIDIC* 18 (1985), pp. 10-11.
Amaladoss, Michael, "Secularization and India: Modernization and Religion in an Eastern Country," *Exchange* 21 (1992), pp. 34-48.
Anderson, B. W., "The New Covenant and the Old," in *The Old Testament and Christian Faith: A Theological Discussion* (New York: Harper & Row, 1963), pp. 225-245.
Anderson, H., *The Gospel of Mark* (Greenwood, S.C.: Attic Press, 1976).
Andover, Newton, "I Believe in the Resurrection of the Body," *Interpretation* 46 (1992), pp. 42-52.
Anonymous, *The Prayers of Jesus in Their Contemporary Setting* (London: The Study Center for Christian-Jewish Relations, 17 Chepstow Villas, n.d.)
Arichea, D. C., "Peace in the New Testament," *The Bible Translator* 38 (1987), pp. 201-206.
Balthasar, H. Urs von, *Die Gottesfrage des heutigen Menschen* (München-Wien: Herold, 1956).
_____, *Dare we Hope, "That All Men Be Saved"?* (San Francisco: Ignatius Press, 1988).
_____, *The Glory of the Lord: A Theological Aesthetics*, vol. 7, Theology: The New Covenant (Edinburgh: T & T Clark, 1989).
Barclay, W., *Beatitudes and the Lord's Prayer for Everyone* (New York: Harper & Row, 1963).
Barret, C. K., *The Holy Spirit and the Gospel Tradition* (London: SPCK, 1947, reprint 1958).
Barth, Karl, *Kirchliche Dogmatik* II/1 (Zollikon-Zürich: Evangelischer Verlag, 1957).
Basset, B., *Let's Start Praying Again* (New York: Herder & Herder, 1972).
Bausch, William J., *Storytelling: Imagination and Faith* (Mystic, Conn.: Twenty-Third Publications, 1991).
Beasley-Murray, G. C., *Jesus and the Kingdom of God* (Grand Rapids, Mich.: Eerdmans Publishing Company, 1986).
Berdyaev, Nicholas, *Christianisme, Marxisme* (Paris: Centurion, 1975).
Beyreuther, E., and G. Finenrath, "Joy," in *The New International Dictionary of New Testament Theology*, vol. 2, ed. Colin Brown (Exeter: Paternoster Press, 1976), pp. 352-561.

Black, M., *Romans* (London: NCB, 1973).

Boff, Clodovis and Leonardo, *Salvation and Liberation: In Search of a Balance between Faith and Politics* (Maryknoll, N.Y.: Orbis Books, 1985).

Boff, L., *Jesus Christ Liberator: A Critical Christology for Our Time* (Maryknoll, N.Y.: Orbis Books, 1978).

_____ , *Teologiá del cautivero y de la liberación* (Madrid: Ediciones Paulinas, 1978).

_____ , *The Lord's Prayer: The Prayer of Integral Liberation* (Maryknoll, N.Y.: Orbis Books Books, 1979).

_____ , *Church Charism and Power: Liberation Theology and the Institutional Church* (London: SCM Press, 1985).

Bonhoeffer, D., *Gesammelte Schriften,* vol. 3 (München: Kaiser Verlag, 1958).

_____ , "Thy Kingdom Come," in *Preface to Bonhoeffer,* D. Godsey (Philadelphia: Fortress Press, 1965).

Bonino, J. M., "Historical Praxis and Christian Identity," *Frontiers of Theology in Latin America,* ed. G. Gibellini (London: SCM Press, 1979), pp. 260-283.

_____ , ed., *Faces of Jesus: Latin American Christologies* (Maryknoll, N.Y.: Orbis Books, 1983).

Borg, Markus. J., *Jesus, a New Vision: Spirit, Culture, and Life of Discipleship* (San Francisco: Harper & Row, 1987).

Boucher, M. I., *The Parables,* New Testament Message 7 (Dublin, 1971).

Bowker, John, "The Human Imagination of Hell," *Theology* 85 (1982), pp. 405-410.

Bredin, Eamonn, *Rediscovering Jesus: Challenge of Discipleship* (Quezon City, Manila: Claretian Publications, 1990; originally published Dublin: Columba Press, 1985).

Bright, John, *The Kingdom of God: The Biblical Concept and Its Meaning for the Church* (Nashville: Abingdon Press, 1953).

Brown, Colin, "Child," in *The New International Dictionary of New Testament Theology,* vol. 1, pp. 280-285.

Brown, Delwin, *To Set at Liberty: Christian Faith and Human Freedom* (Maryknoll, N.Y.: Orbis Books, 1981).

Brown, Harold O.J., "Will the Lost Suffer Forever?" *Criswell Theological Review* 4 (1990), pp. 267-270.

Brown, John Pairman, "Kingdom of God," in *The Encyclopedia of Religion* (New York: Macmillan, 1978), vol. 8, pp. 304-312.

Brown, R. McAfee, *Theology in a New Key* (Philadelphia: Westminster Press, 1978).

Brueggemann, W., "Vine and Fig Tree: A Case Study in Imagination and Criticism," *Catholic Biblical Quarterly* 43 (1981), pp. 188-204.

_____ , *Prophetic Imagination* (London: SCM Press, 1992; original 1978).

Brueggemann, Walter, Sharon Parks, and Thomas H. Groome, *To Act Justly, Love Tenderly, Walk Humbly: An Agenda for Ministers* (New York: Paulist Press, 1986).

Bruners, Wilhelm, *Wie Jesus Glauben Lernte* (Freiburg i. Br.: Christophorus-Verlag, 1989).

Buchanan, G. W., *The Consequences of the Covenant* (Leiden, 1970).

Bultmann, Rudolf, "Zur eschatologishchen Verkündigung Jesu," *TLZ* 12 (1947), cols 271-274.

_____ , *Theology of the New Testament,* vol. 1 (New York: Scribner's Sons, 1951).

_____ , *Jesus and the Word* (New York: Scribner's Sons, 1958).

Cabello, R., "El Reino de Dios," *Christus* 50 (1985), pp. 16-22.

Chilton, Bruce, and J.I.H. McDonald, *Jesus and the Ethics of the Kingdom* (Cambridge: University Press, 1987).

Clarke, Th. E., "The Kingdom of Justice," *The Way* (July 1984), pp. 208-216.

Cobb, John B., Jr., *Sustainability: Economics, Ecology, and Justice* (Maryknoll, N.Y.: Orbis Books, 1992).

Collins, John J., "The Kingdom of God in the Apocrypha and Pseudepigrapha," in *The Kingdom of God in 20th-Century Interpretation*, ed. Wendell Willis (Peabody, Mass.: Hendrickson, 1987), pp. 81-95.

Congar, Yves, *Lay People in the Church* (London: Bloomsbury Publishing Company, 1957).

Coste, Rene, *Marxist Analysis and Christian Faith* (Maryknoll, N.Y.: Orbis Books, 1985).

Crijnen, Ton, "Secularization Seems to Be a Typical (Western) European Phenomenon," *Exchange* 21 (1992), pp. 29-33.

Croatto, J. S., "Biblical Hermeneutics in the Theology of Liberation," in *The Bible and Liberation*, ed. N. K. Gottwald (Maryknoll, N.Y.: Orbis Books, 1983).

Crossan, J. D., *In Parables: The Challenge of the Historical Jesus* (San Francisco: Harper & Row, 1973).

Cullmann, Oscar, *Christ and Time: The Primitive Christian Conception of Time and History* (Philadelphia: Westminster Press, revised edition 1964).

_____ , *Jesus and the Revolutionaries* (New York: Herder, 1970).

Dale, Patrick, "The Kingdom of God in the Old Testament," in *The Kingdom of God in 20th-Century Interpretation*.

Davies, W. D., and S. C. Allison, "Reflection on the Sermon on the Mount," *Scottish Journal of Theology* 44 (1991), pp. 283-309.

De Jonge, Mwarinus, *Jesus, The Servant-Messiah* (New Haven and London: Yale University Press, 1991).

Dentan, R. C., "The Kingdom of God in the Old Testament," in *Interpreter's One-Volume Commentary on the Bible,* ed. Ch. M. Layman (London: Collins, 1971), pp. 1159-1166.

Dodd, C. H., *The Apostolic Preaching and Its Development* (London: Hodder and Stoughton, 1936).

_____ , *The Parables of the Kingdom* (New York: Scribner's Sons, 1961).

Donahue, John R., "Biblical Perspectives on Justice," in *The Faith That Does Justice,* ed. John C. Haughey (New York: Paulist Press, 1977).

Doorly, William J., *Prophet of Love: Understanding the Book of Hosea* (Mahwah, N.J.: Paulist Press, 1991).

Dulles, A. *Models of the Church* (London: Macmillan, 1974).

_____ , "The Meaning of Faith Considered in Relationship to Justice," in *The Faith That Does Justice,* pp. 10-46.

_____ , *A Church to Believe In: Discipleship and the Dynamics of Freedom* (New York: Crossroad, 1982).

Dunn, J.D.G., *Jesus and the Spirit* (Philadelphia: Westminster Press, 1975).

_____ , "Spirit," in *The New International Dictionary of New Testament Theology*, vol. 3, pp. 693-707.

Dunn, James D.J., *Jesus' Call to Discipleship* (Cambridge: University Press, 1992).

Dupuis, Jacques, "The Kingdom of God and World Religions," *Vidyajyoti* 51 (1987), pp. 530-544.

_____ , "Evangelization and Kingdom Values: The Church and the 'Others,'" *Indian Missiological Review* 14 (1992), pp. 4-21.

Duquoc, Christian, *Provisional Churches: An Essay in Ecumenical Ecclesiology* (London: SCM Press, 1986).

Ebeling, G., *On Prayer: The Lord's Prayer in Today's World* (Philadelphia: Fortress Press, 1978).

Eichrodt, Walter, *Theology of the Old Testament II* (Philadelphia: Westminster Press, 1967).

Elliott, Charles, *Praying the Kingdom: Towards a Political Spirituality* (London: Darton, Longman and Todd, 1985).

Esser, H. H., "Mercy," in *The New International Dictionary of New Testament Theology*, vol. 2, pp. 593-600.

Fackre, Gabriel, "I Believe in the Resurrection of the Body," *Interpretation* 46 (1992), pp. 42-52.

Fisher, Neal F., *The Parables of Jesus Glimpses of God's Reign* (New York: Crossroad, revised edition 1990).

Flüglister, N., "Strukturen der alttestamentlichen Ekklesiologie," in *Mysterium Salutis VI,4* (Einsiedeln: Benzinger Verlag, 1972), pp 77-90.

Ford, J. Massyngbaerde, "Shalom in the Johannine Corpus," *Horizons in Biblical Theology* 6 (1984), pp. 67-89.

Fudge, Edward, *The Fire That Consumes: A Biblical and Historical Study of Final Punishment* (Providential Press, 1982).

————, "The Final End of the Wicked," *Journal of the Evangelical Theological Society* 27 (1984), pp. 325-334.

Fuerst, Wesley J., "How Israel Conceived of and Addressed God," in *Our Naming of God: Problems and Prospects of God-Talk Today*, ed. Carl Braaten (Minneapolis: Fortress Press, 1989).

Fuellenbach, John, *Hermeneutics, Marxism, and Liberation Theology* (Manila: Divine Word Publications, 1989).

Fung, Raymond, *The Isaiah Vision* (Geneva: WCC Publication, Risk Books Series, 1992).

Gnilka, Joachim, *Evangelisch-Katholischer Kommentar zum Neuen Testament: Das Evangelium nach Markus (Mk 8:27-16:20)* (Neukirchen: Benzinger/ Neukirchener Verlag, 1979).

————, *Jesus von Nazareth: Botschaft und Geschichte* (Freiburg: Herder, 1990).

Gnuse, R., "Jubilee Legislation in Leviticus: Israel's Vision of Social Reform," *Biblical Theology Bulletin* 15 (1989), pp. 43-48.

Goppelt, Leonhard, *Theology of the New Testament Volume 1* (Grand Rapids, Mich.: Eerdmans Publishing Company, 1981).

Gorbachev, Mikhail, An Address to the United Nations, 7 December 1988.

Graham, G., "The Goodness of God and the Conception of Hell," *New Blackfriars* 69 (1988), pp 477-487.

Grassman, Guenther, "The Church as Sacrament, Sign and Instrument," in *Church Kingdom World*, ed. G. Limouris (Geneva: WCC Publication, 1986).

Green, Robin, "God Is Doing a New Thing: A Theological Reflection on the Practice of Partnership," *International Review of Mission* 80 (1991), pp. 219-229.

Gutiérrez, G., *A Theology of Liberation* (Maryknoll, N.Y.: Orbis Books, 1973).

————, "Liberation Theology and Proclamation," in *Concilium*, New Series, vol. 6, no. 10 (1974), p. 69.

————, *The Power of the Poor in History* (London: SCM Press, 1983).

Hanks, Thomas D., *God So Loved the Third World* (Maryknoll, N.Y.: Orbis Books, 1983).

Harnack, Adolf, *What Is Christianity?* (New York: Harper & Row, 1957).

Harner, Philip B., *Understanding the Lord's Prayer* (Philadelphia: Fortress Press, 1975).

Hendrickx, H., *Peace, Anyone? Biblical Reflection on Peace and Violence* (Quezon City: Claretian Publications, 1986).

————, *The Parables of Jesus: Studies in the Synoptic Gospels* (Manila: St Paul Publications, 1987).

Hengel, Martin, *Was Jesus a Revolutionist?* (Philadelphia: Fortress Press, Facet Books, 1971).

Hobbs, H. Herschel, *The Exposition of the Gospel of Mark* (Grand Rapids, Mich.: Baker Book House, 1970).

Hollenbach, David, "The Church in the World: The Politics of Justice," *Theology Today* 38 (1981/82).

Hollenbach, Paul, "Liberating Jesus for Social Involvement," *Biblical Theology Bulletin* 15 (1985), pp. 151-157.

_____ , "The Historical Jesus Question in North America Today," *Biblical Theology Bulletin* 19 (1989), pp. 12-22.

Horsley, R. A., and John S. Hanson, *Bandits, Prophets, and Messiahs: Popular Movements at the Times of Jesus* (San Francisco: Harper & Row, 1985).

Horsley, R., *Jesus and the Spiral of Violence: Popular Jewish Resistance in Roman Palestine* (San Francisco: Harper & Row, 1987).

Hugh, Anderson, *The Gospel of Mark* (Greenwood, S.C.: Attic Press, 1976).

Hunter, A. M., "The Interpreter and the Parables," *New Testament Issues*, ed. R. Bates (London: SCM Press, 1970).

Hunter, M., *The Parables Then and Now* (Philadelphia: Fortress Press, 1971).

Jeremias, Joachim, *The Sermon on the Mount* (Philadelphia: Fortress Press, 1963).

_____ , *Parables of Jesus* (London: SCM Press, 1963).

_____ , *Jesus Promise to the Nations* (London: SCM Press, 1968).

_____ , *Theology of the New Testament* (London: SCM Press, 1971).

_____ , *The Prayers of Jesus* (London: SCM Press, 1977).

_____ , *The Lord's Prayer in the Light of Recent Research* (London: SCM Press, 1977).

John Paul II, *Redemptoris Missio: On the Permanent Validity of the Church's Missionary Mandate* (Vatican City: Libreria Editrice Vaticana, 1991).

Johnson, Elizabeth A., *Consider Jesus: Waves of Renewal in Christology* (New York: Crossroad, 1990).

Johnston, George, "Kingdom of God Sayings in Paul's Letters," in *From Jesus to Paul Studies in Honor of Francis Beare*, ed. P. Richardson and John C. Hurd (1984), pp. 143-156.

Kaiser, C. W., Jr., "Kingdom Promises as Spiritual and National," in *Continuity and Discontinuity*, ed. J. Feinberg (1988), pp. 289-307.

Kasper, Walter, "Kirche als Sakrament des Geistes," in *Kirche Ort des Geistes*, ed. W. Kasper and Gerhard Sauter (Freiburg: Herder, 1976), pp. 13-55.

_____ , *Jesus the Christ* (London: SCM Press, 1976).

_____ , *Theology and Church* (London: SCM Press, 1989).

_____ , "The Church As Communion," *New Blackfriars* 74 (1993), pp. 232-244.

Kavunkal, J., "Jubilee the Framework of Evangelization," *Vidyajyoti* 52 (1988), pp. 180-191.

Kehl, M., *Die Kirche: Eine katholische Ekklesiologie* (Würzburg: Echter Verlag, 1992).

Kelber, W., *The Kingdom in Mark: A New Place and a New Time* (Philadelphia: Fortress Press, 1974).

Kelly, J.N.D., *Early Christian Creed* (New York: Harper & Row, 1978).

Klein, Günther, "The Biblical Understanding of the Kingdom of God," *Interpretation* 26 (1972), pp. 387-418.

Knitter, Paul, *No Other Name? A Critical Survey of Christian Attitudes Towards The World Religions* (Maryknoll, N.Y.: Orbis Books, 1974).

Koch R., "Spirit," in *Encyclopedia of Biblical Theology, The Complete Sacramentum Verbi*, ed. Johannes Bauer (New York: Crossroad, 1981), pp. 869-889.

Kreutz, Edgar M., "God in the New Testament," in *Our Naming of God: Problems and Prospects of God-Talk Today*, pp. 75-90.

Küng, Hans, *The Church* (New York: Sheed and Ward, 1967).

Kuthirakkattel, Scaria, *The Beginning of Jesus' Ministry according to Mark's Gospel (1:14-3:6): A Redaction Critical Study*, Analecta Biblica 123 (Roma: Editrice Pontificio Instituto Biblico, 1990).

Kuzmić, Peter, "The Church and the Kingdom of God: A Theological Reflection," in *The Church: God's Agent for Change*, ed. Bruce J. Nicholls (Australia: Paternoster Press, 1986), pp. 49-81.

Ladd, Gorge Eldon, *The Presence of the Future: A Revised and Updated Version of Jesus and the Kingdom* (Grand Rapids, Mich.: Eerdmans Publishing Company, 1974).

Lambino, Antonio B., "A New Theological Model: Theology of Liberation," in *Towards Doing Theology in the Philippine Context* (Manila: Loyola Papers 9, 1977), pp. 2-25.

Lane, Dermot A., "Jesus and the Kingdom of God," *Living Light* 19 (1982), pp. 103-114.

Lochert, L., *Die Hölle gehört zur Frohbotschaft* (München: Herold Press, 1981).

Lochman, Jan Milic, "Church and World in the Light of the Kingdom of God," in *Church, Kingdom, World*, pp. 58-72.

_____ , *The Lord's Prayer* (Grand Rapids, Mich.: Eerdmans Publishing Company, 1990).

Lohfink, Gerhard, *The Last Day of Jesus: An Enriching Portrayal of the Passion* (Notre Dame, Ind.: Ave Maria Press, 1984).

_____ , *Jesus and Community* (London: SPCK, 1985).

_____ , "The Exegetical Predicament concerning Jesus' Kingdom of God Proclamation," *Theology Digest* 36 (1989) (103-110); original text: "Die Not der Exegese mit der Reich-Gottes Verkündigung Jesu," *Theologische Quartalschrift* 168 (1988), pp. 1-15.

Lohfink, Norbert, "Religious Orders: God's Therapy for the Church," *Theology Digest* 33 (1986), pp. 203-212.

_____ , *Option for the Poor: The Basic Principle of Liberation Theology in the Light of the Bible* (Berkeley, Cal.: Bibal Press, 1987).

_____ , "Der Begriff des Reiches Gottes vom Alten Testament her gesehen," in *Unterwegs zur Kirche,* ed. Josef Schreider (Freiburg i. B.: Herder, 1987), pp. 33-86.

Lonergan, Bernard. "Theology in Its New Context," in *Conversion,* ed. W. E. Conn (New York: Alba House, 1978), pp. 3-21.

Lord, Elizabeth, "Human History and the Kingdom of God: Past Perspectives and Those of J. L. Segundo," *Heythrop Journal* 30 (1989), pp. 293-303.

Loretz, O. *The Truth of the Bible* (Freiburg: Herder and Herder, 1968).

Mann, C. S. *Mark: A New Translation with Introduction and Commentary,* Anchor Bible (New York: Doubleday, 1986).

Maritain, J., *The Range of Reason* (London: Geoffrey Bles, 1953).

Martyn, J. L., "From Paul to Flannery O'Connor with the Power of Grace," *Katallagete* 7 (1981), pp. 10-17.

Mays, J. L., "Justice, Perspectives from the Prophetic Tradition," *Interpretation* 37 (1983), pp. 5-17.

McBrien, Richard P., *Catholicism* (London: Geoffrey Chapman, 1981).

Mekkel, H., "The Opposition between Jesus and Judaism," in *Jesus and the Politics of His Day,* ed. E. Bammel and C.F.D. Moule (London: Cambridge University Press, 1984).

Merklein, H., *Gottesherrschaft als Handlungsprinzip* (Würzburg: Echter Verlag, 1978).

Meyer, Ben F., *The Aims of Jesus* (London: SCM Press, 1979).

Moltmann, Jürgen, *Theology of Hope* (London: SCM Press, 1964).

_____ , *The Crucified God: The Cross of Christ as the Foundation and Criticism of Christian Theology* (New York: Harper & Row, 1974).

_____ , *The Church in the Power of the Spirit* (New York: Harper & Row, 1977).

_____ , "First the Kingdom of God," *Tripod* 11 (May-June 1991), pp. 6-27.

Morley, Janet, *Bread of Tomorrow* (Maryknoll, N.Y.: Orbis Books, 1992).

Morris, Leon, *Testament of Love: A Study of Love in the Bible* (Grand Rapids, Mich.: Eerdmans Publishing Company, 1981).

_____ , *The Epistle to the Romans* (Grand Rapids, Mich.: Eerdmans Publishing Company, 1988).

Mortimer, Areas, "Mission and Liberation: The Jubilee: Paradigm for Mission Today," in *International Review of Mission* 73 (1984), pp. 34-48.

Moser, A., "Sin as Negation of the Kingdom," *Theology Digest* 30 (1982), pp. 27-30.

Murphy-O'Connor, Jerome, "John the Baptist and Jesus: History and Hypotheses," in *New Testament Studies* 36 (1990), pp. 359-374.

Neusner, Jacob, "There Has Never Been a Judaeo-Christian Dialogue—But There Can Be One," *Cross Currents* 42 (1992), pp. 3-25.

Newbigin, L., *Sign of the Kingdom* (Grand Rapids, Mich.: Eerdmans Publishing Company, 1980).

Newton, A., "I Believe in the Resurrection of the Body," *Interpretation* 46 (1992), pp. 42-52.

Nolan, Albert, *God in South Africa: The Challenge of the Gospel* (Grand Rapids, Mich.: Eerdmans Publishing Company, 1988).

Nordsieck, R., *Reich Gottes Hoffnung der Welt* (Neunkirchen: Neunkirchener Verlag, 1980).

Nowell, Irene, "Mercy," in *The New Dictionary of Theology,* ed. J. A. Komonchak, Mary Collins, Dermont Lane (Dublin: Gill and Macmillan, 1990), pp. 650-652.

O'Donnell, John, "God's Justice and Mercy: What Can We Hope For?" *Pacifica* 5 (1992), pp. 84-95.

Ormerod, Neil, "Renewing the Earth-Renewing Theology," *Pacifica, Australian Theological Studies* 4 (1991), pp. 296-306.

Padilla, R. W., *Mission between the Times: Essays on the Kingdom* (Grand Rapids, Mich.: Eerdmans Publishing Company, 1985).

Pannenberg, Wolfhart, *Jesus, God and Man* (Philadelphia: Westminster Press, 1968).

_____ , *The Apostles' Creed in the Light of Today's Questions* (Philadelphia: Westminster Press, 1972).

_____ , "Doctrine of the Holy Spirit and the Task of a Theology of Nature," *Theology* 75 (1972), pp. 8-21.

_____ , "The Kingdom of God and the Church," in *Theology and the Kingdom of God* (Philadelphia: Westminster Press, fifth printing 1977).

Patrick, Dale, "The Kingdom of God in the Old Testament," in *The Kingdom of God in 20th-Century Interpretation,* pp. 67-79.

Pernia, A. M., *God's Kingdom and Human Liberation: A Study of G. Gutiérrez, L. Boff and J. L. Segundo* (Manila: Divine Word Publications, 1990).

Perrin, Norman, *The Kingdom of God in the Teaching of Jesus* (London: SCM Press, 1963).

_____ , *Rediscovering the Teaching of Jesus* (London: SCM Press, 1967).

_____ , *Jesus and the Language of the Kingdom* (Philadelphia: Fortress Press, 1975).

Pinchas, Lapide, *The Sermon on the Mount: Utopia or Program for Action?* (Maryknoll, N.Y.: Orbis Books, 1986).

Pinnock, Clark H., "The Destruction of the Finally Impenitent," *Criswell Theological Review* 4 (1990), pp. 243-259.

Pixley, G., *God's Kingdom: A Guide for Biblical Study* (Maryknoll, N.Y.: Orbis Books, 1977).

Rad, G. von, "Eirene," *Theological Dictionary of the New Testament*, vol. 2, ed. G. Kittel (Grand Rapids, Mich.: Eerdmans Publishing Company, 1964), pp. 402-403.

Rahner, Karl, "Church and World" in Karl Rahner, et al., eds., *Sacramentum Mundi*, vol. 1 (London: Burns & Oates, 1968), pp. 346-357.

_____ , *Foundation of Christian Faith: An Introduction to the Idea of Christianity* (New York: Seabury Press, 1978).

_____ , *The Church and the Sacraments* (London: Burn & Oates, 1979).

_____ , *The Spirit in the Church* (London: Burn & Oates, 1979).

Rahner, Karl and W. Thüssing, *Christologie systematisch und exegetisch* (Freiburg: Herder, 1972).

Ratzinger, Cardinal Joseph (Sacred Congregation for the Doctrine of the Faith), *Instruction on Certain Aspects of 'Theology of Liberation'* (Vatican City: Vatican Polyglot Press, 1984).

_____ , *Eschatology, Death and Eternal Life: Dogmatic Theology*, vol. 9, ed. J. Auer and J. Ratzinger (Washington, D.C.: Catholic University Press, 1988).

Ringe, Sharon H., *Jesus, Liberation, and the Biblical Jubilee: Images for Ethics and Christology* (Philadelphia: Fortress Press, 1985).

Rosse, Gerard, *The Cry of Jesus on the Cross: A Biblical and Theological Study* (New York: Paulist Press, 1987).

Rottenberg, J. C., *The Promise and the Presence: Towards a Theology of the Kingdom of God* (Grand Rapids, Mich.: Eerdmans Publishing Company, 1980).

Russell, D. S., *Between the Testaments* (London: SCM Press, ninth printing 1986).

Sacchi, P., "Jewish Apocalyptic," *SIDIC* 18 (1985), pp. 4-9.

Sanders, E. P., *Jesus and Judaism* (London: SCM Press, 1985).

Saucy, Robert L., "The Presence of the Kingdom and the Life of the Church," *Bibliotheca Sacra* 145 (1988), p. 30-46.

Schechter, Solomon, *Aspects of Rabbinic Theology: Major Concepts of the Talmud* (New York: Schocken Books, 1961).

Schillebeeckx, E., *The Mission of the Church* (London: Sheed and Ward, 1973).

_____ , *Interim Report on the Book Jesus Christ* (New York: Crossroad, 1981).

_____ , *Church: The Human Story of God* (New York: Crossroad, 1990).

Schmaus, Michael, *The Church as Sacrament* (London: Sheed and Ward, 1975).

Schnackenburg, Rudolf, *God's Rule and Kingdom* (New York: Herder and Herder, 1963).

Schneider, B., "Kata Pneuma agiosunes," *Biblica* 48 (1967), pp. 395-387.

Schneiders, Sandra, "Faith, Hermeneutics and the Literal Sense of Scripture," *Theological Studies* 39 (1978), pp. 719-736.

Schürmann, Heinz, *Reich Gottes-Jesu Geschick* (Freiburg: Herder, 1983).

Schweitzer, Albert, "Die Idee des Reiches Gottes im Verlauf der Umbildung des eschatologischen Glaubens in den uneschatologischen," *Schweizerische Theol. Umschau* 23 (1953), pp. 2-20.

_____ , *The Quest of the Historical Jesus* (New York: Macmillan, 1968; German original 1906).

_____ , *The Kingdom of God and Primitive Christianity* (New York: Seabury Press, 1968.

_____ , *Ausgewählte Werke in Fünf Bänden, Band V* (Berlin: Union Verlag, 1971).

_____ , *The Mystery of the Kingdom of God: The Secret of Jesus' Messiahship and Passion* (Buffalo, N.Y.: Prometheus Books, 1985; German original 1914).

Schweizer, Edward, *The Holy Spirit* (Philadelphia: Fortress Press, 1978).

Scott, B., *Jesus, Symbol-Maker for the Kingdom* (Philadelphia: Fortress Press, 1981).

Segundo, Juan Luis, *The Historical Jesus of the Synoptics* (Maryknoll, N.Y.: Orbis Books, 1985).

Senior, Donald, "Reign of God," in *The New Dictionary of Theology*, pp. 851-861.

Simian-Yofre, H., "Justice," in *Biblical Themes in Religious Education,* ed. J. S. Marino (Birmingham, Ala.: REP, 1983).

Ska, Jean Louis, "Creazione e Liberazione nel Pentateuco," in *Creazione e Liberazione nei libri dell' Antico Testamento* (Torino: Editrice. Elle Di Ci, Leumann, 1989).

Skydsgaard K. E., "Kingdom of God and the Church," *Scottish Journal of Theology* 6 (1959).

Snyder Howard A., *A Kingdom Manifesto: Calling the Church to Live under God's Reign* (Downers Grove, Ill.: InterVarsity Press, 1985).

_____ , *Models of the Kingdom* (Nashville: Abingdon Press, 1991).

Soares-Prabhu, G. M., "The Kingdom of God: Jesus' Vision of a New Society," in *The Indian Church: The Struggle for a New Society*, ed. D. S. Amolorpavadass (Bangalore: NBCLC, 1981), pp. 579-608.

_____ , *Commitment and Conversion: A Biblical Hermeneutics for India Today-A Proposal for Discussion*, unpublished manuscript, 1985.

Sobrino, Jon, *Christology at the Crossroads, A Latin American Approach* (Maryknoll, N.Y.: Orbis Books, 1978).

_____ , "Jesús el Reino de Dios significado y objetivos últimos de su vida y misión," *Christus* 45 (1980), pp. 17-23.

Steidl-Meier, Paul, *Social Justice Ministry: Foundation and Concerns* (New York: Le Jacq Publishing, 1984).

Stendahl, Krister, "Your Kingdom Come," *Cross Current* 32 (1982), pp. 257-266.

Stephen, T. Davis, "Universalism, Hell and the Fate of the Ignorant," *Modern Theology* 6 (1990), pp. 173-186.

Stern, David, "Jesus' Parables from the Perspective of Rabbinic Literature: The Example of the Wicked Husbandmen," in *Parables and Story in Judaism and Christianity*, ed. Clement Thoma and M. Wyschogrod (New York: Paulist Press, 1989). pp. 42-80.

Stock, A., *The Method and the Message of Mark* (Wilmington, Del.: Michael Glazier, 1985).

Strolz, Walter, "Fatherhood of God in Modern Interpretation," in *The Lord's Prayer and Jewish Liturgy,* ed. J. Petuchoswski and M. Brocke (London: Burns & Oates, 1978).

Tappeiner, D. A., "Holy Spirit," *The International Standard Bible Encyclopedia*, vol. 2, ed. G. B. Bromiley (Grand Rapids, Mich.: Eerdmans Publishing Company, 1982), pp. 730-742.

Theisen, Jerome, *The Ultimate Church and the Promise of Salvation* (Collegeville, Minn.: St. John's University Press, 1976).

Theissen, Gerhard, *The First Followers of Jesus* (London: SCM Press, 1978).

Thoma, Clement, and M. Wyschogrod, eds., *Parables and Story in Judaism and Christianity* (New York: Paulist Press, 1989).

Thomas, M. M., "The South Needs a New Vision of Modernization," *Media Development* 39 (1992), pp. 33-35.

Topel, John L., *The Way to Peace: Liberation through the Bible* (Maryknoll, N.Y.: Orbis Books, 1979).

Vidales R., "Methodological Issues in Liberation Theology," in *Frontiers of Theology in Latin America*, ed. R. Gibellini (Maryknoll, N.Y.: Orbis Books, 1979), pp. 34-54.

Villegas, Beltram M., "Bienaventuranzas y Theologia de la Liberacion," in *Dialogo en Torno a la Teologia de la Liberacion* (Santiago de Chile: Editorial Salesiana, Instituto ILADES, 1986), pp. 37-57.

Viviano, Benedict T., "The Kingdom of God in the Qumran Literature," in *The Kingdom of God in 20th-Century Interpretation*, pp. 97-107.

_____ , *The Kingdom of God in History* (Wilmington, Del.: Michael Glazier, 1988).

Wall, Robert W., "The Eschatologies of the Peace Movement," *Biblical Theology Bulletin* 25 (1985), pp. 3-11.

Weiss, Johannes, *Jesus' Proclamation of the Kingdom of God* (Philadelphia: Fortress Press, 1971; German original 1892).

Welker, Michael, "The Holy Spirit," *Theology Today* 46 (1989), pp. 5-11.

Wenz, Helmut, *Theologie des Reiches Gottes: Hat Jesus sich geirrt?* (Hamburg: Herbert Reich Verlag, 1975).

Westermann, Claus, *The Parables of Jesus in the Light of the Old Testament*, trans. and ed. by F. W. Golka and A.H.B. Logan (Edinburgh: T & T Clark, 1990).

Wijngaards, John, *My Galilee: My People Walking on Water* (London: Housetop Publication, 1990).

Wilckens, Ulrich, *Evangelisch-Katholischer Kommentar zum Neuen Testament VI/3 Der Brief an die Römer: Röm 12-17* (Neunkirchen: Neunkirchener Verlag, 1982).

Wilfred, Felix, "Once Again . . . Church and Kingdom," *Vidyajyoti* 57 (1993), pp.6-24.

Williamson, Lamar, "Jesus of the Gospels and the Christian Vision of Shalom," *Horizons in Biblical Theology* 6 (1984), pp. 49-66.

Willis, Wendel, "The Discovery of the Eschatological Kingdom," *The Kingdom of God in 20th Century Interpretation*, pp. 4-5.

Wilson, Bryan R., "Secularization," in *Encyclopedia of Religion*, vol. 13 (New York: Macmillan, 1978), pp. 159-165.

Witvliet, Theo, *A Place in the Sun: An Introduction to Liberation Theology in the Third World* (Maryknoll, N.Y.: Orbis Books, 1985).

Wolf, P., "Gericht und Reich Gottes bei Johannes und Jesus," in *Gegenwart und Kommendes Reich*, ed. P. Fiedler and D. Zeller (Stuttgart: Katholisches Bibelwerk, 1975), pp. 43-66.

Wrembek, Christoph, "Der Heilige Geist und das Reich Gottes," *Geist und Leben* 64 (1991), 167-183 at pp. 173-175, titled "Eine trinitäts-theologische Deutung vom Reich Gottes."

Yoder, Howard, *The Priestly Kingdom: Social Ethics as Gospel* (Notre Dame, Ind.: University of Notre Dame Press, 1984).

Yoder, John H., *The Politics of Jesus* (Grand Rapids, Mich.: Eerdmans Publishing Company, 1972).

Index

Scripture Index